A HISTORY OF RUSSIA

BY GEORGE VERNADSKY
AND MICHAEL KARPOVICH

VOLUME IV

RUSSIA AT THE DAWN OF
THE MODERN AGE

A HISTORY OF RUSSIA

By George Vernadsky and Michael Karpovich

RUSSIA AT THE DAWN OF THE MODERN AGE

BY

GEORGE VERNADSKY

PROFESSOR EMERITUS OF RUSSIAN HISTORY
YALE UNIVERSITY

New Haven: YALE UNIVERSITY PRESS

LONDON: OXFORD UNIVERSITY PRESS

1959

© 1959 by Yale University Press, Inc.
Set in Old Style Number 7 type
and printed in the United States of America by
Vail-Ballou Press, Inc., Binghamton, N.Y.

Library of Congress catalog card number: 59–12704

FOREWORD

HISTORICALLY, Moscow was the nucleus out of which grew modern Russia—the mighty Russian Empire. Moscow's ascendancy had begun in the Mongol age, but its emancipation from Mongol control in the middle of the 15th century cleared the way for the consolidation and further expansion of the Muscovite state. The primary purpose of this expansion was to gather and unify the forces of the Russian people in the latter's struggle with the Tatars, who were to continue to attack Russia and to devastate her border provinces for more than two centuries after the proverbial fall of the Mongol yoke.

The first stage of Muscovite expansion was the unification of Great Russia, achieved under Ivan III and Vasili III. The next stage, also in Ivan's program, was acquisition of control over West Russia (Belorussia and the Ukraine). In its attempt to execute this, Moscow became involved in a conflict with Poland, the repercussions of which have been felt up to the present time.

It is in the post-Mongol period that the foreign policies of Modern Russia and the basic patterns of its political institutions were laid down. A study of events and trends of that period is therefore essential to proper understanding of the subsequent course of Russian history down to our own day.

The post-Mongol period in Russia coincides with the age of Renaissance and Reformation in Europe. For Russia also this era was a period of intense spiritual and artistic fermentation. At one time the Protestant Reformation was on the brink of winning the day in West Russia.

The process of unification of Great Russia is described in Chapters 2–5. The last three chapters deal with the political and social organization of West Russia in the 16th century, the struggle between Moscow and Poland for the control of West Russia, the rise of the Ukrainian Cossacks in the late 16th century, and the Church Union of 1596.

I intend to discuss in the next volume the evolution of Muscovy under the tsars Ivan the Terrible and Boris Godunov, and the main aspects of Russian culture of the late 15th and the 16th centuries.

In the preparation of the present volume, I have profited much from the advice of friends and colleagues, who have helped in many ways. I am especially grateful to Nikolay Andreyev, Oswald P. Backus, Roman Jakobson, Akdes Nimet Kurat, Philip Lozinski, V. F. Minorsky, Lev Okinshevich, S. G. Pushkarev, P. N. Savický, and Simon Szyszman. I alone am responsible for my conclusions, however.

My thanks are due the staff of the Yale Library for their kind cooperation; and to the editorial department of the Yale University Press, in particular to David H. Horne, for their assistance in preparing the manuscript for the printers. Mr. Horne also made the indexes. I am likewise indebted to Michael Karpovich, who generously helped me to read the proofs. The maps have been drawn by Robert L. Williams.

The publication of this volume would not have been possible without the financial support of the Humanities Fund of New York City. It is my pleasant duty to express my gratitude to that organization.

G. V.

New Haven, Connecticut
  December 1958

CONTENTS

MAPS

RUSSIA AT THE DAWN OF THE MODERN AGE

INTRODUCTION

RUSSIA IN THE MIDDLE OF THE FIFTEENTH CENTURY

ON MARCH 27, 1462, the Grand Duke of Moscow, Vasili II, died after ordering kindled touchwood to be applied to various parts of his body. This, as the chronicler remarks, was the usual cure for tabes in Russia. In Vasili's case the cure proved more dangerous than the illness, for the burns caused gangrene. Feeling the approach of the end, he expressed his desire to take monastic vows, but for some unknown reason was not allowed to do so and died a layman.

Vasili lived and died in the old wooden palace in the Kremlin, small and stuffy. Later rulers were to build stone palaces and sumptuous cathedrals and engage Western architects and technicians, as well as Western physicians. Under Vasili's successors the Moscovite state as well as the city of Moscow grew rapidly, and within a few decades Moscow was both the capital of a large nation and one of the important centers of international diplomacy—and intrigue.

Tenacious, unscrupulous, and cruel, Vasili II seems to have lacked the qualities of a good ruler, yet had a definite purpose behind his policies: the unification of all the possessions of the Moscow branch of the Rurikids (House of Daniel) under a single rule. In this he was supported by the church, by a strong group of servitor princes, by the gentry, and by a number of boyars. With their help, by the end of his rule his main goal had been achieved.[1] Moreover, during his reign the Moscow state became *de facto* if not *de jure* independent of the authority of the Tatars; and the Moscow Church became independent of the authority of the Patriarch of Constantinople. The foundations were laid upon which the mighty edifice of the Tsardom of Moscow was soon to be erected. Because of all these things, Vasili's

1. *Mongols and Russia*, pp. 311-332.

reign may be considered one of the important turning points in Russian history.

By the time of his death, the Grand Duchy of Moscow was but one of several Russian states and lands. Side by side with it there existed two other East Russian grand duchies—Tver and Riazan. In the Northwest (looking from Moscow) there were two thriving city-states—Novgorod and Pskov. Novgorod's dominions occupied the whole northern part of Russia, stretching up to the shores of the Arctic Ocean and the northern section of the Ural Mountains in the North, and beyond them to the lower Ob River in the East.

West of Muscovy, the land of Smolensk, the present-day Belorussia, and most of the present-day Ukraine were under the authority of the grand dukes of Lithuania. Eastern Galicia was part of Poland (annexed to it in 1349). Carpatho-Russia belonged to Hungary. (At present, all these territories are part of the Soviet Union, distributed between Soviet Belorussia and Soviet Ukraine, except for Smolensk, which is part of Soviet Russia.)

From the linguistic point of view, by the middle of the 15th century the differentiation of the three present-day East Slavic languages —Russian (Great Russian), Ukrainian (Little Russian), and Belorussian—took definite shape. However, Church Slavonic remained the language of the church in both East and West Russia. It also constituted the foundation of the literary language of each of the three groups. It was characteristic of the people of both East and West Russia that they continued to call themselves Russians and their land Russia (Rus'). This practice was also reflected in the titles of the rulers of the two major states which emerged in the Old Rus' territory—to wit, Moscovy and Lithuania. Beginning with Ivan I (1328–41), the rulers of Muscovy had called themselves "grand dukes of Moscow and all Russia," while those of Lithuania were known as the "grand dukes of Lithuania and Russia." An interesting example of the existence of the concept of the unity of the Russian land, despite its political division, among the Russian literati of this period is the "List of All Russian Cities, Distant and Near" which is inserted among various notes that precede the text of one of the variants of the First Novgorodian Chronicle.[2] The manuscript is dated in the middle of the 15th century, and the list may have been compiled in the late 14th or early 15th century. The names of the Russian cities are arranged in seven groups corresponding to the

2. Pages 475–477.

following areas: (1) the lower Danubian region, including Iasskii Torg—the "Alanic Market" (present-day Iași in Rumania) and Kolomyia; (2) the Kievan area, including Chernigov; (3) Volynia, including Lvov and Galich; (4) Lithuania, mostly Belorussian cities; (5) the Smolensk region; (6) the Riazan region; and (7) the Zalesie ("Beyond-the-Forest") area—that is, Suzdalia (including Moscow), Novgorod, and Pskov.

The Tatar danger was somewhat lessened by the separation (around 1445) from the old khanate (the "Golden Horde") of two new khanates, of the Crimea and Kazan. However, these three khanates taken together continued to control the South Russian and Ukrainian steppes, as well as the middle and lower Volga region. Immense herds grazed in the rich *chernoziom* (black-soil) belt of South Russia, preventing its use for agriculture. Each of the three khanates was strong enough to constitute a perennial threat to either Muscovy or Lithuania. (Had these latter two united their forces, they could have curbed the Tatars then and there.) In both Lithuania and Muscovy there were statesmen and soldiers who understood the importance of building up a united Christian front against the Tatars, but they were not able to overcome mutual suspicions nurtured by the ruling groups of the two states. The people at large in both East and West Russia instinctively felt the necessity of uniting against the Tatars or, failing this, of the formation of a strong Russian state centering either in West or in East Russia and controlling at least part of the resources of both. Because of this, each strong ruler trying to unify Russia could count at that time on the support of a considerable part of her population.

Around 1425, the year in which Vasili II's father, Vasili I, died, it seemed likely that the role of uniting most of the Russian lands would be performed by the Grand Duke of Lithuania rather than by the Grand Duke of Moscow. At that time, Vasili II was a boy of ten and there was no unity in the Moscow princely clan. One of the boys' uncles contested his right to the throne. Trouble could be foreseen even before Vasili I's death. To prevent it, Vasili I in his testament (made in 1423) entrusted his wife and sons to the protection of his father-in-law, the mighty Grand Duke of Lithuania, Vitovt. This gave Vitovt an excuse to insinuate himself into the affairs of the Grand Duchy of Moscow after Vasili I's death. Moreover, within a few years, the grand dukes of both Tver and Riazan recognized Vitovt as their suzerain. The possibility of permanent extension of the authority of the Grand Duke of Lithuania over all East Russia did not materialize, however. After the death of Vitovt in 1430, trouble started in both West and East Russia, but when Vasili II overpowered his rivals in Muscovy in 1447, he emerged as the strongest ruler in East Russia, and in 1449 a treaty of friendship and non-aggression was concluded between Moscow and Lithuania. Tver was brought within the Lithuanian sphere of influence, but not Riazan. This treaty, an important landmark in the relations between East and West Russia, signified the end of the short-lived predominance of Lithuania in East Russian affairs, and the ground was thus cleared for the ascendancy of Moscow.

Three distinct patterns of government and administration developed at this time. In Muscovy the tendency was to strengthen the authority of the grand duke. This affected first of all the Moscow princely clan itself. Most of the apanages of the lesser princes were confiscated by Vasili II, and these princes had to recognize the grand duke as their sovereign. Some of the princes of other branches of the House of Rurik as well as a number of the Lithuanian-Russian princes of the House of Gedymin entered the service of the Grand Duke of Moscow and eventually became mixed with Moscow boyars. The grand duke was assisted by the boyar *duma* (state council) in both legislation and administration, but the duma had no clearly defined authority of its own. In many cases the grand duke used the *diaki* (state secretaries) instead of the boyars as his agents. These were appointed by the grand duke from among the commoners and were entirely dependent on him.

As the former vassals of the Mongol khan and his actual successors in supreme power over Muscovy, the grand dukes assumed the khan's authority in regard to taxation and army administration, including conscription. Both Dmitri Donskoy and his son Vasili I used the conscription system in 1380 and 1396 respectively. Under Vasili II no general conscription took place; he depended on the small but well trained body of guards—the *dvor* (literally "palace" or "yard"), comparable to the Mongol *ordu*. However, the Grand Duke of Moscow never abandoned his right of conscripting troops, and the system was revived under Vasili II's successors, especially under his great-grandson, Ivan IV.

For the administration and judiciary of local districts the grand duke relied upon his *namestniki* (lieutenants) and *volosteli* (agents in rural districts). These were paid no salary from the grand ducal treasury but had to "feed themselves" off the country (the *kormlenie* system)—that is, they were entitled to receive maintenance from the local people as well as to keep for themselves a share of the court fees and taxes collected in each district.

That old Russian institution the *veche* (city assembly) was shattered by the Mongol khans, with the assistance of the Russian princes, in the 14th century and ceased to function except in cases of enemy attack or other emergency.

In contrast to the growth of the authoritarian and centralized regime in Muscovy, the government of the Grand Duchy of Lithuania was based on the principles of federation and constitutional rights. After the first treaty of union between Poland and Lithuania (1385), the constitution of Lithuania was revised according to the Polish pattern. The grand duke was assisted by a council of dignitaries known as the *pany-rada* (lords in council), corresponding to the boyar duma of Muscovy but with much more authority. In Poland alongside this aristocratic body there arose a representative assembly of the provincial gentry, the *posolskaia izba* (chamber of deputies). Together, the two bodies formed the *seim* (diet). The diet controlled Poland's budget, including expenditure for the army. Without the approval of the diet the king could make no important decisions in state affairs. Similar institutions gradually developed in the Grand Duchy of Lithuania as well.

The grand duchy was not a centralized state but a loose federation of "lands" and principalities. Each land enjoyed far-reaching autonomy guaranteed by a *privilei* (special charter). In local as in federal affairs, the aristocracy occupied a predominant position.

The veche was gradually curbed in West Russia and then ceased to function altogether. Instead, major cities were granted corporate municipal government of the German type, on the basis of the so-called Magdeburg law (see below, pp. 212–214).

The third type of government in 15th-century Russia—a type which with certain reservations we may call democratic—was that of the city-state, comparable in many respects to the Ancient Greek *polis*. The Russian city-state, based on the authority of the veche, prevailed in North Russia in Novgorod, Pskov, and Viatka. Viatka was a republic; Novgorod and Pskov had princes, but their authority was limited, and the supreme power belonged to the city, not to the prince. Symbolically, the state of Pskov was called "Lord Pskov," and Novgorod, "Lord Novgorod the Great" (*Gospodin Velikii Nov-*

gorod) or "Sovereign Novgorod the Great" (*Gosudar' Velikii Nov-gorod*). The veche was the main source of authority in both Novgorod and Pskov; all state officials were elected by the veche, not appointed by the prince.

Jointly with the veche there existed in both Novgorod and Pskov a smaller council of notables, the *gospoda* (lords). Legally it was not the upper chamber but a committee of the veche. Actually, however, especially in Novgorod, it succeeded in exerting considerable influence on the decisions of the veche and thus contributed much to the continuity of Novgorod's policies.

It should be noted that Pskov was originally a *prigorod* (by-town) of Novgorod—that is, under Novgorod's sovereignty. In 1347 the Novgorodians granted independence to Pskov, and after that, the latter was sometimes called "Novgorod's younger brother." The Pskov Church, however, remained subordinated to the archbishop of Novgorod.

The city of Novgorod was a commonwealth consisting of five communes or boroughs (*kontsy*, literally "ends"). Accordingly, the basic territory of Novgorod was divided into five parts, known as *piatiny* (fifths).[3] Outer provinces were called *volosti* (possessions). Of these, the Torzhok district was claimed now by Tver, now by Moscow, but the Novgorodians succeeded in keeping control of it until the end of Novgorod's independence. Farther east there were the Dvina land and other territories stretching to the Ural Mountains. Novgorod thus was not merely a city-state but a vast empire dominated by the city.

In both East and West Russia owners of large landed estates constituted the top layer of Russian society. This top group was known in the Kievan period as the boyars, and the term continued to be used in East Russia during the Muscovite period. In West Russia, gradually changing its connotation, it was applied only to certain groups of the lesser gentry, and "boyar" in the old sense became *pan* (lord). The lesser gentry was in the process of formation in both East and West Russia out of various groups of petty landowners and princely servitors who in West Russia became known by the Polish name *szlachta*. In East Russia some of them were called *deti boyarskie* (boyar sons); others, *dvoriane* (that is, belonging to the prince's *dvor,* in the military connotation of that word).

3. On their origin see *Mongols and Russia*, pp. 231–232.

The townspeople were made up of two main groups, the merchants and the artisans. In Poland and Lithuania (and in some parts of West Russia) there were many Germans and Jews among the urban population. Most of the merchants and artisans of East Russia were native Russians. In Novgorod and Pskov the merchant class enjoyed considerable prestige and was influential in forming governmental policy. The upper strata tended to merge with the boyars. In Moscow by contrast only a few of the richest dealers in foreign trade (known as *gosti*) occupied a similar position.

It should be noted that as a result of the Mongol invasion the prosperity of the Russian cities at large was greatly lessened. Many large cities, like Kiev, and Vladimir-in-Suzdalia, were completely destroyed by the Mongols; and after the onslaught, Kiev remained a minor town for a long time. Novgorod was the only major city that not only escaped destruction, but even profited in some respects from the Mongol rule.

On the whole, the proportion of the urban population to the total population of Russia decreased markedly. Even before the Mongol invasion, around 85 per cent of the people of Russia had lived in rural districts. After the invasion the rural population became pro-portionately even greater (probably over 95 per cent), with the exception of the Novgorodians.

The bulk of this population in the 15th century may be called peasants in the general sense of that word, although not all were tillers of soil. Since the steppes of South Russia were controlled by the Tatars, most of the Russians lived in the forest zone, only a part of which was cleared and fit for plowing. Besides agriculture, the peasants depended on fishing, hunting, beekeeping, and various forest industries such as the production of diverse utensils, carts, and boats, as well as tar and potash.

According to the old Russian notion, the tiller had rights of his own on the plot of land he tilled (the so-called *trudovoe pravo,* "toiler's right") irrespective of whom the land legally belonged to. But since a large proportion of land belonged to the state, and in addition, the princes and boyars, as well as the monasteries, owned large landed estates, there was a multiplicity of rights. A peasant living on such an estate retained a claim to his plot as long as he tilled it, and could be ousted only by court decision. On the other hand, he was free to leave his plot (thereby losing his rights to it) and move wherever he pleased.

In East Russia the peasants in the middle of the 15th century were free men. They were, however, subject to state taxes and certain liabilities, and those living in the private or church estates had to perform a certain amount of work in lieu of rent. During the Kievan period a group of peasants—the *smerdy,* who resided on state lands—had been under a special jurisdiction of the princes. This group survived in Novgorod dominions (as well as in Pskov), under the same name; it was under the jurisdiction of the state (not that of the prince) of Novgorod and Pskov.

During the Kievan period there was no difference in social status and position of the peasants of the East and West Russian lands, but in the 15th century the government of the Grand Duchy of Lithuania began curbing their freedom of movement, and the *Privilei* (Charter) of 1447 forbade the peasants to move from private estates to state land. This ordinance presaged serfdom.

Along the southern boundaries of both East and West Russian principalities, in the wooded steppe zone, and at places within the steppe zone itself free communities of a new type emerged in the 15th century—those of frontiersmen, who became known as the *Cherkasy* (Circassians) or the *Kazaki* or *Kozaki* (Cossacks).[4] The earliest mention of them in the Russian chronicles is A.D. 1444: the Riazan Cossacks.

A survey of the old Russian social stratification is not complete without mention of those outside the pale of free society. From the legal point of view, of course, slaves were not persons but chattels. That the ancient institution of slavery survived in both East and West Russia down to modern times is one of the peculiarities of Russian social history; but the truth is, slaves were a fairly numerous group even as late as the Kievan period. After that, their proportion to the total population must have decreased considerably (no exact figures are available for the 15th century). Most were owned by the princes and boyars, and were used as household servants or, in the larger estates, as agricultural workers.

In the spiritual life of the 15th-century Russians two main traditions may be discerned: the ancient, which may be called Old Slavic, and the younger, the Byzantine Christian. Notions of the Old Slavic religion—sun worship and clan cult—were deeply en-

4. On the origin of the terms *Cherkas* and *Kazak* see *Mongols and Russia,* pp. 291–292.

trenched in the people's hearts and minds. In many places in rural districts the Russians, although officially Christians, still secretly worshiped the ancient gods, and especially the clan progenitor and the genitrices—*Rod* and *Rozhanitsy*. The folk literature, based on the oral tradition, was permeated with pre-Christian beliefs, and the folk arts followed the patterns of the Scytho-Alanic era.[5] On this ancient foundation, Byzantine Christianity was superimposed in the 10th century. During the Kievan period, although all of the Russians were officially converted, Christianity took firm roots only in the cities and churches were scarce in the rural districts. It was not until the Mongol period during the 14th and 15th centuries that a serious effort was made to establish churches and parishes all over the country. But with the coming of Christianity, Byzantine literature and art penetrated into Russia; in contrast to the oral literature, written literature sponsored by the church was based on Christian notions and traditions, and in both architecture and painting the spirit of Byzantine Christianity found a glorious expression on Russian soil.

The two currents of medieval Russian culture could not but affect each other in the course of time. On the one hand, Christian literature and arts were, to a certain extent, influenced by pre-Christian folk motifs. Some of the tales of Christian saints, for example, resembled the *byliny* (epic tales) in both form and content. The old Slavic gods were not renounced outright by the clergy and monks but were considered *besy* (evil spirits or demons), with whom the faithful had to wage permanent war. Most of the old Slavic festivals were still celebrated, though somehow adapted to the Christian calendar. Thus the folk ritual of the *koliada* (winter solstice) merged with the celebration of Christmas.

Although the East Slavic culture of the 15th century was basically self-contained, it was open to outside influences. In the first place, Byzantium, which had been the primary source of Russian Christianity, continued to exert its impact on Russia, either directly or through the Southern Slavs (Bulgarians and Serbs) and Rumanians, as well as through the Crimea. It is also through Byzantium and the Balkans that many Christian and non-Christian apocrypha and tales of both Oriental and Western origin reached Russia.

Because of Russia's Eurasian background as well as because she

5. On the Old Slavic religion and its survival in oral tradition, folk music, and arts, see Vernadsky, *The Origins of Russia*, pp. 108–173, 305–316.

had been for a long time controlled by the Mongols, it is natural to expect a considerable impact of Oriental patterns on Russian life and culture of that period, even though the sharp difference between Christianity and Islam precluded the possibility of any decisive Oriental influence on Russian religious life. But in the sphere of epic poetry and folk art the Oriental impact was both strong and fruitful; and of course the Muscovite administrative system and the organization of the army followed Mongol patterns in many respects. Quite a number of Russian terms bearing on financial administration were borrowed from the Tatars (for example, *tamga,* customs duties; *denga,* money).[6] Moreover it should be noted that in the reign of Vasili II several groups of Tatars were settled in Russia (mostly along the southern border) as vassals or servitors, the most important of which was the group under Tsarevich Kasim. This situation led to friendly personal contacts between Russian and Tatar army officers. Many Tatar princes of the House of Chingis-Khan joined the ranks of Russian aristocracy.

Even though the foundations of Christian culture in Russia and in Catholic Europe were identical, the schism between the Greek Orthodox and Roman Catholic denominations resulted in the gradual building up of a cultural barrier between Russia and the West. This barrier was not impenetrable, however. Both Novgorod and Pskov maintained brisk commercial relations with the Baltic Germans and the Hanseatic League, as well as with the Island of Visby. There was a settlement of German merchants (*dvor,* the German *Hof*) in Novgorod, and one of Scandinavians (the *Varangian dvor*). Some of the Novgorodians became familiar with both the German and the Latin languages, and Western influences may be discerned in Novgorodian art, literature, and technology.

West Russia, through her affiliation with the Grand Duchy of Lithuania, likewise was not isolated from the West. Following the first Union of Poland and Lithuania (1385), Roman Catholicism became the official religion of the Grand Duchy of Lithuania, and only with great difficulty did the Russians in this state assert their right to remain Greek Orthodox (which became known as the "Russian Faith"). In Lithuania proper the Roman Catholic Church soon became firmly entrenched, and through this church Western notions spread rapidly among the Lithuanian nobility. Because of the close ties between the Lithuanian and the Polish nobility, Polish cultural

6. See *Mongols and Russia,* chap. 5, esp. pp. 344–366.

influence became paramount in Lithuanian society, and the West Russian aristocracy could not but be affected by it in the course of time. An attempt was made, following the Florentine Union of 1439,[7] to subordinate the West Russian Orthodox Church to the pope. After some hesitation, the West Russian bishops remained true to the Orthodoxy, but the church placed itself under the authority of the Patriarch of Constantinople instead of remaining dependent on the Metropolitan of Moscow. Later, in 1596, a union between the West Russian Church and Rome was established, but even after that the majority of the Ukrainian people remained loyal to Greek Orthodoxy for a long time. However, the Greek Orthodox Church in Ukraine eventually became itself a channel of Western culture, by accepting many features of the Roman Catholic educational system, including the study of Latin.

Of all the Russian lands Western influence was weakest in Muscovy. This may be explained partly by the geographic background —Moscow's remoteness from the West—and partly by the fact that the Mongol domination lasted for one century longer in East Russia than it did in West Russia. We also have to bear in mind the important role played by the Orthodox Church in the creation of the Moscow state; from the middle of the 14th century the church had been the spiritual leader of Russian resistance to the Tatars and the struggle for independence. Because of this the majority of the Muscovites were suspicious of the proselytizing policies of Roman Catholicism, especially after the Florentine Union. Yet in spite of all this, Moscow was not completely isolated from the West. In the late 14th and throughout the 15th centuries several Lithuanian princes married East Russian princesses, and vice versa. Moreover, quite a number of Lithuanian and West Russian princes migrated to Muscovy and entered the service of the Grand Duke of Moscow. The Grand Duchy of Lithuania, still thought of as Rus', was not considered a foreign country by the East Russians at that time. Through it, contact between Moscow and the West, even though indirect, was always possible.

While the Muscovites were warned not to listen to Roman Catholic propaganda, they were not opposed on principle to anything Western. Among other things, Moscow military leaders were always eager to adopt new weapons and techniques, irrespective of their place of origin. Consider, for example, the introduction of firearms

7. *Ibid.*, pp. 307–309.

into Muscovy. The Russians first became acquainted with firearms of the Oriental type at the siege of Bulgar in 1376. Not satisfied with these, they apparently made inquiries in the West, and obtaining a number of cannon of Western type to reinforce the defenses of Moscow, used them there for the first time in 1382.

The chances of closer cultural contacts between East Russia and the West brightened during the brief period of Vitovt supremacy. In 1429 a number of Russian princes, including the Grand Duke of Tver, attended an international conference at Lutsk, Volynia, sponsored by Vitovt. Among those present were Sigismund, Emperor of the Holy Roman Empire, and Iagailo (Jagiello), King of Poland. The pope, the Byzantine Emperor John VIII, the King of Denmark, and the Teutonic Order each sent representatives to Lutsk. All enjoyed the lavish reception and entertainment offered by their mighty host. From the practical point of view the conference was not a success, however. In the next year Grand Duke Vasili II of Moscow and the grand dukes of Tver and Riazan, on the occasion of the expected coronation of Vitovt, attended another impressive gathering in Vilno, Lithuania, which miscarried, since the Poles detained Emperor Sigismund's messengers bringing the crown.[8]

Soon afterward, an event occurred that prepared the way for direct contact between Moscow and Italy—the Ferrara-Florence Church Council of 1438–39 (recognized by the Roman Catholics as the 17th Ecumenical Council). The Russian Church was represented there by Metropolitan Isidor, a Greek born in Salonika, who was accompanied by about a hundred Russian clergymen and laymen. (One of them left a description of their journey to Florence.) Isidor signed the Florentine declaration of the Union of Churches, but when he returned to Moscow he was not accepted by the Moscow authorities and had to flee from Russia.[9] In spite of the failure of the Muscovites to recognize the Union, the whole episode proved an important landmark in the progress of mutual acquaintanceship of Russia and the West.

8. *Ibid.*, pp. 296–297.
9. *Ibid.*, pp. 307–309, 311–312.

CHAPTER I

THE BYZANTINE MARRIAGE OF IVAN III

1. MAN AND RULER

VASILI II's eldest son and successor, Ivan III, was twenty-two at the time of his father's death. To secure his succession in advance Vasili II had proclaimed him grand duke and co-ruler as early as 1449. In his testament Vasili "blessed" Ivan with his *otchina* (patrimony), the grand duchy. No confirmation of Ivan's authority by the khan of the Golden Horde was asked.

Throughout his reign Ivan III was conscious of his rights and of the prestige of his realm. When in 1489 the envoy of the German emperor offered Ivan the royal crown, the latter answered: "We are aboriginal sovereigns in our land, from our first progenitors, and we are installed by God—our ancestors and we . . . And we never sought induction from anyone else, and now do not want any." [1]

Ivan's mother was a Russian princess of the Serpukhov branch of the House of Daniel (the Danilovichi clan) and thus a distant relative of his father. This does not mean, however, that Ivan III was a pure Russian by blood. His progenitor, Vladimir the Saint of Kiev, was of Norse extraction. In between Vladimir and Aleksandr Nevsky much non-Slavic blood was added through intermarriages of the Russian princes with foreign princesses. Among Ivan III's distant ancestresses there were one Swedish princess, one Byzantine, one Polovtsian, and one Ossetian. [2] Furthermore, Ivan's grandfather (Vasili I) had married a Lithuanian princess, daughter of the Grand Duke Vitovt, so that Ivan's father was half Lithuanian by blood.

We have a brief description of Ivan's physical characteristics by the Italian traveler Ambrogio Contarini, who saw him in Moscow in the winter of 1476–77: "The Duke may be thirty five years of age [he was thirty-six]; he is tall and thin, and handsome." [3] There is a

1. *PDS, 1,* 11–12; Bazilevich, pp. 263–264.
2. See Genealogical Chart I.
3. Contarini. p. 163.

representation of Ivan III kneeling before the pope in the wall paintings of Santo Spirito in Rome, which is a pure fantasy of the painter.[4] Ivan's portrait (an engraving) in profile in A. Thevet's *Cosmographie universelle* (1555) [5] likewise cannot be considered authentic, since it represents a different type of face and beard than we find in the likeness of Ivan III (*de trois quarts*) in a group on a contemporary embroidery, in colors (1498).[6] (It should be noted, however, that the technique of embroidery is not a convenient medium for an accurate naturalistic portrait.)

Physically, Ivan seems to have been vigorous and active. Contarini says, "It is his custom to visit the various parts of his dominions every year." [7] And indeed, Ivan was absent during Contarini's visit to Moscow, from the end of September to the end of December 1476. There are stories, in connection with Khan Ahmad's war against Moscow in 1480, that Ivan lacked physical courage. These stories are hardly valid (see below, p. 75). The fact was, Ivan did not seek military glory as such and preferred to achieve success by calculation rather than by chance.

We have little information concerning his inner personality and character. His diplomatic letters and statements were probably written by his secretaries, though he must have told them what to write. The personal element in them is subordinated to the political, even in his letters to his daughter Elena, who became Grand Duchess of Lithuania in 1495. Only fragments of other people's impressions of him can be found in documents of the period. No private letters to him or private memoirs concerning him have been preserved. Thus we may judge of his character mainly from his policies and his actions as reflected in state papers of various kinds as well as in the chronicles. Here again we cannot be sure to what extent, in each case, the initiative was his own and to what extent he was influenced by his advisers; there seem to have been extremely gifted men among them.

As a result of all this, our picture of Ivan as man and ruler cannot be definitive; but in spite of the lack of evidence he may be called one of the ablest Muscovite rulers, and probably the very ablest. He seems to have had broad vision and a definite political

4. Pierling, *1*, 159.
5. Reproduced in *Ocherki* 3, p. 103.
6. Reproduced in *Ocherki* 3, facing p. 206.
7. Contarini, p. 159.

program. He prepared his plan of action well in advance, and never making a rash move knew the value of waiting quietly until the situation was ripe. He relied more on diplomacy than on war. He was persistent, cautious, reticent, and cunning. Though resorting to stern measures against his opponents when he deemed it necessary, he was not excessively cruel by the standards of the time. He seems to have enjoyed art, in any case architecture. With the help of Italian and Pskovian architects he changed the face of Moscow, especially of the Kremlin. Among the sumptuous buildings he sponsored were the new Cathedral of Dormition in the Kremlin (built in 1475–79 by Aristotle Fioravanti), that of the Annunciation (built by Pskovian masters in 1482–89), and the Hall of the Facets (*Granovitaia Palata*), built by Italians in 1473–91 and destined as the audience chamber of the grand duke.

Ivan was interested in religious problems, but his basic approach to church affairs was apparently motivated by political rather than religious considerations. A family man, he seems to have had deep respect for his mother and to have loved his first wife. His second marriage was dictated by political considerations and brought him much trouble, resulting in family discord and political intrigues, especially toward the end of his life and reign. Ivan's advisers and assistants admired his abilities and had great respect for him; they usually spoke of him as *Derzhavny* (the Ruler). But it seems that few really loved him.

In studying any important historical character—in fact, in studying any man—we are faced with the problem of determining what is individual in his personality and what is hereditary.[8] In the case of Ivan III the dearth of authentic evidence makes it extremely difficult to answer the question. As for heredity, the Danilovichi used to marry Russian princesses down to Ivan III's grandfather Vasili I, whose wife, as has been said, was a Lithuanian princess (of the House of Gedymin). This marriage, introducing new genes into the family, constituted an important event in the family history. In both biological and political senses it predetermined the destiny of Ivan's father and of Ivan himself.

The progenitor of the Danilovichi—the first prince of Moscow, Daniel, youngest son of Aleksandr Nevsky—as well as his immediate descendants reigned during the trying conditions of Mongol

8. Among the recent works on personality and heredity see L. Szondi, *Schicksalanalyse* (Basel, 1944); M. de Ferdinandy, *Ahnen and Schicksal* (Munich, 1955).

domination over a dismembered Russia. For survival they had to use, depending on circumstances, now complete subservience to the khan and now daring disregard of the khan's orders. In their relations to other Russian princes they proved tough and greedy. They never let go the possessions they acquired. They were good managers of their huge landed estates, which constituted the economic foundation for the aggrandizement of their political power.

While concentrating on material things, they had at the same time political vision. In 1317 Daniel's eldest son, Iuri III, obtained the khan's *yarlyk* (patent) for the Grand Duchy of Vladimir. A few years after his assassination by a prince of Tver, Iuri's younger brother Ivan I succeeded in getting a similar patent, in 1332. After that, the Muscovite princes considered the throne of Vladimir their patrimony.[9] The grand duke was recognized as the senior of the family, but such was the weight of the clan traditions that his relatives—the lesser Danilovichi—received each an apanage of his own, over which he reigned in his own right. This presaged potential conflicts, and a violent family feud took place in the reign of Ivan III's father, Vasili II, who finally overcoming his rivals, confiscated most of the apanages of the lesser princes and proclaimed his suzerainty over those who remained in power. These now became the grand duke's vassals. Among the factors which contributed to the establishment of the new order, the Lithuanian background of Vasili II— specifically, the protection given him by his father-in-law Vitovt— undoubtedly were of great importance.

Some of Ivan III's traits, like his tenacity and his firm grip on acquired possessions, were common to most of the Danilovichi. He lacked, however, the daring characteristic of a number of the members of the family, especially Daniel himself, Iuri (Daniel's eldest son—not a direct ancestor of Ivan III), and Dmitri Donskoy. On the Lithuanian side, Ivan's cautiousness, his thoroughness in preparing ground for his actions, as well as his reticence make him more like Vitovt's uncle, Olgerd. If Ivan actually inherited these traits from the Lithuanian ancestors of his grandmother, we should look for them in the ancestry of Vitovt's grandfather (Olgerd's father) Gedymin. Too little is known, however, about the personal characteristics of Gedymin's ancestors to venture to make any definite conclusions about it.

The question of the original, the individual, in Ivan III's char-

9. See *Mongols and Russia,* pp. 199–202.

acter is the hardest to answer. It seems in any case that the sense of dignity of his authority and his office was the new element he brought to the Moscow throne. For his father, the centralization of the grand-ducal authority was a matter of necessity. For Ivan, it was not only a political program but a matter of principle. More than that, is seems to have been based on deep personal feelings, which may be partly explained by the painful experiences of his early childhood. In 1446, when Ivan was a boy of six, his father was arrested and blinded by Vasili II's cousin and rival, Dmitri Shemiaka. Ivan and his younger brother Iuri (then only five) were likewise seized and imprisoned by Shemiaka. They were released only at the insistence of the primate of the Russian Church, Iona, then Bishop of Riazan.[10]

As regards Ivan III's advisers and assistants, he at first kept in office those who had directed the affairs in the later part of the reign of his father. The most respected among them was the wise old Metropolitan Iona, but he died in 1461. His successor, Metropolitan Feodosi (Theodosius), was a saintly man, who tried to raise the moral and intellectual level of the clergy but had no taste for politics. In 1464 Feodosi expressed his desire to retire into a monastery and was replaced by Philip I. The most influential of Vasili II's boyars was Prince Ivan Iurievich Patrikeev, a descendant of the Grand Duke Gedymin of Lithuania. His father, Prince Iuri Patrikeev, married one of Vasili II's sisters. Prince Ivan Iurievich was thus Ivan III's first cousin. Several other princes, of the House of Gedymin as well as Rurik, served Vasili II and then the young Ivan III as councilors and generals. Members of a few old Muscovite nonprincely boyar families likewise exercized considerable influence on affairs both before and after Vasili II's death. Among the Muscovite military leaders of this time, Konstantin Bezzubtsev and Prince Ivan Striga-Obolensky were prominent.

2. Sophia Paleologus

The basic tendencies of Ivan III's political program became evident even in the first years of his reign. In 1463 the last Iaroslavl princes lost their independence, and their principalities were absorbed into the Grand Duchy of Moscow. The next year Ivan gave his sister Anna in marriage to the young Prince of Riazan. This

10. *Ibid.*, pp. 322–323.

diplomatic marriage opened the way for the future absorption of
Riazan by Moscow. In his dealings with Novgorod and Pskov, Ivan
III proceeded at first with extreme caution. Not long before his
father's death the latter had imposed on the Pskovians a prince
whom they did not want and soon ousted. Ivan allowed the Pskovians
to elect a prince at their will and at the same time acted as a
mediator in church affairs between Novgorod and Pskov and convinced the Pskovians to respect the authority of the Archbishop of
Novgorod. It was only in 1471 that Ivan made his first move against
Novgorod. Much attention had to be given to Tatar affairs. Both the
Khanate of the Golden Horde and that of Kazan constituted a
perennial danger for Muscovy. Ivan, trying to forestall it by military force and diplomacy, used as his main tool his Tatar vassal,
Tsarevich Kasim. Through the khans of Kasimov, Ivan was able
to participate in Kazan affairs and to prepare ground for building up
a friendship with the khans of the Crimea.

Ivan III's first wife, Princess Maria of Tver, died in 1467. She
had borne him, in 1456, one son, Ivan Junior (*Molodoy*), who
around 1470 received the title of grand duke and was recognized as
his father's co-ruler. Left with only one son, and that a minor, Ivan
III must have been worried about the security of the succession to
the throne. Suggestions for a second marriage of the young ruler
(Ivan was twenty-seven at the time of Maria's death) were probably
offered from many quarters. The fact that the second marriage took
place not immediately but five years after the end of the first may be
indicative of Ivan III's reverence of the memory of his first consort.
Besides, as we know, he was not one to make quick decisions: it is
also possible that he decided to wait for a suitable opportunity of
marrying a foreign princess. Such a marriage, it could be argued,
would raise the prestige of the ruler of Moscow and place him and
his family above the local Moscow aristocracy. It also could be useful from the point of view of international affairs and diplomacy.

Before long, opportunity knocked. In 1468 Gian-Battista della
Volpe (known in Moscow as Ivan Friazin), the Italian whom Ivan
III had put in charge of coinage in Moscow, sent to Italy two agents,
the Italian Niccolò Gislardi (or Gilardi) and the Greek George
(Iuri). Their primary task was to engage more Italian technicians
for Ivan III.[11] Volpe's agents were received in Rome by Pope Paul
II, who decided to use them for opening negotiations for a marriage

11. Bazilevich, p. 76.

between Ivan III and the Byzantine princess Zoe Paleologus, a niece of the last Byzantine emperor Constantine XI. Zoe's family had accepted the Florentine Declaration of Union, and Zoe herself had become a Roman Catholic. The pope was her guardian. In February 1469 (the date according to the Russian chronicles) the Greek Iuri returned to Moscow bringing with him two Italian technicians, Volpe's brother Carlo, and Antonio Gislardi (Anton Friazin). Iuri also delivered a letter to Ivan from Cardinal Bessarion, Zoe's tutor, offering Zoe's hand to Ivan.

In arranging for Zoe's marriage with Ivan, the pope had a twofold purpose: to promote Roman Catholicism in Russia and to make the Moscow grand duke his ally against the Ottoman Turks. Under the threat of the Ottoman danger the pope (as well as the Venetian senate) was at that time enlisting every possible ally, including the rulers of the Golden Horde and Iran. Volpe's agents seem to have given the pope an exaggerated idea of Muscovy's strength and an entirely wrong notion of Ivan III's willingness to combat the Turks. Volpe himself had an ambitious plan of his own—to become the pope's and Venice's main agent in the East. To achieve this aim he would not mind deceiving both the pope and the Grand Duke of Moscow if it served his plans.[12] When he had arrived in Muscovy he had agreed to be converted to Greek Orthodoxy, but he secretly remained a Roman Catholic. Now he assured the Muscovites that Zoe was a Greek Orthodox, and at the same time he let the pope believe that Zoe's Catholicism would not be an obstacle to her becoming Ivan III's consort.

After receiving Bessarion's message, Ivan III consulted his mother as well as Metropolitan Philip and the boyars. With their approval he sent Volpe to Rome in 1470, to talk the matter over with Zoe herself and, of course, with Pope Paul and Cardinal Bessarion. Zoe agreed to marry Ivan, and the pope and the cardinal approved her choice. Volpe brought to Moscow Zoe's portrait. In the winter of 1471–72 the plan of marriage was again discussed by Ivan III and his councilors and was finally accepted. On January 16, 1472, Volpe left for Rome once more, this time to bring Ivan's fiancée to Moscow. (Pope Paul II died in 1471. The news had reached Moscow before Volpe's departure, but the name of the new pope was erroneously given to the Muscovites as "Kalistus." That name was consequently mentioned in Ivan III's official letter to the pope. However, when Volpe

12. On Volpe see E. Shmurlo, "Volpe," *ES, 13* (1892), 147; Pierling, *1*, 130–134.

and his companions reached Italy they were informed that the new pope's name was Sixtus, not Kalistus. Volpe found an easy way out of the difficult situation: he erased, in Ivan's letter, the wrong name and inserted the right one instead.)

On May 24, 1472, the Muscovite ambassadors were received by Pope Sixtus IV. On June 1 a solemn ceremony took place in the Vatican—Zoe's betrothal to Ivan III (Volpe acting as proxy for the Grand Duke of Moscow). Some historians call this ceremony a wedding, not a betrothal. P. Pierling prefers to speak of it as a "marriage d'Ivan au Vatican." However, he admits that the documents are equivocal.[13] As a matter of fact, Pierling himself cites the pope's letter to the Duke of Modena, of June 21, 1472, in which the pope says that Zoe was recently "affianced" to Ivan.[14]

On June 24 Zoe—accompanied by the papal legate Antonio Bonumbre, by Volpe, by the Greek Dmitri Ralev (Rhalli; he was to represent Zoe's brothers at the wedding in Moscow), by another Greek Iuri Trakhaniot (whom the Russian chroniclers call her "boyar"), and by numerous attendants—set forth from Rome through Florence and Nuremberg for Lubeck. There Zoe and her party boarded a ship that brought them to Reval (in Russian, Kolyvan) on October 21. The sea voyage took eleven days. The itinerary Zoe had to choose is a good illustration of the havoc wrought in the communications between Italy and Eastern Europe by the Ottoman conquest of Constantinople and the Balkans. Both the sea route from Italy to the Black Sea and the overland route through the Balkans were barred by the Turks. From Nuremberg, Zoe could have chosen the overland route through Poland and Lithuania, but just at that time the relations between Ivan III and Casimir of Poland and Lithuania were tense because of the Novgorodian conflict (see below, pp. 49–50). Also, the roads through Lithuania were very bad, especially in the autumn.

From Reval, Zoe and her suite rode to Pskov, where the clergy, the boyars, and the whole population greeted her. Although Zoe was accompanied by the papal legate, she apparently had made up her mind, even before starting her voyage, to please the Russians by accepting their customs and their faith. This might have been the result of the advice of her boyar, Iuri Trakhaniot, who according to

---

13. "Les documents s'expriment d'une manière équivoque," Pierling, *1*, 150.
14. *Ibid.*, p. 162.

the Pskovian Chronicle was a relative of the Bishop of Tver.[15] Before entering Pskov, therefore, Zoe donned Russian royal vestments, and in Pskov without consulting the papal legate she visited the Holy Trinity Cathedral and reverenced the icons. The legate, who found himself in an embarrassing situation, nevertheless went with Zoe to Moscow. There he was customarily preceded by an attendant who carried what the Russian chroniclers call a "Latin cross" (crucifix). This nearly created a crisis, since Metropolitan Philip objected violently to a public display of the Latin cross in Moscow and threatened to leave the city. In spite of Volpe's objections, the legate was forbidden to have the crucifix publicly carried before him.

The very day Zoe had entered Moscow, November 12, 1472, her Orthodox wedding with Ivan had been performed, after a solemn mass, in the small temporary structure being used during construction of the Cathedral of Dormition. The metropolitan himself officiated, and Zoe's name was changed to Sophia. While the papal legate understood that Zoe had been lost to the Roman Catholic cause, he stayed in Moscow for eleven more weeks, trying to secure Ivan III's assistance against the Turks. He finally left Moscow, carrying with him back to Italy rich gifts but no political agreement.

Although Sophia became Ivan III's consort, the man to whose labors she owed her new position, Gian-Battista della Volpe, got into serious trouble. As has been said, both the pope and the Venetian senate were eager to secure the assistance of the Khan of the Golden Horde against the Ottoman Turks. In 1471 the senate decided to send its secretary, Gian-Battista Trevisano, to the Golden Horde via Moscow. He was instructed to consult Volpe in Moscow and to follow his advice. Trevisano was well received in Moscow, but Volpe convinced him not to reveal to Ivan his capacity of Venetian ambassador to the Golden Horde but to represent himself as Volpe's nephew with no official status. When Sophia arrived in Moscow, the Italians in her suite inadvertently disclosed the true meaning of Trevisano's coming to Moscow. Ivan was angered by the deceit and assumed that Volpe and Trevisano had had secret contacts with the Golden Horde, to the detriment of Moscow's interests. Volpe was arrested and deported to the town of Kolomna (southeast of Moscow). Trevisano was sentenced to death, and only the papal legate's personal intervention saved him. He was interned and put under the surveillance of a

15. Pskovian Chronicle, p. 74.

Russian official, Nikita Beklemishev, until the matter was cleared
through negotiations with Venice. When Ivan received assurances
from the Venetian senate that Trevisano's mission was to arouse the
Golden Horde against the Turks, not against Moscow, Trevisano
was freed (1473) and allowed to proceed to the khan. But Volpe's
career in Muscovy had come to an end, and his subsequent fate is
not known.[16]

3. Zoe in Moscow

For Sophia (Zoe) her transplantation from Italy to Moscow signified a most drastic change in her way of life. Her childhood had
not been a happy one. Her father, Thomas Paleologue, brother of
the last Byzantine emperor, Constantine XI, had been the ruler
(despot) of Morea until 1460, when he fled to the Island of Corfu to
escape the advancing Turks.[17] Leaving his wife and children in
Corfu, Thomas went to Italy, where he tried in vain to have his
rights to the Byzantine throne recognized by the pope. He was given
a decent pension (3,600 ducats from the Roman curia, 2,400 ducats
from the college of cardinals, and 500 ducats from Venice annually),
with which, however, he was not satisfied. Both Thomas and his wife
died around 1462. Their children—two boys, Andrew and Manuel,
and the youngest, the girl Zoe—were brought to Italy. Zoe was
then around fourteen. Of her brothers, Manuel later recognized the
authority of the Ottoman sultan and returned to his native land.
The eldest, Andrew, remained in the West, offering to sell his rights
to the Byzantine throne to the highest bidder. In fact, he sold them
at least three times, each time to a different person.

The pope entrusted Cardinal Bessarion, a prominent Greek scholar
converted to Roman Catholicism (he had ardently supported the
Florentine Union) with the task of supervising the education of
Thomas' children. One of the two teachers appointed by Bessarion
was a Greek; another apparently was an Italian (the teacher of
Latin). Besides, two Catholic priests were to take care of the children's religious indoctrination. In his instructions to the teachers
Bessarion ordered that the children be advised not to boast of their
royal origin but always to remember that they were refugees, or-
phans, and paupers; that they should be virtuous, humble, and

16. On the Volpe and Trevisano episode see Bazilevich, pp. 105–106.
17. On the title "despot" see *Mongols and Russia,* p. 306.

grateful to their benefactors; and that they should be diligent students.[18] One of the good fruits of this system was that the children, in addition to their native tongue—the Greek—mastered both Latin and Italian. On the other hand, they hardly could have enjoyed constant reminders of their humble situation and of the gratitude they owed their benefactors. Such a system could only result in the development of either an inferiority complex or hypocrisy, or both, and could develop in the children a cynical attitude toward life. In the case of Zoe, it seems probable that her ostentatious devotion to Roman Catholicism was not sincere.

When all is said, while Zoe could not have been happy in the days of her youth, she was fortunate to have spent them in the most civilized and artistic country of Europe. When she reached Moscow, the contrast between Italy and Russia must have been quite a shock, even though her new position was one of power and wealth. But having been accustomed from her childhood to constant changes of fortune, she, as it seems, adapted herself rapidly to the new conditions of life. No one heard any complaints from her; at least, no one recorded such complaints. As a gifted linguist she must have mastered Russian without great difficulties.

Although Zoe, now Sophia, seemed contented in Moscow, she enjoyed every opportunity of conversing with Italian visitors and Italian residents of Moscow. They called her "Despina" (feminine of "Despot"), in the Greek way. Contarini says that he paid her a visit at Ivan's request, and had a long conversation with her. "She treated me with great kindness and courtesy, and entreated me earnestly to recommend her to my Illustrious Seignory." [19]

Sophia's portrait, brought to Moscow by Volpe in 1470, has not yet been found. She was also represented, kneeling before the pope, in the wall paintings of the Santo Spirito.[20] In the group on the Moscow embroidery of 1498 (mentioned above) Sophia (like the others in the group) is depicted in conventional style. Her face may be called pretty, but we do not know whether it is an accurate likeness (she was around fifty at that time). The Italian princess Clarissa Orsini, who called on her in Rome in 1472, found her beautiful, though the Florentine poet Luigi Pulci, who was present at this meeting, described her in a letter to a friend of his as abhorrently fat. But Pulci,

18. See Savva, pp. 43–45.
19. Contarini, p. 164.
20. Pierling, *1*, 159.

in love with Clarissa, was ready to find fault with Sophia. Besides, Sophia offered neither food nor drink to her visitors during the whole evening and perhaps the poet's hunger accounts for his disparagement.[21]

There cannot be any doubt that Sophia's coming to Moscow displeased some of Ivan's courtiers. Sophia must have been regarded as an intruder and a schemer eager to dominate her husband and to undermine the position of his former advisers. But with her adaptability and tact, she apparently succeeded in establishing good relations with her mother-in-law, outwardly at least. On the other hand, her stepson, Ivan Junior, who was sixteen at the time of Sophia's arrival, was suspicious of her. It is obvious that Sophia did not like him either. Contarini says that Ivan Junior "is not in great favor, on account of his bad conduct." [22] This statement apparently reflects some gossip at Sophia's court in 1476. An indication of the resentment against her in certain circles of the Muscovite society may be found in Russian chronicles, in their description of the Russo-Tatar conflict of 1480. Some of the chroniclers criticized Sophia for having left Moscow at the time of danger and fleeing to North Russia for safety.[23]

Sharp attacks against Sophia were made in the 16th century by the opponents of her son Vasili III and of her grandson Ivan IV. Baron Sigismund von Herberstein, who visited Russia twice, in 1517 and 1526, was told (apparently by resentful boyars) that Sophia was "very astute" and that Ivan III "did many things at her instigation." [24] Ivan Bersen-Beklemishev (son of Nikita Beklemishev, mentioned above) told the scholar Maxim the Greek around 1520 that "when Grand Duchess Sophia came here with your Greeks, our land became confused and great disorders started." He explained that the causes of these disorders were the haughtiness of the grand duke and his refusal to seek the advice of the old boyars. In this case, however, he meant Ivan III's son Vasili, not Ivan himself. He said that Ivan had been kind to his councilors and appreciated frank criticism of his actions. Prince Andrei Kurbsky, who broke with Vasili's son Ivan IV and went over to the Lithuanian side, called Sophia a "Greek sorceress" and deplored her evil influence on Ivan III.

21. *Ibid.*, pp. 150–152; Savva, p. 42.
22. Contarini, p. 163.
23. *PSRL, 4,* 154; *6,* 21 and 232. Cf. Savva, p. 30.
24. Herberstein-Backus, p. 10.

Kurbsky also accused her of poisoning her stepson Ivan Junior (who died in 1490).[25]

Under the influence of the 16th-century critics of Sophia, as well as on other grounds, most of the 18th- and 19th-century historians attributed to Sophia an extremely important role in Russian affairs during the reign of Ivan III. It was asserted that through his marriage to Sophia Ivan acquired the right to the Byzantine throne (F. I. Uspensky); that one of the after effects of the marriage was the creation of the theory that Moscow was the "Third Rome" (Pierling); that following the marriage, Byzantine court etiquette was introduced in Moscow (Prince Shcherbatov, Karamzin, Bestuzhev-Riumin, Ikonnikov); that both the annexation of Novgorod and the "overthrow of the Mongol yoke" were the results of Sophia's advice (Prince Shcherbatov, Karamzin, Ternovsky, Pierling). On the other hand, S. M. Soloviev, while admitting a degree of influence of Sophia on Ivan, pointed out that most of Ivan's moves followed traditional lines of Muscovite policies. Such was also V. O. Kliuchevsky's opinion. In 1901 the problem of Sophia's role in Muscovite politics was carefully re-examined by V. I. Savva, who came to the conclusion that Sophia's alleged influence on her husband and on Moscow affairs was greatly exaggerated by the historians. Recently, K. V. Bazilevich expressed the same opinion.[26]

Savva's and Bazilevich's conclusions seem basically sound to me. Indeed, there is no reason whatsoever to ascribe to Sophia's influence either the annexation of Novgorod or the achievement of the *de jure* independence of Muscovy from the Golden Horde. Ivan III's first move against Novgorod was made in 1471, one year before his marriage to Sophia. As for the Tatars, Moscow became *de facto* independent around 1452, in the reign of Ivan's father, Vasili II. After that, the shedding of the legal skin of Mongol rule was only a matter of time and skillful diplomacy. And the rights to the Byzantine throne were not held by Sophia; her eldest brother Andrew considered himself entitled to them and, as has been mentioned, was eager to sell them. Andrew visited Moscow twice, in 1480 and 1490. We may suppose that he offered the rights to Ivan, but no transaction was concluded.

On the whole it may be said that during the first two decades of Sophia's stay in Moscow she could hardly have had any serious

25. See Savva, pp. 36–37.
26. *Ibid.*, pp. 1–57; Bazilevich, pp. 83–88.

political influence on state affairs. True, she proved very useful to
Ivan in his dealings with his Italian architects and technicians. These
Italians could always plead for her intervention and protection in
case of misunderstandings between them and the Russians. And the
mere fact that the Despina was in Moscow encouraged more Italians
to come there. It seems that Sophia was greatly interested in the
vast building program started by her husband in Moscow. While
she could not have known the real splendor of the Byzantine court
(she was born around five years before the fall of Constantinople),
she did see the splendor of Italian palaces and quite naturally desired
to have something similar built in Moscow for her own use as well
as for the reception of foreign ambassadors. Only after that had
been done could one think of introducing a more elaborate ceremonial
at the court of Moscow.

The only possible way for Sophia to acquire political influence
was through palace intrigue. This way was opened for her in 1479
when her first son, Vasili, was born (her first two children were
girls). Through him Sophia might hope, under lucky circumstances,
to achieve real power. But she had to wait patiently for these circumstances. In 1485 when Ivan III's mother passed away, Sophia
became the first lady of the Moscow palace. Five years later, Ivan
III's eldest son (Sophia's stepson), Ivan Junior, died. This event,
abruptly changing the whole palace situation, made Sophia's dream
of securing the throne for her son a possibility, even though a distant
one. Ivan Junior left one son, Dmitri, who was six years old in 1490.
Sophia's son Vasili was eleven at that time. There was no definite
law of succession in Muscovy, and it was not clear which of the two
boys had the right of succession.

An intense struggle for power started between the two mothers—
the Byzantine princess Sophia (mother of Vasili) and the Moldavian
princess Elena (mother of Dmitri). At first, the Moldavian seemed
to have better chances, but the Despina was eventually victorious. In
1502 Vasili was proclaimed grand duke, coruler with his father, and
heir to the throne; and Elena and Dmitri were arrested. Sophia,
however, was not to enjoy the fruits of her victory for long: she
passed away in 1503. Ivan III died two years later, and Vasili III
ascended the throne in 1505.

Sophia's main impact on the course of Russian history was made
by the fact of her giving birth to the man who was destined to become the father of Ivan the Terrible.

CHAPTER II

NOVGOROD

1. CULTURAL TRADITIONS

THE TWO CITY-STATES in North Russia—Novgorod and Pskov—were not directly affected by the Mongol invasion of the 13th century and succeeded in maintaining their integrity and autonomy throughout the Mongol rule. Novgorod had to pay its share of the tribute to the khan, but otherwise was not molested by the Mongols. On the contrary, the Mongols guaranteed its old political privileges and the freedom of its commerce.

Throughout the Mongol period Novgorod maintained lively trading with the Island of Visby as well as with Riga and the Hanseatic League. Pskov likewise traded with Riga. Novgorodian and Pskovian merchants also dealt with Tver, Vitebsk, and Smolensk, and with what they called the "lower towns" (*nizovye goroda*) in the upper Volga-Oka region. The Novgorodians were obviously interested in opening the whole course of the Volga River down from Nizhni-Novgorod to the Caspian Sea for their commerce. It should be mentioned in this connection that merchants of certain other Russian cities were also interested in the Oriental trade at this time. One of them, Afanasi Nikitin of Tver, left a remarkable account of his journey to India (1466–72).[1] It was in the interest of Novgorodian, Pskovian, and Tverian merchants not to let barriers interfere with their trade, and therefore they supported and tried to revive the old traditions of the free Russian federation as a bulwark against the growing cleavage between East and West Russia.

Both politically and culturally the Novgorodian and Pskovian society cherished the heritage of the Kievan period. The only manuscript of the *Igor Tale* (*Slovo o polku Igoreve*) which had survived down to 1812 (when it perished in the big Moscow fire during Napoleon's invasion) was a copy made in Pskov in the 16th

1. *Khozhenie za tri moria Afanasiia Nikitina*, B. D. Grekov and V. P. Adrianova-Peretts, eds. (Moscow and Leningrad, 1948).

century by a Pskovian copyist—an indication of the lively interest
in the literature of the Kievan period among the Pskov scholars as
late as the 16th century. It should be noted in this connection that
the story of the Battle of Orsha (1514) in the Pskovian Chronicle[2] is
written in the style of the *Igor Tale,* which shows that its author
was quite familiar with it and imbued with its spirit.

In view of the democratic form of government in both Novgorod
and Pskov, we may suppose that a considerable number of the citizens of these two states understood the importance of maintaining
the old traditions of political freedom and of unity through federation of all the Russian lands. In that federation, Novgorod (many
a Novgorodian dreamed) was to play an important role—as it had in
the past. It is against this background of intense political thought
and reverence to the great cultural traditions that the significant rise
of Novgorodian literature and arts in the late 14th and the 15th
centuries may be best understood.

A prominent leader in this movement was the Archbishop of
Novgorod, Evfimi II. Evfimi was elected by the Novgorod veche
for this position in 1429 but his candidacy was not approved by
Metropolitan Foti (Photius) of Moscow, who was then primate of
the Russian Church in both Muscovy and Lithuania; and the Novgorodian see remained vacant for some time. Foti died in 1431. Next
year the council of East Russian bishops nominated Bishop Iona of
Riazan for the metropolitan see. The Grand Duke of Lithuania submitted the name of his own candidate, Bishop Gerasim, to the Patriarch of Constantinople, to whom, at that time, the right of ordaining
metropolitans of Russia belonged. The patriarch ordained Gerasim.
When the Muscovites refused to accept him, Gerasim established his
residence in Smolensk; it was to him that the Novgorodians addressed themselves for approval of Evfimi's candidacy to the see of
Novgorod. Evfimi was duly ordained Archbishop of Novgorod, by
Metropolitan Gerasim in 1434. Next year Gerasim was burned at
the stake by order of the Grand Duke of Lithuania,[3] and the Russian metropolitan see again became vacant. It remained so for some
time—until a new metropolitan, Isidor, was sent from Constantinople
to Moscow. After Isidor's acceptance of the Florentine Union the
Muscovites repudiated him too, and in 1448 Bishop Iona of Riazan
was again elected Metropolitan of Russia by a council of East Rus-

2. Pskovian Chronicle, p. 98.
3. See *Mongols and Russia,* p. 299.

sian bishops. This time no approval of the Patriarch of Constantinople was asked. Evfimi did not attend the electoral council but sent his written agreement to Iona's election. Evfimi died in 1458 after having been the head of the Novgorodian Church for twenty-four years. His position had been unique, since he had been ordained not by the Metropolitan of Moscow but by a metropolitan who for all practical purposes was primate of the West Russian Church. In contrast to many a Muscovite clergyman, Evfimi entertained no suspicions against foreigners. According to his "Life"—compiled by a Serbian scholar who emigrated to Russia in 1440, Pakhomi Logofet —Evfimi welcomed all newcomers from foreign lands and was friendly and helpful to them. In the German sources he is called "good protector and defender of the German merchants." [4]

Until 1448 Muscovite political and religious affairs had been in a state of confusion, and Evfimi's authority over the Novgorodian Church was practically unrestricted. The new metropolitan, Iona, was at first uncertain about his own powers (being unrecognized by the Patriarch of Constantinople) and so made no drastic attempt to curb the rights of the church. True, he addressed two epistles to Novgorod, one to Archbishop Evfimi, the other to Novgorodians at large, admonishing them to desist from their widespread habit of public fisticuffs, which often resulted in bloodshed and murder. Iona's epistles were in the form of advice, however, not of peremptory orders.[5] On the whole, the period of Evfimi II was that of rapid growth of the spirit of freedom and self-reliance in the Novgorodian Church and Novgorodian society at large. Evfimi's successor, Archbishop Iona (d. 1470), followed the tradition.

Among the literary works sponsored by Evfimi was a cycle of tales centering around the lives and miracles of two distant predecessors of Evfimi, Archbishop Ivan (Ioann, around 1170) and Archbishop Moisei (1325–29 and 1352–59). Their purpose was to glorify the Novgorodian saints and thus enhance the prestige of the Novgorodian Church. At the time of Ivan, one of the tales recounted, Novgorod was attacked by the Suzdalian armies, led by several princes under the command of Prince Andrei Bogoliubsky. On Ivan's advice, the Novgorodians took a venerated icon of Our Lady from the church to which it belonged and placed it on the top of the wall, facing the Suzdalians. It was hoped that the latter would then desist

---

4. Nikitsky, *Ocherk vnutrennei istorii tserkvi v Velikom Novgorode*, pp. 44–45.
5. See Makari, *Istoriia Russkoi Tserkvi*, 7, 123–125.

from their attack. The Suzdalians, however, continued to shoot arrows, and some of the arrows hit the icon. Tears are reported to have poured from the eyes of Our Lady. The Suzdalians were struck by blindness and fled from Novgorod. The motif of this tale was used in the composition of the icon of Our Lady of the Sign of the late 15th century.[6] The author of the tale bitterly complained that the allied princes, in attacking Novgorod, broke the unity of the Russian people and the Christian faith.[7]

The same idea of the unity of Russian people lay at the basis of the Novgorodian historical literature of the 15th century. Under Evfimi (around 1448) an ambitious scholarly project was undertaken, that of compiling, on the basis of earlier Russian annals (both Novgorodian and other), a comprehensive history of Russia. In modern historical literature this compilation is known as the Novgorod-Sophian Digest (*Novgorodsko-Sofiisky Svod*).[8] A novel feature of it is the inclusion of various historical, geographical, and juridical notes, among others the "List of the Russian Cities" mentioned above (pp. 2–3). The *Svod* was not preserved as a whole, but parts of it survived in some Novgorodian annals of lesser scope, especially in the Fourth Novgorodian Chronicle and the First Sophian Chronicle. The "List" as well as other notes of similar character, were also included in a variant of the First Novgorodian Chronicle,[9] where we find also a "List of Russian Metropolitans." The last name in this list is that of Gerasim, who had ordained Evfimi. Among the other notes in that section of the codex is a list of the Russian "grand princes" (from Rurik to Vasili II) as well as a list of the Novgorod princes, mayors (*posadniki*), chiliarchs (*tysiatskie*), and archbishops.

Another aspect of Evfimi's activities is shown by his interest in architecture. He sponsored the building of churches and palaces in Novgorod; many of these churches were built in the style of the 12th century. It is obvious that Evfimi tried to revive the old traditions of Novgorodian architecture.[10] As far as I know, there is no evidence of Evfimi's personal interest in painting, but his period

6. Hamilton, plate 54B.
7. Gudzii, p. 456.
8. See Likhachev, *Russkie letopisi,* pp. 312–316.
9. First Novgorodian Chronicle, pp. 475–477.
10. Likhachev, *Russkie letopisi,* p. 341. For pictures of the 12th-century Novgorodian architecture see Hamilton, plates 8 and 9; for the 15th century see Grabar, *1,* 212–214. See also Grabar (2d ed., *2,* 30–44, 63–71, text and illustrations).

nevertheless saw the blossoming of icon painting of the Novgorodian School.

2. BETWEEN MOSCOW AND LITHUANIA

Novgorod's prosperity and the flowering of her culture depended on her freedom as well as on her being a part of the Russian world. In conformity with this, her political program consisted of two main points—the preservation of Novgorodian institutions and the revival of the Russian federation. Most of the Novgorodian political leaders realized that Novgorod could survive only within the framework of a community of all the Russian lands.

Was this ideal attainable? The odds were against it, since by the middle of the 15th century two large states—the Grand Duchy of Moscow and that of Lithuania—had absorbed most of the formerly independent Russian principalities. Had Novgorod been a strong military power, on a par with Muscovy and Lithuania, she could think of sponsoring a federated union of the three major states—herself, Lithuania, and Muscovy—in which the minor states (Pskov, Tver, and Riazan) could also take part. However, Novgorod never succeeded in building up a strong military establishment, and this proved fatal to her in the hour of crisis.

Under the circumstances, Novgorod's only hope of survival was to balance Muscovy against Lithuania, and to support centrifugal forces in both these large states. On the Lithuanian side, the Novgorodians tried to cultivate friendly relations with some of the lesser princes of the House of Gedymin, notably, with those of Kiev. On the Moscow side, during the struggle between Vasili II and his uncle Iuri (and afterward, Iuri's son Dmitri Shemiaka and the latter's son, Shemiachich) in the 1430's and 1440's,[11] the Novgorodians supported Vasili's opponents. Vasili, not unnaturally, resented their attitude and after his victory attempted to restrict Novgorod's freedom in retaliation.

The Novgorodians, for obvious reasons, feared the power of the Grand Duke of Moscow and centralization of the Muscovite army and administration; at the same time they failed to realize the underlying purpose of Muscovite policies and the support a considerable part of the Muscovites gave these policies. The people of Moscow were weary of the civil war. Even more important, they suffered

11. See *Mongols and Russia*, pp. 299–301, 318–325, 327–329.

under the constant strain of Tatar attacks and devastation and therefore understood better than anyone else the necessity of strong leadership and building up a strong army. For them it was a struggle for
survival, and the people felt that they needed security from enemy
attacks more than anything else. Vasili II's rival, Dmitri Shemiaka,
at one time tried to use against Vasili both Novgorod and the
Khanate of Kazan. Novgorodian sympathies for Shemiaka were thus
linked, in the eyes of the Muscovites, with Shemiaka's friendliness
toward the Tatars. Novgorod was safe from the Tatar menace because it was screened from the Tatars by Muscovy. Few Novgorodians gave sufficient thought to this situation and even fewer understood the effect of the Tatar menace on Moscow's political
program.

Since Lithuania was a constitutional monarchy and the Russian
lands subject to the authority of the grand duke enjoyed far-reaching autonomy, Novgorod had much less to fear politically from
entering into a union with Lithuania than from recognizing the authority of the Grand Duke of Moscow. From the point of view of
economics, however, Novgorod was more closely connected with
Muscovy than with Lithuania. In the first place, the Novgorod area
did not produce enough grain for her population, and she therefore
had to buy most of her grain in the lower towns. Any conflict with
Muscovy meant shortage of bread and consequently famine. Besides, the main road to the East, down the Volga River, was controlled by Moscow, and it was mainly through Muscovy that the
Novgorodian merchants could obtain the Oriental goods that constituted a valuable item in their trade with the West. As to the Baltic
trade, West Russian and Lithuanian cities had their own outlets to
the Baltic and were in some respects Novgorod's rivals.

Furthermore, the relations between Novgorod and Lithuania were
complicated by Lithuania's union with Poland. True, between 1447
and 1569 the union was effected only through the person of the
ruler. With few exceptions, Poland and Lithuania elected to their
respective thrones the same man, known as "king" in Poland and
"grand duke" in Lithuania. Internally, Lithuania was a separate
state, but Lithuanian policies could not but be affected by Polish
interests. With this the religious problem was closely connected,
Poland being the main bulwark of Catholicism in Eastern Europe.

According to the stipulations of the first treaty of union between
Poland and Lithuania (1385) Roman Catholicism officially became

the state religion in the Grand Duchy of Lithuania, and only Roman Catholics were to enjoy political rights. As a result, the Lithuanians were converted to Roman Catholicism. The West Russian nobility, however, objected violently to any attempt to convert them to Roman Catholicism or deprive them of their former political status. In 1432 the Grand Duke of Lithuania had to make concessions to his Russian subjects and to abrogate the clause denying them political rights. The existence of the Greek Orthodox Church in Lithuania was thus indirectly recognized. (The execution of Metropolitan Gerasim, in 1435, mentioned above, was motivated by political not by religious reasons.)

Following the Florentine Union an attempt was made to subordinate the West Russian Church to the authority of the pope. It should be noted that after Iona's election in Moscow to the metropolitan see (1448), Casimir—Grand Duke of Lithuania since 1440; King of Poland since 1447—at first recognized Iona's authority over the West Russian Church. Ten years later, in Rome, however, the Greek Uniate patriarch in exile, Gregory Mammas, at the advice of Cardinal Isidor (former Metropolitan of Moscow) ordained the latter's pupil Grigori (a Bulgarian) Metropolitan of Russia. Pope Pius II confirmed Grigori and sent him to Casimir. As King of Poland, Casimir did not find it possible to refuse the pope's plea and admitted Grigori as Metropolitan "of Kiev and all Russia." The Moscow authorities refused to accept him, but the West Russian bishops reluctantly agreed to cooperate with him. Only one of them refused to recognize Grigori and emigrated to Muscovy. As a matter of fact, none of the West Russian bishops accepted the union wholeheartedly, and the congregations were openly against it. After ten years of unsuccessful attempts to entrench the idea of union among his flock, Grigori finally gave up and in 1469 dispatched an envoy to Constantinople asking for the blessing of the Greek Orthodox patriarch. The latter confirmed Grigori in his office and sent messages to Moscow and Novgorod urging that Grigori be recognized as metropolitan in all Russia. The Moscow authorities refused to do this. On the other hand, some of the Novgorodians, as we shall see, were inclined to comply with the patriarch's demand. The result of the controversy was the division of the Russian Orthodox Church into two bodies: the autocephalous Church of Moscow and the Kievan diocese of the Patriarchate of Constantinople.

The religious problem was closely connected with the general position of the Russian people within the framework of the Grand Duchy of Lithuania. Numerically, the Russians constituted the majority of the population of the grand duchy. Politically, however, their position was greatly weakened after Lithuania's union with Poland, the conversion of the Lithuanians to Roman Catholicism, and the gradual Polonization of the Lithuanian aristocracy. As the Ukrainian historian Mikhail Hrushevsky pointed out, in spite of the *Privilei* of 1432, at first only few Russians were admitted to any high position in the state. While Roman Catholic bishops played an important role in the *rada* (council of the lords), we find no Greek Orthodox bishops there.[12] On the other hand, the Lithuanian lords were not in a position to exclude Russian laymen from the government of the grand duchy, since Lithuania needed their support now against Poland and now against Moscow. In 1441 Casimir had to recognize his uncle Svidrigailo, popular among the Russians, as Prince of Volynia, and his cousin, Aleksandr (Olelko), as Prince of Kiev.[13] These concessions were the result of the shaky position of Casimir at the beginning of his reign and the existence of rival candidates to the throne. Later on, Casimir and the Lithuanian lords attempted to curb the ascendancy of the Russian element in the grand duchy, which resulted in the opposition to Casimir of a number of the defenders of the Russian rights.

It was in the mutual interest of the Russians in both the Grand Duchy of Lithuania and Novgorod to coordinate their policies. That the Novgorodians attempted to do, but with no great success.

3. THE CONSTITUTION

Novgorod was politically connected with Moscow through the person of her prince, who usually was at the same time Grand Duke of Moscow. The prince in Novgorod, however, had an entirely different status than in Moscow. In the first place, the princely office in Novgorod was elective. Secondly, the prince in Novgorod had but a limited authority. Each prince, after being elected, had to take a special oath and to sign a contract, in the form of a treaty, by which he pledged to preserve the Novgorodian institutions and to limit his actions to a strictly defined sphere of competence. In case

12. Hrushevsky, *Istoriia Ukrainy-Rusi*, 4, 225–226.
13. *Ibid.*, p. 200.

the Novgorodians did not like the prince, they had the right to depose him—to "show him the way out," as the expression ran.

The main reason why the Novgorodians needed a prince was military. Their own forces, on many occasions, proved inadequate to ward off the attacks of their enemies—the Germans, the Lithuanians, and the Swedes. Another important function of the prince was judicial; as an outsider, he could be expected to be less partial than the Novgorodian authorities. Also, he was authorized to participate in the higher administration of Novgorod, though his competence was strictly limited by treaties. The prince might function only in conjunction with the Novgorodian authorities. In each princely treaty with Novgorod we find the expression addressed to the prince: "And you shall not judge, or appoint provincial governors, or issue any charters, without the concurrence of the *posadnik* [mayor]." It was stipulated, furthermore, that the prince could act, as Prince of Novgorod, only while he stayed in Novgorod; no decision on any Novgorodian affair could be taken while he was residing in his other principality (Suzdalia or Moscow). In contrast, the Novgorodian officials could and did act without the prince's advice, and the Novgorodian city assembly (veche) could and did issue new laws and charters (*vechnye gramoty*) without the prince's approval. He had to promise not to trade with the German merchants in Novgorod except through the Novgorodians. He had no right to close the German Yard, or to send his constables there.[14]

As remuneration for his services the prince was entitled to receive an annual *dar* (gift) from the Novgorodian outside *volosti* (provinces) but not from the basic territory of Novgorod (the *piatiny;* see above, p. 6). The prince in addition received a share in court fees and was assigned a number of hunting and fishing preserves for his exploitation. All of his revenues were audited by Novgorodian officials.

The Novgorodians took every precaution to prevent the prince from firmly entrenching himself in Novgorod. He was treated as an

14. Novgorod's treaties with the grand dukes of Vladimir and Moscow are published in *GNP*. See also Soloviev, *Ob otnosheniiakh Novgoroda k velikim kniaziam.* On Novgorod at large see N. I. Kostomarov, *Severnorusskie narodopravstva, 1, 2;* Nikitsky, *Istoriia ekonomicheskogo byta Velikogo Novgoroda; idem,* "Ocherki iz zhizni Velikogo Novgoroda," *ZMNP, 145* (1869), 294–309, and *ZMNP, 150* (1870), 201–224; Kliuchevsky, *Kurs Russkoi istorii, 2;* Porfiridov, *Drevnii Novgorod; Ocherki 2.*

2. Novgorod's Five Provinces (*Piatiny*)

outsider. The office and residence buildings he was assigned were situated outside the city, in a locality known as *Gorodishche* ("Old Town Site"). He, his family, and his retinue were forbidden to acquire landed property in the Novgorodian territory or to establish their patronage over Novgorodian peasants or workers.

When all is said, it is clear that the Novgorodian prince was not a ruler of Novgorod; he was a hired official with a limited competence. Actually, Novgorod was a republic—Lord Novgorod the Great (*Gospodin Velikii Novgorod*). The Sancta Sophia Cathedral was its spiritual center, and it was believed that Novgorod was protected by the "Divine Wisdom" (*Sancta Sophia*).

The supreme power was vested in the city assembly. This body elected the mayors, the chiliarchs, and other high officials who acted in the name of Novgorod. It was convened by the pealing of a special bell—the veche bell, main symbol of Novgorodian liberty. The veche chancellery was located at the so-called Iaroslav Yard, and the assembly met in the square in front of the chancellery.

In its meetings all male Novgorodian citizens had the right to participate, and a "unanimous" decision was required in each case, meaning that if there was a clear majority vote on any question, the dissidents had to acquiesce. If, on the contrary, there were two disagreeing groups of about equal size, fisticuffs would often result. In a critical situation, the archbishop acted as moderator, but if nothing worked the decision had to be postponed. We should not think, however, that the assembly was an amorphous crowd. The people were arranged in the square in accordance with the subdivisions of the city. As has been mentioned, the city of Novgorod was an association of five communes, or boroughs, known as *kontšy*. Each *konets* (singular) consisted of two *sotni* (hundreds); each *sotnia* of several *ulitsy* (streets); each *ulitsa* of several *riady* (rows). The smaller communes were like neighborhood associations. Usually, artisans of the same trade, and in general people of similar status or profession, settled in the same section of the city, so that some of the sectional communes resembled artisan guilds.

Most of the important affairs, before being submitted to the consideration of the veche, were discussed in the sectional communes. More often than not a preliminary agreement would be reached at the borough level. At the meetings of the veche, men of each borough kept together, and within the borough each smaller group had its own place. When all of the boroughs were unanimous, the veche was able to arrive at a final decision without any trouble. Only when there was a disagreement among the boroughs was the veche torn by dissension.

The work of the veche was also aided by the existence of its special committee, the council of lords, which met in the archbishop's palace and was presided over by the archbishop. It consisted of the highest officials of the city—the senior mayor, assistant mayors, and chiliarchs; and of the *starosty* (elders) of the kontsy and sotni. All in all, these were about fifty members of the council, collectively known as the boyars.[15] The council prepared matters for the discussions of the veche and, generally speaking, maintained a continuity of Novgorodian policy. It should be added that the highest positions in the administration of the judiciary were filled, by election, with candidates from among the social set that centered around the council.

Political conflicts in Novgorod were often tinged with social emotions arising from the divergence of interests among the various classes of the Novgorod people. The Novgorod society was not a feudal one. There were no "estates" in Novgorod in Western terms, no *Stände* in the German sense (the corresponding Russian term of the Imperial period is *sostoianie* or *soslovie*). What differences there were among the various social classes in Novgorod were founded on economic position—greater or lesser wealth.

The basic social cleavage in Novgorod was between the rich and the poor—in S. M. Soloviev's words, between the consumers of wheat bread and those of rye.[16] The former group was numerically smaller than the latter but much more influential economically and politically. There were two subdivisions in the wealthy class. The top group was the boyars; the next, *zhityi liudi* (well-to-do people). People of the lowest group—the rye-bread eaters—were *molodshie liudi* (junior men) or *chernye liudi* (black people). In the Novgorod Charter of Justice of 1471 we find a scale of fines for riotous attack on any of the Novgorod high officials or judges. According to this

---

15. See Nikitsky, "Ocherki iz zhizni Velikogo Novgoroda." As regards the Novgorod mayors (*posadniki*), it is usually considered in scholarly literature that there was only one mayor (*stepennyi posadnik*); other mayors mentioned were considered "old" ("late") mayors, not officially in power. In my opinion, there were several mayors in Novgorod at any given time. The senior one was called *stepennyi posadnik;* the others were known as just *posadniki. Stepennyi* is derived from *stepen'*, "rostrum," from which official statements were announced.

16. Soloviev, *Istoriia Rossii s drevneishikh vremen, 5,* 19.

scale, a boyar had to pay, for the offense he committed, a fine of
fifty rubles; a *zhityi*, twenty rubles; and a junior man, ten rubles.[17]
This scale does not reflect the exact proportion of disparity in the
distribution of wealth between the upper and lower classes in
Novgorod, for the actual difference was certainly much greater.

The two main sources of wealth of the Novgorod upper classes
were trade and landed estates. It should be noted that the land
regime in Novgorod was not feudal. Land was freely bought and
sold, and citizens of any social group could own it. Actually, the
largest landed estates belonged to the boyars, but some of the
zhityis also owned estates of considerable size. Because of the poor
soil and harsh climate of the Novgorodian area, the value of a
landed estate was not so much in agriculture as in the exploitation
of natural resources of the forests and lakes: producing tars and
ashes (later of potash), extracting and smelting iron, making salt
(through evaporation), and exploiting various fishing and hunting
preserves. Among agricultural products, flax was of great importance. All these products were in constant demand on the market.
We may say, therefore, that in Novgorod the production of the large
landed estates was oriented in trade.

Merchants in Novgorod did not constitute a separate group;
many of the boyars and zhityis undoubtedly were engaged in trade.
A merchant could be counted as a boyar or as a zhityi depending
on the amount of his capital. And there was a professional organization, the Guild of St. John, the entrance fee of which was high
(50 silver *grivny* in the 12th century; no figure is available for
the later period). This was obviously a corporation of the wealthy
wholesale merchants. Retail merchants of smaller means were organized in associations known as "hundreds." It is this lower group
of merchants, called *kuptsy* (merchants), that is referred to in the
preamble to the Novgorod Charter of 1471, where it is listed below
the zhityis.

The church people in Novgorod formed a social group of their
own, and a very influential group it was. At the head stood the
Archbishop of Novgorod. Next to him in importance was the
Archimandrite of Novgorod (the title of the Abbot of St. George's
Monastery). Of considerable importance also were the clergy of
the Sancta Sophia Cathedral and the abbots of major monasteries.
In addition to the clergymen, some of the laymen in the archbishop's

17. Vernadsky, *Medieval Russian Laws*, p. 84 (art. 6).

service were fairly influential in both church and city affairs. All
people connected with the church were under the archbishop's special jurisdiction. With all this, the clergy did not constitute a closed
estate in Novgorod. Any Novgorodian citizen might be ordained,
and there was no law against a clergyman's, even of a monk's, returning to the ranks of laymen. The church was rich. The archbishop's see as well as the major monasteries owned vast landed
estates and industrial establishments. The Archbishop of Novgorod
thus controlled, directly or indirectly, a substantial share of
Novgorod's national income.

The lower classes of the city consisted of artisans and manual
workers of various trades. Physical labor was the main source of
their income.

So far we have been dealing with Novgorod's society in the proper
sense of the word—the people of Novgorod herself, consisting of
full-fledged Novgorod citizens. Some of them resided outside the
city, in the smaller towns (*prigorody,* literally "by-towns") or on
their farms, but they had the right to participate in the veche
whenever they were physically able to attend its meetings. However, besides the citizens there were certain other groups, whom
we may call subjects rather than citizens. In the first place, in the
basic area of Novgorod there was a group of peasants—settled on
state lands—who, though personally free, had no political rights.
These were known as *smerdy* (a terminological leftover of the
Kievan period).

Then, we should not forget the provinces (*volosti*), and Novgorod's
vast empire in North Russia, stretching east to the Ural Mountains.
The people of these regions were ruled by agents, and having no
voice in the veche could not influence Novgorod's policies in normal
times, though in time of crisis—especially during the struggle with
Moscow—the attitude of these people toward the metropolis was
of considerable importance: they could either support Novgorod
wholeheartedly or refuse her support. In the latter case they could
and to a certain extent did become Moscow's tools.

Finally, it should be noted that in Novgorod, as in all other
Russian lands, slavery was a recognized institution. Slaves were
owned mainly by the boyars and rich merchants. The number of
slaves in Novgorod was greater than in Muscovy, but the Muscovite
society was also a slave-owning society, and therefore Moscow was
not in a position to promote any abolitionist policy on principle.

But individual discontented slaves of the Novgorod boyars could be used by Moscow agents as informers against their masters.

Apart from the peripheral population of the dominions, the social cleavage between rich and poor in Novgorod could not but gravely affect politics, especially in time of crisis. While the poor constituted the majority in the veche, the rich controlled the council of lords, and when the sectional communes could not agree among themselves, the opinion of the council would prevail in the veche. Moreover, the boyars had various ways by which they could directly or indirectly influence public opinion. If nothing else worked, attempts would be made to bribe influential commoners to accept policies recommended by the boyars. It was enough for the boyar party to secure support of even one or two of the kontsy to break the unity of the veche.

Another aspect of the Novgorod government where the influence of the wealthy prevailed was the judiciary. Novgorod, as well as Pskov, had a well balanced system of courts and firmly established rules of procedure. All of the citizens were equal before the law and were tried in the same manner. However, as the judges were chosen mostly among the wealthier section of the people, the poor complained, on many occasions, of being denied fair justice. Eventually, this situation made it possible for the Grand Duke of Moscow to increase his judicial prerogatives and in this way to drive another wedge between the Novgorodian aristocracy and the commoners.

Novgorod's original political program had, as mentioned, two basic points—maintaining the city's freedom and reviving the Russian federation; from the available evidence we may think this program was supported by a great majority of citizens irrespective of what social group they belonged to. However, when the plan of federation had proved unattainable and when, in the harsh terms of practical politics, Novgorod was faced with the dilemma of siding with either Lithuania or Moscow, the Novgorodians found themselves in a state of confusion, and dissensions started among them.

The boyars, most of them in any case, were for an agreement with Lithuania, since they thought that Novgorod's freedom would be best protected this way. On the other hand, most of the clergy were reluctant to enter into a union with Lithuania, because they were afraid of the possibility of Roman Catholic pressure on the Novgorod Church. Many of the commoners had the same doubts. Besides, good relations with Moscow meant cheap and plentiful bread. Furthermore, some of the lower-class people were not against granting the Grand Duke of Moscow added jurisdiction in the Novgorodian courts. On the whole, it may be said that the pro-Lithuanian party in Novgorod was sponsored mostly by the boyars, and the pro-Moscow party by a section of the lower classes. The majority of citizens could not make up their minds and preferred avoiding a showdown as long as possible.

As has been mentioned, Novgorod's main weakness was in her military establishment. Traditionally, the Novgorodians expected the prince they had elected to protect the city. The Grand Duke of Moscow was not in a position—and had no wish—to reside permanently in Novgorod. Besides, he was prevented, by treaties, from keeping a permanent army in Novgorod. He was expected to send his troops there whenever the latter was attacked by the Swedes or Livonian Knights. This proved not entirely satisfactory to the Novgorodians, since the grand duke's troops could not always reach Novgorod in time. For securing her defense, she needed troops on the spot, and therefore hired "service princes" from time to time. Some of these princes belonged to the House of Rurik, others to the House of Gedymin. Each was supposed to bring with him his retinue, a well trained body of horsemen. But the Novgorodians also needed to build up an armed force of their own. The Novgorod Church agreed to produce a cavalry detachment, known as *vladychnyi stiag* (the prelate's banner), and in case of emergency, all of the citizens could be mobilized to form an infantry army, under the command of the tysiatsky. As a result of those arrangements, Novgorod was in position to gather, when needed, a large army—the majority of whose soldiers, however, were poorly armed and trained, and over which there was no unity of command. Such a force proved no match for Moscow.

4. CONFLICTS WITH MOSCOW, 1456 AND 1470–71

Moscow's political program, like that of Novgorod, was based on the notion of unity of the Russian people. Her methods for achieving the unity were, however, quite different from those proposed by Novgorod. Moscow offered the Russian people unity through its subordination to the political and military authority of the grand duke. All of Russia was regarded in Moscow as the patrimony of the grand ducal crown. Thus, in opposition to the republican idea of a free Russian federation (sponsored by the Novgorodians), Moscow offered the monarchical idea of a centralized Russian state. In view of such divergence in basic political goals, a conflict between Novgorod and Moscow seemed inevitable.

While the Muscovite grand dukes, like the Suzdalian and Tver grand dukes before them, pledged to secure Novgorodian freedoms "in accordance with the *starina*" (old customs), they were anxious gradually to increase their authority over Novgorod by offering their own notion of starina. Since the reign of Daniel's son Ivan I, the Novgorodians, with few exceptions, had always elected grand dukes of Moscow (descendants of Ivan I) to the Novgorodian princely office. This preference they gave to Moscow may be explained by their hope that they could obtain better protection against their enemies from the Grand Duke of Moscow than from any other prince. The time came, however, when Moscow itself emerged as a menace. Especially was this clear to the Novgorodians after Vasili II's victory over his opponents. Vasili considered the fact that so many of his ancestors were princes of Novgorod a precedent for enhancing Moscow's authority over it. This was his conception of starina in the Muscovite-Novgorodian relations, and because of it he insisted that the Novgorodians pledge to keep the grand-ducal power *chestno i grozno* (in esteem and respect).

When Vasili's chief rival and opponent, Dmitri Shemiaka, after having been finally defeated by Moscow's generals (1452) fled to Novgorod, and the Novgorodians gave him refuge, Vasili regarded this act as a breach of faith on the part of the Novgorodians. The next year Shemiaka was secretly poisoned by Muscovite agents. The Novgorodians gave his body a state funeral in the St. George Monastery, which Vasili II considered another offense. He also resented the fact that the Novgorodians accepted, as their service-prince, one of the princes of the House of Suzdalia, Vasili Grebenka Shuisky, who formerly had been in his service. Moreover, Vasili II complained to the Novgorodian authorities that they failed regularly to pay him his share of the court fees. Receiving no satisfactory reply from Novgorod, Vasili II led his armies against what he considered a rebellious city. A small detachment of the Muscovite troops commanded by Prince Ivan Vasilievich Striga-Obolensky and the "boyar son" Fedor Basenok seized and looted the rich town of Rusa south of Lake Ilmen. The Novgorodians sent their cavalry corps, five thousand strong, to rescue Rusa. These horsemen wore heavy plate armor and were equipped with long lances. Their horses, however, were not protected. It is said that only two hundred of the Muscovites were at hand to meet the Novgorodians, the other Muscovites having gone back to the main army with their loot. As the Novgorodians approached, the Muscovites aimed their arrows at the horses, not the horsemen. A large number of mounts fell, others stampeded, and the battle ended in complete victory for the Muscovites.[18]

The Novgorodians could not muster further resistance and sent Archbishop Evfimi to the grand duke's camp to plead for peace, which was granted, but on harsh conditions. They accepted nevertheless (1456), and a new treaty was concluded in the name of Vasili II and his son Ivan III, then a lad of sixteen.[19] This was a master stroke of Muscovite diplomacy, for it enabled Ivan, later on, to claim Novgorod as his *otchina* (patrimony). The Novgorodians had to pay a fine of 8,500 rubles and permit the grand duke to collect a special tax, the so-called *cherny bor* (black collection), a leftover of the Mongol tribute, from some of the Novgorodian provinces. The veche was deprived of its old right of issuing charters without the prince's approval. The grand duke's seal was to be applied to all charters. Finally, the Novgorodians had to promise not to admit to Novgorod Shemiaka's son (who fled to Lithuania after the death of his father), nor any of Vasili II's other enemies (*likhodei,* literally "wrongdoers"). By that, the Novgorodians not only abandoned their old rule of giving refuge to anyone who asked for it but also accepted Moscow's political control over their relations with all the Russian princes not subject to the authority of the Grand Duke of Moscow. More than that, by this clause of the treaty a new concept was introduced into the relations between Moscow and Novgorod: "treason." Any association of the Novgorodians with any of the grand duke's wrongdoers could now be considered by the Muscovite authorities as a political crime against the duke, to whose discretion it was left to determine what was treason and what was not. His now was the sole power to punish offenses he considered criminal. Nothing was said about participation of Novgorodian officials in political trials.

The Treaty of 1456 proved a serious blow to Novgorod's freedom. It meant that the first round in the struggle with Moscow had been

18. *PSRL, 12,* 111.
19. For the texts of the Treaty of 1456 see *GNP,* pp. 39–43.

won by the latter. This prepared the ground for Ivan III's attack on Novgorod fifteen years later.

The story of the Moscow-Novgorodian conflict of 1470–71 is known to us mainly from Muscovite sources. Only an excerpt from the Novgorodian records of the events was preserved in the Fourth Novgorodian Chronicle. Some additional information may be culled from the Pskovian chronicles. The Muscovite accounts are not unnaturally biased in favor of Ivan III, and some of them read like political pamphlets expounding the Muscovite doctrine of state and church. Undoubtedly, pamphlets of such nature were also written in Novgorod to explain and defend the Novgorodian political program, but none has reached us.

For obvious reasons, the Novgorodians could not be expected to accept the terms of the Treaty of 1456 as final; they determined to get rid of the oppressive clauses of the treaty at their first opportunity. An influential group of Novgorodian boyars now looked to Lithuania for assistance. At the head of this boyar group stood a woman—"Martha, the Mayoress" (Marfa Posadnitsa). Marfa Boretskaia was undoubtedly one of the most remarkable Russian women of that age. Legally, she was not a mayoress—only men might be elected mayors in Novgorod. She was, however, widow of a mayor and mother of a mayor, and her influence on Novgorodian policies, especially on the policies of the boyar party, was apparently considerable. Unfortunately, very little evidence on her is available, since after the fall of Novgorod the archives of the Boretskys as well as those of most of the Novgorodian boyars were destroyed or confiscated. Part of the state papers from the Boretskys' archive were taken to Moscow. Private correspondence was apparently destroyed.

The Muscovite chroniclers speak of Marfa with obvious bias and hatred. They say that Marfa and her sons "were taught by the Devil." [20] They liken her to Jezebel, to Delilah, to Herodiad, and to the Byzantine Empress Eudocia, who persecuted St. John Chrysostom.[21] They alleged that she wanted to ruin the Greek Orthodox faith and convert Novgorodians to Roman Catholicism. Furthermore, they accused her of personal vanity and asserted that she intended to marry the Lithuanian grandee whom Casimir was to send to Novgorod as his lieutenant and thus to rule Novgorod

20. *PSRL, 12,* 126.
21. Fourth Novgodorian Chronicle, p. 503; *PSRL, 6, 5.*

in Casimir's name. This latter charge sounds ridiculous, since Marfa was well advanced in years. Her husband, Isaak Andreevich Boretsky had been an important Novgorodian official as early as 1428; in 1439, as the then mayor of Novgorod, he signed a treaty with the German merchants.[22] He died before 1459. His and Marfa's eldest son, Dmitri, was the mayor of Novgorod in 1471. At that time Marfa probably was 65 if not more.

While active in politics, Marfa did not neglect family affairs. The Boretskys were among the wealthiest landowners. They had huge estates in various parts of the Novgorodian empire, among other places at the coast of the White Sea opposite the Solovki Islands. After her husband's death, Marfa ruled the family possessions with a firm hand. She was the boss; her sons merely assisted her. In view of the accusations of the Moscow chronicles of Marfa's treason to Greek Orthodoxy, it should be pointed out that at least on two occasions she donated valuable tracts of land, with fishing grounds, to the Solovki Monastery. One of these tracts was given some time between 1459 and 1469; the other, in 1469–70.[23]

It is interesting to note that the memory of these deeds survived among the *pomory* (people at the coast of the White Sea) until recently. Around 1908 the coast fishermen told the writer Mikhail Prishvin that the Solovki monks had very old rights on the fishing grounds—in fact, "from the time of Marfa the Mayoress."[24]

In conformance with Novgorodian political traditions, the boyar party first intended to deal not with the Grand Duke of Lithuania but with some lesser prince of the House of Gedymin, one who would represent the Russian element in the Grand Duchy of Lithuania. Accordingly, some time in 1470 they invited Prince Mikhail Olelkovich (son of Olelko, i.e. Aleksandr) to come to Novgorod with his retinue in the capacity of a "service prince."

Mikhail's father and grandfather had been princes of Kiev, and his elder brother Simeon had occupied the Kievan throne from around 1454. Simeon was very popular in Pskov, and presumably in Novgorod too. On the occasion of his death in 1470, the Pskovian chronicler remarked that he "defended, with honor, his patrimony, Kiev, from the Golden Horde and other Tatars, and his name was highly esteemed both in Russia and in foreign lands."[25] It should

22. *GNP*, p. 113.
23. *GNP*, pp. 242–243, 300.
24. M. Prishvin, *Izbrannoe* (Moscow, 1946), p. 23.
25. *PSRL, 4*, 236.

be noted that Simeon's and Mikhail's mother was Vasili II's sister, and they were therefore Ivan III's first cousins.

Mikhail accepted the Novgorodian offer and arrived at Novgorod on November 8, 1470, with his retinue.[26] In the Nikon Chronicle it is said that King Casimir (Grand Duke of Lithuania) sent him to Novgorod.[27] In the Fourth Novgorodian Chronicle it is recorded only that Mikhail "came to Novgorod." [28] As a matter of fact, the relations between Casimir and the Olelkovichi (sons of Olelko) were not at all cordial, and the Olelkovichi might have hoped to strengthen their position by an agreement between Kiev and Novgorod. Casimir hardly could have been happy about it.

A number of Kievan merchants came to Novgorod with Mikhail, among them several Jews.[29] One of these, Zechariah (Skharia), was a learned man, well versed in philosophy and astronomy; and in his talks with Novgorodian scholars he sowed the seeds of the intellectual current in Russia that eventually became known as the "Heresy of the Judaizers."

It is presumably Mikhail Olelkovich or someone in his retinue who arranged for a trip of Novgorodian painters to Kraków, Poland. To them belongs the wall painting of the Last Supper in the Holy Cross chapel of the Kraków Cathedral, dated 1471.[30]

The Moscow government could not help being worried about Mikhail Olelkovich's coming to Novgorod. Political tension between Moscow and Novgorod was aggravated by religious discord. Three days before Mikhail's arrival, Archbishop Iona died in his palace, and ten days after his death the veche met in the Sancta Sophia square for the election of a new archbishop. No unanimous decision was reached. Three candidates were nominated, all of them monks closely associated with the late Iona, namely, Iona's confessor Varsonofi; the archbishop's steward, Pimen; and the chief vestry-

---

26. *PSRL, 4,* 235.

27. *PSRL, 12,* 126. Bazilevich (p. 91) says that the Pskovian Chronicle likewise considers Mikhail Casimir's agent, quoting the phrase "from the king's hand." This is a misunderstanding. The phrase refers not to Michael's arrival at Novgorod but to the installation, by Casimir, of Olelko and his clan on the throne of Kiev (*PSRL, 4,* 235).

28. Fourth Novgorodian Chronicle, p. 446.

29. In the Grand Duchy of Lithuania of this period both Rabbinical Jews (Talmudists) and Karaites were called "Jews." The question whether Zechariah and his companions were adherents of Rabbinical Judaism or were Karaites will be discussed in Vol. 5.

30. See picture of it in Grabar, *6,* 261.

man, Feofil. The matter was decided by lot, which fell on Feofil, who was therefore recognized as archbishop-elect.

The next move was to notify Moscow of the election and ask safe conduct from the Moscow authorities for Feofil to come to Moscow to be ordained by Metropolitan Philip. The Moscow government agreed to accept Feofil without any hesitation. However, by the time the message reached Novgorod, the city was in riotous turmoil. The boyar party objected to the subordination of the Novgorod archbishop to the Metropolitan of Moscow and insisted on sending the archbishop-elect to Kiev instead, to be blessed by Metropolitan Grigori of Kiev. Feofil flatly refused to be ordained by Grigori. The latter, as has been said, had been originally ordained by the Greek Uniate patriarch and the pope in Rome and only later (in 1469) was blessed by the Orthodox Greek patriarch. Feofil apparently doubted the sincerity of Grigori's conversion to Orthodoxy. The Moscow authorities, as we know, refused to recognize Grigori.

However, Pimen, Feofil's fellow candidate to the archbishop's see, although not favored by lot now declared that he was ready to go to Kiev for Grigori's blessing. In his position of steward of the archbishop's palace, Pimen controlled large amounts of money, and according to the Muscovite chronicles he let Marfa Boretskaia use part of the sums to bribe people in favor of the boyar party. Prince Mikhail Olelkovich seems to have been in close touch with both Marfa and Pimen. The plan of ordaining Pimen to the Novgorod see was certainly a violation of Novgorodian laws, since Feofil had been already proclaimed archbishop-elect and without a new action of the veche could not be deposed. It is thus understandable that there should be a great deal of indignation in Novgorod, especially among the commoners, about the actions of the boyar party. A huge crowd broke into the archbishop's palace, Pimen was beaten and arrested, and part of the archbishop's treasury was "looted," as the chonicler says (possibly, taken in custody to prevent further use of the money in favor of the boyar party).

In spite of this episode, the boyar party decided to recommend to the veche a formal agreement with Lithuania to secure her assistance against Moscow. According to the Muscovite chroniclers, the boyars bribed as many people to support them as they could. After a riotous session the veche voted to conclude a treaty with King Casimir (in his capacity of Grand Duke of Lithuania). An embassy was then sent to Casimir and the treaty concluded on conditions quite agreeable to Novgorod.[31] The general form of the pact followed the pattern of the previous Novgorodian treaties with Russian grand dukes, but the sphere of competence granted Casimir was much more limited than that granted the Russian grand dukes even in the old times before Vasili II. In the text of the treaty the Novgorodians called themselves *muzhi volnye* (free men). There were several new clauses required by religious considerations. Casimir promised not to harm Greek Orthodoxy in Novgorod and to allow the Archbishop of Novgorod to be ordained whenever the Novgorodians pleased. Casimir's lieutenant in Novgorod was to be an Orthodox Christian. In addition, Casimir pledged not to build any Roman Catholic churches in Novgorod territory. Most important for the Novgorodians was of course the military convention. Casimir and the Lithuanian lords pledged to protect Novgorod against Moscow with the full might of the Lithuanian army. The treaty was signed early in 1471, probably in February.

It should be noted that in the Treaty of 1471 the question of where and by whom the Archbishop of Novgorod was to be ordained was left to the discretion of the Novgorodians. This shows that while the boyars succeeded in achieving their political aims, they had to compromise with Feofil in church matters. It was only on that condition that Feofil approved the treaty and agreed that his name could be mentioned in the preamble.

The conclusion of Novgorod's treaty with Casimir could not have satisfied Mikhail Olelkovich. The latter had his own political plans and apparently did not want to remain in Novgorod merely as Casimir's tool. Mikhail's elder brother, Prince Simeon of Kiev, died in December 1470, and Mikhail expected to take his place. However, Casimir, under pressure of the Lithuanians, refused to grant Kiev either to Mikhail or to Simeon's son Vasili, and appointed instead one of the mightiest Lithuanian lords, Martin Gashtovt, his lieutenant in Kiev. According to the Polish chronicler Dlugosz, the Kievans strongly resented the degradation of Kiev from the status of principality to that of lieutenancy, and on religious grounds they objected to the appointment of a Roman Catholic as their new governor. Moreover, the Olelkovichi clan was popular in Kiev and the Kievans wanted Mikhail as their new prince.[32]

31. For the text of Novgorod's treaty with Casimir (1470) see *GNP,* pp. 130–132.
32. Hrushevsky, *Istoriia Ukrainy-Rusi, 4,* 224–225.

The evidence on the relations between Novgorod and Mikhail Olelkovich is scant. It may be supposed that Mikhail expected the Novgorodians to help him obtain the Kievan principality, possibly to insist on that point in their negotiations with Casimir, but no such clause was inserted in Novgorod's treaty with Casimir. On March 15, 1471, Mikhail left Novgorod and led his retinue back to Lithuania. On their way, his retainers looted the rich town of Rusa and a number of villages.[33]

By offending Mikhail and letting him depart to Lithuania, the Novgorodians deprived themselves of the services of an able captain and an efficient body of warriors. To be sure, they expected to receive, instead, the support of the whole Lithuanian army. In this, as future events showed, they were to be bitterly disillusioned.

From the point of view of the Novgorodians, their treaty with Casimir was not contrary to their old starina (traditions), according to which Novgorod had the right of choosing her prince at will. On the other hand, from the point of view of the Muscovites, Novgorod was bound to Moscow by both treaty and precedent. By their agreement with Casimir, the Novgorodians—as the Muscovites thought—broke the starina and committed treason. And because Casimir was a Roman Catholic, the Novgorodians, by accepting him as their prince, endangered the integrity of the Greek Orthodox faith and thus violated the religious starina in addition to the political. It was on these two premises that Ivan III built up the powerful propaganda drive against Novgorod that prepared the ground for his political and military moves. Metropolitan Philip supported the grand duke wholeheartedly and addressed several epistles to the Novgorodians urging them to be faithful to Orthodoxy.

Probably in April 1471 Ivan III called for advice his mother, the metropolitan, and the major boyars. At that small conference war against Novgorod was decided in principle. Following, Ivan sent invitations to come to Moscow to his brothers and to all bishops, lesser princes dependent on him, boyars, army generals (voevody), and "warriors" (vsia voi svoia)—that is, we may think, all the "boyar sons" and dvoriane (squires) in his service.[34] This amounted to gathering a national assembly of church and state leaders, aristocracy and gentry. Even though neither the merchants nor the peasants were summoned to take part in the discussions, the conference may

33. *PSRL, 4,* 237.
34. *PSRL, 12,* 129.

be called the prototype of the "national council" (*zemsky sobor*, literally "assembly of the land") of the 16th and 17th centuries. It met in Moscow in May, and the decision to wage war against Novgorod was confirmed without debate. The only question discussed was of the time of the expedition. Because of the nature of the Novgorodian country—abundance of lakes, rivers, and swamps—winter and not summer was usually considered the proper season for attacking Novgorod. However, after protracted deliberation it was decided to begin the campaign immediately. Metropolitan Philip and all the clergy present blessed the undertaking.

The diplomatic ground had been prepared well in advance. Pskov, Tver, and Viatka agreed to support Ivan III. The Novgorodians counted on an alliance with Pskov, and the news of Pskov's siding with Moscow was a severe blow to them. With the help of Pskov they could expect to hold against the Muscovite armies until the arrival of Casimir's forces. They now urged Casimir to lead the Lithuanian army to their rescue as soon as possible and sent messenger after messenger to Casimir, but the latter did not move.

There were several reasons for his inactivity. In the first place he apparently did not want to break with Pskov. The only way for the Lithuanian army to reach Novgorod and avoid Pskov was through the possessions of the Livonian Knights. Casimir asked the Livonian magister to let the Lithuanian troops through; but the magister, after considerable delay, refused to grant permission. Moreover, so says the Polish chronicler Dlugosz, Casimir was waiting for Poland's help.[35] According to the Nieszawa Statutes of 1454, the King of Poland needed the approval of the provincial assemblies of the szlachta (*sejmiki*) to mobilize the Polish armies.[36] This meant another delay. Finally, Casimir was at that time preoccupied with Czech and Hungarian affairs.[37] Be all this as it may, Novgorod was left without allies, and the Novgorodians had to depend on themselves.

It was tragic for Novgorod that even at that fateful hour the people could not agree among themselves. The boyars, of course, prepared for defense wholeheartedly. But the clergy and many commoners were confused by the religious issue, and many of them were impressed by Metropolitan Philip's epistles. Archbishop-elect Feofil

35. Dlugosz, *14*, 698. See Bazilevich, pp. 98–99.
36. On the Nieszawa Statutes see Wojciechowski, *État Polonais*, pp. 254–256, 290.
37. See Bazilevich, p. 99.

refused to send his cavalry division ("the archbishop's banner") against Ivan III and allowed its use only against the Pskovians.

The Moscow army was reinforced by Tatar cavalry brought by Ivan III's vassal Tsarevich Danyar of Kasimov, and in June several columns of Muscovite and Tatar troops invaded Novgorod territory from three sides. Ivan himself set forth from Moscow on June 20, accompanied by Tsarevich Danyar. They reached Torzhok on June 29. Tver troops joined them there in July, and the Pskovian army began the campaign on July 10.

The war actually was a combination of local campaigns. There were several battles and skirmishes. Later on, the chroniclers tried to build up an account of the war on the basis of local reports, but the picture is somewhat confused. It seems certain in any case that the decisive battle took place on the banks of the Shelon River southwest of Novgorod. The description of this battle in the Nikon Chronicle [38] substantially differs from that in the Novgorodian sources.[39] According to the Nikon Chronicle, the boyars mobilized in Novgorod 40,000 artisans and workers, put them on horses, and led them against the Muscovite advance guard, 5,000 strong, commanded by Prince Mikhail Kholmsky (of the Tverian princely branch). The small but well trained Muscovite cavalry force easily defeated the improvised Novgorodian horse. Twelve thousand Novgorodians are said to have been killed, and two thousand captured.

According to the Fourth Novgorodian Chronicle, the Novgorodians in this battle had no cavalry at all because of the refusal of the archbishop-elect to send his banner against the Muscovites. Nevertheless, the Novgorodians succeeded in pushing Moscow's troops back across the Shelon River, at which juncture they were ambushed by Danyar's Tatars and suffered a terrible defeat. Many were killed, some fled, others were captured. No exact figures are given.

As may be seen, there are two main points of discrepancy between the Muscovite and the Novgorodian accounts: (1) The Nikon Chronicle, contrary to the Fourth Novgorodian, fails to mention the participation of the Tatars in the Shelon battle; (2) The Fourth Novgorodian, contrary to the Nikon Chronicle, states that the Novgorodians had no cavalry in this battle.

The Novgorodian account of the course of the battle is more

38. *PSRL, 12,* 133–135.
39. Fourth Novgorodian Chronicle, pp. 446–447.

credible than the Muscovite. The latter seems to be an imitation of the description of the battle of Rusa of 1456. As for the results, sources of both sides agree that the Novgorodians lost the day and that their casualties were heavy, also that among the Novgorodians taken prisoner were one of Marfa Boretskaia's sons, Dmitri Isakovich Boretsky, and several other Novgorodian boyars.

Ivan III expected that Novgorod would now sue for peace. The Novgorodian boyar party, however, insisted on continuing the struggle. A Novgorodian, Upadysh, who had proved to be an agent of Moscow, was executed. Riots started and, as the chronicler remarks, "There was no rye bread in the market, only wheat bread, and little of that, too." [40] The people began blaming the boyars for Novgorod's misfortunes. Meanwhile news was received that the Moscow and Viatka troops had defeated the Novgorodian forces in the Dvina land and the Pechora region. The whole Novgorodian empire crumbled.

The time seemed ripe for Ivan's final action. To frighten the boyar party, he ordered Dmitri Boretsky and three other Novgorodian boyars among his prisoners to be executed. Other captive boyars and zhityis were deported to Moscow and imprisoned there. Captive junior men were set free and allowed to return to Novgorod. This proved a psychologically skillful move, for it strengthened the pro-Moscow party in Novgorod. Finally, the "rye-bread eaters" there overcame the "wheat-bread eaters," and the veche authorized Archbishop-elect Feofil to go to Ivan's camp at the mouth of the Shelon River to sue for peace.

Peace was granted on conditions less severe than might have been expected under the circumstances. The Novgorodians had to pay a fine of 15,500 rubles and to cancel their treaty with Casimir. In the Treaty of August 11, 1471, the most important clauses of the Treaty of 1456 were repeated.[41] In addition, the Novgorodians solemnly pledged never to seek protection of the King (Grand Duke) of Lithuania and never to accept service princes from Lithuania. Furthermore, the Novgorodians had to repeat the promises given by them to Ivan III's father in 1456—never to accept any of the descendants of Shemiaka or any other of the grand duke's "wrongdoers."

The Novgorodians still called themselves, in the text of the treaty,

40. *Ibid.*, p. 447.
41. For the text of the Treaty of 1471 see *GNP*, pp. 45–51.

"free men" but had to recognize Novgorod as an *otchina* (patrimony) of the grand dukes of Moscow. The Novgorodian Charter of Justice (*Gramota o Sude*) was to be re-issued in the name of the grand duke and sealed by him.[42]

Ivan returned to Moscow on September 1, 1471. On November 30 the Archbishop-elect of Novgorod, Feofil, came to Moscow, and on December 15 was solemnly ordained by Metropolitan Philip. On that occasion all of the Novgorodian prisoners were set free and allowed to return home.

5. SURRENDER, 1478

The results of the war of 1471 were disastrous for Novgorod. Many of its provinces were devastated. Not only were the most offensive clauses of the Treaty of 1456 confirmed by the new treaty, but the Novgorodians had to recognize the permanent dependence of Novgorod on Moscow. For all that, Novgorod remained a semi-autonomous state, and had the Novgorodians now become united in the defense of what remained of their old institutions, they would have stood a chance of warding off further encroachments by Moscow, at least for some time. Unfortunately, the dissensions among the Novgorodians did not end, and the boyar party still thought of revolting against Ivan III at the first opportunity.

The prestige of the boyars had been greatly lowered by the dismal failure of their policies in 1470–71. At that time the zhityis had supported the boyars, and only the lower classes (junior men) tried to oppose the agreement with Lithuania. Now most of the zhityis accepted Ivan's new regime in Novgorod, and even some of the boyars doubted the wisdom of opposing Moscow.

The leading boyars no longer dared show openly their animosity to Moscow at the meetings of the veche. Instead, they tried to obtain firm control of at least some of the sectional communes. When persuasion or bribery did not work, they applied force. In the autumn of 1475 the mayor, Vasili Ananin, accompanied by eighteen other boyars with their retinues organized a punitive expedition against the people of two "street communes" (of Slavkova and Nikitina streets). The force attacked a number of the members of

---

42. For a fragment of the revised text of the Novgorod Charter see Vladimirsky-Budanov, *Khristomatiia, 1,* 172–185; *PRP, 2,* 212–218; for the English translation see Vernadsky, *Medieval Russian Laws,* pp. 83–92.

these communes (some were beaten to death) and looted their property, the damage being estimated at 1,000 rubles. About the same time the elder (starosta) of the Pamfilov street commune, accompanied by two boyars (of the same group who seconded Mayor Ananin), attacked the house of two recalcitrant boyars—the brothers Polinarin—and plundered it. Damages were estimated at 500 rubles.[43]

The motive of these attacks, in each case, obviously was to intimidate the opponents of the boyar party. However, from the case of the brothers Polinarin we may see that even some of the boyars refused to follow their leaders. On the other hand, it may be concluded that the elder of the Pamfilova street commune sided with the boyars. This commune must have been dominated by the boyar party, as probably some others were. The majority of the sectional communes must have been reluctant to recognize the boyar leadership. The boyar party certainly played a dangerous game, since its opponents could now turn to Ivan III for arbitration, and did so. People of the middle class (zhityis) and lower classes (molodshie) sent a delegation to Moscow to ask Ivan for justice.[44]

On October 22, 1475, Ivan set forth from Moscow to Novgorod with a large retinue.[45] In Vyshni Volochek he was greeted by Archbishop Feofil's envoy carrying gifts. Simultaneously, a delegation from the Novgorod citizens offended by the boyars brought their complaints. Ivan then proceeded to Novgorod slowly. More complaints against the boyars were presented to him on his way. Apparently there had been many other cases of offense committed by the boyars besides the two recorded in the chronicles and described above.

At a point about 60 miles from Novgorod, Ivan was met by Novgorod's state delegation, consisting of Archbishop Feofil, the service-prince Vasili Grebenka Shuisky, Mayor Vasili Ananin, and many other notables. On November 21 they all reached Novgorod and in conformity with the old treaties Ivan established his headquarters at Gorodishche. He refused the archbishop's invitation for dinner and instead entertained the archbishop and the Novgorodian notables at Gorodishche. Many Novgorodians rushed to present their com-

43. *PSRL, 12,* 163.
44. Soloviev, *Istoriia, 5,* 23.
45. For the following see *PSRL, 6,* 200–205, and *12,* 158–168; Fourth Novgorodian Chronicle, p. 449.

plaints. They were told to wait for a few days. On November 23 Ivan visited the city of Novgorod, attended mass at the Sancta Sophia, and then dined at the archbishop's. Rich gifts were presented to him.

On November 26 Ivan held a session of the supreme court in Gorodishche for the trial of the two cases of boyar violence mentioned above, acting in concurrence with Archbishop Feofil and the mayors. The senior mayor Ananin was naturally not allowed to be a member of the court, since he was a defendant himself. Both the plaintiffs and the defendants were invited to state their cases, and the court, recognizing the validity of the plaintiff's complaints, found the defendants guilty. The leading men among them, including Ananin, were arrested; others were let out on bail. So far Ivan had acted within his prerogatives as established by the Treaty of 1471 and had not violated the Novgorodian notion of starina.

After the session of the tribunal, Ivan ordered two boyars (not among the defendants), Ivan Afanasiev and his son, to be arrested for propaganda in favor of Casimir of Lithuania. This action was unlawful from the point of view of starina, since Ivan's order was not seconded by any Novgorod official.

From Ivan III's point of view, the treaties of 1456 and 1471 gave him full authority to act at his discretion in handling cases of treason. It was only now that the Novgorodians realized the full meaning of the political clauses of those fateful treaties.

Three days later Archbishop Feofil and the mayors asked Ivan to pardon the arrested boyars and to set them free. Ivan not only refused to satisfy their demand but ordered that the mayor Ananin and three of his associates be deported to Moscow and imprisoned there. This was certainly a violation of starina, but the Novgorodians were now helpless to do anything about it. Several days later Ivan agreed to pardon the lesser offenders who had been previously let out on bail. They had to pay the damages to the plaintiffs, however, as well as the court fees to Ivan. A new senior mayor was elected to replace Ananin, and the Novgorodian notables then fêted Ivan at a series of lavish banquets, at each of which rich gifts were presented to him. Among the notables was a widow, Anastasia Ivanovna Grigorieva—"the glorious Anastasia," as some chroniclers call her.

On January 26, 1476, Ivan left Novgorod and on February 8

returned to Moscow. In accordance with the treaties he demanded no gifts from the local people on his way back.

Ivan's sojourn in Novgorod greatly enhanced his popularity among the middle and lower classes there, and even a number of the boyars seem to have been favorably impressed by his actions. Many Novgorodians who, after Ivan's departure for Moscow, presented their complaints to the Novgorod courts and were not satisfied by the verdict, were inclined to appeal to Ivan. According to starina the Grand Duke of Moscow could judge the Novgorodians only when he resided in Novgorod and had no right to accept any complaints when he was in Moscow. It is probable that many of the discontented Novgorodians urged him to come again to Novgorod to hold another session of the supreme court, but Ivan showed no desire to undertake another voyage so soon after the first; hence the only thing for impatient Novgorodians to do was to present their cases to Ivan in Moscow.

In February 1477 a Novgorod mayor Zakhar Ovin, with a number of discontented Novgorodians appeared in Moscow to seek justice there. By doing so they shattered one of the most important foundations of their own starina. "No such thing had been done since the very beginning of Novgorod," noted the chronicler.[46] Soon afterward, several other boyars, zhityis, and small landowners likewise broke the old rule by coming to Moscow. One of the boyars, Vasili Nikiforov, entered Ivan's service.

In March, an episode took place that still remains somewhat mysterious. Two minor Novgorodian officials, the constable (*podvoiski*) Nazar and a certain Zakhar (not to be confused with the mayor Zakhar Ovin) who called himself the secretary of the veche (although he apparently was only a minor clerk), arrived at Moscow and submitted a petition to Ivan in which they addressed him as Novgorod's *gosudar* (sovereign) instead of the traditional form *gospodin* (lord). In the Nikon Chronicle [47] it is said that Nazar and Zakhar had been officially sent to Moscow by "Archbishop Feofil and the whole Novgorod the Great," but this cannot be accepted, in view of the low position of both Nazar and Zakhar in the Novgorodian administration. Surely, much more important men would have been chosen for a mission of such character. Most likely,

46. *PSRL, 12,* 169.
47. *PSRL, 12,* 169–170.

Nazar and Zakhar's trip was engineered by some Moscow agent in Novgorod, possibly on a hint from Moscow.

In Moscow, as might be expected, Nazar and Zakhar's mission was accepted on its face value. On April 24 Ivan sent to Novgorod an embassy consisting of two Muscovite boyars and the *diak* (state secretary) Vasili Tretiak Dalmatov, one of Ivan's ablest assistants. They appeared at the veche and referring to Novgorod's acceptance of Ivan III as her sovereign, stated Ivan's conditions: the grand duke should have full judicial control in Novgorod, and the Novgorodian officials should not interfere with his judicial commands; the grand duke's office in Novgorod should be in Iaroslav's Yard, not in Gorodishche.[48] The Novgorodians were stunned. Archbishop Feofil "and the whole Novgorod the Great" immediately announced that Nazar and Zakhar had not been authorized to offer to Ivan sovereignty over Novgorod and openly called the Moscow ambassadors' version of Nazar and Zakhar's mission a lie.

The whole city was now in commotion. Actual and alleged friends of Moscow were accused of treason to Novgorod. The boyar Vasili Nikiforov, who had entered Ivan's service, was summoned to the meeting of the veche, sentenced to death, and killed on the spot. Mayor Zakhar Ovin (who had been the first to come to Moscow with complaints) was killed in the archbishop's yard. Many Novgorodians insisted on again seeking Casimir's protection. Pskov's offer of arbitration was rejected. Ivan III's envoys were not molested, however, and after a six-week delay were allowed to return to Moscow to communicate to Ivan Novgorod's official answer: she recognizes Ivan as her lord but not as her sovereign, and wants to be governed on the basis of the Treaty of 1471.

After receiving Novgorod's answer, Ivan announced that the Novgorodians themselves had offered him sovereignty and now called him a liar, which showed that they were rebels and perjurers. On September 30 Ivan sent to Novgorod his declaration of war.[49] On October 9 he began the campaign. Both the Kasimov Tatar horsemen and the Tver troops joined the Muscovite army. When Ivan reached Torzhok, he was met by two Novgorod boyars, the brothers Klementiev, who petitioned Ivan to accept them into his service—a clear indication of the lack of unity and the demoralization of the Novgorodians.

48. Karamzin, *Primechaniia*, n. 147 to Vol. *6*.
49. For the following see *PSRL*, *6*, 207–221; *12*, 171–179.

Ivan reached the outskirts of Novgorod on November 27. The Novgorodians, having fortified the city, refused to surrender. With his usual cautiousness Ivan did not venture to storm it but encircled it tightly with his troops, hoping that lack of food would soon break the spirit of the defenders. Several times the Novgorodians sent messengers to Ivan, each time offering more concessions. Ivan rejected all offers and insisted on recognition of his full sovereignty. Specifically, he demanded that the veche be dissolved and the veche bell taken away; that the office of mayor be abolished; that the grand duke have the same power in Novgorod as in Moscow. On December 29 the Novgorodians accepted Ivan's conditions, and on January 13, 1478, the Novgorodian notables took the oath of loyalty to their *gosudar*. The Novgorod service prince Vasili Grebenka Shuisky annulled his oath to Novgorod and pledged allegiance to Ivan. After having taken the oath, the Novgorodian notables asked Ivan to announce his "favors" to the people of Novgorod. Ivan let Prince Ivan Iurievich Patrikeev be his spokesman. In the grand duke's name Prince Patrikeev declared that in view of the complete submission of Novgorod the grand duke changed his anger to benevolence and was ready to treat the Novgorodians with favor. After that, all of the people of Novgorod took oath in each borough. On January 18 the Novgorodian boyars and the zhityis petitioned Ivan to accept them in his service.

Two *namestniki* (lieutenants) were appointed by Ivan to govern Novgorod. They were two princes Obolensky—Ivan Vasilievich Striga, the noted general, and his brother Iaroslav, who immediately established themselves at Iaroslav's Yard. Novgorod was deprived of all its eastern dominions, and the Novgorodians were compelled to cede to the grand duke all the rural districts of Torzhok province; the archbishop ceded ten of the rural districts belonging to his see. Furthermore, the people of the rural districts in all that was left of Novgorod's provinces had to pay tribute to the grand duke. Ivan agreed, however, that the Novgorodians themselves could collect this tribute and hand him the proceeds at the rate agreed upon.

Before leaving Novgorod, Ivan ordered that several Novgorodian boyars be arrested and deported to Moscow, and all their property confiscated. Among them was Marfa Boretskaia and one of her grandsons. On February 17 Ivan set forth for Moscow, arriving on March 5. The Novgorod veche bell was shipped to Moscow and hung in one of her belfries.

According to the Polish chronicler Dlugosz, Ivan brought from
Novgorod immense booty, consisting of silver, gold, precious stones,
silk fabrics, cloth, and furs. Part of it was taken from the archbishop's treasury and part from the confiscated property of the arrested boyars. Three hundred carts were used to transport it to
Moscow.[50] In another source the value of the booty is estimated at
14,000,000 florins.[51] It should be noted that most of the riches
brought to Moscow must have been intended for the grand-ducal
treasury, not for Ivan personally. The archbishop's treasury was
brought for safekeeping only and was returned to Novgorod in
1524.[52]

6. REVOLT AND FINAL SUBMISSION

While the majority of the Novgorodians submitted themselves to
their fate, albeit gloomily, some of the boyars tried to find ways to
overthrow Moscow's control. Afraid now to come out in the open,
they resorted to underground methods. Archbishop Feofil himself
was in the plot. All of them realized that Novgorod could be liberated
only with the help of strong allies. In spite of Casimir's failure to
come to Novgorod's rescue in 1471, the conspirators were ready
again to turn to him for assistance. Casimir too was looking for
allies against Moscow and in 1479 negotiated with Khan Ahmad of
the Golden Horde for a joint attack on Muscovy. The boyar leaders
in Novgorod undoubtedly were informed of these plans.

The boyar party also attempted to establish contact with Ivan
III's brothers. Ivan's favorite brother, Prince Iuri of Dmitrov, had
died in 1473. Iuri, born in 1441, was one year younger than Ivan.
After his death there remained three others—Andrei Senior, Prince
of Uglich (born in 1446); Boris, Prince of Volok (born in 1449);
and Andrei Junior (born in 1452). The former two, being against
Ivan's political program of centralization and in favor of securing
more rights for the lesser princes, sympathized with Novgorod's
plight. There is hardly any doubt that they also were in secret contact with Casimir, just as were the boyar leaders in Novgorod.

Apparently, in October 1479, Ivan received from his spies in Nov-

---

50. Dlugosz, *14*, 697–698; Karamzin, *Istoriia*, *6*, 131, and *Primechaniia*, *6*, n. 182.
51. Karamzin, *Istoriia*, *6*, 131, and *Primechaniia*, n. 182 to Vol. *6*, referring to Arnt,
Liefland Chronicle.
52. Nikitsky, *Ocherk vnutrennei istorii tserkvi v Velikom Novgorode*, p. 128.

gorod a report of the boyar conspiracy there. On October 26 he set forth for Novgorod with a small force of 1,000 warriors, without any declaration of war, so as not to arouse any suspicions. He left orders for his son, Ivan Junior (then twenty-three), to mobilize more troops and follow. It is probable that either Prince Andrei Senior or Prince Boris warned the Novgorodians of Ivan's intentions. In any case, they were not taken unaware. The conspirators now came out into the open, convoked the veche, and restored Novgorod's old forms of government.[53]

Ivan had to wait until more troops had been mobilized. Even when Novgorod was surrounded with his forces, the Novgorodians at first refused to submit themselves again. Before long, however, they saw that further resistance was futile, opened the city gate, and pleaded for mercy. Ivan entered the city around January 15, 1480, promising to pardon all except the ringleaders. Fifty of the latter were immediately seized. Under torture some of them disclosed more names of conspirators, including that of Archbishop Feofil. On January 19 Feofil was arrested, deported to Moscow and interned in a cell in the Chudov Monastery. More arrests were made, and 100 boyars were executed; 100 zhityis and merchants with their families were deported to Suzdalia. At that juncture Ivan received news that his brothers Andrei Senior and Boris had revolted against him, besieged some of the Muscovite towns, and plundered the country. He returned to Moscow in haste and quickly checked the revolt; in April 1480 the rebellious princes fled to Velikie Luki in the former Novgorod area close to the Lithuanian border and asked Casimir for protection. Casimir promised to intervene in their favor and meanwhile assigned to their wives the city of Vitebsk for residence. On his part Ivan III sent his envoys to Velikie Luki urging Andrei Senior and Boris to return to Muscovy and offering them two towns in addition to their respective principalities.

Ivan was eager to reach an agreement with his rebellious brothers as soon as possible because the news had come that Khan Ahmad's army was heading for the Oka River. In September, Andrei Senior and Boris came to Moscow and were well received by Ivan. At the time Moscow was getting ready for Ahmad's attack, which seemed imminent. It did not materialize, however, and Ahmad's whole campaign proved a failure; on November 11, 1480, the khan hastily retreated to his capital, Sarai (see below, p. 76).

53. *PSRL, 4,* 152–154; *6,* 19–20; *12,* 197–200; Fourth Novgorodian Chronicle, p. 516.

The Tatar danger being over, Ivan III could once more turn his attention to Novgorodian affairs.[54] In 1481 four more boyars were arrested. Three years later Ivan received a report that some of the Novgorodians had corresponded with Casimir. On the basis of this report thirty Novgorodian boyars and zhityis were arrested and tortured. Each accused the others. They were all sentenced to death, but when they were brought to the gallows, each asked pardon of the others for false accusations. When Ivan heard of it, he commuted all sentences to imprisonment. About the same time, two more notables were arrested: "the glorious Anastasia" who had entertained Ivan in 1476 and the boyar Ivan Kuzmin, who had fled to Lithuania in 1478 but receiving no favors from Casimir had soon returned to Novgorod. The property of both Anastasia and Kuzmin was confiscated.

With the arrest of Archbishop Feofil the autonomy of the Novgorod Church came to an end, and the see was left vacant for four years. In 1483 Feofil was induced to write a statement in which he admitted his inability "to lead Christ's flock" and renounced his title.[55] This cleared the way for ordaining a new archbishop. Feofil's successor was selected by Moscow authorities among the Muscovite monks.[56] To keep a semblance of the old Novgorodian procedure, the grand duke and Metropolitan Geronti (successor of Philip I, the latter having died in 1473) nominated three candidates, the choice among them to be decided by lot. The monk Sergei of Trinity Monastery was favored by the lot and became the new Archbishop of Novgorod, but snubbed by the Novgorodian clergy he finally had a nervous breakdown, was deposed at the metropolitan's order, returning to Trinity Monastery. Archimandrite Gennadi, of the Chudov Monastery (one of the two other candidates nominated in 1483) was then ordained Archbishop of Novgorod to replace Sergei. Gennadi was an energetic and well educated man of strong will, but even he could not break the opposition of the Novgorod clergy at once and had to make some concessions to their traditions.[57]

After the arrests and executions of the Novgorodian boyars in 1480–84, the backbone of the boyar resistance had been broken. Ivan

54. Soloviev, *Istoriia*, 5, 37–39.

55. Karamzin, *Primechaniia*, n. 198 to Vol. 6; Nikitsky, *Ocherk . . . Novgorode*, p. 127; *AAE, 1*, 476.

56. *PSRL, 12*, 214–215.

57. Fourth Novgorodian Chronicle, p. 467; Nikitsky, *Ocherk . . . Novgorode*, pp. 132–134.

III and his advisers now turned their attention to the Novgorodian middle classes. In 1487 fifty wealthy merchants were deported to Vladimir. The next year the grand duke's lieutenant in Novgorod, discovering a conspiracy among the zhityis, ordered several of the ringleaders executed at once. Following that, over 7,000 zhityis were brought to Moscow, some of them being executed there. The bulk were settled in Nizhni-Novgorod, Vladimir, Rostov, and other towns of the Upper Volga-Oka region. To replace them, Muscovite "boyar sons" and merchants were sent to Novgorod and settled there.[58]

As a result of all these measures, the top layer of Novgorodian society was skimmed off and most of the middle class dispersed. The commoners were left without leaders or political rights, and the church was subjected to Moscow's control. This was the end of Novgorod the Great, politically. Yet, even after all these repressive changes, the spirit of the Novgorodians was not completely broken. Instead of in politics, they now expressed themselves in literature, art, and religious disputation. Until the middle of the 16th century Novgorod remained one of the important centers of Russian spiritual culture.

7. LEGENDS

The fall of Novgorod produced an immense impression on its contemporaries, both in Novgorod itself and in Muscovy. It was reflected in a number of legends, some of which might have originated even before the war of 1471. Most of them seem to have been created in an ecclesiastical milieu and represent a continuation of the literary traditions of Archbishop Evfimi II and his circle.

The legends may be classified into two main groups, portents and prophetic visions, and tales intended to enhance the prestige of the Novgorodian Church and its saints.

To the first category belongs the story about the concealed meaning of a detail in the fresco of Christ Pantocrator in the dome of Sancta Sophia of Novgorod. In the representations of the Pantocrator in Greek and Russian religious art, especially in the icons, the Saviour's right hand is usually "open"—that is, the fingers are in the attitude of blessing. In the fresco of Pantocrator in Novgorod the hand is "closed." The fresco was supposedly painted in 1144 (the cathedral was built in 1045–52), repainted in the 16th century, and

58. Soloviev, *Istoriia, 5,* 39–40.

renovated in the 19th century.[59] The closed hand survived reno-
vating. According to N. P. Kondakov, the shut hand was usual in
11th-century mosaics and was passed on to the 12th-century fresco.[60]
In the Third Novgorodian Chronicle, however, a story of the painting of the fresco—inserted under A.D. 1045, the year when the building of the Sancta Sophia of Novgorod was begun—has it that the
painters tried three times to represent Our Lord's hand in the
blessing position, but each time, when they returned to work, the
hand had miraculously reverted to the closed position. Finally, a
voice from above called to the designers, telling them to paint the
figure with the right hand not open but closed, "for in this my hand
I hold Novgorod, and when this my hand will open, Novgorod will
come to an end." [61] The interpretation of the secret of the shut hand
could have come to the minds of the Novgorodians only when Novgorod's position became hazardous. In my opinion, the story might
have been composed soon after the war of 1456, possibly in 1460
when Vasili II visited Novgorod and the Novgorodian fears and
hatred were again aroused. The Novgorodians planned to kill him at
that time but were stopped by the thought that Ivan III (whom
Vasili had left in Moscow) would avenge the murder.[62]

It seems that both the Novgorodians and the Muscovites felt at
that time that Ivan was the man destined to crush Novgorod.
These feelings were reflected in the story of the prophecy of the
monk Mikhail of the Klopsky Monastery near Novgorod. Mikhail,
as it seems, migrated to Novgorod from Moscow in his youth. He
told no one of his origin but there were rumors that he belonged by
blood to the Moscow princely clan. He did not conceal his pro-
Moscow sympathies, and at the time of the civil war of the 1440's
he upbraided Shemiaka for the latter's revolt against Vasili II.
Mikhail died in 1452. According to the story, Archbishop Evfimi II
visited Mikhail in the Klopsky Monastery on January 22, 1440. As
soon as Evfimi entered his cell, Mikhail told him that "there is great
rejoicing in Moscow today." He then explained that he had had a
vision that a son had just been born to Grand Duke Vasili and was

59. According to V. N. Lazarev, the fresco in the form in which it was known in the
19th century dates back to the 16th century. It perished during the German occupation of Novgorod in 1943–44 (Grabar, 2d ed. 2, 73–74).

60. Kondakov, *Ikonografiia Spasa*, pp. 50–51, and *The Russian Icon*, p. 94. For the
picture of the fresco see Kondakov, *Ikonografiia Spasa*, p. 50; Grabar, 6, 130.

61. Kondakov, *Ikonografiia Spasa*, p. 50; *PSRL*, 3, p. 211.

62. *PSRL*, 6, 182.

named Ivan. "He will destroy the customs of the Novgorod land and will bring ruin to our city." [63] We are not in a position to say whether the story is authentic or not. If it was made up, it was probably composed around 1460.

Another story of a prophecy of Novgorod's impending misfortune is that of the vision of the sexton Tarasi of the Khutynsky Monastery (one of Novgorod's major monasteries, founded by St. Varlaam in the late 12th century). On one occasion Tarasi had to go to the monastery church at midnight. As he entered, all the candles lit up by themselves, and Tarasi saw St. Varlaam coming out from his sepulcher. For three hours Varlaam prayed before the icons. Tarasi was overawed. Then Varlaam approached him and told him to ascend to the top of the church to see by what means God intended to smite Novgorod. From the top of the church the terrified Tarasi saw that Lake Ilmen had spread high above the city. When Tarasi reported it to Varlaam, the latter prayed for three more hours and then sent Tarasi once more to the top of the roof. This time Tarasi saw a host of angels shooting fire arrows. A third omen was of burning clouds. Varlaam then told Tarasi that Novgorod would be stricken by flood, plague, and great fire. There are several versions of this story. [64] In my opinion, the earliest might have originated in the period 1456–70.

A case of a more concrete vision, narrower in scope, is related in the "Life" of Saints Zosima and Savvati, founders of Solovki Monastery. On one occasion, Zosima had to go to Novgorod on the monastery's business. Among other things, he had to see Marfa Boretskaia to complain of offenses to the monastery people on the part of the Boretskys' stewards. According to the story, Marfa at first refused to receive Zosima. As he went away, he told his pupils who accompanied him: "the time is near when the doors of this house will be closed and the house will be empty." Marfa repented, called Zosima back to her house, asked for his blessing, and invited him for dinner. As Zosima sat at the table he saw that among the boyars present six had no heads. He bent his head and did not touch any food after that. Soon after, so the story goes, the Novgorodians were defeated at the Shelon River (1471), and six boyars were taken prisoner by the Muscovites and executed. [65] A short version of the story of the Zosima's prophetic vision was inserted in the Nikon

63. Kliuchevsky, *Kurs Russkoi istorii, 2,* 109.
64. *Pamiatniki SRL, 1,* 283–284; Gudzii, pp. 261–262.
65. Gudzii, p. 261.

Chronicle.[66] There, four boyars are mentioned rather than six, in accordance with the chronicler's account of the number of the executed. It was apparently at the time of Zosima's visit that Marfa decided to make her second donation to the Solovki Monastery (see above, p. 46).

Let us now turn to the other group of legends, the tendency of which is to raise the prestige of the Novgorodian saints and the Novgorodian Church. Some of the legends of this kind originated in the milieu of the monks of Khutynsky Monastery, and one was inserted in the Novgorodian Chronicle under A.D. 1461.[67] According to it, when Ivan III once visited the Monastery, he ordered the sepulcher of St. Varlaam, the founder, to be opened. When Ivan's assistants tried to do it, a flame rose from the sepulcher, and the terrified Ivan fled from the church, leaving his staff behind. The half burned staff was later shown to visitors.[68]

Another legend of this type concerns the monk Sergei, who, it was said, was appointed Archbishop of Novgorod by the Moscow authorities to replace the deposed Feofil in 1483. As we know, Sergei was met with much hostility on the part of the Novgorodians. As may be seen from the legend, the Novgorodians accused him, among other things, of offending the memory of Archbishop Moisei (who lived in the 14th century). In Moisei's "Life," written by Pakhomi Logofet, it is related that Sergei once came to the church where Moisei was buried and ordered the sepulcher opened so that he could see Moisei's relics (a motif similar to the story of Ivan III and the sepulcher of Varlaam). The priest refused to open the sepulcher and told Sergei that only a bishop would be entitled to do so. Whereupon Sergei went away saying, "I have no desire to look at the body of that boor" (meaning Moisei). Afterward, Sergei lost his reason and the metropolitan had to call him back to Muscovy. Some of the Novgorodians thought that Sergei was miraculously punished, for his disrespect of Moisei, by another Novgorodian saint, Archbishop Ivan (of the 12th century). The Muscovites accused the Novgorodians of inflicting mental illness on Sergei by sorcery.[69]

66. *PSRL*, *12*, 137–138.
67. *PSRL*, *4*, 127.
68. Gudzii, p. 260.
69. Kliuchevsky, *Zhitiia*, pp. 151–152; Gudzii, pp. 259–260.

CHAPTER III

IVAN III'S FOREIGN POLICIES

1. UNDERLYING FACTORS

IVAN's main purpose in life was to build up a united Russian state ruled by a single sovereign, strong enough to survive in a hostile world. To the achieving of that goal all his moves, both internal and external, were oriented. We therefore cannot draw any sharp dividing line between his national and international policies. When he became Grand Duke of Moscow, Great Russia was not yet united and the traditions of the Kievan period were not dead. Not only the other Great Russian states, like Tver, Riazan, and Novgorod, but even the lesser Muscovite princes themselves were reluctant to accept Ivan's sovereignty.

When it became clear to Ivan's Russian opponents that they lacked strength to prevent the growth of the grand duke's power, they turned to the outside states—Lithuania and the Golden Horde —for assistance. From Ivan's point of view this was treason, and thus his Russian national policy merged with his foreign diplomacy. This could not but affect the course of the struggle between himself and his opponents in Russia.

The dovetailing of national and foreign problems is especially clear in the case of the fall of Novgorod. Ivan probably would have preferred to have subjected Novgorod gradually to his authority, but the alliance between Novgorod and Lithuania prompted him to act quickly and decisively. Likewise, attempts of the Tver grand duke and of the lesser Muscovite princes (including two of Ivan's own brothers) to side with Casimir of Lithuania against Ivan only accelerated his drastic measures against them. It is thus on the success of Ivan's foreign policies that the process of unification of Great Russia depended, and vice versa.

After achieving virtual independence from the Golden Horde in the reign of Ivan's father Vasili II, around 1452, Muscovy became an important factor in the international politics of Western

Eurasia and Eastern Europe, and its importance as such grew steadily during the reign of Ivan. After the fall of Novgorod, the Moscow state reached the Gulf of Finland and thus became a Baltic power.

Except for the extreme North, Muscovy at that time had no safe national boundaries and was all but surrounded by Oriental and Western states, many of whom were her actual or potential enemies. The Muscovite army was not strong enough to withstand all these enemies at the same time. Hence the Muscovite government had a perennial diplomatic task of preventing the formation of any coalition of foreign powers against Moscow, and when such a coalition was nevertheless formed, of breaking the unity of potential or actual enemies by a separate agreement with some of them and by opposing to the enemy bloc a coalition of its own. In this way Ivan often succeeded in handling his enemies one at a time—the secret of many of his successes.

It should be added that more often than not, some of the foreign powers themselves sought Ivan's support against their enemies and thereby added to the complexity of the diplomatic situation. In his turn, Ivan was always eager to turn such opportunities to his own advantage, though he flatly refused to participate in any combination which, from his point of view, was against Moscow's real interests. Thus he remained cool to all attempts on the part of the pope and the German emperor to involve him in a conflict with Turkey. With the latter power he tried, on the contrary, to establish friendly relations.

For the understanding of the intricate diplomatic moves of both Ivan and his enemies it is necessary briefly to survey the ring of foreign powers around Muscovy. To begin with the Tatar khanates in the East and the South, the Tatar Khanate of Tiumen in Western Siberia posed no immediate threat to Muscovy; on the contrary, it was useful to Moscow on certain occasions in her conflicts with the Golden Horde. The latter represented at first the greatest danger. Later, the Khanate of Kazan became more troublesome. An unpredictable factor was the Nogay Horde, which controlled the area east of the Lower Volga and the basin of the Yaik (Ural) River.

In the South, the Khan of the Crimea possessed not only the Crimean Peninsula itself but the section of the steppes between the Lower Dnieper and the Sea of Azov. In 1475 the Khan of the Crimea had to recognize the suzerainty of the Ottoman Sultan and became his vassal. Besides, the Turks occupied outright the important trading city of Kaffa (modern Feodosia) in the Crimea as well as Kerch (on the strait of the same name) and Azov (at the mouth of the Don River).

West of Muscovy lay Lithuania and behind it, Poland. In the Northwest, following the fall of Novgorod, Livonia became Muscovy's neighbor. Livonia did not constitute a united state. From the military point of view, the Livonian branch of the Teutonic Order was the strongest element in the German control of the country, but the Archbishop of Riga was independent of the magister of the Order, and the Livonian cities (Riga, Derpt, and others) had their own rights. Finland, at that time, belonged to Sweden. Novgorod, and Moscow afterward controlled the whole course of the Neva River, down to its mouth, but beyond that the whole northern littoral of the Gulf of Finland was held by the Swedes. To the shores of Lake Ladoga Sweden had no access at that time. Neither did the Swedish boundary reach the Arctic Ocean. Pechenga (Petsamo) Bay belonged to the Russians, and in that region, Muscovy had direct contact with Norway.

It should be noted that in any clash of interests between the German Empire and Poland the emperor was inclined to seek a rapprochement with Muscovy. Moreover, during the reign of King Matthew Corvin (1458–90), Hungary—squeezed as it was between the Turks and the Hapsburgs—in its turn tried to establish contact with Moscow.

In regard to the Tatar khanates, Ivan's policy was aimed at using one or more of them against the others. He eventually succeeded in establishing friendly relations with the Khan of the Crimea, Mengli-Girey. On his part, Casimir of Lithuania concluded an agreement with Khan Ahmad of the Golden Horde. Each partner of each side occasionally tried to reinsure himself by separate negotiations with a partner of the other side, which mostly led nowhere but at times endangered the stability of the whole combination.

Commercial interests constituted an important aspect of Ivan's diplomacy, both in the East and in the West. Kazan and the Crimea were important centers of international trade and attracted yearly great numbers of Russian merchants. The Moscow government took considerable pains to protect them and to keep the routes open for them. The khans of the Golden Horde were in position to cut the Don River way from Moscow to the Crimea whenever they wanted, and in fact often did cut it. The Muscovite merchants had then to use the Western route to the Crimea via the Middle Dnieper area; but that was at the mercy of Lithuania. As a matter of fact, the control of these routes played an important role in the conflicts of Moscow with the Golden Horde and Lithuania.

In Ivan's Baltic policies commercial interests were likewise clearly noticeable. Ivan's main objective was to break the monopoly of the Hanseatic League in Russia's Baltic commerce. This eventually led to a rapprochement with Denmark.

In both the 15th and the 16th centuries religious conflicts were an important factor in international politics. The basic difference between the Byzantine-Russian world and the Western world was, of course, that between Greek Orthodoxy and Roman Catholicism. The Florentine Union, though it did not prevent the fall of Constantinople, nevertheless served as a basis for further attempts to establish the pope's authority over the East Slavic Church. These attempts, however, had no lasting results until the Council of Brest of 1596. Not only did Moscow reject the Union at once, but the majority of the clergy and congregations in Western Russia strongly opposed every new Uniate move in the Russian lands of the Grand Duchy of Lithuania.

In the conflict between Roman Catholicism and Greek Orthodoxy Ivan assumed the role of the protector of Orthodoxy and a staunch opponent of Roman Catholicism. As we have seen (above, p. 50), this attitude greatly helped to break the unity of the Novgorodians. It also attracted the sympathies of a number of West Russian princes and thus served Ivan's interests in his conflict with Lithuania.

By contrast, Ivan never mixed religion with politics in his relations with the Oriental world, and in his dealings with the Tatars carefully avoided any interference with the latter's religious beliefs —no attempt was ever made to convert forcibly any of his Moslem vassals.

Another aspect of Ivan's religious toleration was his friendly attitude toward the Jews.[1] The Jew Khozia Kokos was Ivan's commercial and diplomatic agent in the Crimea in the 1470's and the 1480's. In 1484 and again in 1487 Ivan invited another Jew,

---

1. It will be recalled (see above, p. 47, n. 29) that in this period no clear distinction was made in the Grand Duchy of Lithuania between Rabbinical Judaism and Karaism. This is also true of East Russia.

Zechariah, then also residing in the Crimea, to come to Moscow.[2]
For a number of years Ivan was reluctant to take any drastic measures against the spread of the so-called "Heresy of the Judaizers." It
was only toward the end of his life, when his son Vasili became his
co-ruler (1502), that Ivan had to withdraw his tacit protection from
both the Judaizers and the *Zavolzhskie Startsy* (Hermits of beyond
the Volga), a mystic group in the Russian Orthodox Church (see below, p. 119).

2. Struggle with the Golden Horde

At the time of the Novgorodian crisis (1470–71) King Casimir
had concluded an alliance against Moscow with Khan Ahmad of the
Golden Horde. Though Casimir failed to support Novgorod in 1471,
he continued to prepare himself for a war against Moscow and urged
Ahmad to take part in it.

Of all of the Tatar khanates of this period, the Golden Horde,
although only a fragment of the once mighty Mongol Empire, represented best the old traditions of the Mongol age. All of the ruling
dynasties of the Tatar khanates descended from Chingis-Khan, but
it is the rulers of the Golden Horde who were at that time especially
conscious of their ancestry. In his letter to Sultan Fatih Mehmet
(Mohammed II, the Conqueror) of 1477, Ahmad, assuring the
Sultan of his "brotherhood and love," proudly called himself a
"son" (*ogul*) of Chingis-Khan.[3]

Ahmad belonged to the House of Juchi, the eldest son of Chingis-
Khan. More specifically, Ahmad's father, Kuchuk-Mahmed was a
descendant of Urus-Khan (a descendant of Juchi).[4] Kuchuk-
Mahmed undertook no major campaign against Moscow and apparently never collected much tribute from Muscovy, if any. It
seems that after 1452 Grand Duke Vasili II paid no regular yearly
tribute to any of the rival khans. However, the grand dukes felt
that they might be obliged to pay the tribute to some Tatar khan any
time and because of this kept the tax collectors busy. The year when

2. It should be noted that a number of scholars are of the opinion that this Zechariah was an Italian and not a Jew. Be this as it may, Ivan III twice addressed him as
"Zechariah the Jew"; see *Sbornik, 41*, 41, 71.
3. Kurat, p. 49, line 17. Bazilevich (p. 112, n. 2) gives a wrong page reference to
Kurat's publication.
4. See *Mongols and Russia*, p. 430, Genealogical Table VI.

no payment to any horde was made they just deposited the collected money into their own treasury. In his testament Vasili II advised his wife and sons to make, after his death, a census of their lands for the collection of the tribute. He added, however, that in case "God changes (the power of) the Horde," each prince shall keep the collected tribute for himself.[5] In Ivan III's treaty with Prince Mikhail Andreevich of Vereia (around 1463), we find the following clause: "It is I, the grand duke, who knows the Horde [that is, handles the tribute] . . . And when I, the grand duke, give no tribute to the Horde, I shall take no tribute money from thee."[6] No regular tribute payments to any khan are mentioned in the Russian chronicles for the period of the reign of Ivan III.

Ahmad's program consisted of two main points: restoration of the khan's suzerainty over the Grand Duke of Moscow and reimposition of the annual tribute on Muscovy. To achieve these aims he undertook several campaigns against Moscow. According to the "Kazan History" (*Kazanskaia istoriia*), Ahmad, after he became khan, sent his envoys to Grand Duke Ivan III "in accordance with the old custom of his fathers, with his *basma*-portrait, to demand tribute for the past years. The grand duke showed no fear of the tsar [i.e. khan], took the *basma*-portrait of the tsar, spit on it, threw it to the ground, and stamped on it with his feet."[7] The episode is said to have taken place in 1480—that is, the year of the final conflict between Ivan and Ahmad.

Taking into consideration that the Kazan History—compiled around 1565 as a historico-political pamphlet written for the glorification of Ivan the Terrible—includes a number of legends as well as much valuable information on the history of the Kazan Khanate, we may assume that there is no more than a grain of truth in the above story, underlying later embellishments. Ahmad became khan not later than 1460 (when his name is first mentioned in Russian chronicles). It is quite probable that he began his reign by sending his envoys to the Grand Duke of Moscow to demand obedience. At that time, Vasili II was still alive. However, Ivan was his co-ruler and also had the title of grand duke. It is possible that he received Ahmad's envoys, and rejected Ahmad's demands, but

5. *DDG*, p. 197.
6. *DDG*, p. 209.
7. *Kazanskaia istoriia*, p. 55. See also G. N. Moiseeva, "Avtor Kazanskoi Istorii," *TODRL*, 9 (1953), 266–288.

the description of his reaction to these demands in the Kazan History
is of course fantastic. It is obvious that the compiler or editor of the
work had no clear notion of the badges of authority granted by the
khans to their vassals and servitors. He speaks of such a badge as a
basma-portrait of the khan. In Turkish *basma* means "stamp," "impression." In old Russia the term was applied to the metal frame of
the icon (usually in *repoussé* silver). A *basma*-portrait would then be
a metal representation of a face in bas-relief. No such portraits were
ever used by any Mongol khans in the investiture of their vassals.
The compiler of the Kazan History must have confused *basma* with
baisa, the latter term deriving from the Chinese *paitze,* the "tablet
of authority," as Marco Polo calls it. This was, depending on the
degree of the authority of the functionary to whom it was granted by
the khan, a golden or silver tablet with some design, such as a tiger's
or falcon's head, and a brief inscription incised on it.[8] It is such a
tablet that Ahmad's envoy might have brought to Ivan, to hand
to him if he agreed to recognize Ahmad's suzerainty. As Ivan apparently refused to become Ahmad's vassal, the tablet must have
been kept by the envoy and returned to the khan. The dramatic
description of Ivan's stamping on the *baisa* is therefore fiction.

His demands being rejected by the grand duke, Ahmad attacked
the city of Pereiaslavl in Riazan principality with a large force (in
1460, according to the Nikon Chronicle).[9] The Russians succeeded
in repulsing him. Ahmad, five years later, concentrated his troops
in the Middle Don region for a campaign against Moscow but was
himself attacked by Haji-Girey, the Khan of the Crimea, which
upset all his plans.[10] In 1472, encouraged by Casimir, Ahmad undertook another drive against Muscovy. Instead of using the direct
route to Moscow through Kolomna, Ahmad led his army westward
to the town of Aleksin, close to the Lithuanian boundary. He apparently expected that Casimir would join him there with the
Lithuanian army. The Tatars burned Aleksin and crossed the Oka
River but met with strong Russian resistance on the opposite bank.
As no Lithuanian army came to his assistance, Ahmad retreated
back into the steppes.[11]

In order to forestall further attacks of the Golden Horde, Ivan,
through the Jew Khozia Kokos, entered in negotiations with the

8. See *Mongols and Russia*, pp. 125–126.
9. *PSRL, 12,* 113.
10. *PSRL, 12,* 116–117.
11. Bazilevich, pp. 99–101.

Crimean Khan Mengli-Girey, son and successor of Haji-Girey. Ivan offered Mengli-Girey an alliance against both Ahmad and Casimir. The ground was well prepared for a treaty when the Turks appeared in the Crimea in 1475 and Mengli-Girey was seized by them. In the ensuing turmoil Ahmad at first attempted to put a relative of his on the Crimean throne, but the Turkish Sultan decided instead to install Mengli-Girey as his vassal (1478). As already noted, the Turks kept several Crimean towns, including Kaffa, for themselves. A Turkish governor now resided in Kaffa. In April 1480 a treaty of friendship and mutual assistance was finally concluded between Ivan and Mengli-Girey.[12] Even before that the khan's two brothers, Nur-Dawlet and Haydar, who at first had sought protection of King Casimir, came to Moscow and entered Ivan's service.

The conclusion of the alliance with Mengli-Girey took place at a time when a new conflict seemed imminent between Ivan, on the one hand, and Casimir and Ahmad, on the other. In the fall and winter of 1479 Ivan was faced with a conspiracy in Novgorod (in favor of Casimir) and the revolt of two of his brothers (see above, pp. 60–61). Moreover, in January 1480 the Livonian Knights invaded Pskov territory. In all probability the Livonian magister had an agreement of some kind with both Casimir and Ahmad.[13] News reached Moscow in the summer of 1480 that Ahmad was about to begin his campaign, and in October Ahmad led his army to the banks of the Ugra River, a tributary of the Oka, west of Kaluga, thus coming even farther west than in 1472. One of his two motives was to avoid Russian troops and fortifications along the northern bank of the Oka River; the other was to join forces with Casimir.

The accounts in the historical literature of the ensuing war between Ahmad and Ivan were, until recently, based mainly on reports in the Muscovite chronicles, and on Bishop Vassian of Rostov's epistle to Ivan. Some of the historians also credited the *basma* story of the Kazan History. As K. V. Bazilevich has shown,[14] many of the reports of this war in the Russian chronicles are later interpolations. Only scattered pieces of authentic contemporary evidence can be discerned in the mid 16th-century digests of annals, such as the Voskresensk and Nikon chronicles. Their basic source, the

12. *Sbornik, 41,* 16–20.
13. See Bazilevich, p. 133.
14. Bazilevich, pp. 134–147.

"Story of Ahmad's Invasion," must have been written around 1498
—that is, almost twenty years after the war.

In the chronicles, as well as in Vassian's Epistle, Ivan III is accused of cowardice. It is alleged that he did not dare to fight the
Tatars and was prepared to abandon Moscow and retreat to North
Russia. The chronicler puts the blame for Ivan's behavior on two
of his councilors, Ivan Oshchera and Grigori Mamon, who are represented as traitors—rich men afraid of losing their wealth. It is
asserted that it was only at the insistence of his son, Ivan Junior,
and his confessor, Bishop Vassian of Rostov, that Ivan decided to
lead his troops to the Ugra River. Bazilevich, rightly in my opinion,
refuses to accept the validity of the "Story of Ahmad's Invasion,"
but he seems to admit the authenticity of Vassian's "Epistle," which
is closely connected with the "Story." I believe that the Epistle,
in the form we know it, must likewise have been compiled around
1498. It is quite probable that Vassian had actually addressed an
epistle to Ivan in 1480 but that his original text was later replaced
by a different version, which amounted to a political pamphlet.
(Vassian died in 1481.) It should be noted that while the so-called
Vassian's Epistle was inserted into some chronicles, no separate
manuscript of it has so far been found.[15]

According to the Vologda-Perm Chronicle (not yet published
in full) Ahmad attempted to cross the Ugra River on October 8,
1480, but met with strong resistance on the part of Russian troops
equipped with small firearms. These troops were under the command of Grand Duke Ivan Junior and his uncle, Prince Andrei
Junior. After four days of intense fighting, Ahmad realized that further effort was futile and retreated two verstas (a mile and a half)
west, pitching his camp in Lithuanian territory.[16] He decided to
wait for the arrival of Casimir with the Lithuanian army. Casimir,
however, failed to appear, in the first place because he had not received sufficient support from Poland, and in the second place his
attention was distracted by Khan Mengli-Girey's raid on Podolia.
Furthermore, there was much opposition among some Russian
princes in Lithuania to Casimir's plans. A conspiracy was formed

15. For the text of Vassian's epistle (in the form we know it) see *PSRL, 6*, 225–230;
12, 203–212. See also I. M. Kudriavtsev, "Poslanie na Ugru Vassiana Rylo," *TODRL,
8* (1951), 158–186.
16. Bazilevich, p. 147.

against Casimir in which both Prince Mikhail Olelkovich and Prince Fedor Ivanovich Belsky took active part. In 1481 Mikhail Olelkovich was arrested and executed, and Belsky fled to Muscovy.[17]

Receiving no aid from Casimir, Ahmad's Tatars looted the territory of the "upper towns" (on the Upper Oka basin): Odoev, Belev, Mtsensk, and others. The Russian princes of this region were Casimir's vassals and, as Bazilevich thinks,[18] may have taken part in the conspiracy against Casimir. In looting this region Ahmad might have had two purposes, to prevent any open uprising in the rear of his camp and to recompense his troops for the unsuccessful campaign.

On November 7, 1480 (the date in the Vologda-Perm Chronicle)[19] Ahmad led his army back to Saray. According to the Kazan History,[20] during the stalemate that followed Ahmad's unsuccessful attempt to cross the Ugra River, Ivan sent across the steppes a combined Russo-Tatar cavalry detachment, under the command of Nur-Dawlet and Prince Vasili Nozdrevaty, to raid Saray. The news of this raid might have accelerated Ahmad's retreat.

To save face, Ahmad dispatched a letter to Ivan saying that he had retreated temporarily because of the approaching winter. He warned Ivan that he would return and take prisoner Ivan and his boyars unless Ivan agreed (1) to pay tribute in the amount of 60,-000 altyns within forty days (1 altyn was equal to 6 dengas, or three-hundredths of a ruble), 20,000 altyns the next spring, and 60,000 altyns the next autumn; (2) to wear "Batu's sign" on his *kolpak* (cap); and (3) to remove Tsarevich Danyar from Kasimov. Ahmad's letter is preserved in Russian translation only.[21] There is no doubt, however, that the translation was made from the original Tatar text soon after the letter was received in Moscow. The "Batu's sign" mentioned in the document is, of course, the *baisa* (tablet of authority). Ahmad's demand to abolish the Khanate of Kasimov is quite understandable in view of the important role that khanate played in Ivan's Tatar policies.

17. Hrushevsky, *Istoriia Ukrainy-Rusi, 4,* 228–229; Bazilevich, pp. 150–153; Jablonowski, pp. 118–123.

18. Bazilevich, p. 154.

19. Bazilevich, p. 159, n. 3.

20. *Kazanskaia istoriia,* p. 56.

21. See text in Bazilevich, pp. 164–165. See also *Zolotaia Orda,* p. 427. K. V. Bazilevich's article "Yarlyk Akhmed-khana Ivanu III," *Vestnik Moskovskogo Universiteta* (1948), No. 1, is inaccessible to me (quoted in *Zolotaia Orda,* p. 426).

The amount of the tribute demanded by Ahmad (140,000 altyns, 840,000 dengas) is quite modest if we compare it to that paid by the Moscow grand dukes to the khans in the earlier period. 840,000 dengas make 4,200 rubles. This is but a fraction of the sum collected by Khan Tokhtamysh from the Grand Duchy of Vladimir in 1382 (around 85,000 rubles).[22]

Ahmad was not destined to continue his struggle against Moscow. According to the Ustiug Chronicle,[23] when Khan Ivak (Aybek) of Tiumen (Western Siberia) heard that Ahmad returned to Saray from Lithuania with rich booty, he decided to attack him stealthily. The Nogay Horde joined Ivak in his enterprise. As Ahmad's people did not expect any attack, they had no time to organize any resistance. Ivak easily reached Ahmad's white tent and personally killed Ahmad. The Tiumenians and the Nogays then sacked Ahmad's headquarters and seized most of his Lithuanian loot, including many captives, Ivak receiving the lion's share of the loot.

After Ahmad's assassination, his sons divided among themselves the power in the Golden Horde, thus intensifying the centrifugal forces in the Horde, which was considerably weakened. Nevertheless, it remained a menace to both Moscow and the Crimea for about twenty more years.

The events of 1480–81 are often spoken of in historical literature as "the fall of the Tatar yoke." Actually, Moscow asserted its independence almost thirty years earlier, in the reign of Vasili II, and Ahmad's campaign was merely an attempt to restore the former suzerainty of the khans over Moscow. The failure of the attempt showed that Moscow had grown too strong ever to be dominated again by the Tatars.

The Tatar danger was not over by any means, however. Ivan III had to use all his diplomatic skill to cultivate friendly relations with the Khanate of the Crimea and to keep the Golden Horde and the Khanate of Kazan in check. While no regular annual tribute to the Tatars was paid any more, Ivan, as well as his successors, had to spend large sums of money as *pominki* (presents) to various khans, including the vassal khans of Kasimov. Because of this, taxes still had to be collected, and their purpose for a long time was defined as *vykhod* (tribute).[24]

22. See *Mongols and Russia*, p. 231.
23. Ustiug Chronicle, pp. 93–94.
24. On the term *vykhod* see *Mongols and Russia*, p. 228.

3. Relations with Turkey, the Crimea,
and Kazan, to 1487

Ottoman Turkey, which established itself on the ruins of the Byzantine Empire, was, in the second half of the 15th and the first half of the 16th century, the mightiest state in what is traditionally called the Near East. It controlled both Asia Minor and the Balkans and constituted a serious danger to Italy, Austria, Hungary, Wallachia, Moldavia, and Poland. After the Crimean campaign of 1475 the Ottoman sultans were in position to supervise, and partly to direct, the policy of the khans of the Crimea (now their vassals). Because of the important role of the Crimea in Ivan III's diplomatic system Turkey became a factor with which Moscow had to reckon.

The period of the reign of Sultan Mohammed II the Conqueror (1451–81) was characterized by dynamic expansion and fierce aggressiveness of the Ottoman Empire. In contrast, the reign of Mohammed's son and successor, Bayazit II "the Saint Sultan" (1481–1512) was a period of comparative quiet and consolidation of the gains made before. In his *Discourses* Niccolò Machiavelli, a contemporary of Bayazit, mentions Bayazit to illustrate his thesis that "if an able and vigorous prince is succeeded by a feeble one, the latter may for a time be able to maintain himself; but if his successor be also weak, then the latter will not be able to preserve his state." Machiavelli says that Bayazit, "although preferring peace to war, yet could enjoy the labors of his father Mahomet, who, having like David crushed his neighbors, left him a firmly established kingdom, which he could easily preserve with the arts of peace." [25] (Bayazit's successors—his son Selim the Dread and grandson Suleiman the Magnificent—continued the militant policies of Mohammed II.) Bayazit was a philosopher on the throne, a Sufi, more interested in religious meditations than in military exploits. [26]

In spite of the peaceful disposition of Sultan Bayazit, under him the Turks took certain measures to strengthen their position in the Black Sea area. In 1484 they seized Kilia in the Danube delta and Akkerman (Belgorod) in the Dniester estuary. [27] Simultaneously,

25. N. Machiavelli, *The Prince and the Discourses* (Modern Library ed., C. E. Detmold's translation), pp. 172–173.
26. See Krymsky, p. 108.
27. Bazilevich, p. 239.

in the northeastern corner of the Black Sea they occupied the Taman Peninsula (ancient Tmutorokan) and subdued the Circassians.[28] Following that, they obtained full control of the whole Black Sea, which was shortly afterward closed to all foreign ships. Eventually, a special Turkish doctrine was formulated according to which the Black Sea was a "virgin" not to be violated by Christian ships. It was only in 1774, during the reign of Catherine II in Russia, that the Turks were finally compelled to abandon this position.

In his letter to the citizens of Raguza of August 2, 1484, Bayazit called Kilia the key and gate to Moldavia and Hungary, and Akkerman the key and gate to Poland, Russia, and Tataria.[29]

As regards Ivan III's policies, the Turks were now in a position to watch closely the exchange of envoys between Moscow, on the one hand, and Moldavia and Hungary, on the other. In 1482 a Hungarian envoy came to Moscow to discuss a joint action against King Casimir. Ivan was pleased with this opportunity of strengthening Moscow's position in the West and sent one of his best diplomats, Fedor Kuritsyn, to Hungary to conclude an alliance with King Matthew Corvin. Ivan also was eager to establish friendly relations with the Voevoda Stephan of Moldavia. In 1482 an agreement was reached between Ivan and Stephan concerning the marriage of Stephan's daughter Elena to Ivan III's son Ivan Junior. The wedding took place in Moscow on January 1, 1483. It should be noted that Elena's mother was a daughter of Prince Olelko of Kiev and thus a sister of Prince Mikhail Olelkovich, executed by Casimir in 1481.

Kuritsyn stayed in Hungary over a year and collected a great deal of information on Central European and Balkan affairs. On his way back he conferred with the Voevoda Stephan and then set out for the Crimea in the fall of 1484—that is, soon after the seizure of Akkerman by the Turks. Since the relations between the Turks and the Hungarians were strained, the Turks became suspicious of Kuritsyn's mission, arrested him, and kept him imprisoned in Akkerman for more than two years. It was only in the summer of 1487 that he was able to return to Moscow.

The Turkish occupation of the Taman area did not immediately affect Russian interests at that time. From the historian's point of

---

28. See R. Loewe, *Die Reste der Germanen am Schwarzen Meere* (Halle, 1896), pp. 38–40.

29. Bazilevich, p. 239, referring to *MHH, VI*, No. 33.

view, however, the event was significant because it meant that Turkey had staked its claims on that region (where the Russian principality of Tmutorokan had flourished in the 11th century) before Russia was in position to present her counterclaims. It should be noted in this connection that in 1487 a former prince of Taman, an Italian named Zechariah de Guizolfi—formerly a vassal of the Genoese—after being dispossessed by the Turks asked Ivan III to permit him to come to Moscow and become the grand duke's servitor. Ivan approved his petition, but for various reasons Zechariah never reached Moscow.[30]

About the same time, the Georgians attempted to establish contact with Moscow. A Russian translation of a letter of the Kakhetian King (Tsar) Aleksandr to Ivan III has been preserved. It contains names of Georgian envoys to Moscow and is dated 1483. No information about this embassy is available in Russian sources, in which the first mention of a Georgian mission to Moscow is dated 1492.[31]

Prior to the destruction of the Italian colonies in the Crimea by the Turks, in 1475, the Crimean trade was controlled mostly by the Genoese.[32] Muscovite merchants profited much by the Crimean commerce, in which they took active part. After 1475 the Kaffa trade was controlled by the Turks, but the Russian merchants continued to visit the Crimean markets. Because of this, maintaining good relations with the Crimea was essential for Russian commercial interests.

From the political angle, the alliance between Moscow and the Crimea against Lithuania and the Golden Horde continued throughout the reign of Ivan III. For Mengli-Girey the main purpose of the alliance with Ivan was to curb the aggressiveness of the Golden Horde. The Crimea was not directly threatened by Lithuania, but the state of war with her was profitable to Mengli-Girey, since it enabled him to raid periodically the southern provinces of Lithuania —actually, the Ukrainian lands. One of the most terrible attacks of the Crimean Tatars was that on Kiev in 1482. It was thoroughly devastated and did not recover for many years. Raids on neighboring countries, it should be noted, constituted an important source of income of the Tatar khanates of this period. Much gold and

30. See *Sbornik, 41,* pp. 72–73, 77.
31. Bazilevich, p. 410.
32. See N. L. Ernst, "Konflikt Ivana III s Genuezskoi Kafoi," *TOIAE, 1* (1927), 167–180.

jewelry was usually seized in the churches and the noblemen's mansions; but the staple item were the captives—men, women, and children. These were driven to Kaffa and sold there, to be shipped to Turkey, Egypt, and Italy. Mengli-Girey's raids on the Ukraine distracted Casimir's attention from other matters and more often than not upset his plans for a war against Moscow. This made Mengli-Girey a valuable ally for Ivan. The threat to Moscow on the part of the Golden Horde subsided after the death of Ahmad. It was now not the Golden Horde but the Khanate of Kazan that presented the main danger for Moscow, especially since the Kazan Tatars were in convenient position to raid the Muscovite provinces adjacent to them. In the area beyond the Volga the Tatars penetrated far to the North and established contact with the Russian republic of Viatka. From the economic point of view, Kazan was an important center of Oriental trade and in the periods of peace was visited by a great number of Russian merchants.

In his attempts to curb the power of the Khanate of Kazan, Ivan at first tried to use his vassal, Tsarevich Kasim, as his tool. The first Khan of Kazan, Mahmudek, was Kasim's brother. After Mahmudek's death his son Ibrahim became khan and Kasim married Mahmudek's widow (Ibrahim's mother).[33] In 1467 Kasim was invited by a group of Kazan princes to occupy the throne. However, Khan Ibrahim refused to vacate the throne, and most of the Kazan army backed him. Ivan sent Russian troops to support Kasim's claims. Three campaigns were undertaken against Kazan. The first two proved failures; the third resulted in a treaty of peace. Ibrahim remained Khan of Kazan. Kasim died during or soon after the third campaign (around 1469).

Around 1482 Ibrahim in his turn died and was succeeded by Ilgam (also called Ali-Khan), his son by one of his less important wives. Ibrahim's chief wife was Nur-Saltan, daughter of Prince Temir of the clan of Mangkyt.[34] By her, Ibrahim had two sons, Mohammed-Amin and Abdul-Letif. About three years after Ibrahim's death Nur-Saltan married the Khan of the Crimea, Mengli-Girey, and became his chief wife. She was a clever and energetic woman and exerted considerable influence on the policies of her new husband, supporting the pro-Moscow orientation in the Crimea.

33. See *Mongols and Russia*, p. 431, Genealogical Table VII; Veliaminov-Zernov, *1*, 3–4, 13–14, 58–59.

34. On Nur-Saltan see Bazilevich, pp. 177–178; B. S. Ischboldin, "Tsaritsa Tatarskaia Nursultana," *Novik* (1951), pp. 11–15.

Ivan, on his part, tried to promote friendship with her and her kin. Her father, Prince Temir, called Ivan his "son," and Ivan addressed Temir as "father." Both Nur-Saltan and her father were sent rich presents from Moscow every year.

Nur-Saltan was scheming to oust from the Kazan throne her step-son Ilgam in order to put there the eldest of her own sons by Ibrahim, Mohammed-Amin. This suited Ivan's plans perfectly. In the Khanate of Kazan, like that of the Crimea, the khan's authority was actually limited by the princes—heads of aristocratic Tatar clans. Without the concurrence of at least some of them, the khan was not able to act. When the most influential clans supported the khan, affairs ran smoothly. When there was a disagreement among the leading clans, the ground was laid for intrigues and even for palace revolutions. Ivan III and his advisers understood well the mechanics of the Tatar government. Both in the Crimea and in Kazan, Ivan cultivated friendly relations with a number of influential princes. Nur-Saltan helped him in the Crimea and—through her agents—also in Kazan. For several years, a stubborn struggle went on in Kazan between the followers of Ilgam and those of Mohammed-Amin. In 1486 Mohammed-Amin fled to Moscow and personally asked Ivan III to intervene in his favor.

On May 18, 1487, a strong Russian army under the supreme command of Prince Daniel Kholmsky appeared before Kazan. After a siege that lasted for fifty-two days Khan Ilgam surrendered. He was arrested and later deported to Vologda, and several of the Tatar princes who had supported him were executed. Mohammed-Amin was then installed Khan of Kazan, as Ivan III's vassal. Immediately upon receiving news of this event Ivan dispatched a messenger to the Crimea to notify Mengli-Girey and Nur-Saltan of Mohammed-Amin's enthronement. It is noteworthy that thereafter the official correspondence between Kazan and the Crimea was allowed only via Moscow. There all letters from Kazan to the Crimea and vice versa were read and translated into Russian, after which the originals were duly forwarded to the addressees.[35]

4. MOSCOW AND LITHUANIA, 1487–95

The curbing of the power of the Khanate of Kazan enabled Ivan to pay more attention to Lithuania. No war was declared, but a

35. Bazilevich, p. 206.

series of border incidents occurred in 1487 and the following years in the Smolensk area as well as in the region of the upper towns. Moscow officially was not involved in this "small war." On the surface the initiative belonged to Ivan III's son, Prince Ivan Junior (at that time Prince of Tver); to Ivan's brother Prince Andrei Senior of Uglich and Mozhaisk, in his capacity of the Prince of Mozhaisk; and to governors of the districts adjacent to the upper towns. The Lithuanians retaliated from time to time, but on the whole the Muscovites had the upper hand. Thousands of people were seized in the raided areas, deported to the Muscovite territory, and settled there. It should be noted that a number of petty Russian princes both in the Viazma region and in the upper towns were in opposition to Casimir and demanded wider rights and privileges. While Ivan III carried on a policy of centralization in Muscovy, he supported the claims of local princes in the Grand Duchy of Lithuania, since the opposition of these princes to Casimir weakened the latter's position. As a result of Ivan's policies several Russian princes of the upper towns, among them the Vorotynskys and the Belevskys went over to Moscow's side.

Simultaneously, Ivan worked for a diplomatic encirclement of Poland and Lithuania, to be ready in case the small war should develop into a great war. Besides his negotiations with Hungary, Ivan also made contact with the German Empire. In 1486 a German knight, Nicholas Poppel, visited Moscow to acquaint himself with the situation there. In 1489 he returned to Moscow as an official envoy of Emperor Frederick III, authorized by Frederick to offer Ivan the royal crown. Ivan's acceptance would have meant inclusion of Muscovy in the system of the Holy Roman Empire. Ivan refused the crown but expressed his willingness to conclude a treaty of alliance with the Empire. After further exchange of embassies, Frederick's son, King Maximilian I, approved the treaty (1491), but soon after its conclusion Maximilian made peace with Casimir's son, Wladyslaw, King of Bohemia and Hungary. The Moscow alliance now had no value for him, and the treaty was not put into effect.

The contact with the German Empire in these years proved beneficial for the development of mining in Russia. As early as 1482 Ivan had asked King Matthew Corvin of Hungary to dispatch to Moscow mining engineers for the search of deposits of metals in Russia. If Hungarian engineers were sent, they were not able to reach Moscow because of Kuritsyn's arrest by the Turks on his way back from Hungary. In 1491 two mining specialists were brought by Ivan's envoys from Germany. They are mentioned only by their first names in Russian sources (Ivan and Victor). Accompanied by two Russian officials, these Germans went to North Russia and discovered deposits of silver and copper at Ust-Tsylma on the lower Pechora River.[36] The next year the German Michael Snups came to Moscow with letters of recommendation from King Maximilian I and the latter's uncle, Archduke Sigismund of Innsbruck. They asked Ivan to let Snups undertake a journey beyond the Ural to the Ob River for geographic reasearch. Ivan refused, under the pretext that he could not guarantee Snups' safety in the wild countries where he intended to go. Apparently Ivan was suspicious of the true purpose of Snups' mission.[37]

When all is said, Khan Mengli-Girey of the Crimea proved Ivan III's only useful ally against Lithuania, even though he was not always reliable. In 1492 Mengli-Girey decided to build a stronghold which could serve as an advance base for any future operations against Poland and Lithuania. He selected a suitable place on the northern side of the Dnieper estuary and called the new fortress Ochakov. News of its building caused great anxiety in Poland and Lithuania. In Moscow the news must have been met with mixed feelings. The fortress undoubtedly improved Mengli-Girey's position against Moscow's Western enemies. At the same time, however, Ochakov could be considered a perennial threat to Kiev and other Ukrainian lands on the future of which Ivan III had designs of his own.

The fortress was eventually taken over by the Turks and served as an important base for them in their wars against Russia in the late 17th and the 18th centuries. It was finally stormed by the Russians in 1788 and annexed to Russia by the Treaty of Iași, 1792. The seizure of Ochakov by the Russians was greatly resented in Great Britain at that time. An American historian, J. H. Gleason, has recently suggested that this event should be connected with the genesis of Russophobia in England.[38]

On June 7, 1492, Casimir died in Grodno. He left several sons, the eldest of whom, Wladyslaw, was King of Bohemia (from 1471) and Hungary (from 1490). Of Casimir's other sons, Jan Albrecht,

36. Karamzin, *Istoriia*, 6, 227, and *Primechaniia*, nn. 360, 361 to Vol. 6.

37. Karamzin, *Istoriia*, 6, 228–229, and n. 362 to Vol. 6.

38. J. H. Gleason, *The Genesis of Russophobia in Great Britain* (Cambridge, Harvard University Press, 1950), pp. 9, 11, 15, 19.

after Casimir's death, was elected King of Poland, and the next in seniority, Aleksandr, became Grand Duke of Lithuania. As a result, the dynastic tie between Poland and Lithuania was temporarily severed. (It was renewed in 1501 when, after the death of Jan Albrecht, Aleksandr was elected King of Poland, remaining at the same time Grand Duke of Lithuania.) While Poland had not given much support to Lithuania even under Casimir, the separation of the two states nevertheless weakened Lithuania's position *vis-à-vis* Moscow.

A few remarks should be made at this juncture concerning the change of Lithuanian policies toward the Jews after Casimir's death. In the 15th century Jews constituted an important element in the urban population of both Poland and Lithuania. In the 13th and 14th centuries the Polish kings had issued several charters by which Jews were authorized to engage freely in trade throughout Poland. In the 15th century Casimir confirmed the old charters and gave the Jews some new privileges. On the other hand, the Catholic Church in Poland tended to restrict the rights of Jews. There was also some resentment in Poland against the activities of Jews as usurers. By the Statutes of Nieszawa (1454) usury was forbidden; but these statutes were valid in Poland only, not in Lithuania.[39]

In Lithuania, during the whole period of Casimir's reign, Jews enjoyed the same privileges as in Poland. It should be noted that the Karaite settlements were subject to the same laws as those of the Rabbinical Jews. The Karaite communities of Troki were given the privilege of the Magdeburg law, which otherwise was applied only to the Christians.[40]

In 1492 Jews were forbidden to live in Kovna. Three years later Grand Duke Aleksandr issued an edict by which both Rabbinic Jews and Karaites were ejected from the Grand Duchy of Lithuania. These anti-Jewish measures may be partly ascribed to the influence on Aleksandr of the Roman Catholic clergy. But there is also a possibility that Aleksandr's advisers considered the Jews potential agents of Ivan III. It is known that in 1490 the Lithuanian Jews rejoiced at the progress of Judaism in Russia.[41] It should also be noted that Grand Duke Aleksandr revoked his anti-Jewish edict in 1503 —that is, at the very time the conservatives of the Russian Greek

39. Wojciechowski, pp. 238–240; Liubavsky, *Ocherk*, pp. 117–118.
40. See Szyszman, "Die Karäer in Ost-Mitteleuropa," pp. 37–38.
41. *AFED*, p. 377.

Orthodox clergy overcame the opposition of the "Beyond the Volga Hermits" which presaged the curbing of the Judaizers (see below, p. 131).

In 1493 negotiations were begun between Lithuania and Moscow for the conclusion of a treaty that would end the impossible situation of the undeclared border war. To secure better relations with Moscow, the Lithuanians suggested that Ivan's daughter Elena be given in marriage to Grand Duke Aleksandr. In the course of these negotiations Ivan III, for the first time in his relations with a foreign power, called himself "Sovereign of All Russia" (*Gosudar vseia Rusi*). The phrase "of All Russia" was not invented by him, however. His forefather, Ivan I (Grand Duke of Vladimir, 1332–41) added it to his title, in imitation of the title of the metropolitans of Russia.[42] Following that, the phrase occurred in the title of the Moscow grand dukes on several occasions in the interprince treaties, as for example, in the treaty of Grand Duke Simeon with his brothers around 1350; [43] in that of Vasili I with his brother Iuri around 1390; [44] and in several treaties of Ivan III with lesser princes in 1483–86.[45] But in 1493 Ivan for the first time included the phrase "of All Russia" in his title in negotiations with a foreign country and, what was especially significant, with a country in regard to which the phrase sounded like a challenge, since the ruler of that country himself had "Russia" in his title ("Grand Duke of Lithuania and Russia," *Veliki Kniaz' Litovsky i Russky*).

After protracted bargaining and bickering, the treaty of friendship and alliance between Lithuania and Moscow was signed in Moscow on February 7, 1494.[46] Ivan's title "of All Russia" was accepted by the Lithuanians. Both Aleksandr and Ivan promised not to interfere with each other's possessions. Aleksandr abandoned all claims to Novgorod, Pskov, Tver, Rzhev, Viazma, Aleksin, and Riazan. Ivan relinquished his claims to Smolensk, Liubutsk, Mtsensk, and Briansk. Of the petty Russian princes of the upper towns, Aleksandr abandoned his suzerainty over the Odoevskys, the Vorotynskys, the Belevskys, and one branch of the Mezetskys. Ivan, on the other hand, agreed to recognize Aleksandr's suzerainty over the other branch of the Mezetskys.

42. See *Mongols and Russia*, p. 201.
43. *DDG*, p. 11.
44. *DDG*, p. 39.
45. *DDG*, pp. 290, 295, 301, 315, and 332.
46. For the text of the treaty see *DDG*, pp. 329–332. Cf. Bazilevich, pp. 326–329.

The treaty as a whole was undoubtedly more favorable to Moscow than to Lithuania. True, most of what Aleksandr renounced (Novgorod, Pskov, Tver, Riazan) did not actually belong to him, but he also had to cede an important section of the disputed border territory, including Viazma and part of the upper towns. Furthermore, he had to recognize Ivan's title "of All Russia," without actually knowing what it comprised.

It is obvious that the Lithuanians made these important concessions to Ivan in the hope that in this way they would secure firm peace in the East. They also believed that the marriage between Aleksandr and Ivan's daughter would make the relations between the two rulers more friendly. Elena's engagement to Aleksandr took place on the eve of the signing of the political treaty. Aleksandr was represented by proxy. The main condition of Ivan's agreement to his daughter's marriage was that she should remain a member of the Greek Orthodox Church. There were many details still unsettled even after the engagement, and it was not until eleven months later that the Lithuanian ambassadors who were to take the fiancée to Vilna arrived at Moscow (January 6, 1495). Ivan in his turn appointed Prince Semen Ivanovich Riapolovsky and other Muscovite officials to accompany Elena, with their wives. A Muscovite priest, Foma (Thomas) also was in the party, to serve as Elena's chaplain in Vilna. The festive train left Moscow on January 13.

Elena's journey to Vilna and her wedding there are vividly described in the report of the Moscow envoys to Ivan of February 1495.[47] When Elena's train reached the new Moscow possession of Viazma, Elena was solemnly met by all of the princes Viazemsky, offering her rich gifts. No less cordial a welcome awaited her in the first major town in Lithuanian territory, Smolensk. She was greeted by Aleksandr's lieutenant there and by all the boyars and burghers of Smolensk, as well as by the Russian clergy. She stopped in Smolensk for two days and attended mass in the Russian cathedral.

Similar events occurred on her way through the West Russian lands of the Grand Duchy of Lithuania in Polotsk and Vitebsk. When she reached the Lithuanian territory proper, near Krevo, she was met by Aleksandr's special representatives, Prince Konstantin Ivanovich Ostrozhsky and princes Ivan and Vasili Glinsky. They offered Elena a luxurious coach Aleksandr had sent her to continue her journey. It was driven by eight gray stallions in beautiful harness.

47. *Sbornik, 35,* 182–187. Cf. Bazilevich, pp. 332–334.

However, Elena had strict instructions from her father not to use the Lithuanian carriage (the offer of which had apparently been expected) unless Aleksandr's mother was there to greet her and to accompany her. Since this was not the case, Elena refused to move over to the Lithuanian coach and stuck to the sturdy vehicle she had traveled in from Moscow, the *tapkana*.[48] Two miles before Vilna Aleksandr personally met his fiancée, riding on a horse. When he approached the tapkana, he ordered that a piece of red cloth be laid on the ground between his horse and Elena's carriage. The Moscow boyars, thinking fast, put a piece of damask over the section of cloth closest to the tapkana. Thus, when the groom alighted from his horse and Elena from her carriage, he stepped on his cloth and she on her damask—that is, symbolically, she remained on Moscow territory.

After the groom and the fiancée had greeted each other, Elena returned to her tapkana and Aleksandr rode at her side on horseback. Arriving at Vilna, Elena went to the Russian church of the Nativity of the Holy Virgin and Aleksandr to the Roman Catholic cathedral where the wedding was to take place. In front of the Russian church Elena was greeted by the Orthodox Metropolitan of Kiev, Makari. In the church Elena attended at the Te Deum (the mass was just over). Then, according to old Russian wedding custom, the boyars' wives who accompanied Elena unplaited her hair, combed and made it up, put the *kika*[49] on her head, and sprinkled Elena with hops. Elena's chaplain, the priest Foma, then read the prayers and blessed her. After that, Elena went to the Roman Catholic cathedral where Aleksandr waited for her. The priest Foma walked before her, carrying the cross with which he blessed her. A Roman Catholic bishop with a crucifix met Elena in front of the church but did not bless her. They all then entered the cathedral, where Elena took her place alongside Aleksandr. The bishop performed the Roman Catholic rite of marriage. Metropolitan Makari was present but was forbidden by Aleksandr to take any part in the service. The priest Foma, however, stood by and recited prayers in Slavonic; Princess Maria Riapolovskaia held the wedding crown over Elena's head according to the Russian fashion. Both the bishop and Aleksandr himself angrily protested to

48. The word *tapkana* may derive from the Ossetic language. In Ossetic *tapka* means "shed, canopy." *Tapkana* must have been a covered wagon, or a sleigh (Elena traveled in January).

49. *Kika*, woman's headgear in Old Russia. A variation of it is known as *kokoshnik*.

Prince Riapolovsky against Princess Maria's and Foma's interference with the service. Riapolovsky made an attempt to persuade Foma and Maria to desist, but they both stubbornly continued to do what they considered their duty. After the wedding Aleksandr went to his apartment in the palace and his bride, to hers. Soon after, Aleksandr invited the Russian boyars to a banquet. In the conclusion of their report to Ivan, the boyars noted that Elena wore her Russian dress at the wedding ceremony and added, with obvious satisfaction: "And today is the fourth day after the wedding and the Grand Duchess still wears her own dress and her kika."

5. THE NEAR EAST AND KAZAN, 1490–96

The establishment of Ivan's suzerainty over Kazan greatly enhanced his prestige in the East. In August 1490 princes (*murzy*) of the Nogay Horde sent an embassy to Moscow offering Ivan an alliance against "Ahmad's sons"—that is, the Golden Horde. The offer was accepted. Moreover, Ivan allowed his vassal, Khan Mohammed-Amin of Kazan, to marry the daughter of a Nogay prince and to give his (Mohammed-Amin's) daughter in marriage to another Nogay prince.[50] By encouraging friendly relations between Kazan and the Nogays, Ivan apparently hoped not only to strengthen his position against the remnants of the Golden Horde but also to open a new path of communication with the Middle East through the Yaik River basin. It is probably through that region that an envoy of Hussein-Mirza, the ruler of Herat, came to Moscow on September 28, 1490.[51]

In 1492 a Georgian (Kakhetian) embassy visited Moscow.[52] As has been mentioned, this apparently was not the first Georgian mission to Ivan III.[53] King (Tsar) Aleksandr of Kakhetia's letter to Ivan, which has been preserved in Russian translation only, seems to belong to the previous embassy (1482). Both missions must have been identical in purpose. Aleksandr conveyed his greetings to Ivan as if Ivan were the protector of all the Orthodox Christians oppressed by the Moslems.[54]

50. Bazilevich, pp. 206–208.
51. *PSRL, 8*, 220; Bazilevich, p. 413.
52. *PSRL, 12*, 232.
53. See above, p. 80; and Bazilevich, pp. 409–411.
54. For the text of Tsar Aleksandr's letter see Karamzin, *Primechaniia*, n. 370 to Vol. *6;* Belokurov, *1*, pp. xxi–xxii.

Through the Crimea, Ivan III tried to establish friendly relations with the Mameluk Sultan of Egypt.[55] In 1491 the Khan of the Crimea, Mengli-Girey, wrote to Ivan that he had received a message from the Sultan of Egypt in which the latter asked Mengli-Girey to send him presents, to promote friendly relations between them. Mengli-Girey explained to Ivan that he had used his (Ivan's) gifts of this year for the presents he sent to the Ottoman Sultan Bayazit and had now nothing suitable left for the Sultan of Egypt. Therefore he urged Ivan to send him (Mengli-Girey) some valuable gifts, such as sables and walrus tusks, for reshipping to Egypt.[56] Presumably, Ivan sent to Mengli-Girey the required goods. Then in 1493 a Muscovite official, Mikhail Munekhin, went to Palestine and Egypt. Nikolay Andreyev suggests that the purpose of his mission was to distribute alms from the grand duke to Orthodox churches there.[57] This might have been one of Munekhin's tasks, but his main duty was probably that of bringing more presents to the Sultan of Egypt, this time without the intermediary of Mengli-Girey. After his journey Munekhin became known as Misiur-Munekhin (from the Arabic name for Egypt, Misr, in Russian transcription *Misiur*).

While the relations between Ivan III and Mengli-Girey continued to be friendly, Muscovite merchants who dealt with the Crimea resented high customs duties established by the Turks as well as various abuses on the part of the Turkish officials. Prior to the arrival of the Turks in the Crimea, Russian merchants paid customs duties (*tamga*) reckoned at 7 per cent ad valorem to the Khan of the Crimea, and a special duty of 16 dengas per man to Prince Shirin (the Shirins were the mightiest clan among the Crimean Tatar aristocracy). If the Russians had to undertake a sea voyage from Kaffa, they paid a tamga of 5 per cent ad valorem, which exempted them from any other duties upon their return to Kaffa. Now the Turks raised the amount of all the customs duties and established a new tamga at Ochakov, which they collected even if the Russian merchants went directly to Perekop, not stopping at Ochakov. Furthermore, the Russians complained that the Turks drafted Russian merchants for the work of building fortresses whenever they needed labor, as in Azov. If a member of the company of Russian merchants fell ill while staying in a Turkish town, the goods of the

55. In Ivan's time the Mameluk Sultanate was still an independent state. It was conquered by the Ottoman Sultan Selim the Dread in 1517.

56. *Sbornik, 41,* 107.

57. Andreyev, p. 318.

whole company were immediately sealed. After the merchant's re-
covery, only half the goods was returned to the company. If the
merchant died, all the goods were confiscated.[58]

In retaliation Ivan III, in 1492, forbade trading by Russians in
the Crimea. Simultaneously, he dispatched through Mengli-Girey
a letter to Sultan Bayazit asking him if he knew of the abuses of
his subjects and suggesting that a Turkish envoy be sent to Moscow
to talk over the matter. It is not known whether Ivan received any
answer from the Sultan, but three years later Bayazit decided to
reorganize the Turkish administration in the Crimea and sent one
of his sons, the young *shah-zadeh* (literally "sovereign's son")
Mehmet (Mohammed) to Kaffa as his viceroy. A tutor was appointed to advise Mehmet. Mengli-Girey then informed Ivan that
Mehmet was authorized to deal with Ivan's complaints concerning
the offenses against the Russian merchants. Soon after (in the
winter of 1495–96) Mehmet sent an envoy to Ivan, but this envoy
was arrested in Kiev by order of Grand Duke Aleksandr of Lithuania
and not allowed to proceed to Moscow. Taking advantage of this
opening of negotiations by Turkey, even though it was a failure,
Ivan sent his envoy, Mikhail Pleshcheev, to Kaffa, to thank Mehmet
for his friendliness, and then to Constantinople to negotiate with
Sultan Bayazit himself.

Pleshcheev had strict instructions from Ivan not to disclose the
aim of his embassy to the Turkish pashas prior to the audience
with the Sultan; also, not to kneel before the Sultan. Pleshcheev's
refusal to comply with the requirements of the Turkish protocol
infuriated the pashas. A. Krymsky aptly remarks that had such an
incident occurred under Mohammed II, the envoy might have been
executed,[59] but luckily for Pleshcheev, Bayazit was of a mild disposition and agreed to receive him (in May 1497).[60] In his answer
to Ivan, Bayazit said that some of the complaints of the Russian
merchants were lies, but that he had nevertheless ordered his son
Mehmet in Kaffa to take strict measures for preventing offenses
against Russian merchants and securing justice for them.

In 1499 Ivan sent to Constantinople another envoy, Aleksandr
Golokhvastov. He was to thank Bayazit for his readiness to facilitate
trade conditions and also to suggest that a Turkish envoy be sent

58. *Sbornik, 41,* 312–313; Bazilevich, pp. 417–418.
59. Krymsky, p. 113.
60. On Pleshcheev's mission to the Sultan see *Sbornik, 41,* 231–236, 241–249.

to Moscow directly by Bayazit and not by Mehmet of Kaffa.
Golokhvastov was well received by Bayazit. However, in his reply
to Ivan the Sultan, while expressing friendship, did not say anything
about sending his envoy to Moscow. Further relations between
Moscow and Constantinople in Ivan's reign continued through
Kaffa.[61]

Turning once more to Kazan affairs, we see that Moscow's sway
over that khanate was challenged in 1495 by Mamuk, brother of
the late Khan Ivak (of the House of Shiban) and his successor as
Khan of Tiumen. Mamuk concluded an agreement with a number
of Nogay princes and with their support attacked Kazan in the
autumn of 1495. Undoubtedly, Mamuk had also had a secret understanding with some Kazan princes who were opposed to Mohammed-
Amin. Mamuk succeeded in ousting Mohammed-Amin, but when he
himself tried to seize power in Kazan, most of the Kazan princes
rose against him and sent messengers to Ivan III asking him to
send them a new khan, Mohammed-Amin's younger brother Abdul-
Letif. Ivan agreed, and in April 1496 Moscow officials brought
Abdul-Letif to Kazan and installed him in office. To Mohammed-
Amin, Ivan granted three Russian towns, including Kashira and
Serpukhov, for "feeding." [62] Eight years later Ivan called Abdul-
Letif back to Moscow and sent Mohammed-Amin back to Kazan.

6. CONFLICTS WITH SWEDEN, LITHUANIA, AND LIVONIA, 1492–1503

After the annexation of Novgorod, Muscovy became a Baltic
power and new problems arose for Ivan III. His main objectives in
the Baltic area were threefold: to break the commercial monopoly
of the Hanseatic League, to make Novgorod and Pskov secure from
the attacks of the Livonian Knights, and to make the outlet to the
Gulf of Finland, via the Neva River, safe from the encroachment
of Swedes.

In 1492 Ivan ordered a new Russian fortress, called Ivangorod
(Ivan Town), built on the eastern bank of the Narova River, close
to the mouth and opposite the German town of Narva. In addition
to its military importance, it quickly assumed considerable eco-

61. On Golokhvastov's mission see *Sbornik, 41,* 280–282.
62. Bazilevich, p. 399.

nomic significance as a new harbor for commercial ships plying the Baltic Sea.

A Danish envoy appeared in Moscow in July 1493 to prepare ground for an agreement between Denmark and Muscovy on Baltic affairs. Ivan III reciprocated by sending his envoys to Denmark, and on November 8 a treaty of alliance between King Johannes (Hans) of Denmark and Ivan III was signed in Denmark.[63] The two rulers pledged to assist each other "as much as is feasible." Specifically, they announced a joint action against the ruler of Sweden, Sten Sture, a usurper from the point of view of King Hans, who claimed the crown of Sweden for himself. For Ivan III the value of the Danish alliance was twofold: it strengthened his position in relation to the Hanseatic League, and it gave him an opportunity to weaken Sweden's hold over Finland. A year later Ivan closed the Hanseatic Yard (*Hof*) in Novgorod, and in 1495–96 the Russians participated in Hans' war against Sweden. Russian armies raided Finland and reached the Gulf of Bothnia twice. The war was won by the allies, and Hans was crowned King of Sweden (1497).[64]

Meanwhile, new misunderstandings arose between Muscovy and Lithuania. Elena's marriage to Aleksandr, instead of making the relations between Ivan III and Aleksandr more cordial, sowed the seeds of a new conflict. Ivan, never one to allow family feelings to interfere with his policies, was ready to sacrifice his daughter's personal happiness to Russia's national and religious interests as he understood them. On the other side, the pope and the Roman Catholic clergy in Lithuania exerted constant pressure on Aleksandr either to convince his consort to accept Roman Catholicism or to repudiate her.

Before long a new attempt to subordinate the West Russian Church to the pope was made by the Lithuanian government. In 1497 the Metropolitan of Kiev, Makari, was killed by the Crimean Tatars during one of their raids on West Russian lands. To replace him, Grand Duke Aleksandr appointed the Bishop of Smolensk, Iosif Bolgarinovich (1498). The new metropolitan belonged to a noble West Russian family and was a relative of Ian Sapega, secretary of Grand Duke Aleksandr. Sapega, originally Greek Orthodox, had been converted to Roman Catholicism in 1492.

Iosif Bolgarinovich was in favor of the union of the West Russian

63. Forsten, pp. 597–598; Bazilevich, p. 379.
64. Bazilevich, pp. 387–393.

Church with Rome. After a preliminary exchange of messages with
Rome, in 1500 he sent an official letter to the pope announcing his
willingness to accept the Florentine declaration of union.[65] Even
before that, the Greek Orthodox in Lithuania were complaining to
Ivan that their religious rights were curtailed.

In 1499, in anticipation of a new conflict with Lithuania, Ivan
III deemed it necessary to discuss with his ally, the Khan Mengli-
Girey, the question of division of the respective spheres of influence
of Muscovy and the Crimea in the Ukrainian lands of the Grand
Duchy of Lithuania. Mengli-Girey agreed that Kiev and Cherkasy
should belong to Ivan.[66]

In April 1500 two Russian princes of the Chernigov-Severian
region, Simeon Ivanovich Mozhaisky and Vasili Ivanovich Shemiachich, went over to Ivan's side. Both of them were descendants of
old foes of Vasili II, and their dramatic shift from Lithuanian
suzerainty to Muscovite was of concern to both sides.

In May 1500 Ivan III sent to Vilna his declaration of war,[67]
motivated by the failure of the Lithuanian government to observe the
conditions of the treaty of 1494, and by the pressure on his daughter,
Elena, to abandon her faith. On the diplomatic side, Lithuania had
alliances with Livonia and the Golden Horde. Also, in 1501
Aleksandr, after the death of his brother Jan Albrecht, became
King of Poland and the dynastic union between Poland and Lithuania was thus restored. Muscovy had alliances with the Crimean
Horde and with Denmark. Actually, in the ensuing war Mengli-
Girey's attention was distracted by the Golden Horde (which he
crushed in 1502), and he gave little direct assistance to Ivan against
Lithuania. King Hans of Denmark gave Ivan no assistance at all,
for in 1501 Sweden revolted and he had to send more troops against
it.

It so happened, then, that Muscovy had to wage two wars at
once—with Lithuania and with Livonia—all by herself. The Livonian war, fought mostly in the Pskov region, was of limited significance—except that Ivan had to divert part of his forces from the
Lithuanian theater to the Pskovian, which could only weaken the
Muscovite effort in the main theater. There the Muscovites admin-
istered a crushing defeat to the Lithuanian army on the banks of

65. Makari, 9, 100–102.
66. Sbornik, 41, 288; Bazilevich, p. 446.
67. Bazilevich, p. 451.

the Vedrosha River in the first year of the war (July 14, 1500). The Muscovite troops were commanded by the boyar Iuri Zakharievich Koshkin and Prince Daniel Shchenia; the Lithuanians by a West Russian noble, Prince Konstantin Ivanovich Ostrozhsky (who was taken prisoner).[68] In the late summer of 1500 Muscovite troops occupied most of the Chernigov-Severian area. On the other hand, Moscow's attempt to storm Smolensk, in October 1502, was a failure, since the Muscovite artillery proved too weak for the task.[69]

The successful defense of Smolensk enabled the Lithuanian government to begin negotiations for peace without losing face. Pope Alexander VI offered to serve as mediator, purposing to include both Lithuania and Moscow in the Anti-Turkish League he was trying to organize. Ivan, however, preferred to negotiate directly with Aleksandr of Lithuania. Both the Lithuanian and the Livonian envoys arrived in Moscow on March 4, 1503. Ivan refused to deal with the Livonian envoys, referring them to his lieutenant in Novgorod. The talks with the Lithuanians started immediately, but it soon became obvious that neither side was ready to make concessions important enough to secure a stable peace. Therefore, instead of a peace merely an armistice for six years was concluded (April 2, 1503). According to it all the border provinces of the Grand Duchy of Lithuania occupied by Muscovite troops during the war (and still held by them at the time of the armistice) remained under Ivan's authority for the duration of the armistice.[70]

In that way Moscow retained Dorogobuzh and Belaia, in the Smolensk area; Briansk, Mtsensk, Liubutsk, and a number of other upper towns; and most of the Chernigov-Severian land (the basins of the Desna, Sozh, and Seim rivers); also the town of Liubech on the Dnieper River, north of Kiev. Moscow thus obtained control of the overland route to the Middle Dnieper region, which greatly facilitated access to the Crimea by Muscovite merchants and diplomatic agents.

Soon after the effecting of the Moscow-Lithuanian armistice an armistice with the Livonian Order was signed in Novgorod. This involved no territorial changes but contained an obligation on the part of the Bishop of Derpt to pay an annual token tribute to Ivan III as suzerain of Pskov, in consideration of old custom.[71]

68. *PSRL, 12*, 252.
69. *PSRL, 12*, 257; Bazilevich, pp. 494–495.
70. *Sbornik, 35*, 398–402; Bazilevich, pp. 518–521.
71. Karamzin, *Primechaniia*, Note 551 to Vol. *6*.

CHAPTER IV

IVAN III'S NATIONAL POLICIES

1. UNIFICATION OF GREAT RUSSIA

IVAN's main objective in his internal policies was to extend the grand ducal authority over all of Great Russia, ultimately over all Russia. His policies, therefore, affected not the Grand Duchy of Moscow alone but many other parts of Russia as well. His objectives may be characterized as national Russian not as specifically Muscovite. The old phrase in the title of the grand dukes of Moscow, *Vseia Rusi* (of All Russia), now took on added significance.

The task that faced Ivan in carrying out his national policies was twofold: he had to annex to Moscow hitherto independent Russian states, and he had to reduce the power of his brothers and other apanage princes. As we know, he avoided snap decisions whenever possible, preferring to move slowly and concentrate attention on one particular task at a time in order to deal with each separately whenever feasible. Because of this, the process of the unification of Great Russia went on through Ivan's whole reign, and some minor tasks were left unfinished for his son and successor Vasili III to complete.

It will be recalled that in 1462—the year of Ivan III's accession to the throne—Great Russia was still far from political unity. In addition to the Grand Duchy of Moscow there existed two other grand duchies (Tver and Riazan), two principalities (Iaroslavl and Rostov), and three city-states (Novgorod, Pskov, and Viatka).

The Grand Duchy of Moscow itself was not entirely united. Although Ivan III's father, Vasili II, had confiscated the apanages of Dmitri Iurievich Shemiaka (Galich in Kostroma region), of Ivan Andreevich of Mozhaisk, and of Vasili Iaroslavich of Borovsk and Serpukhov, he agreed to leave Prince Mikhail Andreevich in Vereia and Beloozero to reign there as the grand duke's vassal ("younger brother"). Mikhail addressed Vasili II as his *gospodin* (lord) and "elder brother." [1]

1. Treaty of 1450; see *DDG*, p. 164.

In the first or second year of his reign Ivan III in his turn concluded a treaty with Mikhail with approximately the same conditions as those of the Treaty of 1450. The same terminology was employed to show the political dependence of Mikhail on the grand
duke: [2] in the Treaty of 1472 Ivan called himself Mikhail's "elder
brother" and his "lord." Similar terms were used in the Treaty of
1482.[3] In the Treaty of 1483 Mikhail had also to recognize Ivan
III's son, Ivan Junior, as his "elder brother." [4] It may be seen that
Ivan III steadily tightened the grand ducal authority, which was
reflected in the change of terms of subordination. Around 1483
Mikhail Andreevich wrote a will in which he called Ivan III not
only his lord but his *gosudar* (sovereign); moreover, he added the
phrase "of All Russia" to Ivan's title.[5] What was even more important for Ivan, Mikhail bequeathed him the principalities of
Vereia and Beloozero. Mikhail died in 1486, and the two principalities were then legally incorporated into Muscovy.

All of Vasili II's brothers had died in their childhood (except one
who died at the age of 21) and had left no offspring. Thus no problem of apanages within the grand duke's family arose during Vasili's
reign. Vasili left five sons, including Ivan III. So strong was the old
Russian notion according to which all the sons should have a share
in the father's estate that Vasili II had to reckon with it. In his last
will and testament Vasili "blessed" his eldest son Ivan III with the
Grand Duchy and assigned more than half its territory for his immediate rule: fourteen towns as against twelve that were divided
among four other sons.[6]

Of Ivan III's brothers, Iuri became Prince of Dmitrov; Andrei
Senior, Prince of Uglich; Boris, Prince of Volok; and Andrei Junior,
Prince of Vologda (see above, p. 60).

Although Ivan III honored his father's will and recognized the
apanage rights of his brothers, he had no intention of increasing
their possessions. When Iuri of Dmitrov died in 1473 leaving no offspring, Ivan ruled that his apanage was to revert as escheat to the
grand duke. This was contrary to the old traditions, according to
which each of the remaining brothers could claim a share in the de-
ceased brother's estate. Then again, in 1478, Ivan refused to grant

2. *DDG,* p. 207.
3. *DDG,* p. 277.
4. *DDG,* p. 293.
5. *DDG,* p. 301.
6. *DDG,* pp. 193–198.

his brothers any share in the districts acquired from Novgorod. Princes Andrei Senior and Boris resented Ivan's policy, and as we have seen (above, p. 61), they actually revolted against Ivan the next year. The immediate cause of the revolt was their conflict with Ivan III over the case of Prince Ivan Vladimirovich Obolensky-Lyko.[7] Prince Obolensky was the grand duke's lieutenant in the town of Velikie Luki. The townspeople were irritated by Obolensky's abuses and complained to the grand duke. Ivan III dismissed Obolensky from his position and ordered that he be tried. The offended Obolensky then left Ivan and entered the service of Prince Boris of Volok, availing himself of the old boyar privilege of freedom of service. Ivan, however, no longer recognized the principle and sent his agents to seize Obolensky by force and bring him to Moscow for trial. Not unnaturally, Prince Boris and Prince Andrei Senior resented the grand duke's action. However, in 1480, at the time of Khan Ahmad's invasion, Boris and Andrei, under the influence of their mother and of Bishop Vassian of Rostov, agreed to a peace with Ivan. Ivan had to make some concessions. He granted to Andrei Senior the important town of Mozhaisk in addition to his Uglich apanage, and to Boris a small town of Vyshgorod in the Dmitrov district, with a few villages in addition to Volok. Both Mozhaisk and Vyshgorod had belonged to the late Prince Iuri's apanage. In spite of this settlement, the relations between Ivan and these two brothers remained strained.

In 1481 Prince Andrei Junior of Vologda died childless. His apanage, like that of Iuri's formerly, was escheated. This could not improve Ivan's relations with Andrei Senior and Boris, and in 1491 Andrei Senior failed to take part in a campaign against the Golden Horde. Both he and Boris were then accused of treason. Ivan pardoned Boris, but Andrei was imprisoned and his apanage confiscated;[8] he died in prison in 1493. The next year Prince Boris of Volok died, leaving two sons. One of them was not married and died in 1504; the other, married but with no sons, died in 1513. This was during the reign of Vasili III, who appropriated Volok as escheat, and is one of the times when Vasili III completed his father's work.

Of the outside rulers, the Iaroslavl princes ceded their rights to Ivan III in 1463, and the Rostov princes sold their rights to Ivan eleven years later. In 1456 Grand Duke Ivan IV of Riasan died,

7. *PSRL, 6*, 222.
8. Bazilevich, p. 340.

leaving an eight-year-old son, Vasili, whom he entrusted to the care of the Grand Duke of Moscow, Vasili II. In 1465 Ivan III married his sister Anna to the young Vasili of Riazan. After that, Riazan, while formally independent, became Moscow's satellite. Vasili died in 1483, leaving two sons, Ivan V and Fedor. The latter bequeathed his half of the Riazan principality to Ivan III of Moscow (1503), and Ivan V died in 1500, but was succeeded by his son Ivan VI.

Ivan III's most important achievement in the process of unification of Great Russia was the annexation of Novgorod (1478). Novgorod (see above, pp. 57-60) was subdued only after a protracted struggle and a series of coercive measures applied to the citizens for several years after 1478. Still, the work was done, even though at the price of destruction of Novgorod's traditions.

The conquest of Tver proved much easier. It should be noted that Mikhail, the Grand Duke of Tver (brother of Ivan III's first wife), helped Ivan III in the latter's campaigns against Novgorod. For his assistance he expected to receive part of the Novgorodian territory as a reward, but this was denied to him. Around 1483 Mikhail concluded an alliance with Casimir of Lithuania against Moscow. As soon as the news of this pact reached Ivan II, he sent troops against Tver (1484). Receiving no assistance from Casimir, Mikhail sued for peace.[9]

By the Treaty of 1485 Mikhail recognized Ivan III "of All Russia" as his lord and elder brother and Ivan Junior as his elder brother.[10] Mikhail had to promise never to conclude any agreement with Casimir. Although Mikhail had signed the treaty, he did not intend to honor it and continued secret negotiations with Casimir. Before long, one of Mikhail's letters to Casimir was intercepted by Moscow agents, following which Ivan personally led his army to Tver (August 24, 1485). The city capitulated on the third day of the siege, and Mikhail fled to Lithuania. To make the transition to the new regime easier for the Tverians, Ivan appointed a new prince to Tver—his son, Ivan Junior.

After the subjugation of Tver, Ivan turned his attention to the small northern republic of Viatka. Originally a colony of Novgorod, Viatka achieved independence in the late 12th century.[11] The town of Khlynov became its capital. The Novgorodians resented the loss

9. *Ibid.*, pp. 226–228.
10. *DDG,* pp. 295–301.
11. See Kostomarov, *Narodopravstva, 1,* 241–242.

of the valuable region, and the Viatkans were always on the alert to prevent any attempts on the part of Novgorod to dominate them. These Viatkans were men of independent spirit and great arrogance. They succeeded in quarreling with almost all their neighbors, including the people of the Dvina region, (who were Novgorod's subjects) and those of the city of Ustiug, which had been annexed to Moscow during the reign of Vasili I. The Viatkans gradually expanded their authority southward, down the course of the Viatka River, a tributary of the Kama. Some Finnish clans of the tribes of Votiaki and of the Cheremisy became Viatka's satellites. After the foundation of the Khanate of Kazan, the Kazan Tatars, expanding northward, penetrated into the lower Viatka region, as a result of which clashes occurred between them and the Viatkans.

Maintaining a balance between Novgorod and Kazan, the Viatkans on many occasions looked to Moscow for protection. When they understood that such protection could threaten their independence, however, they attempted to establish friendly relations with the Khanate of Kazan instead. During the civil war in Muscovy, in 1451–52, the Viatkans supported Dmitri Shemiaka against Vasili II. After his victory over Shemiaka, Vasili sent a detachment of troops to Viatka. The first Muscovite campaign against Viatka proved a failure. In the second campaign, the Muscovites defeated the Viatkans, and the latter pledged allegiance to Vasili (1460),[12] but soon after the departure of the Muscovite troops the Viatkans again asserted their independence.

When Ivan III, in 1468, asked the Viatkans to send auxiliary troops to support the Muscovite campaign against Kazan, they refused to do so and proclaimed their neutrality in the Moscow-Kazan conflict. Three years later, however, they agreed to join the Muscovite drive against Novgorod. This was a mistake, of course, since in spite of their dislike of Novgorod its very existence was a certain curb on Moscow's policy of annexation. In 1486 the Viatkans raided Ustiug, a Muscovite possession. A year later they again refused to participate in Moscow's campaign against Kazan. Ivan III then asked Metropolitan Geronti to address an epistle to the Viatkans. The metropolitan urged the Viatkans not to help the Moslems against Christians and threatened them with excommunication.[13] Receiving no answer, Ivan III sent a detachment of troops against them, but

12. See *Mongols and Russia*, p. 329.
13. Kostomarov, *Narodopravstva*, 1, 248–249.

the campaign was not decisive and in 1489 Ivan sent a strong army under the command of Prince Daniel Shchenia and the Boyar Grigori Morozov. Contingents of Tverian, Ustiugan, and Dvinian troops participated in this campaign together with the Moscow army, which included a cavalry squadron. Ivan's vassal Khan Mohammed-Amin of Kazan sent 700 Tatar horsemen. It will be recalled that both the Ustiugans and the Dvinians had had their own grievances against Viatka and were therefore eager to punish it.

On August 16, 1489, the combined Muscovite army appeared before Khlynov. The Moscow generals required that the Viatkans pledge obedience to Ivan III and hand over three of their leaders. After three days of hesitation the Viatkans surrendered. The three leaders were arrested and given in custody to the Ustiugans. This was not all, however. On September 1 all Viatkan citizens with their families (there were probably several thousand of them) were ordered to leave their homes and were driven to Moscow via Ustiug. The three leaders were executed in Moscow. All other Viatkans had to enter the grand duke's service. Some were granted *pomestia* (military fiefs).[14] Such was the end of Viatka.

As a result of these events, by the end of Ivan III's reign only half the principality of Riazan and the city of Pskov remained separate states in Great Russia. Neither Riazan nor Pskov presented any danger to Moscow. Pskov needed Moscow's support against the Livonian Knights and therefore might be expected to remain permanently loyal to the grand dukes of Moscow.

2. REGIONAL CHARTERS AND THE SUDEBNIK

The extension of grand-ducal political authority over the formerly independent Great Russian states was only the first step toward the unification of Great Russian government and administration. It established the new form of the national Great Russian state, but that form was yet to be filled with a new content. The Moscow grand duke had thus an immense task before him: adjusting the administration of the newly acquired regions to national needs and coordinating the central and regional agencies of the government.

In these matters, as in many others, Ivan III preferred to move slowly and cautiously. The noted historian of Russian law and institutions M. F. Vladimirsky-Budanov rightly observed that for

14. Ustiug Chronicle, pp. 97–98.

some time after the annexation of each state to Moscow the regional administration of newly acquired territory followed certain old features, and the region thus retained for a while a degree of administrative autonomy.[15] Of course, regional affairs were now under the authority of the grand duke's lieutenants and not of the former rulers. The Moscow administrative patterns were extended to the whole of Great Russia only gradually. In that process, Muscovite methods of government and administration themselves underwent a series of changes, which were to culminate in the great reforms of the 1550's.

In the first half of the 15th century the Muscovite administration was a combination of two different systems, each based on a different principle.[16] One of two branches may be called state administration in the proper sense of the term; the other, "manorial" or "palace" management. To the state administration belonged the handling of the tribute (formerly collected by the khans), the army conscription system, and the judiciary. To the palace administration belonged the maintenance of the grand duke's guard troops and the management of the grand-ducal estates and various special departments (*puti*) such as the falconry, the stables, the hunt, and the supply of food and drinks to the grand-ducal palace.

When the authority of the Grand Duke of Moscow was extended over all Great Russia and he became the ruler of a national state, the palace administration took on national significance as well. The two systems—state and palace—did not merge, however, but continued to coexist. Each had its own set of offices and officials. Agencies of both branches were gradually established in the annexed regions.

As regards the state administration, its main agents in the provinces were the grand duke's *namestniki* (lieutenants) and *volosteli* (district chiefs). A lieutenant was appointed to each major town and a district chief to each rural district. The chief function of the namestnik and the volostel was judicial. They received no salary from the grand duke and therefore were entitled to keep for themselves at least part of the court fees they collected, also being allowed to "feed" themselves off the town or district to which they were appointed. This was the so-called *kormlenie* (see above, pp.

15. Vladimirsky-Budanov, *Obzor*, p. 192.
16. See *Mongols and Russia*, pp. 358–362.

4–5).[17] The amount of food and other items the people had to supply to the officials was established by custom. With the aggrandizement of the Grand Duchy of Moscow, it became necessary to determine more precisely the obligations of the local people toward the grand duke's officials, especially in the newly acquired regions where the people were not accustomed to the Moscow administrative system. The earliest lists of the people's liabilities toward the *kormlenshchiki* (the officials rewarded by *kormlenie*) date from the middle of the 15th century.[18] During the reign of Ivan III it was decided to issue special charters to the people of the newly acquired regions in order to prevent misunderstandings between the officials and the people. One such charter, granted by Ivan III to the people of the Beloozero region in 1488, reached us in full. We may think, however, that this was not the only one enacted during his reign. In Article 38 of the *Sudebnik* (Code of Laws) of 1497 it is said that the lieutenants and the district chiefs shall collect court fees "according to the charters" (*gramoty,* plural). This clearly shows that by 1497 several such charters were in existence.[19]

It will be recalled that the last Prince of Beloozero, Mikhail Andreevich, had bequeathed his principality to Ivan III. When Mikhail died (1486), Moscow officials were sent to Beloozero to reorganize the former principality into a Muscovite province. Their first task was to collect information on local laws and customs. These materials were carefully studied in Moscow and used in the preparation of the charter determining the competence of the Muscovite lieutenants and district chiefs in Beloozero province; it was promulgated in March 1488.[20] This Beloozero *ustavnaia gramota* (statutory charter) of 1488 is an important document of the Muscovite administrative law of this period.[21]

The charter sets forth certain rules for the apprehension and trial of criminals as well as the amount of certain court fees. To prevent

17. *Ibid.,* p. 359.

18. S. B. Veselovsky, pp. 270–271.

19. The earliest regional charter issued by a Moscow grand duke is the "Charter of the Dvina Land," issued by Vasili I in 1397. For the English translation of its text see Vernadsky, *Medieval Russian Laws,* pp. 57–60.

20. See Cherepnin, *Russkie feodalnye arkhivy, 2,* 33–34.

21. For a recent study of the Beloozero charter and English translation of its text see H. W. Dewey, "The White Lake Charter: A Mediaeval Russian Administrative Statute," *Speculum, 32* (1957), 74–83. For the Russian text of the Beloozero charter see *PRP, 3,* 170–174.

abuses on the part of the officials, the charter establishes the amount of subsistence payments (*korm*) to the officials by the local people and the terms of delivery of korm (twice a year, at Christmas and on St. Peter's day). The payments had to be collected by elected representatives of the rural communities (the hundredmen), not by the officials directly. An important article (19) of the charter requires that the local people be represented in the court by the hundredmen and "good men" (*dobrye liudi,* those elected by the communities). The judge had to consult them during the trial. Another significant clause (23) rules that in cases of offense against Beloozero people (burghers or peasants), the injured ones "shall themselves set a time of court appearance for the namestniki and the volosteli and their agents." In this way, a namestnik could not evade responsibility by indefinitely postponing the case against him. In the conclusion of the charter it is said that anyone who violates the charter shall be punished by the grand duke. This presupposes the right of the local people to send to the grand dukes complaints against the officials if regular procedure should be barred by the latter.

Regional charters proved to be only the first stage in the path of unification of administrative methods and legal procedure. There was obviously a need for a more comprehensive code of laws that would be applicable for the whole of Great Russia. Such a sudebnik was promulgated on September 1, 1497. There is no doubt that the preliminary work on the compilation of the code was started at least one year before its final approval by the grand duke and the boyar duma, probably not less than two years before. Until recently it was assumed that the chief architect of the sudebnik was Vladimir Gusev, since in one of the chronicles—the so-called Synodal Printing Office copy—Gusev's name is mentioned immediately after the report on the publication of the sudebnik.[22] Most of the scholars thought that Gusev was *diak* (state secretary). However, N. P. Likhachev, in his work on the diaks (published in 1885), stated that the name "Vladimir Gusev" does not occur among the diaks of this period known to us.[23] In 1939 S. B. Veselovsky, in his article on Vladimir Gusev, showed that Gusev's family belonged to the gentry.[24]

22. *PSRL, 24,* 213.
23. Likhachev, *Razriadnye diaki,* p. 133.
24. S. B. Veselovsky in *IZ, 5* (1939), 31–47.

In 1940 I. S. Lurie expressed his opinion that the name of Vladimir
Gusev in the Tipografskaia Chronicle was mentioned merely as a
note concerning the next entry, that on Gusev's execution in 1497
(of which more will be said later), and not in connection with the
preceding entry on the compilation of the sudebnik.[25] Lurie's conclusion has been accepted by L. V. Cherepnin.[26] According to
Cherepnin, the task of compiling the sudebnik had been entrusted
by Ivan III not to Gusev but to a committee headed by Prince Ivan
Iurievich Patrikeev. The materials collected by the committee might
have been edited by the diak Vasili Tretiak Dalmatov.[27] Cherepnin's
argument seems valid to me.

In its essence, the Sudebnik of 1497 is a collection of rules of
procedure and of selected norms of law, intended primarily as a
guide to the judges, those of both the higher and the local courts.[28]
Three kinds of higher courts are mentioned in the sudebnik: (1)
the supreme court, headed by the chairman of the boyar duma, in
which both boyars and state secretaries participated; there was no
appeal to the decisions of this court. (2) The boyar court, which
had to report the matter to the grand duke, to whom the final decision
belonged. (3) The special-cases court, presided over by a judge (a
boyar or state secretary) who was specially appointed for each such
case; this judge had to report the matter to the supreme court for
final approval of the judge's decision. The administration of justice
in the provincial towns and districts was left in the hands of the
kormlenshchiki. As in the Beloozero charter, representatives of the
local people had to participate in the trials (sections 37 and 38 of
the sudebnik).

As for norms of law, the sudebnik established a scale of punishment for various types of crimes as well as rules for litigation over
landed estates and merchants' loans, relations between employers
and employees and between owners of landed estates and peasants,
and slavery. Most of the sudebnik's articles are quite laconic. Many
are based on the earlier Russian codes of law—the *Russkaia pravda*

25. I. S. Lurie, "Iz istorii politicheskoi borby pri Ivane III," *Uchenye Zapiski,* Leningrad University, Section of Historical Sciences, *10* (1940).

26. Cherepnin, *Russkie feodalnye arkhivy, 2,* 273, 289–303.

27. *Ibid.,* 306–310.

28. For a general characterization of the sudebnik see H. W. Dewey, "The 1497
Sudebnik," *ASEER, 15* (1956), 325–338; and M. Szeftel, "Le Justicier (Sudebnik) du
Grand Duc Ivan III," *RHDFE* (1956), pp. 531–568 (with French translation). For
the Russian text of the sudebnik see *Sudebniki,* ed., B. D. Grekov, pp. 17–29; *PRP, 3,*
346–357.

(Russian law) of the Kievan period and the Pskov charter of the 14th and 15th centuries.[29]

Of great significance for the strengthening of grand-ducal authority was article 9 of the sudebnik, which decreed capital punishment for major state crimes, especially for everyone guilty of armed rebellion and conspiracy against the sovereign.[30]

The death penalty was unknown to Russkaia pravda but existed in Novgorodian and Pskovian law. The grand dukes of Moscow had ordered execution of recalcitrant boyars and traitors on several occasions in the late 14th and early 15th centuries.[31] According to the Dvina Land Charter of 1397, the penalty for the third theft was death by hanging. Ivan III, as we know, executed a number of Novgorodian boyars, as well as the ringleaders of the Viatkan rebellion. However, there was no general law of capital punishment for state crimes in Great Russia until the Sudebnik of 1497.

From the point of view of social and economic development of Great Russia, one of the most important clauses of the sudebnik is article 57, dealing with the right of the peasants to move from one estate, or district, to another. This article consists of two parts. The first contains the general rule that the peasants are free to move from one locality to another once a year, during the period of two weeks around "The Autumn St. George's Day," November 26. The second part of the clause deals with a special case and concerns only those peasants who lived in the houses (*pozhilye dvory*) built for them by the owner of the landed estate. If such a peasant wanted to move at the end of his first year of residence, he had to pay to the

29. For the English translation of *Russkaia pravda* and the Pskov charter see Vernadsky, *Medieval Russian Laws*, pp. 26–56, 61–82.

30. *Gosudarskii uboitsa i koromolnik.* It should be noted that the phrase *gosudarskii uboitsa* in article 9 has been interpreted by modern scholars in different ways. The term *gosudar* (from which the adjective *gosudarskii* derives) means "sovereign," but also has the connotation of "lord" (lord of the slaves, lord of the peasants settled on an estate). The term *uboitsa* likewise has various connotations. It may mean "murderer, assassin." Herberstein, who paraphrased part of the sudebnik into Latin in the 16th century, understood the phrase *gosudarskii uboitsa* in the sense of "slayer of his masters" (Herberstein–Backus, p. 60). A number of modern historians, including Cherepnin, Dewey, and Szeftel, accepted Herberstein's interpretation and asserted that the phrase refers to rebellious slaves. In my opinion, this interpretation is wrong. In the first place, article 9 as a whole deals with the crimes against the state and the church (it is based on article 7 of the Pskov charter). Moreover, the adjective *gosudarskii* in article 9 of the sudebnik obviously refers not only to the noun *uboitsa* but to the following noun *koromolnik* as well. It deals with armed insurrection and conspiracy against the sovereign.

31. See *Mongols and Russia*, pp. 355–357.

landlord, for the use of the house, one-fourth the cost of the house. If the peasant stayed for two years, he had to pay one-half the cost of the house; if he stayed for three years, he had to pay three-fourths the cost; if he wanted to leave after staying in the house for four years, he had to pay the full amount. The standard full price of the house was set at one ruble in the prairie regions (where timber was expensive) and half a ruble in forest regions.

It seems obvious that article 57 was enacted in order to safeguard the interests of the owners of the landed estates and the peasants, as well as those of the grand duke. For the peasants, it was important that their freedom of moving from one locality to another be officially confirmed. The term set for moving (around November 26) corresponded to the end of the agricultural season in Great Russia. By that time the harvesting had been done and the grain stored. The peasant was thus in position to settle all his accounts with the owner of the landed estate and pay his taxes to the grand duke. An earlier enactment of this kind is to be found in article 42 of the Pskov charter (with a slightly different term for moving—November 14, instead of November 26). As regards the special case of the peasants who used the houses built by the landowners, the requirement of a refund for the use of the house by the peasant in case he wanted to leave the estate was of course intended primarily to guarantee the landowner from any damages to the house done by the peasant during his stay. However, the estimate set for the cost of the house was not excessively high. Moreover, if the peasant left the estate after staying more than four years, he had to pay no more than standard amount, and thus so much less per year.

On the whole, article 57 must be considered an ordinance quite fair to both the owners of the landed estates and the peasants. In my opinion, V. B. Eliashevich is right when he says that the article was intended not to deprive the peasants of their freedom to move but to regulate the peasants' migration in accordance with the conditions of agricultural economy.[32]

32. Eliashevich, *1*, 139. For a different interpretation of article 57 see L. V. Cherepnin's commentaries on the article in *Sudebniki*, B. D. Grekov, ed. According to Cherepnin, the sudebnik "created the juridical prerequisites for the strengthening of serfdom and for the rise of feudal exploitation" (p. 96).

3. LANDOWNERSHIP, THE ARMY, AND THE
RISE OF THE GENTRY

Even after the political unification of Great Russia and the establishment of a uniform framework of the judiciary, there remained many obstacles to the exercise of direct grand-ducal authority over the people. There existed in the Russia of that period deeper contradictions than political, to wit contradictions of the social and economic order.

That order is now usually characterized, especially by Marxist historians, as feudal. But the term "feudalism" has become a kind of shibboleth and so far as Russia is concerned, it is on the whole misapplied.[33] There were undoubtedly in Russia in the 15th century certain analogies to the feudal regime of the Western type. Prior to the unification of Great Russia, the relations between the grand duke and the lesser princes may be explained in terms of suzerainty and vassalage. One of the mainstays of economic feudalism is the large landed estate, and this certainly was a widespread institution in 15th-century Russia. As in the West, the lord of the manor exercised certain manorial and judicial rights over the population of the estate. However, in Russia the peasants were not at that time bound to the estate and were still free to move from one locality to another. Moreover, the basis of landownership was not feudal. Until the introduction of the system of pomestie in the latter part of Ivan III's reign, the lord of the estate had full ownership rights on the land.

The concept of rights on land in Old Russia differed considerably from the notions of the modern period. It is only with reservations that we may apply modern legal terms to Russian landownership of the 15th century. The best analysis of the problem is that by V. B. Eliashevich. Simplifying somewhat his conclusions, we may speak of the following main categories of land in Old Russia: (1) state land (usually called *chernye zemli,* "black land"); (2) grand-ducal land (usually known as *dvortsovye zemli,* "palace land"); (3) *votchiny* (patrimonial estates) of the lesser princes, which they kept even after they had renounced their sovereign right and became service princes under the authority of the grand duke; (4) *boyarskie*

---

33. See Vernadsky, "Feudalism"; and Vernadsky, "Serfdom."

zemli, (boyar land); and (5) church land, including monastery land.

It should be noted that not only land owned by the boyars but all land belonging to individuals under full ownership rights was called boyar land. Thus "boyar land" was the equivalent of "privately owned land," in contrast to state land or church land.[34] To this category then, belongs alike the votchina of a boyar, the much smaller estate of a member of lower gentry (so-called "boyar son"), and the tiny estate, the owner of which sometimes personally tilled the land. Such petty landowners were known in Novgorod as *svoezemtsy* (self-owners of land). They existed in Muscovy as well, although their number there declined steadily.[35] Neither the boyar sons nor the svoezemtsy represented any threat to grand-ducal authority. The boyars and the service princes, on the other hand, could cause—and at times actually caused—much trouble for the grand duke. Their strength was in their patrimonial estates. Ivan III understood this clearly; in accordance with his cautious nature, however, he avoided any direct attack on the patrimonial rights of the service princes and boyars. Instead, he attempted to establish, side by side with the old forms of landed estates, a new type of landholding—the pomestie.

The patrimonial rights of the service princes and boyars interfered with grand-ducal authority in the administration of both the judiciary and the army. The Russian judiciary, as we know, was based in this period on the kormlenie system. Lacking money for the salaries of the judges, the grand duke could not abolish the system, in any event not all at once. Instead, as we know, he tried to regulate it by three different methods. In the first place, through the regional charters and the sudebnik, rules were established concerning the subsistence payments to which the judges were entitled. Secondly, definite norms of procedure were confirmed. Thirdly, the local people were allowed to participate, through their elected representatives, both in the collection of subsistence payments and in the functioning of courts. All this concerned the people settled on state land and palace land, as well as the petty landowners. The patrimonial estates of the service princes and boyars, as well as the church and monastery landed estates, were not, at first, greatly affected by the new legislation.

From the time of Vladimir the Saint, the Russian Church had en-

34. Eliashevich, *1*, 232–233.
35. *Mongols and Russia,* pp. 374–375.

joyed semi-autonomous status and a number of special privileges. On the basis of Vladimir's Church Statute and other enactments, "church people" were subject to the jurisdiction of the metropolitan, not the prince. By "church people" not merely the clergy and members of their families were meant but also certain other groups who either served the church in one way or another or needed its protection.[36] After the Mongol invasion, the Mongol khans, in accordance with Chingis-Khan's Great Yasa, granted the church special *yarlyks* (charters) of immunity.

The landed estates of the churches and monasteries with all people employed on them were exempt from taxation; all of the church people were exempt from military service. The Mongol agents were forbidden, under penalty of death, to seize any church lands or require any services from the church people.[37] After the decline of the Golden Horde and the rise of the authority of the Moscow grand duke, the church had to turn to the latter for confirmation of its privileges. A number of grand-ducal charters were issued in the 14th and 15th centuries granting the church administrative and judicial immunity, but subjecting the peasants on the church estates to state taxes. Thus, paradoxically enough, the immunity of the church was curbed when Christian rulers took over power from the Buddhist, Shamanist, and Mohammedan khans.[38]

As regards the patrimonial estates of the service princes, the latter (if and when they retained their former lands after they had abdicated their sovereign privileges) had a traditional right of exercising judicial authority over the people settled on their domains. The grand dukes, at first, tacitly recognized their rights.

As a contrast, the nontitled boyars and the lesser landowners needed grand-ducal confirmation of their judicial authority. A number of judicial immunity charters were granted to such landowners by the grand dukes in the course of the fifteenth century. The grand duke's motive in issuing these charters was twofold. In the first place, he did not have enough trained agents to supply judges for all the boyar estates. Secondly, by granting the charters he was in position to limit the judicial rights of the boyars whenever he deemed it necessary. In most of the charters, trial of the major crimes was exempt from the authority of the landowner. Besides, all litigation

36. See *Kievan Russia*, pp. 151–152.
37. See *Mongols and Russia*, pp. 165–166.
38. *Ibid.*, pp. 375–376.

between the grantee and his neighbors was subject to the authority of the grand duke.[39]

Although in the domain of the judiciary the grand duke could be satisfied, for the time being, with a compromise agreeable to both sides, the situation in the army was quite different. Great Russia's desperate struggle for survival required a centralized army administration more than anything else. The Moscow grand duke, as we know, inherited from the Mongol khans the authority for a general conscription in the time of need. On the basis of this authority Dmitri Donskoy ordered a general levy in the whole Grand Duchy of Moscow in 1380, and his son, Vasili I, did the same in 1396.[40]

However, no national army on a permanent basis was created by either Dmitri or Vasili I. The success of general mobilization depended on the cooperation of the lesser princes and boyars, and of course, on the response of the people at large. Because of this, general mobilization was possible in that period only at a time of national emergency and popular enthusiasm. During the interprince struggle in the first part of Vasili II's reign, no large armies were mobilized and the grand duke had to rely chiefly on his *dvor* (retinue or palace guards).[41]

From the evidence available, we think that in the second half of the reign of Vasili II the grand-ducal dvor was considerably expanded. A number of service-bound retainers (*slugi pod dvorskim*) [42] were transferred from their other duties to military service. These *dvoriane* (servitors of the dvor) were usually granted small landed estates either in full ownership or as temporary holdings. The earliest known case of a princely servitor provided with land for the time of his service is recorded in the testament of Grand Duke Ivan I (around 1339). Says Ivan I: "and concerning the village I bought for Borisko Vorkov, if he chooses to serve one of my sons, he keeps the village; if he does not, the village is to be taken from him." [43] Presumably, there were other such arrangements in the 14th century and even more of them in the first half of the 15th century.

However, even a considerable expansion of the grand-ducal dvor was not enough to create a strong army. Other methods had to be

---

39. Eliashevich, *1*, 259–263.
40. *Mongols and Russia*, pp. 259–262 and 275–276.
41. On the *dvor* as a military establishment see *Mongols and Russia*, pp. 254, 364, 371.
42. See *Mongols and Russia*, p. 371.
43. *DDG*, p. 10.

tried. One of the most successful in the reign of Vasili II was engaging for grand-ducal service Tatar princes with their respective
retinues. When such princes belonged to the House of Chingis-Khan,
they were known in Russia as *tsarevichi* (tsar's sons). For their
subsistence, each received a town (with the surrounding district) to
feed himself. Here we have a case of the use of the kormlenie system
for the needs of the army rather than for the administration of the
judiciary. These Tatar troops were usually very efficient and proved
a great help to both Vasili II and Ivan III.

In the first half of Ivan III's reign, Moscow, as we know, had to
wage several wars, namely those against the Khanate of Kazan
(1468–69); against Novgorod (1471 and 1478); and against the
Golden Horde (1472 and 1480). On the basis of the description of
these wars in the chronicles as well as on that of other sources, the
following observations on the composition and organization of the
Moscow armed forces in this period may be submitted.

The core of the Muscovite army consisted of the grand-ducal
dvoriane and the boyar sons associated with the dvor, under the
command of the grand duke himself or of a *voevoda* (general) appointed by the grand duke. This branch of the army may be called
the gentry militia. The grand-ducal brothers had to come to the
grand duke's assistance, with their respective retinues, whenever
called. The grand duke's service princes and the Moscow boyars had
to participate in a campaign when ordered, each with his retinue.
They expected to receive appointments to the commanding posts in
accordance with their seniority in the service and the social status of
their respective clans. The grand duke was bound by tradition in
this respect. Next should be mentioned the auxiliary Tatar troops
commanded by the Tatar tsarevichi holding various towns on the
basis of the kormlenie system, as well as the Tatar troops of the
vassal Khan of Kasimov.

All the above troops were horsemen. In addition, on many occasions infantry troops were used. In 1469 Ivan III mobilized, for
the campaign against Kazan, all able-bodied Moscow merchants and
burghers as well as the burghers of a number of smaller towns. They
served under the command of a separate voevoda (subordinated to
the voevoda of the gentry troops, who was the commander-in-chief).
This town militia fought on foot. Another type of infantry troops
were the Cossacks, first mentioned in Russian chronicles in the

Riazan area under 1444.[44] In 1468 a group of Cossacks was sent against the Kazan Tatars to the Kama region from Moscow. Presumably, this group had been temporarily stationed at that time in or near Moscow. Their abodes must have been not in Moscow but somewhere beyond the Oka River, on the northern fringe of the steppes. The Cossacks fought under the command of their own elected *ataman* (chieftain), who in 1468 was Ivan Runo.

A remarkable feature of the Great Russian army of this period was the spirit of initiative of the soldiers as well as their participation in the planning of a campaign. A good example is the spring campaign against Kazan in 1469. The Russian army, under the command of the senior voevoda, the boyar Konstantin Aleksandrovich Bezzubtsev, was concentrated in Nizhni-Novgorod. For some reason Ivan III at the last moment decided to postpone the main drive on Kazan and send troops forward to reconnoiter. He ordered Bezzubtsev to stay in Nizhni-Novgorod with his staff and let those soldiers who would volunteer for a raid against Kazan go ahead. When Bezzubtsev announced the grand duke's wish to the soldiers, they all volunteered to fight the Tatars "for the benefit of the whole of Christendom." They first ordered a *Te Deum* mass which they all attended, and then elected their own commander for the campaign, the Cossack ataman Ivan Runo. They then went down the Volga in boats and reached the outskirts of Kazan on May 22. The Tatars counterattacked, and the Russians suffered many casualties, but on the whole the raid served its purpose and prepared ground for a major campaign against Kazan, which took place in August and ended on September 1 in a treaty of peace between Kazan and Moscow.[45] Another example of the participation of army officers and soldiers in the planning of a campaign is the conference of the boyars and the gentry troops gathered by Ivan III in 1471 on the eve of his drive against Novgorod (see above, pp. 50–51).

In the second part of his reign Ivan was faced with the problem of integrating the manpower of the newly acquired territories (Novgorod, Tver, Beloozero) with that of the old Grand Duchy of Moscow. His main emphasis now was on the expansion of the gentry militia. His policies in this respect were dictated by both military and political considerations. From the military point of view the

44. *Mongols and Russia,* p. 316.
45. *PSRL, 12,* XII, 121–123.

gentry troops, being under the direct authority of the grand duke, served better the purpose of centralization of the army setup and unity of command than the detachments of troops supplied by the princes and the boyars. On the political side, the gentry could be expected to support loyally the grand duke's government against any encroachments of the aristocracy.

To perform their military duties efficiently the gentry troops needed means of subsistence, and these could be supplied at that time only in the form of landholdings. Hence, Ivan III's basic problem in the second half of his reign was how to obtain sufficient land to distribute to his gentry soldiers.

Theoretically, the grand duke had authority over all state land. Actually, most of it, especially in North Russia, was virginal forest. The tilled portion was populated by peasants, who according to the old Russian notion had rights of their own on the land they tilled. Since they paid state taxes, they were an important source of state revenue. The palace land was needed for the upkeep of the grand duke and his court. Because of these considerations the grand duke would prefer not to use state land for the pomestie fund. There were, however, two more vast categories of land—the boyar patrimonial estates and the church and monastery land.

The grand duke was not in position to touch the boyar estates, since the boyars were the leading force in Great Russian government and administration. Any attempt to abolish the patrimonial rights of the boyar class might be expected to end in the overthrow of the grand duke himself. And an open attack on boyar rights would have been contrary to Ivan's very nature. Besides, the gentry—who were to serve as the grand duke's ally in the latter's struggle against the boyars—were not yet sufficiently strong or properly organized. In spite of these factors, Ivan lost no opportunity to seize the estates of individual boyars guilty of treason or misbehavior, and did so in the 1480's when a number of Muscovite boyars incurred his disfavor.

The situation was different in the newly annexed areas. There the grand duke was not bound by traditions and could act as a conqueror. Since the Novgorodian boyars had headed the opposition against him in Novgorod, Ivan III attempted to destroy them as a class. As we know, after the annexation of Novgorod a number of its boyars were executed, the bulk of the other were deported to

Muscovy, and their estates were seized by the grand duke. In this way Ivan III obtained a considerable amount of lands he could use as he pleased. It is estimated that prior to 1470 about 33 per cent of tilled land in the Novgorod area belonged to sixty-eight boyar families.[46] In 1489 the smaller estates, those of the zhityis, were also confiscated.

Not satisfied with this new land fund, Ivan turned his attention to the Novgorodian Church and the monasteries. In 1478 the Archbishop of Novgorod was required to cede to Ivan ten districts (*volosti*) belonging to his see, as well as the six of the richest Novgorodian monasteries—half of the church land.[47] In 1491 and 1492 Muscovite officials were sent to Novgorod to make a cadastre of all of the Novgorodian lands. They worked for several years, during which more land belonging to church and monasteries was turned over to the grand duke. In 1500 Ivan obtained the blessing of Metropolitan Simon of Moscow to secularize all the church and monastery lands in the Novgorod area he wanted.[48]

According to S. B. Veselovsky, by 1500 Ivan had obtained in the Novgorod area, through the confiscation of boyar and church land, around 1,000,000 *desiatiny* (2,700,000 acres) of tillable land.[49] Most of this land the Moscow government distributed to the gentry soldiers, the majority of whom were boyar sons. In addition, a number of the former servitors of the disgraced Moscow boyars as well as those of some Novgorodian boyars were also settled in the Novgorod area and now became the grand duke's servitors.

We have no exact figures of the total number of gentry troopers settled in the Novgorod area in the period between 1487 and 1500, but we may suppose that no less than 8,000 men received landholdings there in that period. It is known that 9,000 Novgorodian boyars, zhityis, and merchants were deported from Novgorod in 1489, and to take their place an equal number of Muscovite boyars, merchants, and boyar sons were sent to Novgorod.[50] The Novgorodian cadastre books have reached us, although there are some gaps in them. According to S. B. Veselovsky, 2,000 landholdings of the Muscovite settlers (boyars, boyar sons, and former boyar servitors) are registered in

46. *Ocherki*, 3, p. 36.
47. See Nikitsky, *Ocherk* . . . *Novgorode*, pp. 125–126.
48. *Ibid.*, pp. 193–194.
49. Veselovsky, p. 289.
50. *PSRL, 12*, 220.

the cadastre books available to us. Bazilevich gives a smaller figure
—1,800.[51] Most of the new landholdings ranged between 20 and 60
obzhi per man—that is, between approximately 100 and 300 *de-siatiny*.[52]

It should be noted that most of the Novgorodians deported from
Novgorod were enrolled in the grand duke's service and received
landholdings in various districts of the original Grand Duchy of
Moscow. On the whole, this was a two-way resettlement operation
of vast proportions. On the basis of available information, it seems
that the undertaking was organized carefully and carried off
smoothly. The historical importance of this mass resettlement for
Russian political and social history is tremendous, for in the process
of resettlement a new type of conditional landholding was created,
the kind of military fief known as pomestie. Neither the Muscovite
settlers in the Novgorod area, nor the Novgorodian settlers in the
Muscovite area were granted land in full ownership. They received
land to enable them to perform their duties as army officers, and
held it conditional on their service to the state. While the legal nature of the pomestie was more precisely defined in the middle of
the 16th century, the purpose of a pomestie grant was well understood by both the grantor and the grantee in Ivan's time.

The grantee of a pomestie became known as *pomestnik* or
pomeschik, (later familiarized in the form *pomeshchik*), that is, one
who has been "placed" (from *mesto*, "place"; *pomestiti*, "to place").
The term is mentioned in article 63 of the Sudebnik of 1497. It is
characteristic that the pomeshchik is mentioned not in the first part
of the article (where the boyars and the monasteries are dealt with),
but in the second, where the "black" (state) peasants are mentioned.
Moreover, the pomeshchik is defined as one "who holds grand-ducal
lands." The legislator thus emphasized clearly that the pomestiia
(plural form) belonged in the category of state land, not privately
owned land.

4. THE BOYAR DUMA AND SECULARIZATION
OF CHURCH LAND

Although a deep social upheaval took place in the second half
of Ivan III's reign, which was to bring to the surface the class of

51. See Veselovsky, pp. 288–299; Bazilevich, pp. 340–345.
52. Veselovsky, pp. 287 and 296. Cf. *Ocherki, 3,* 39.

the middle gentry (dvoriane), Great Russian government and central administration was still at that time in the hands of the boyars. But a profound change took place in the composition of that social class as well. Alongside the old clans of the Moscow boyardom, the service princes now surrounded the throne. Some of them were descendants of Rurik, others of Gedymin.

Before long, the two aristocratic groups—the service princes and the nontitled boyars—merged, forming a single ruling group known collectively as the boyars. The process of adjustment was not always smooth, since some of the old nontitled boyar clans objected to being pushed aside by the newcomers and continued to claim for themselves the highest positions in the army and administration. In 1500, in the campaign against Lithuania, the boyar Iuri Zakharich Koshkin refused to occupy the position of the commander of the watch regiment when Prince Daniel Shchenia (a descendant of Gedymin) was appointed commander of the main division. Koshkin protested that it was not proper for him to be subordinated to Shchenia—"to guard Prince Daniel," as he put it. Ivan answered that Koshkin was to guard not Prince Daniel but the grand duke himself (in other words, that each officer served the state, not his immediate superior).[53] Koshkin obeyed Ivan's order in this case, but Ivan did not succeed in generally breaking the aristocratic traditions in the army and administration. Eventually, an elaborate scale of offices was established and a corresponding scale of seniority of princely and boyar clans. The system became known as *mestnichestvo* (literally "place order"), and both the grand duke and the boyars had to recognize its validity.

The boyars ruled Russia jointly with the grand duke through the state council, known in modern historiography as the boyar duma. The members of this body were appointed by the grand duke, but the latter was bound by tradition to choose them among the senior princely and boyar families. As we know, in 1471, the grand duke consulted both the boyars and the gentry in preparing his campaign against Novgorod (see above, pp. 50–51). This conference may be regarded as the prototype of the Zemsky sobor established by Ivan III's grandson, Ivan the Terrible. In Ivan III's reign the experiment was not repeated as far as we know. The boyars were still mighty, and the gentry not strong enough.

Though not in position to establish a permanent council of the

53. Bazilevich, p. 454.

gentry to counterbalance the influence of the boyar duma, Ivan III used other methods to control the boyar administration. He relied more and more on diaks (state secretaries), usually chosen by the grand duke from among the commoners. Some of them, like Fedor Kuritsyn, were learned men; most received a good education by Russian standards of that age. The grand duke could appoint and dismiss the diaks without consulting the boyar duma; the success of a diak in the service therefore depended on his own abilities and on his loyalty to the grand duke. Most of the diaks were able and some may be called outstanding statesmen. They served as secretaries for both the grand duke and the boyar duma, and under Ivan III the duma diaks were recognized as full-fledged members of the duma. The management of the grand duke's treasury and the foreign office was usually entrusted to them, and as may be seen from the Sudebnik of 1497 (article 1), they participated in the activities of the supreme court.

The boyar duma was the highest body of government and administration in Great Russia. It served as a legislative council and directed both internal and foreign affairs, as well as army administration. The grand duke presided over its meetings whenever he pleased, usually when an important decision was about to be confirmed and promulgated. Routine meetings were directed by one of the boyars, known as the *pervosovetnik* (first councilor).[54] We may call him the chairman of the duma. During most of Ivan's reign, down to 1499, Prince Ivan Iurievich Patrikeev filled that office.

We would be mistaken to believe that the boyars thought only of their class interests. Historically, the Moscow boyars were a major factor in the building up of the Grand Duchy of Moscow. They were expanding it now, together with the service princes, into a Great Russian state. They supported the grand duke wholeheartedly in the latter's policy of unification. They also proved ready to cooperate with the grand duke in expanding the gentry militia and providing it with land—as long as their rights on their own lands were not affected.

Large as the land fund obtained by Ivan III from Novgorod seemed to be, it was not sufficient for the full potential expansion of the pomestie plan. Besides, all the Novgorod land fund was concentrated in one area, North Russia. This could serve for the defense

54. See Maksimovich, p. 141.

base of the Novgorod and Pskov areas against the Baltic Germans and the Swedes. However, other potential war fronts—the Lithuanian in the West and the Tatar in the South and Southeast—likewise required attention. A more equal distribution of pomestie landholdings throughout the whole of Great Russia was needed to facilitate rapid mobilization of the gentry army in case of emergency on any front. Thus more land for the gentry militia was needed in the central part of Great Russia, as well as on the western and southeastern border regions.

The success of the secularization of the church and monastery land in the Novgorod area encouraged Ivan and his advisers to consider the possibility of secularizing at least part of the church land in the basic area of the Grand Duchy of Moscow itself.

It should be noted that during the reign of Ivan III the Church of Moscow, while emancipating itself from the authority of the Patriarch of Constantinople and becoming a national Russian Church, proved unable to define clearly its interrelations with the growing Russian state. The Grand Duke of Moscow was regarded as its protector. More than that, in many cases, and especially in the choice of the metropolitan, Ivan III acted as head of the church administration. The metropolitan was elected by the council of bishops, though with the approval of the grand duke. In one case (that of Metropolitan Simon, 1494), Ivan solemnly led the newly ordained prelate to the metropolitan's throne in the Cathedral of Assumption, thus emphasizing the prerogatives of the grand duke.[55]

In view of Ivan's prominent role in Russian Church administration, the achievement of at least partial secularization of church land in Muscovy seemed feasible. Of great importance also was the fact that the right of the monasteries to own land and other riches was questioned, on moral and religious grounds, by a group of clergymen themselves. Prominent among them were the so-called *Zavolzhskie startsy* (Trans-Volga Hermits), who represented a mystical current of thought in Russian Orthodoxy of this period. They were influenced by the teachings of the noted Byzantine theologian of the 14th century, St. Gregory Palamas, and his followers.

The problem of the church lands was widely discussed among laymen as well as clergymen. Many laymen, including some of the boyars, sympathized with the Trans-Volga Hermits in the latter's

55. *PSRL, 6,* 39–40; Karamzin, *Istoriia, 6,* 203–204.

activities aimed at a spiritual revival and a purification of the church. Prince Ivan Patrikeev's son Vasili, who was made monk in 1499 (see below p. 127), became prominent among the Hermits, under the name of Vassian. Presumably, the whole Patrikeev clan sympathized with the movement.

The right of the monasteries to own land was also challenged by another religious movement, which in fact attacked the whole institution of the Orthodox Church: the Heresy of the Judaizers (above, p. 71). It has been initiated by the learned Jew (possibly Karaite) Zechariah, (Skharia) who came to Novgorod in 1470. There were several undercurrents in the heresy, ranging from Karaism to a rationalistic refutation of the church's dogmas and ritual.[56] A number of high officials in Moscow, including the diak Fedor Kuritsyn, secretly supported the heresy.

It is not likely that Ivan III personally sympathized with the heresy on religious grounds. But he apparently considered at least one of its tenets—the denial of the church's right to own land—useful for his policies. As the protector of the Orthodox Church, Ivan was not in a position to sanction openly the activities of the Judaizers. Rather, according to the prevailing notions of the age, his duty was to suppress the movement by stern measures. In 1375 the Novgorodian government did not hesitate to inflict death penalties on three leaders of an earlier heretical movement, the so-called Strigolniki.[57] In contrast, for as long as possible Ivan III avoided taking any drastic measures against the Judaizers.

It seems that Archbishop Gennadi of Novgorod became aware of the existence of the heresy in the late 1470's.[58] It was not until 1487, however, that Gennadi, having collected more information, arrested two priests and two diaks, accusing them of blasphemy. He sent all four to Moscow, asking the grand duke and the metropolitan to punish them. In Moscow three of the accused were found guilty of execrating holy icons, and one was acquitted. The question of heresy as a whole was not raised. In 1488 the three accused men (two priests and one diak) were knouted and all four sent back to Novgorod. Gennadi was told to make further inquiries but at the same time was forbidden to apply torture to the suspects or to make false accusations. No inquiry of the spread of the heresy

56. The "Heresy of the Judaizers" will be discussed in Vol. 5 of the present edition.
57. *PSRL*, 4, 72.
58. *AFED*, p. 109.

in Moscow was ordered. On September 26, 1490, the monk Zosima, considered a secret sympathizer of the heresy, was ordained Metropolitan of Moscow. On the other hand, under the pressure of Archbishop Gennadi and other conservative clergymen who demanded energetic action, a *sobor* (church council) was convoked in Moscow to discuss measures for stopping the further expansion of heresy.

The council tried several more Novgorodian priests and diaks accused by Archbishop Gennadi of heresy on the basis of his investigation. Ivan did not choose to attend the trial, sending instead three boyars (including Prince Ivan Patrikeev) and one diak to represent grand-ducal authority. All of the tried were pronounced guilty, and the priests among them were unfrocked. All were sentenced to flogging and sent back to Novgorod for administration of the punishment. Gennadi paraded them in a mock procession through the streets of Novgorod before having them flogged. No heretics in Moscow itself were either arrested or tried at that time.

Gennadi and his followers could not be satisfied with such half-measures and now began a campaign against Metropolitan Zosima, whom they accused not only of heretical views but of drunkenness. In 1494 Ivan let Zosima quietly retire from his office and then, as has been mentioned, appointed Simon as his successor. Simon was staunchly Orthodox but a timid man, ready to comply with Ivan's orders. It was obvious that the government's basically tolerant attitude toward the heresy would continue as long as Ivan was in full power.

5. POLITICAL AND DYNASTIC CRISIS, 1497–99

Throughout most of Ivan III's reign the Moscow government worked smoothly without any sharp division within the ruling group. The situation changed in the 1490's. Religious dissension confused the people at large and caused much bitterness. The arrest of Ivan's brother Andrei Senior in 1491 and his death in prison in 1493 made a martyr of him in the eyes of many supporters of the rights of the lesser princes, especially the former servitors of such princes. As regards foreign policies, the bulk of the nation wholeheartedly supported Ivan III in the latter's struggle against the Tatars, the Germans, and the Swedes, but there was no such unanimity on his conflict with Lithuania. All this created convenient psychological ground for the growth of opposition to Ivan. The opposition was not united in its purpose and would have represented no serious threat to Ivan and his government had not that government been plagued at this time with palace intrigues and a dynastic crisis, as a result of which Ivan himself finally lost his temper.

As we know (above, p. 18), in 1470 Ivan proclaimed his son (by his first wife) Ivan Junior his co-ruler, with the title of grand duke. Twenty years later Ivan Junior died (there were rumors that he had been poisoned by his stepmother, Sophia Paleologus), and this reopened the question of succession to the throne. The court was divided into two factions, one favoring the candidacy of Ivan Junior's son (Ivan III's grandson), Dmitri; and the other, that of Ivan III's eldest son by Sophia Paleologus, Vasili (born in 1479). Behind all this was the personal rivalry of two women—Sophia, mother of Vasili, and Elena of Moldavia, mother of Dmitri.

For a number of years Ivan III could not make up his mind which of the two boys he should appoint his successor. Among Ivan's chief advisers both Prince Ivan Patrikeev and the diak Fedor Kuritsyn supported Dmitri's candidacy. On the other hand, Sophia, not unnaturally, intrigued in favor of her son. Some of Ivan's opponents likewise preferred Vasili to Dmitri. Among them were the former retainers of the apanage princes as well as some of the conservative orthodox clergymen distressed by Ivan III's tolerant attitude toward the Heresy of the Judaizers. It was known that Sophia's rival, Princess Elena of Moldavia, joined the heresy. Under the circumstances, it could be expected that Sophia and Vasili would try to get in touch with Ivan's political and religious opponents.

Sophia's connections with the lesser Muscovite princes started long before the conflict of the 1490's. In 1480 her niece Maria (daughter of Sophia's brother Andrew Paleologus) married Prince Vasili Mikhailovich, son of Prince Mikhail Andreevich of Vereia. This marriage had unexpected repercussions four years later as a factor in a quarrel between Sophia and Ivan III. After his marriage, Ivan had let Sophia use one of the jewels of his first wife. When, in 1483, Dmitri (son of Ivan Junior and Elena of Moldavia) was born, Ivan III asked Sophia to return the jewel, since he wanted to give it to Elena. Sophia considered this request an insult and refused to hand over the jewel. She explained that she had few jewels left for herself, since she had had to give many to her brother Andrew (who, it will be recalled, was always in need of money) and others to her niece Maria for the latter's dowry. Ivan was infuriated and sent his agents to Vereia to confiscate Maria's dowry, which they did. Vasili and Maria then fled to Lithuania, asking Grand Duke Casimir for protection.[59]

This episode naturally fanned Sophia's hatred against Elena and the boy Dmitri. As long as Dmitri's father was living, the boy himself did not represent any immediate threat to Sophia. It was only after Ivan Junior had died that Dmitri became an obvious obstacle in Sophia's and her son Vasili's path.

The obstacle could be removed only by desperate measures. As a matter of fact, a conspiracy aimed at Dmitri's assassination was discovered in 1497. Presumably it had been formed after Prince Andrei Senior's arrest in 1491 or after his death in prison in 1493. The conspirators had decided to strike when they received news in 1497 that Ivan III had finally decided to proclaim Dmitri his coruler and successor.

Evidence about the conspiracy in the chronicles is scant and confusing. For obvious reasons the editors of the digests of annals compiled during the reigns of Vasili III and of the latter's son Ivan IV must have been instructed to delete the data implicating Sophia and Vasili. However, a fragment of the original records survived in some manuscripts.[60]

According to the story as described in this fragment, Ivan III, after receiving information of the conspiracy and of Vasili's role in it, was enraged and interned Vasili in the latter's house, under guard. Vasili's adherents were arrested. The investigation disclosed the following facts.

Some time before (probably in September or in October), Vasili was informed by the diak Fedor Stromilov that his father (Ivan III) had decided to grant Dmitri the title of Grand Duke of Vladimir and Moscow. Following the advice of Afanasi Eropkin, Vasili gathered a conference of his followers, most being boyar sons; among them was Vladimir Gusev (who, until recently, was erroneously considered the compiler of the sudebnik). All of them, and some others, pledged their allegiance to Vasili. It was decided that Vasili with his followers should break allegiance with his father, go to North Russia, and seize the reserves of the grand-ducal treasury that were stored in Vologda and Beloozero. Meanwhile, Dmitri was to be murdered.

59. *PSRL, 6,* 335.
60. *PSRL, 6,* 279; *12,* 263.

Simultaneously Ivan received reports that Sophia had been in touch with some "evil women" who supplied her with poison. The implication is that Sophia—as her part in the plot—intended secretly to poison Dmitri, and perhaps even Ivan himself. Ivan ordered that the "evil women" be arrested and drowned in the Moscow River at night. He then disgraced Sophia and, as the chronicler says, "from this time took special measures of precaution for his safety." [61] Vasili likewise fell into disfavor and was closely watched.

As for the leaders of the conspiracy, Ivan first of all referred the matter to Metropolitan Simon and the council of bishops.[62] The council of bishops authorized the supreme court to conduct the trial. All of the participants in the plot were found guilty. The diak Fedor Stromilov, Afanasi Eropkin, Vladimir Gusev, and three more ringleaders were sentenced to death and beheaded on December 27. This was the first case of application of article 9 of the sudebnik. Many other adherents of Vasili were imprisoned.

As L. V. Cherepnin has convincingly shown, all of the leaders of the plot and their families were connected, at one time or another with the courts of the apanage princes, such as Andrei Senior of Uglich, Boris of Volok, and Mikhail of Vereia and Beloozero. It should also be noted that the ancestors of both Gusev and Stromilov had supported Dmitri Shemiaka and Ivan of Mozhaisk against Ivan III's father.[63] Thus the conspiracy of 1497 seems to have been a revival of the old tradition of the federative idea as opposed to the autocracy.

There is no reason to believe that Ivan's son Vasili sympathized with the rights of the lesser princes. Later, after becoming ruler of Muscovy, he continued the centralizing policies of his father. It is obvious that his alliance with Gusev's group was a desperate gamble. The conspiracy seemed to be the only possible way for Vasili to seize power. He lost the game, but as future events were soon to prove, not finally. For the moment the important thing was that his life was spared.

As soon as the conspiracy had been suppressed, the preparations for Dmitri's installation were completed. Elaborate ritual for the crowning had been drafted well in advance. The ceremony took

61. *PSRL, 6,* 279.
62. *PSRL, 22,* 513; Cherepnin, II, p. 302.
63. Cherepnin, *Russkie feodalnye arkhivy, 2,* 292–303. See also Bazilevich, pp. 360–364.

place in the Cathedral of the Dormition in the Kremlin on February 4, 1498. Metropolitan Simon and the bishops officiated. Three thrones were placed in the center of the church: for Ivan, for Dmitri, and for the metropolitan. Ivan and the metropolitan sat on their thrones; Dmitri stood before his place. Ivan, addressing himself to the metropolitan, explained that according to the old custom, each of his ancestors used to hand down the grand duchy to his first son. Since Ivan's first son had died, Ivan was now blessing that son's first son Dmitri with the grand duchies of Vladimir, Moscow, and Novgorod. The metropolitan then laid his hand on Dmitri's head and read the prayer of anointment, following which he blessed the regalia—the *barmy* [64]—and the cap. [65] Ivan then put the regalia on Dmitri's shoulders and head, Dmitri sat on his throne, and the *Te Deum* was sung. Then, in a brief oration, Ivan admonished his grandson to be obedient to God, to love justice, and to take good care of all the Orthodox people. [66]

With Dmitri's solemn coronation it seemed that the political crisis had been overcome and the government's stability firmly re-established and, moreover, sanctioned by the metropolitan and the council of bishops. Actually, however, the wound was not healed. The disclosure of the conspiracy and especially of Sophia's and Vasili's role in it, painfully affected Ivan's mind and strained his nerves. If we choose to credit Herberstein's story about Ivan's drunkenness, we may think that he took to drinking at this time. Says Herberstein: "He used to drink so much at dinner that he was overcome with sleep. In the meantime all those invited were frightened and silent." [67] Herberstein collected much valuable information during his trips to Moscow, but also repeated mere gossip, and some of his stories are obviously untrue. This particular story seems psychologically possible, but only if we assume it refers to the last years of Ivan's life; there is no evidence of excessive drinking during the earlier part of his reign. The Italian Ambrogio Contarini, who was three times invited to dinner by Ivan in 1476–77, found that the dinner "was certainly served in good style." Contarini liked the dishes served. As to drinks, he says only that after he had dined at Ivan's for the third time (shortly before his departure), he had

---

64. *Barmy* is described by Herberstein as a collar of broad form made of black silk overlaid with gold and jewels (Herberstein–Backus, p. 24).
65. The so-called "Monomach's Crown." See *Mongols and Russia*, p. 386.
66. *PSRL, 6,* 241–243; *12,* 246–248. See also Herberstein–Backus, pp. 22–24.
67. Herberstein–Backus, p. 13.

been presented, after the dinner, "with a large cup of silver filled
with their beverage made of honey." Contarini was able to drink
only about a quarter of it. Ivan did not insist that he drink all of
it, and "ordered the cup to be emptied and given back to him." [68]

Although Sophia and Vasili had been disgraced and were presumably under close surveillance, they could not have been completely isolated. Vasili's next younger brother Iuri (born in 1480)
was not disfavored (nor were the youngest of Sophia's children).
Iuri even took part in the ceremonies of Dmitri's crowning. Vasili's
sister Elena was Grand Duchess of Lithuania and any open violence
against her mother could result in a diplomatic incident. Prior to
the disclosure of the conspiracy of 1497, both Ivan and Sophia regularly corresponded with Elena. Following Sophia's disgrace, she
stopped writing to her daughter. Ivan, however, continued to write
Elena and to convey his greetings to both Elena and her consort,
Grand Duke Aleksandr. On March 29, 1498, Ivan's ambassador to
Lithuania, Prince Vasili Romodanovsky, was instructed to convey
greetings to Aleksandr, in the following order: from Ivan himself,
from Dmitri, from Sophia, and from Dmitri's mother Elena of
Moldavia. Greetings to Elena of Lithuania were to be made in the
same order.[69]

After the first shock of their disgrace was over, both Sophia and
Vasili must have started trying, through their friends among the
courtiers and the clergy, to re-establish themselves in the grand
duke's favor. To achieve that it was necessary to arouse Ivan's
suspicions against those boyars who had been instrumental in the
trial of the conspirators in 1497 and in Dmitri's elevation to power,
in the first place against Prince Ivan Patrikeev. The obvious line of
argument would be that Vasili had been a victim of calumny. This
is exactly the line taken in the digests of annals of the 16th century.
In the Nikon Chronicle we read that Ivan III disgraced Vasili and
Sophia under the influence "of the Devil's sorcery and the advice
of evil men." [70] We may be certain that Prince Ivan Patrikeev was
considered one of those evil men.

The Byzantines were past masters in court intrigue, and Sophia
must have had the art in her blood. We may think that at first she
did not try to argue with Ivan directly but let some third person,

68. Contarini, pp. 163–165.
69. *Sbornik, 35,* 250–253.
70. PSRL, *6,* 43; *12,* 246.

supposedly neutral in the conflict, gradually undermine Ivan's confidence in Prince Patrikeev, through seemingly casual remarks in the midst of conversation on other matters. It so happened that just at this time a difference of opinion arose between Ivan and Prince Patrikeev on the course of Russian foreign policy. As we know (above, pp. 82–86), after the subjugation of the Khanate of Kazan, in 1487, Ivan made the annexation of West Russian lands his next objective. This presaged a conflict with the Grand Duchy of Lithuania. The marriage of Ivan's daughter Elena to Aleksandr of Lithuania (in 1495) was on Ivan's part only a diplomatic move intended to strengthen the Russian Orthodox party in Lithuania. On the contrary, Prince Ivan Patrikeev and some other leading boyars, like Prince Semen Ivanovich Riapolovsky and Prince Vasili Vasilievich Romodanovsky, were in favor of a rapprochement with the Grand Duchy of Lithuania. They hoped that Elena's marriage to Aleksandr could cement the friendship between the two countries, who would then be in a better position to fight the Tatars and the Turks.[71]

It seems that Patrikeev and Riapolovsky, who often were entrusted with negotiations with Lithuania, did not always follow Ivan's instructions closely but tried to stick to their own line of policy in order to avoid war between Moscow and Lithuania. When Ivan realized this, he considered it "treason" (the expression used in the Ustiug Chronicle).[72] The upshot was that in January 1499 Ivan ordered Prince Ivan Patrikeev, his son Vasili, and Prince Semen Riapolovsky to be arrested. On February 5 Riapolovsky was executed. The two Patrikeevs were made monks. In April, Prince Vasili Romodanovsky was imprisoned.[73]

All the orders were issued in this case by Ivan III personally, without the approval of the boyar duma (of which Prince Ivan Patrikeev was chairman). Thus, in contrast to the executions of 1497, the execution of Prince Riapolovsky was an arbitrary act not compatible with the spirit of the sudebnik. A new chairman of the duma was soon appointed—Prince Vasili Danilovich Kholmsky (of the Tver branch of the Rurikids). A year after (on February 13, 1500), Ivan gave his daughter Feodosia (born in 1485) in

71. Bazilevich, pp. 371–375.
72. Ustiug Chronicle, p. 100.
73. *PSRL*, *6*, 43; *12*, 248–249; Ustiug Chronicle, p. 100; Karamzin, *Primechaniia*, Note 451 to Vol. *6*.

marriage to Kholmsky. It should be noted that Vasili Kholmsky's father, Prince Daniel Dmitrievich Kholmsky, distinguished himself as army leader in the war against the Kazan Tatars and the Livonian Knights, but in spite of this was disgraced by Ivan in 1474. Ivan returned his favor to Prince Daniel only after the latter had signed a special pledge never to leave the Muscovite service. Prince Daniel died in 1493. His son Vasili (the new chairman of the duma) was likewise an outstanding general.

Soon after the arrest of Riapolovsky and the Patrikeevs, Ivan again bestowed his favor on Sophia and Vasili, and on March 21 Vasili was proclaimed Grand Duke of Novgorod and Pskov.

Before long, Sophia resumed writing to her daughter, Elena of Lithuania. However, a change in the nature of her letters may be noticed. Previously, they were intimate letters of mother to daughter; now Sophia's letters had a religious and political tone. She exhorted Elena to keep firmly her Orthodox faith. "Do not accept Roman faith even if they threaten thee with pain and death, otherwise thy soul will perish" (May 30, 1499).[74] Obviously, Sophia followed in her letters to Elena of this period the official line of Ivan's diplomacy.

At his coronation in 1498 Dmitri had received the title of Grand Duke of All Russia. Specifically, Ivan III "blessed his grandson with the Grand Duchies of Vladimir, Moscow, and Novgorod." Now, a little over a year after Dmitri's coronation, Ivan proclaimed his son Vasili Grand Duke of Novgorod (and Pskov), thus breaking the unity of "All Russia" and depriving Dmitri of one of his grand duchies. Ivan's action presumably was approved by the boyar duma under its new chairman. In any case there is no evidence of objection. On the other hand, a vigorous protest against Vasili's new title came from some of those directly affected by it. Novgorod was now in fact a Muscovite province, and the Novgorodians had no voice in politics. Pskov, however, was still a free city, although under Ivan's suzerainty. Ivan sent an envoy to Pskov to deliver the following message: "I, Grand Duke Ivan, favored my son Vasili and granted him Novgorod and Pskov." The Pskov veche refused to accept Vasili and sent a delegation consisting of three mayors and three boyars to Moscow to petition the grand dukes Ivan and Dmitri not to violate the old custom according to which the Grand Duke of Moscow was the suzerain of Pskov. (Both Ivan and Dmitri were grand dukes of Moscow; Vasili was not.)

74. *Sbornik, 35,* 275; Bazilevich, p. 375.

When the Pskovian delegates presented their petition to Ivan, the latter became angry and retorted: "Am I not free to take care of my grandson and my sons? I grant princely power to whom I please; and I please to grant Novgorod and Pskov to Vasili." He arrested two members of the Pskovian delegation, though he allowed all the others to return to Pskov. The Pskovians then sent another delegation with a new petition, this one addressed to "Ivan, Grand Duke of Novgorod and Pskov." Ivan told the delegation to go back to Pskov and promised to send a special envoy to Pskov with his answer. That envoy, the boyar Ivan Chobotov, duly came to Pskov and announced to the veche that the grand duke would observe the old customs in regard to Pskov. The text of the message brought by Chobotov is not recorded in the Pskovian Chronicle. Apparently, Ivan explained to the Pskovians that he continued to be their suzerain and that Vasili's title was nominal only. The next Pskovian delegation to Moscow petitioned the grand dukes Ivan and Vasili to release from prison the two members of the first delegation (still interned in Moscow). This was done immediately,[75] and the conflict between Pskov and Moscow thus came to an end. Vasili, however, was deeply offended by the Pskovians' unwillingness to accept him unreservedly as their grand duke; and his feelings were to affect his own policies toward Pskov when he became the sole ruler of Great Russia.

6. IVAN'S LAST YEARS

Neither Sophia nor Vasili intended to acquiesce in their partial success, and the struggle for power inside the grand-ducal palace continued unabated. The odds now were decidedly against Dmitri. The latter was still in his teens (born in 1483). After the fall of the Patrikeevs and the execution of Riapolovsky, Dmitri's only influential protector among the high officials was Fedor Kuritsyn. However, Kuritsyn, being a diak, depended entirely on the grand duke's favor and was not in position to contradict Ivan. If he had dared to defend Dmitri openly, he would have been removed from his office at once. Kuritsyn is last mentioned in the sources available to us in 1500. He apparently died before 1503.

Soon after bestowing on Vasili the title of Grand Duke of Novgorod and Pskov, Ivan began neglecting Dmitri.[76] An impossible sit-

75. Pskovian Chronicle, pp. 83–84.
76. Soloviev, Istoriia, 5, 180.

uation arose at the court, which could not avoid confusing both the boyars and the people at large. Finally, on April 11, 1502, Ivan disgraced Dmitri and the latter's mother Elena of Moldavia; both of them were interned in their apartments and kept under guard. Three days later, with the blessing of Metropolitan Simon, Ivan proclaimed Vasili "Grand Duke of Vladimir and Moscow and Autocrat of All Russia." [77]

The news must have been met in Great Russia with mixed feelings. It caused considerable excitement abroad and generated all kinds of rumors. The disgrace of Elena of Moldavia and her son strained the relations between Moscow and Moldavia. The Voevoda Stephan, Elena's father, bitterly complained to his and Ivan's ally, Khan Mengli-Girey of the Crimea. Through his envoy to the khan, Ivan tried to defend his action against Dmitri on the following ground: "I, Ivan, at first had favored my grandson Dmitri, but the latter became rude to me. Everyone favors that one who serves well and tries to please his benefactor; there is no sense in favoring a man who is rude to you." Ivan's envoy to Lithuania was instructed to give a similiar explanation to anyone who would ask questions about the meaning of the Moscow events. Besides, the envoy was to emphasize that Vasili was now, together with Ivan himself, the suzerain of all Russian states.[78]

After that, in some of the documents Ivan was referred to as "the greater suzerain." This is probably the reason why Herberstein called him "the Great." [79] Actually, we may think, Ivan, while receiving all the outward honors, had to cede much real authority to Vasili (Sophia died on April 7, 1503). It is evident that Vasili established close contact with the leaders of the conservative group of Russian clergymen. They, in their turn, expected Vasili to support the drive against the Heresy of the Judaizers and also to help them ward off any further attempts to secularize the church land.

It is under Vasili's influence that Ivan agreed to receive the chief spokesman of the conservative clergy, Abbot Iosif Sanin of Volok.[80] Ivan had three talks with Iosif during Easter week of 1503.[81] We know of these talks from Iosif's letter to Archimandrite Mitrofan, who was Ivan III's confessor in the last years of his life. Iosif wrote

77. *PSRL, 6,* 48; *12,* 255.
78. Soloviev, *Istoriia, 5,* 81.
79. Herberstein–Backus, p. 13.
80. Khrushchov, pp. 178–179.
81. On the date of the talks see *AFED,* p. 205.

to Mitrofan in April 1504—that is, about a year after his meeting with Ivan. Iosif might have recalled at that time the main lines of his conversations with Ivan pretty well, but we cannot be sure that all his statements are correct in detail.[82] According to Iosif, during their first meeting Ivan admitted that he conversed with the heretics and asked Iosif to forgive him. Ivan added than the metropolitan and the bishops had forgiven him. Iosif answered that God would forgive Ivan if from now on he would combat the heresy. In their second talk Ivan explained to Iosif what kind of heresy was led by the archpriest Alexis and what kind was led by Fedor Kuritsyn. Ivan also acknowledged that his daughter-in-law Elena had been converted to heresy by Ivan Maksimov. Ivan then, allegedly, promised to take strong measures against the heresy. However, at their third meeting Ivan asked Iosif if it was not a sin to punish the heretics. When Iosif started to argue in favor of punishment, Ivan abruptly ended the conversation.

In August and September 1503 the *sobor* (church council) met in Moscow. Iosif and his adherents apparently hoped that this council would sanction the suppression of the heresy. Ivan, however, did not include the question of the heresy on the agenda of the sobor, which under Ivan's direction dealt with certain minor reforms in church administration. One of them concerned the fees required by bishops from the candidates for priesthood, at their ordaining. This, incidentally, was one of the targets of the criticism of the Russian Church by the heretics. The sobor ruled to abolish these fees. When the sobor was about to close, the spokesman of the Trans-Volga Hermits, Nil Maikov of the Sora Hermitage, brought a new matter to the attention of the sobor by moving that the monasteries should be deprived of the right to own landed estates. There can be little doubt that Nil's motion was made with Ivan's cognizance.

The proposal met with violent opposition. Metropolitan Simon, who three years ago had blessed the seizure of church land in Novgorod, now cried out against the possibility of such an act applied to the whole of Russia. As we know, prior to 1503 Simon never dared to oppose Ivan openly. Now, however, Simon could count on Vasili's protection. The opponents of Nil made every effort to defeat his motion. Iosif Sanin, who had left Moscow a day before Nil's speech, was hastily summoned back to Moscow. The majority of the sobor

82. For the text of Iosif's letter to Mitrofan see *AFED,* pp. 436–438.

proved to be against Nil. Ivan tried three times to overrule the council but finally was obliged to retreat after Iosif and other defenders of the established order had presented Ivan with a voluminous set of quotations from church fathers and Byzantine law statutes in support of their position.[83]

The sobor's refusal to allow further secularization of church land was a serious blow to Ivan's plans of expanding the pomestie land fund and, through it, the gentry militia. Since Vasili apparently had supported the decision of the sobor, Ivan was helpless to do anything about it. As a minor satisfaction, Ivan was soon able to strike back against one of the staunchest enemies of the heretics, Archbishop Gennadi of Novgorod. Gennadi signed the decision of the sobor abolishing the bishop's fees for ordaining priests; but when he returned to Novgorod, he could not prevail upon his secretary to stop collecting the fees. Complaints immediately were rushed to Moscow. Under different circumstances Gennadi might have extricated himself or at the most escaped with a minor penalty or a reprimand. Now Ivan demanded prompt action from Metropolitan Simon, and Gennadi was immediately dismissed from his see.[84]

After Gennadi's removal, Iosif Sanin took upon himself the direction of the struggle against the heresy. In his above-mentioned letter to Ivan's confessor, Mitrofan, of April 1504, Iosif urged Mitrofan to use every means of persuasion to convince Ivan of the necessity to suppress the heresy. Iosif argued that if Mitrofan failed to do so, both he (Mitrofan) and Ivan would be punished by God.[85] Vasili, on his part, must have urged his father to convoke a new church council to condemn the heresy. Finally Ivan yielded. It is noteworthy that about this time (not later than June 16, 1504) Ivan made his will, in which he "blessed" Vasili with "all the Russian grand duchies." Vasili's younger brothers were admonished to consider Vasili "their father" and to obey him in everything. Dmitri was not mentioned at all in this will. The testament was witnessed by four persons: Ivan's confessor, Archimandrite Mitrofan; the chairman of the boyar duma, Prince Kholmsky; Prince Daniel Vasilievich Shchenia; and the boyar Iakov Zakharich Koshkin.[86]

The sobor against the heretics gathered in Moscow in December

83. See Pavlov, *Ocherk*, pp. 39 ff.; Vernadsky, "Heresy," p. 146.
84. *PSRL, 6*, 49; *12*, 258; Nikitsky, *Ocherk . . . Novgorode*, p. 187.
85. *AFED*, p. 438.
86. *DDG*, pp. 353–364.

1504. This time Vasili nominally presided over the meetings jointly with his father, but in fact was the only presiding officer. The ringleaders of the heresy were sentenced to death by burning at the stake. Three of them, including Fedor's brother Volk Kuritsyn and Ivan Maksimov, were burned in Moscow on December 27. Soon afterward, several other heretics were executed in Novgorod.[87] Elena of Moldavia died in prison on January 18, 1505.

The refusal of the sobor of 1503 to allow the secularization of church land and the harsh punishment of the heretics decreed by the sobor of 1504 could not but painfully affect Ivan's feelings. He must have been overcome by remorse and frustration, and must have blamed himself for his past mistakes. It was too late now, however, to undo anything. Mechanically, he continued to exercise his royal duties. Ivan's vassal, Khan Mohammed-Amin of Kazan, revolted against Ivan and massacred a large number of Russian merchants residing in Kazan. In September the Kazan Tatars attacked Nizhni-Novgorod but were repulsed. As regards family affairs, on September 4, 1505, Vasili married Solomonia Saburova, daughter of a Moscow boyar. Metropolitan Simon officiated. Ivan was present at the marriage.

Had Ivan had any thoughts of restoring Dmitri in power? Rumors about it circulated in Moscow as late as 1517, at the time of Herberstein's first visit to Moscow. Herberstein relates that when Ivan was dying, "he ordered Dmitri brought to him, and said: Dear grandson, I have sinned against God and you, because I have harmed you by having you thrown in prison and because I have deprived you of your rightful inheritance. Therefore, I beseech you to forgive the injury done you by me. Go therefore and enjoy your right. Dmitri was moved by this speech and easily forgave his grandfather the wrong. However, as he was going out, he was seized by the order of his uncle Gabriel [i.e. Vasili] and thrown into prison." [88]

Ivan passed away on October 27, 1505.

87. *PSRL, 6,* 49–50 and 244; *12,* 258; *AFED,* pp. 216–217.
88. Herberstein–Backus, p. 11. It should be noted that "Gabriel" was Vasili's Christian name and "Vasili" was his "princely name." In the Kievan period the princely names were usually Slavic or Norse (see *Kievan Russia,* p. 311). In the Mongol and post-Mongol periods both names were those of Christian saints.

Chapter V

THE REIGN OF VASILI III

1. Vasili and His Advisers

Vasili III's personality, as well as the significance of his rule, has been obscured by the period of constructive achievements of the preceding reign (his father, Ivan III) and by the intense drama of the subsequent age (his son, Ivan IV). Hemmed in between the two Ivans, Vasili seems at first glance a colorless character, and his reign is often characterized merely as a continuation of his father's or a prelude to his son's. One is inclined to speak of his age as a period of transition, a term to which the historian often has recourse when not willing to take the trouble to analyze properly a stage of historical development.

For Western scholarship Vasili has been saved from oblivion by one of the many Western envoys who came to Moscow during his reign and who proved a keen observer and competent writer. Moreover, being familiar with the Slavic language, the envoy, Baron Sigismund von Herberstein, succeeded in understanding Russia of the Russians more thoroughly than any other of his fellow diplomats. In his famous book on Russia, based on a serious study of Russian history and institutions, as well as on his personal impressions, Herberstein noted that "in the control which he exercises over his people" Vasili "easily surpasses all the rulers of the entire world." According to Herberstein the Russians "publicly declare that the will of the prince is the will of God and that whatever the prince does is done by the will of God. . . . Likewise also, if someone questions about something uncertain or doubtful, they are accustomed to answer, both God and the Great Prince know." [1]

Vasili's high opinion of his authority was instilled by both his farsighted father and his crafty mother, the Byzantine princess. Byzantine subtleness can indeed, be felt in all Vasili's policies, especially in foreign affairs. In the suppression of the opposition to his

1. Herberstein–Backus, pp. 16 and 18.

rule inside Russia he used brutal force or deceit or a combination of both. It should be noted, however, that while many of his opponents were imprisoned or exiled by his orders, only a few were executed, in sharp contrast to the wave of terror which was to engulf Russia during the reign of his son, Tsar Ivan IV.

Personal vanity was not Vasili's sole motive for his stern policies of the unification of his realm. Like his father, he undoubtedly was guided by considerations of state interest. Vasili was convinced that the tense international situation, and especially the lack of security in the South and the Southeast, made centralization of the Russian administration imperative. That conviction was shared by most of his advisers and by the majority of the Great Russian people.

Like his father, Vasili was an enthusiastic builder. He sponsored many new churches, including the Cathedral of the Archangel Michael in the Moscow Kremlin (the foundations for which were laid in the last months of his father's reign), and a number of new fortifications, for example the stone walls in Nizhni-Novgorod and Tula. A new grand-ducal palace was completed in 1508, and Vasili moved there with his consort Solomonia in May of that year.[2] In creating and decorating the churches Vasili, who undoubtedly appreciated art, followed both his religious zeal and his aesthetic urge. When he entered the Cathedral of the Dormition in the Kremlin in 1515, right after the new murals there had been completed, he exclaimed that he felt as if he were in heaven.[3] He likewise seems to have had a taste for the old Russian oral literature and could express himself in its style. According to the Pskovian Chronicle, Vasili finally decided to divorce his first wife, Solomonia (because she was barren), during his travels in North Russia. He saw a bird's nest on a tree above the road and said: "I feel sadness. To whom could I liken myself? Not to the birds—they bear offspring; not to the animals—they are prolific; not to the streams—they play with waves and abound in fish." Then he looked down at the ground and added: "Oh Lord! And not to the earth can I liken myself, since it produces fruit and thus glorifies Thee!"[4] A few letters of Vasili to his second wife, Elena, née Princess Glinskaia, have been preserved. He dictated them to his secretary, but the style is obviously his own—informal and lively. These letters evidence the

2. Karamzin, *Istoriia, 7,* 190.
3. *Ibid.,* 190; *PSRL, 6,* 280.
4. Pskovian Chronicle, p. 103.

warmth of his personal feelings toward his wife and his boy son Ivan (the future Tsar Ivan IV) as well as his keen solicitude for their health.[5] Like his father, Vasili was physically sound and active. He traveled much, either on business or on pilgrimages visiting various monasteries. Hunting was his passion.

In accordance with both his political views and his character, Vasili III insisted on directing personally the policies of his administration. Some of his moves must have been suggested to him by his advisers, but in all important matters the final decision came from him. Among his advisers, to begin with clergymen, was his former enemy, Vassian (formerly Prince Vasili Ivanovich Patrikeev), who had been made monk by order of Ivan III in 1499. Around 1509 Vasili III allowed him to return to Moscow. For about twelve years the grand duke and the monk were friendly, but around 1521 Vassian lost his influence and in 1531 fell in disgrace. He was a supporter of the Trans-Volga Hermits and a staunch opponent of "Josephism" (*Iosiflianstvo*), as the belief of Iosif Sanin's followers was called.

Iosif Sanin had died in 1515 but his policies were continued by his disciple Daniel, who succeeded Iosif as Abbot of the Volok Monastery. In 1522 Daniel was ordained metropolitan and with his ascension to the see of Moscow Josephism firmly established its sway over the church and state of Russia. In 1531 the monk Vassian, Daniel's chief opponent, was tried by a church sobor and sentenced to prison for life. Daniel gave full and unequivocal support to the grand-ducal authority. He rarely used the metropolitan's traditional right of pleading before the grand duke for the mitigation of severe punishments imposed by Vasili on his opponents. In one case (that of Prince Vasili Shemiakin, 1523), Daniel did not even raise his voice against the arrest of a man whose freedom he had before guaranteed by oath (see below, p. 158). On that occasion, the boyar I. N. Bersen-Beklemishev accused Daniel of perjury (two years later Bersen was executed).

Herberstein described Daniel as a man "with a strong and obese body whose face always glowed in a reddish way. Lest he seem more dedicated to his stomach than to fasting, virtues, and prayers, whenever he was to celebrate some public rite he was accustomed to expose his face to sulphur fumes so that it would grow pale." [6] In

5. *Pis'ma, 1*, 3–5.
6. Herberstein–Backus, pp. 31–32.

terms of the period Daniel was a learned man but certainly not a deep scholar. His writings enjoyed great prestige among the Muscovite readers. In his works he commented on the church dogmas as well as on the moral duties of men and women. He criticized various symptoms of moral laxity in his flock and fulminated against the habits of drinking of the Russians at large as well as against luxury among the boyars. He also reprimanded the mighty for the oppression of the lower classes. In many of these admonitions Daniel gave a vivid picture of the Russian ways of life of the period. In contrast to the elaborate Byzantine style of his dogmatic treatises, his sermons are written, in part at least, in racy Russian, which made them an important factor in the development of the Great Russian literary language. Tsar Ivan IV's epistolary style seems to have been formed under their influence. One of Daniel's epistles—on the manner of joining the fingers for prayers—was to play a significant role in the future troubles of the Russian Church. Basing his teaching on the authority of Theodorit of Cyrrhus, Daniel recommended *dvoeperstie* (joining of two fingers) to symbolize the dual nature of Christ. Incidentally, it was later proved that the old Greek work which Daniel used in a Slavic translation had not been written by Theodorit but was wrongly ascribed to him.

The most important body of Vasili's advisers was of course the boyar duma. The relation between Vasili and the boyars needs clarification. In my opinion, great as Vasili's power was he was not an absolute monarch, since he had to reckon with the boyardom. Historians seem to have attributed too much weight to Herberstein's summary statements as well as to the angry words of Bersen-Beklemishev (see above, p. 24), according to whom Vasili showed no respect to the old advisers and settled all state affairs in his bedroom with one or two assistants. As a matter of fact, Vasili could be rude to a passionate opponent like Bersen-Beklemishev (whose family, incidentally, did not belong to the top boyars) but he was careful not to offend the boyars as a group. The boyar duma was permanently in session during Vasili's reign. Except for cases of *lèse-majesté* no prominent boyar was removed from office by Vasili; even the generals who lost battles through negligence were rarely reprimanded. The leading boyars were given the most lucrative positions of the realm, and no attempt to interfere with the boyars' manorial rights was made by Vasili's government. As a matter of precaution, Vasili III required many service princes to sign pledges of loyalty similar to that given by Prince Daniel Kholmsky to Ivan III in 1474.

At the time when Vasili ascended the throne, the key position of the chairman of the boyar duma was occupied by his brother-in-law, Prince Vasili D. Kholmsky (above, p. 127). It will be recalled that Prince Kholmsky had been appointed to this position by Ivan III in 1499 to replace Prince Ivan I. Patrikeev, the champion of the rights of Ivan III's unlucky grandson Dmitri, who was imprisoned at that time. In 1508 Prince Kholmsky was suddenly arrested and deported to Beloozero, where he was put in prison, dying there in 1524. Obviously, Vasili III must have had special reasons for removing Kholmsky. Most likely, those reasons were dynastic: it may be surmised that Prince Kholmsky attempted to intervene in favor of Dmitri. Even if he had simply recommended the latter's release from internment, Vasili must have become suspicious of his intentions. Incidentally, Dmitri died in prison in the next year.

Kholmsky's successor in the office was Prince Daniel V. Shchenia, one of the ablest Russian generals of the period, and the victor at Vedrosha in 1500. Like the Patrikeevs, Shchenia was a descendant of Gedymin. He was Vassian Patrikeev's cousin, and it is presumably at his request that Vassian was returned to Moscow. Shchenia died in 1515; there is no definite evidence concerning his successor. Around 1520 Prince Dmitri Fedorovich Belsky was appointed chairman of the duma, to remain in office for about thirty years until his death. Belsky belonged to a prominent West Russian princely family. His father moved from Lithuania to Moscow in 1482 and later married a Riazan princess, niece of Ivan III. Dmitri Belsky was thus Vasili III's second cousin once removed. Among other prominent titled boyar families of this period were the Princes Penkov, of the Iaroslavl princely branch; the Princes Shuisky, of the Suzdal branch; and the Princes Obolensky, of the Chernigov branch. Of the nontitled boyar families, the Koshkins, the Cheliadnins, the Vorontsovs, the Saburovs, and the Golovins may be mentioned here. The most colorful figure among the boyars was Prince Mikhail Lvovich Glinsky.[7] The Princes Glinsky were a West

7. On Prince Mikhail Lvovich Glinsky and the clan of the Glinskys see A. E. [A. V. Ekzempliarsky], "Glinsky, Kn. M. L.," *ES, 16* (1893), 866–867; R. V. Zotov, *O Chernigovskikh kniaziakh po Liubetskomu Sinodiku* (St. Petersburg, 1892), p. 131; *Vremennik, 10*, pp. 157–158.

Russian family of Mongol descent and had their apanages in the Severian region, then under the authority of the Grand Duke of Lithuania. Mikhail Glinsky received a brilliant education and in his youth spent twelve years abroad, in Germany, Italy (where he was converted to Roman Catholicism), and Spain. For some time he served in the army of Duke Albrecht of Saxony. After his return to Lithuania he played a prominent role in Lithuanian politics. He also proved a successful army leader in the wars against the Crimean Tatars. A man of great abilities and of even greater ambitions, Glinsky had many supporters among the Russians in Lithuania but made many enemies among the Lithuanian lords. The Polish chronicler Maciej Stryjkowski relates that Glinsky's adherents dreamed of restoring the Kievan state and proclaiming Glinsky Grand Duke of Kiev and all Lithuania.[8] King Aleksandr was under Glinsky's influence but after Aleksandr's death (1506) relations between Glinsky and the crown became strained. Glinsky was accused of conspiracy against Aleksandr's brother and successor, King Sigismund I. In 1508 Glinsky actually revolted against the king and put himself under Vasili III's protection. The revolt failed in spite of Muscovite intervention, and in 1510 Glinsky emigrated to Muscovy with his kin. Because of his knowledge of Western languages and Western ways of life and his intimate acquaintance with Lithuanian and Polish affairs, Glinsky proved an invaluable assistant to Vasili. Glinsky was conscious of this and expected big rewards for his help to Moscow. When a new war broke out between Lithuania and Muscovy and Smolensk was taken by the Muscovites (see below, p. 155), Glinsky demanded the post of viceroy of the conquered region (1514). Another man was appointed instead, and Glinsky decided to go over to Sigismund's side. One of Glinsky's servitors informed the nearest Russian commander of his master's intentions and Glinsky was arrested by the Russians. Brought to Moscow and threatened with execution, Glinsky announced his desire to return to the fold of the Greek Orthodox Church. Death sentence was then replaced by imprisonment. It was only after Vasili III had married Glinsky's niece, Elena, that Glinsky was released from prison (1526). In the last years of Vasili's reign Glinsky became one of the most influential men at the grand duke's court.

While the support of the boyars was politically indispensable to Vasili, he used to choose his most trusted advisers not from among

8. Lappo, *Zapadnaia Rossiia*, p. 123.

the boyars but from among the diaks, even though he was prevented by custom from appointing any of the latter to the top positions of the realm. The diaks were used by Vasili in both the diplomatic services and the internal administration. Prominent among them was Vasili Tretiak Dalmatov, who had started his career under Ivan III. Vasili imposed on Dalmatov the unpleasant task of abrogating the liberties of the city of Pskov in 1510 (see below, p. 144). Any possibility of a rebellion in Pskov was prevented by Dalmatov's crafty methods. The administration of Pskov was then entrusted to another outstanding diak, Mikhail Grigorievich Misiur-Munekhin (under the nominal authority of a boyar). Like Dalmatov, Munekhin started his career as a diplomat, being sent as envoy to Egypt in 1493 (see above, p. 90). Munekhin remained in Pskov until his death in 1528. He belonged to the educated élite of Muscovite society and was closely associated with Abbot Filofei, initiator of the theory of the Third Rome (below, p. 169). Being a deeply religious man, Munekhin was active in church affairs as well. He founded the Crypt Monastery (Pskovo-Pecherski Monastyr) near the Livonian border, around twenty miles west of Pskov. The new monastery was expected to revive and continue the traditions of the old Crypt Monastery of Kiev. It actually became an important outpost of Russian spirituality, facing as it did the Western world.[9]

The subsequent fate of Dalmatov shows the precariousness of the diaks' tenure during Vasili's reign and how little protected they were against abuse by the grand duke. According to Herberstein, a few years after Dalmatov's important services in the Pskov affair Vasili decided to send him as envoy to Emperor Maximilian. Dalmatov refused to serve, arguing that he lacked money for the expensive voyage. By Vasili's order Dalmatov was then exiled to Beloozero and put in prison there.[10] After his death, all his property was confiscated. Though Misiur-Munekhin was not molested during his life, following his death his property, as we know from the Pskov Chronicle, likewise was seized by Vasili.[11]

2. ANNEXATION OF PSKOV

The important historical task of unification of Great Russia was accomplished, in its essence, in the reign of Ivan III. However,

9. On the Crypt Monastery in Pechery see Andreyev, "Pskov–Pechery Monastery." See also L. Zurov, *Otchina* (Riga, 1929).

10. Herberstein–Backus, p. 17.

11. Pskovian Chronicle, p. 105.

there remained many problems still to be solved. The pomestie system had to be expanded, and more land was needed for it. As regards religious life, the debates between the defenders of the monasteries' rights on land, known now as the Josephans, and the Trans-
Volga Hermits (often referred to as the *nestiazhateli*, "Non-Ac-
quirers") continued in spite of Nil Maikov's defeat at the sobor of
1503. The Heresy of the Judaizers, although outlawed, still had
many adherents.

In terms of national policies, regional centrifugal forces were not
entirely suppressed during Ivan III's reign. When Vasili ascended
the throne, the City of Pskov still enjoyed far-reaching autonomy,
and half the principality of Riazan was nominally independent. In
the West, the fate of Severia and of certain border regions had not
been finally decided, since these regions had been left under the
authority of the Grand Duke of Moscow only for the duration of the
six-year armistice between Lithuania and Moscow, concluded in
1503 (see above, p. 95). The Russian princes of the disputed regions pledged vassal allegiance to the Grand Duke of Moscow but
did not become his boyars. The City of Smolensk remained under
Lithuanian control.

By the end of Ivan III's reign no apanage princes were left in
the territory of the Grand Duchy of Moscow except for Ivan's
nephew Prince Fedor of Volok. However, under the influence of
family tradition, Ivan in his testament designated an apanage for
each of Vasili's younger brothers. Vasili's share was sixty-six towns
as against thirty allocated to all four of his brothers together. Of the
latter, Iuri became Prince of Dmitrov; Dmitri, Prince of Uglich;
Simeon, Prince of Kaluga; and Andrei, Prince of Staritsa (in the
former Tver territory). Ivan ruled that the share of each younger
brother, in case each should die without sons, should revert to Vasili
as escheat. No younger brother received the right of coinage. All
were deprived of the right of diplomatic relations with foreign powers. It seems that Ivan took every possible precaution to prevent the
revival of the apanage traditions. Yet eventually there were dissensions between Vasili and three of his younger brothers.

It will be recalled that during the dynastic crisis of 1497–99 the
Pskovians were on the side of Ivan III's grandson, Dmitri. When
Ivan III appointed Vasili Grand Duke of Pskov in 1499, the
Pskovians at first refused to recognize him as such (see above, p.
128). After Ivan's death Pskov accepted Vasili's suzerainty over
her without any open protest. Vasili sent to Pskov Prince Peter V.

Shuisky-Veliky as his lieutenant. However, Vasili did not intend to leave to Pskov its old liberties for long.

On February 15, 1509, Ivan III's grandson Dmitri died in his country estate, where he was interned. Though Dmitri had little chance if any to return to power, his death made Vasili's position more legally secure than before. According to Herberstein, "while Dmitri was living, Gabriel [i.e. Vasili] acted as regent." [12] The validity of Herberstein's statement is questionable, but it may reflect the feelings of the Pskovians. In any case it is only after Dmitri's death that Vasili decided to strike.

Vasili was vindictive by nature and did not forgive the Pskovians for their refusal to accept him as their prince in 1499. His main motive in suppressing the Pskovian liberties was nevertheless more political than personal. Pskovian autonomy was an obstacle to the centralization of the Russian army as well as of the judiciary.

Although the Pskovians needed Moscow's military assistance against the Germans, they were not bound by any permanent treaty to assist Moscow against the latter's enemies. Pskov's only enemies at that time were the Livonian Germans, and the Pskovians eagerly accepted Moscow's assistance against them. Each time Ivan III needed Pskovian help against Novgorod, Sweden, or Lithuania, he had to send a special envoy to Pskov to negotiate a specific convention of alliance, valid only for this particular campaign. The Pskov veche usually approved such conventions, but on its own terms concerning the quota of soldiers to be mustered and the amount of equipment and supplies. The Pskov militiamen were not trained or equipped for long and distant campaigns, and except for wars against the Germans the Pskovians participated in such campaigns only halfheartedly. Their army was a separate unit, not an integral part of the Great Russian army.

As regards the judiciary, the Pskov courts consisted of judges appointed by the veche and of an equal number of judges appointed by the Prince of Pskov (i.e. Grand Duke of Moscow). The court fees were equally divided between the city and the prince. Under this system, the Grand Duke of Moscow had no real control over the court procedures in Pskov. From the financial point of view, court fees constituted an important item of revenue for Russian princes and cities, and many a Moscow official as well as the grand duke himself looked forward to laying hands on the Pskov court fees, which

12. Herberstein–Backus, p. 11.

seemed to be an easy way of improving Moscow's finances. Another important source of Moscow state revenue was the *tamga* (customs duties). Pskov practiced free trade and collected no tamga. This, of course, could be changed in case of the subjugation of Pskov to Moscow.

In preparing their plan for the annexation of Pskov, Vasili III and his chief adviser in this matter, the diak Vasili Tretiak Dalmatov, closely followed the pattern of annexation of Novgorod by Ivan III. It will be recalled (above, p. 58) that Dalmatov was Ivan's assistant in Novgorodian affairs in 1477–78. His plan for Pskov likewise aimed at a wholesale deportation of upper-class families, secretly decided upon in advance. To achieve their aims, Vasili and Dalmatov intended to play on the disagreement between the upper and lower classes in Pskov, which was not as sharp there as in Novgorod but existed nevertheless.

Vasili's opening move in the game was to dismiss his lieutenant in Pskov, Prince Peter V. Shuisky-Veliky, with whom the Pskovians were on good terms, and replace him with Prince Ivan M. Repnia-Obolensky (the ancestor of the Princes Repnin). Following Vasili's instructions, Prince Repnia did not notify the Pskovian authorities in advance of his coming to Pskov; the Pskovians had to accept him without official ceremonies, as a result of which Repnia did not consider himself bound by the old Pskov traditions (he came to Pskov in the summer of 1509). The Pskovian chronicler remarks that Repnia was cruel to the people of Pskov. By this, the upper-class citizens are primarily meant, since Repnia encouraged the commoners to present their complaints against the boyars and the city officials.

On October 26, 1509, Vasili III came to Novgorod with his brother Andrei (Prince of Staritsa) and his boyars.[13] As soon as the Pskovians heard of Vasili's arrival, they sent their envoys to Novgorod to voice their grievances against Prince Repnia. The envoys handed Vasili a small sum of money (150 Novgorodian rubles) as the city's gift to her suzerain. The gift was graciously accepted and the envoys were told that the grand duke was ready to let the Pskovians submit their complaints to him in the presence of Repnia, and if Repnia proved guilty, the grand duke would be ready to punish him.

After a while Repnia was summoned to Novgorod. Meanwhile the Pskov veche recommended to all the Pskovians who had any

13. For the following see the Pskovian Chronicle, pp. 92–97; *PSRL, 4,* 282–288.

kind of complaints to go to Novgorod to ask the grand duke for justice. The result was rather unexpected, since a number of Pskovians, instead of complaining against Prince Repnia, proved ready to accuse their own officials of certain abuses. Even one of Pskov's mayors decided to go to Vasili to complain against his own colleague, another mayor.

Vasili III thus found himself in the position of an arbiter not only between Prince Repnia and the city of Pskov, but between two conflicting groups of the Pskovians themselves. The unity of the Pskovian public opinion was broken. Vasili announced that he would act on the complaints on Epiphany Day, January 6, 1510. By that time all the top officials of the city of Pskov, as well as the most prominent Pskov boyars and merchants and a number of Pskov commoners, had gathered in Novgorod. All were invited to attend the traditional ceremony of the Blessing of Waters on the morning of Epiphany Day. Following that, they were instructed to come to the grand duke's palace in Novgorod. The commoners had to wait in the yard; the notables were let into the palace hall. When all the notables had gathered there, the grand duke's boyars came in and announced: "You are arrested by God and by the Grand Duke Vasili Ivanovich of All Russia." The commoners were handed over to the custody of the Novgorodian authorities.

News of the event soon reached Pskov through a Pskovian merchant who had been going to Novgorod but was warned by the Novgorodians he met on his way. He immediately galloped back to Pskov. Consternation spread among the people. The veche gathered at once. Some Pskovians advocated rebellion against Vasili. Others pointed out that Pskov was bound by an oath of allegiance to the grand duke. Still others reminded the people that they were left without most of their officials and notables and that it would be hard to organize a new government. Finally, it was decided to send a special envoy to Vasili to plead for the grand duke's mercy. Answering the envoy's plea, Vasili sent to Pskov Tretiak Dalmatov to announce the two conditions on which the grand duke was ready to return his favor to Pskov. In the first place, the veche was to be abolished and the veche bell taken out; secondly, Pskov was henceforth to be ruled by two grand-ducal lieutenants. By this latter point Vasili meant that Pskov was to cease to be a separate state governed by a prince of its own. Dalmatov warned the Pskovians that if they rejected these conditions, the grand duke's army was ready to march on Pskov. If they accepted the conditions, the grand duke would favor the Pskovians by a visit to show his respect to the Holy Trinity Cathedral.

The Pskovians were stunned. "Only the infants did not shed tears," remarked the chronicler. And he asked pathetically, "why did not the heart break from its root?" All was in vain. The Pskovians asked to have one day to consider Vasili's conditions. This was granted. The next day the Pskovians accepted the inevitable. They pointed out, however, that while they had kept their oath of loyalty to the grand duke, the latter had not kept his. The Pskovians said that they accepted their fate as God's punishment, voicing in these words a slightly veiled threat of the possibility that the grand duke, in his turn, might be eventually punished by God. On January 13, 1510, the veche bell was taken down from the belfry of the Holy Trinity Cathedral. The people wept as they watched the loss of the symbol of their liberties. On the same night the bell was shipped to Novgorod, with Dalmatov personally escorting it.

Vasili's visit to Pskov was set for Thursday, January 24. In the morning of this day a Muscovite bishop, Vassian of Kolomna came to town and in the name of the grand duke forbade the Pskovian clergy to meet Vasili outside of the city as they had planned. Presumably, the grand duke was afraid that the clergy would use their traditional right of pleading for the oppressed. The laymen met Vasili two miles outside the city. Vasili, according to the usual ritual in such cases, asked them about their health; they answered: "Never mind our health, let thee, our sovereign, be in good health." When Vasili entered the Holy Trinity Cathedral, Bishop Vassian congratulated him on the seizure of Pskov, which was considered a new offense by the Pskovians. It was then announced that all the Pskovians were invited to come to the princely palace next Sunday to hear of the grand duke's favor to them. On that fateful Sunday, the notables were asked to enter the hall and the commoners, to remain in the yard. The former were arrested, the latter set free and told that the grand duke would grant them a special charter of rights.

Those arrested were on the same night sent to Moscow with their families; they were allowed to take along only a few belongings. Those previously arrested in Novgorod had been already deported, and now their families were to join them in their new abodes. Altogether three hundred families were deported from Pskov, and an equal number of Muscovite families were brought in to replace them.

This, however, was only the beginning of the resettlement plan. After the deportation of the top group of Pskovian society, middle-class families were ejected from their houses in the central section of the city and replaced by Muscovites. 6,500 homesteads were thus taken from middle-class Pskovians. Whether all were deported to Muscovy or some allowed to build new homes outside the city walls is not clear. In any case Vasili's objective was achieved by these ruthless measures, and the leading stratum of Pskovian society was transplanted. The remnants of the middle classes as well as the lower classes became an amorphous mass, politically, and no more opposition could be expected from them.

"Thus perished the glory of Pskov," remarked the chronicler. The feelings of the Pskovians were expressed in the poetical "Lament of the City of Pskov" composed by an unknown author in the tradition of the *Igor Tale* of the 12th century. Parts of this poem were incorporated into the Pskovian Chronicle:

"O great Pskov, famous among the cities, why dost thou lament, why dost thou weep?—How can I not lament, not weep? A many-winged eagle, with many talons, flew against me. God allowed him, as punishment for our sins, to take from me my cedar of Lebanon [i.e. my strength], to lay our land waste, to destroy our city, to capture our people, to demolish our market places, and to send our fathers and our kin [to distant lands] where none of them had ever been before."

In their despair, some of the Pskovians were inclined to interpret the meaning of the catastrophe in apocalyptic terms. In one of the variants of the Pskovian Chronicle [14] we find a significant comment on a passage in the Revelation of St. John. In the English version the passage reads: "And there are seven kings: five are fallen, and one is, and the other is not yet come; and when he cometh, he must continue a short space. And the beast that was, and is not, even he is the eighth, and is of the seven, and goeth into perdition" (Revelation 17:10–11). The Pskovian writer explained that "in Russia the sixth kingdom is called Scythia. This is the sixth, and then comes the seventh; and the eighth is the Antichrist. . . . Alas! Let Jesus Christ our Lord save us from all evil and from eternal torment and grant us eternal good." It seems that the Pskovian commentator considered Vasili a representative of the seventh kingdom—that is, a forerunner of the Antichrist.

14. *PSRL, 4,* 282.

Vasili spent four weeks in Pskov, and issued the new charter he had promised the commoners. Its text has not been preserved, but from the chronicler's narrative we may deduce that its essence was an abrogation of the old Pskovian laws and introduction of Moscow's. Besides, the charter must have contained certain guarantees for the taxpayers by establishing a definite rate of payment which the officials were supposed to abide by; and the officials must have been forbidden to demand any money in excess of the prescribed table of collections. Of such a type was Vasili's charter to the peasants of the Pereiaslav district issued in 1506.[15]

Two of the grand duke's lieutenants (both prominent Moscow boyars) and two diaks (one of them was Misiur-Munekhin) were sent to Pskov to rule the city. To assist them, twelve Muscovite and twelve Pskovian starosty were appointed. Moscow *gosti* (financiers) were summoned to Pskov to organize the collection of the tamga. A garrison of 1,000 "boyar sons" and 500 Novgorodian *pishchalniki* (musketeers) was stationed in the city. The new Moscow officials were apparently given instructions to deal ruthlessly with the Pskovians in order to subjugate them completely. "And these lieutenants and their agents drank much Pskovian blood," remarks the chronicle. The Pskovians were at first hampered by their ignorance of Muscovite laws. When they complained of heavy fines and arrests, the Muscovite agents answered derisively, "Keep quiet! This is your new charter." According to the chronicler, most of the foreigners who had previously lived in Pskov went back to their native lands. "Only the Pskovians remained. [Where could they go?] The earth would not burst beneath them, nor could they fly away."

The only way the Pskovians could alleviate their plight was to ask the church authorities to intervene in their favor, as was traditional. Normally, the Pskovians would have asked the Archbishop of Novgorod (to whose see Pskov belonged) to help them, but the Novgorod see had been vacant since 1509.[16] Therefore the Pskovians addressed themselves to Abbot Filofei of the Eleazar Monastery in Pskov, a learned and highly esteemed monk.

To console the Pskovians, Filofei addressed an epistle to them in which he said that they should bear their misfortunes in a spirit of Christian submission to Providence. He reminded them that the saints themselves often had to suffer, that misfortunes were sent by

15. *AAE, 1,* 116–117. It is paraphrased in Soloviev, *Istoriia, 5,* 443–444.
16. On the causes see below, p. 151.

God for the people's past sins, and that they should pray to God for forgiveness.[17]

Simultaneously, Filofei wrote a letter to Grand Duke Vasili III in which he dealt with a number of questions bearing on Pskov affairs directly or indirectly—without, however, mentioning Pskov specifically.[18] I believe that before writing this letter Filofei consulted the diak Misiur-Munekhin. Munekhin could not approve of the wanton cruelty of the new regime in Pskov and might have needed Filofei's support for his own plans to improve the situation of the unfortunate Pskovians. Most likely, Munekhin took upon himself delivering Filofei's letter to the grand duke, together with his own report.

In his letter to Vasili, Filofei discussed primarily the following three questions: (1) the vacancy ("widowhood") of the Novgorod see; (2) the incorrect manner in which some people used the sign of the cross; (3) sodomy. Filofei had explained to Vasili that leaving a see vacant for long is a serious blow to the integrity of the church; he urged the grand duke to remedy the situation at once. Filofei discussed the question in general terms; but he undoubtedly had also in mind the interests of Pskov and of the Pskov Church, which was left without the protection of an archbishop.

The other two items in Filofei's letter (manner of the sign of the cross and sodomy) apparently had some relation to Pskov affairs too. I am inclined to think that some of the Muscovite officials who oppressed the Pskovians were accused of sodomy, as well as of an improper way of crossing themselves. Munekhin certainly knew all about the behavior of his Muscovite colleagues in Pskov; Filofei's comments on the seriousness of the sins committed by them could help Munekhin convince the grand duke of the necessity of removing them.

Alongside the treatise on sins, Filofei, again not mentioning the Pskovians specifically, implored the grand duke to show mercy to the oppressed: "Do turn avarice into generosity and harshness to charity; do comfort the weeping, who wail day and night; deliver the oppressed from the hand of the oppressors." And in an obvious reference to the confiscation of the property of the Pskovians, he warned the grand duke: "Do not rely on gold and glory which are acquired here on earth and remain on earth. Said the wise Solomon:

17. For the text of Filofei's epistle to the Pskovians see Malinin, appendix, pp. 7–24.
18. For the text of the letter see Malinin, appendix, pp. 49–56.

'The purpose of riches and gold is not in keeping them in the coffers but in using them for the assistance of the needy.' " [19]

In conclusion, Filofei asked Vasili to forgive him for taking the liberty of writing and pointed out that after the fall of Constantinople the Grand Duke of Moscow was the sole remaining Orthodox Christian ruler on earth and thus had special responsibilities and duties toward the Orthodox Christian Church. It was in this letter and in this connection that Filofei first formulated his famous theory of the Third Rome (below, p. 169).

Vasili ignored Filofei's plea to terminate the widowhood of the Novgorod see. On the other hand, Vasili "showed mercy" to Pskov and removed his harsh lieutenants, replacing them by two benevolent men—Prince Peter V. Shuisky-Veliky [20] (a former prince-lieutenant of Pskov) and Prince Simeon F. Kurbsky (1511). The diaks remained in office, and Misiur-Munekhin now took the administration of Pskov into his firm and experienced hands. The people felt more easy and secure. Many Pskovians returned to the city, foreigners appeared again, and the city became prosperous once more. But it was not the former Pskov. As Herberstein says, "the more refined and humane customs of the Pskovians were superseded by the more corrupt customs of the Muscovites. The integrity, candor, and sincerity of the Pskovians in business deals was such that all verbosity calculated to defraud the buyer was left out. They pointed to the merchandise itself with but a word." [21] Herberstein's statement is obviously based on the information he obtained from German merchants. The latter must have found the Muscovite tradesmen much sharper dealers than the Pskovians ever had been. Besides, the Pskovians were accustomed to German customs and ways of handling business, while the Muscovites were not.

Such was the impact of Pskov's traditions and of her proximity to the West, however, that as time went on the descendants of the Muscovites settled in Pskov were gradually "Pskovicized" in their manners. The Pskovian people in the late 16th century and throughout the 17th showed evidence of a somewhat different spirit from that of the average Muscovite. They were more independent in their attitude toward the government.

19. Malinin, p. 372.
20. Pskovian Chronicle, p. 97.
21. Herberstein–Backus, p. 88.

3. NATIONAL AND INTERNATIONAL
AFFAIRS, 1505–22

Religious fermentation in Russia did not end after the church councils of 1503 and 1504, and religious problems continued to play an important role in Vasili III's policies. True, the voice of the heretics was now almost stifled, but the Trans-Volga Hermits could not be silenced at once. They had nothing in common with the heresy, dogmatically, but they protested against the executions of the heretics, declaring that the true Christian way to combat heresies was by prayer and persuasion, not by fire and prison. They bitterly reprimanded Iosif Sanin for his brutality toward the heretics.[22]

On his part, Iosif addressed several epistles to Vasili III urging the latter not to slacken his efforts to suppress the remnants of the heresy with harsh measures.[23] Although there is no evidence of any new mass persecution of heretics in the first years of Vasili's reign, it seems that Vasili was favorably impressed by Iosif's fervor, and Iosif's younger brother Vassian was ordained Archbishop of Rostov and Iaroslavl.

Just about this time Iosif found himself in a difficult situation because of the animosity of the Prince of Volok, Fedor, in whose territory Iosif's monastery (founded in 1479) was located. Ecclesiastically, Volok belonged to the jurisdiction of the Archbishop of Novgorod, and at the time Gennadi occupied the see of Novgorod, Iosif could always count on his protection. The removal of Gennadi in 1503 (see above, p. 132) was a serious blow to the security of Iosif's position in Volok, for the new Archbishop of Novgorod, Serapion, was unfriendly.

Prince Fedor of Volok regarded Iosif's monastery as a source of potential revenue. He "borrowed" money from the monastery, frequently visited it with his retinue, and abused Iosif's hospitality. On one occasion, informing Iosif of his impending visit, he asked Iosif to serve him and his retinue mead, not kvas; mead was the favorite alcoholic beverage in Old Russia and was more expensive than kvas.[24] Fedor also expected expensive gifts, such as horses of best

22. *AFED,* pp. 511–513, 522–523.
23. *AFED,* pp. 488–498, 518–520.
24. See *Kievan Russia,* pp. 307–308.

breed, armor, and jewels. It was not long before he actually threatened Iosif with expulsion from the Volok territory.[25]

In despair, Iosif, through his friend the boyar Kutuzov, petitioned Vasili III to exempt his monastery from the authority of Prince Fedor and place it under the direct authority of the grand duke. Simultaneously Iosif asked Metropolitan Simon to sanction such transfer. Simon agreed to support Iosif's petition, and Vasili accepted Iosif's monastery under his protection. There was a hitch, however. From the point of view of canon law, no such transaction could be carried out without the approval of Archbishop Serapion of Novgorod. In any case, the latter had to be notified of the transaction. According to Iosif's biographer, the monk Savva Chorny (the Black), Iosif had intended to notify Serapion but could not do so because of the epidemics of plague in Novgorod. The monk Savva added that the grand duke himself promised to arrange the matter.[26] The validity of these statements is questionable.

When Prince Fedor received news of Vasili III's order, depriving him of the richest monastery in his principality, he was furious, and after consulting the abbot of another Volok monastery he sent a complaint to Archbishop Serapion. The latter expected that Iosif would at least present an explanation. Receiving no apology from Iosif, Serapion sent him a stern message, forbidding him to perform the sacred rites and to partake of the Holy Communion. Iosif immediately complained to Metropolitan Simon, and the latter consulted the council of bishops. It was decided to free Iosif from Serapion's interdiction and to call Serapion to Moscow for explanation. Serapion was tried, found guilty, removed from the Novgorod see, and interned in St. Andronik Monastery in Moscow (1509).[27] The Novgorod see was thereafter left vacant for seventeen years. Apparently, Serapion's actions were interpreted as a kind of rebellion of Novgorod against Moscow.

Prince Fedor of Volok died in 1513, after which his apanage was incorporated into the Grand Duchy of Moscow.

Iosif won the day in his controversy with Serapion, but the means by which he achieved his victory aroused the indignation of many clergymen and boyars and confused even some of his followers. Some of the latter implored him to apologize to Serapion, but Iosif flatly refused to do this.

25. Khrushchov, p. 206.
26. *Ibid.*, pp. 208–209.
27. *Ibid.*, pp. 209–215.

Even Vasili III himself was uneasy about Iosif's methods and the severity of Serapion's punishment. Receiving a report that Metropolitan Simon treated Serapion harshly in the latter's prison cell in St. Andronik Monastery, Vasili ordered that Serapion be transferred to the Holy Trinity Monastery (of which Serapion formerly had been abbot). He lived there rather as a guest than as a prisoner, until his death in 1516.

Another evidence of Vasili's emancipation from Iosif's influence was his change of attitude toward the disgraced monk Vassian Patrikeev. Around 1509 Vassian was allowed to come to Moscow and was put up in the Simonov Monastery. Before long, Vassian acquired Vasili's confidence and favor. On one occasion Vasili called Vassian a "support of his realm" and his "preceptor in philanthropy." [28] It was probably under Vassian's influence that Varlaam, a man agreeable to the Trans-Volga Hermits, was ordained Metropolitan of Moscow to replace Simon, who died in 1511.

The exchange of polemics continued between Iosif Sanin and his opponents, the foremost of whom was now Vassian Patrikeev (Nil Maikov died in 1508). Besides the question of the punishment of the heretics, that of the right of the monasteries to own landed estates was again raised. It seems that Vasili III was reverting to the program of his father in this matter. And indeed, the imperative necessity of expanding the Great Russian army through the pomestie plan was now even greater than in Ivan's times, since Moscow's relations with her neighbors became even more strained than under Ivan.

As we know (above, p. 74), the cornerstone of Ivan III's Eurasian policy was his alliance with the Khan Mengli-Girey of the Crimea. The main value of the alliance for the latter was Moscow's cooperation with him against the Golden Horde. But by the end of Ivan's reign the Golden Horde had disintegrated, and was partly replaced by the much weaker Khanate of Astrakhan, which presented no serious threat either to Moscow or to the Crimea. After that, Mengli-Girey was less interested in the Moscow alliance. For Moscow, the value of the Crimean alliance, besides the Crimean pressure on the Golden Horde and Kazan, was that Mengli-Girey helped Ivan in the latter's struggle against Lithuania. However, when Moscow extended her control to the Severia region, Mengli-Girey was not too pleased, since the Muscovite troops now came too close to his own domain. Moreover, he was now in no position to plunder the

28. Zhmakin, p. 71.

Severia region; and as we know, the possibility of looting the Ukrainian lands, both east and west of the Dnieper River, was for him one of the attractions of his alliance with Moscow. Finally, Vasili, being a miser by disposition, was reluctant to squander as much money on the "presents" to the Crimean Khan and his kin and grandees, as his father—wisely—had done. The Crimeans, not unnaturally, resented such an attitude.

All this resulted in a considerable cooling of friendship between Moscow and the Crimea in the first years of Vasili III's reign, and in 1512 Mengli-Girey broke the alliance with Vasili and went over to the Lithuanian side. As the Crimean Tatars now had to abstain from looting the Ukrainian lands controlled by the Grand Duke of Lithuania, they shifted the direction of their attacks to Severia and the border provinces of the Grand Duchy of Moscow. This was the beginning of the protracted struggle between Russia and the Crimean Tatars, with the latter supported later by the Ottoman Turks. The devastating raids of the Crimean Tatars on the southern borderlands of Russia continued well into the reign of Catherine II.

In the summer of 1521 Mengli-Girey's son and successor, Khan Mohammed-Girey, succeeded in reaching the suburbs of Moscow itself. He received some support from the Grand Duchy of Lithuania. The Starosta of Cherkasy, Ostafi Dashkevich, raided Severia at the head of a detachment of Ukrainian Cossacks in his service (below, p. 255). When Vasili III received news of the Tatar invasion, he retired to Volok to gather more troops and left Moscow under the command of a Tatar prince converted to Greek Orthodoxy—Peter, husband of Vasili's sister Evdokia (she had died in 1513). Moscow was crowded with refugees from the districts around, and disease was rampant. Peter sent rich presents to Mohammed-Girey, and the latter lifted the siege. Herberstein relates that Peter agreed to give Mohammed-Girey a written pledge in the name of the Moscow government to pay a regular annual tribute to the khan, and that later a Russian general, the chief of the Russian garrison at Riazan, succeeded in obtaining that paper by ruse and destroyed it; but the story does not sound credible.[29]

Both the Crimean khan and the Grand Duke of Lithuania tried to undermine Moscow's grip on the Khanate of Kazan. As we know (above, p. 133), Khan Mohammed-Amin of Kazan revolted against

29. On this Tatar raid see *PSRL*, *6*, 263; *13*, 38–43; Soloviev, *Istoriia*, *5*, 365–369; Herberstein–Backus, pp. 107–109.

Moscow shortly before Ivan III's death. In the spring of 1506 Vasili III sent Russian troops against Kazan but the campaign was not successful, and the Russians suffered two severe defeats. Two years later, however, Mohammed-Amin returned the Russian prisoners to Moscow and signed a treaty of friendship with Vasili. After Mohammed-Amin's death, Vasili sent to Kazan the Tsar of Kasimov, Shah-Ali (1519).[30] The Kazanians at first accepted him as their khan but soon, under the influence of Crimean agents, revolted and invited Sahib-Girey, a brother of the Khan of the Crimea, to the throne of Kazan (1521). Shah-Ali was allowed, however, to return to Moscow with all his wives and belongings.[31] As soon as Sahib-Girey arrived in Kazan, he ordered Russians residing in Kazan to be either killed or enslaved.

The break with the Crimea and the constant troubles in Kazan made it imperative for the Russians to strengthen their defense system. Every spring, troops were sent to the *bereg* (bank)—that is, the main defense line along the course of the Oka River. Both along that line and to the south of it, fortresses were built (Zaraisk, Tula, Kaluga). In the border regions (*ukrainy*) south of the Oka line companies of *ukrainniki* (frontiersmen or Cossacks) were settled. On the diplomatic front, Vasili's government tried to entertain friendly relations with the Nogay Horde as well as with the Khanate of Astrakhan.

The deterioration of Moscow's relations with the Tatars made the Lithuanian problem more difficult to handle for Vasili. Yet he continued his father's policy in regard to the West Russian lands. Grand Duke Aleksandr died in 1506; his younger brother Sigismund was now elected King of Poland and Grand Duke of Lithuania. Grand Duchess Elena (Aleksandr's widow and Vasili's sister) had to remain in Lithuania in view of the strained relations between Lithuania and Moscow. After the death of her husband her life became even sadder. She died in 1513, a "victim of political calculations," in K. N. Bestuzhev-Riumin's expression.[32]

Even before the expiration of the six-year truce with Lithuania (concluded in 1503), the war flared again, in connection with Mikhail Glinsky's defection from Lithuania (above, p. 139). A new

30. Veliaminov-Zernov, *1*, 250–252.
31. *Ibid.*, 256–260.
32. *ES, 22*, 600.

truce was concluded, and then war operations started again. In 1514 Russian troops under the command of Prince Daniel Shchenia seized Smolensk after a fierce artillery bombardment of the city.[33] As we know, Vasili III offended Glinsky on this occasion by appointing not him but another man (Prince Vasili Vasilievich Shuisky) his lieutenant of Smolensk.

The capture of Smolensk was an important success for the Great Russians, but about a month afterward the Muscovite army suffered a serious defeat at Orsha.[34] The same prince, Konstantin Ivanovich Ostrozhsky, who had lost the battle at Vedrosha fourteen years ago, now led the Lithuanian troops to victory. All the efforts of the Lithuanians to win back Smolensk failed, however. The situation was the reverse of that during the war of 1500–03. Then, the Great Russians had won the most important field battle but were not able to take Smolensk. Now, even though they lost the battle, they held Smolensk firmly. Skirmishes continued, interrupted by diplomatic negotiations. Emperor Maximilian I tried to arbitrate the conflict, and it was for that purpose that Herberstein was first sent to Moscow (1517). Nothing came of this attempt. In 1522 a new truce for five years was concluded directly between Moscow and Lithuania. Moscow kept Smolensk and all of the gains made by Ivan III.[35]

Vasili's brothers attempted to use the Lithuanian conflict to intrigue against him. In 1511 Vasili received a report that Prince Simeon of Kaluga intended to join Grand Duke Sigismund of Lithuania. Vasili ordered Simeon to come to Moscow at once. Simeon lost heart and asked the metropolitan and the bishops to implore Vasili to pardon him. Vasili agreed not to disgrace Simeon, but the latter had to dismiss all his boyars and attendants and accept a new retinue sent him by Vasili.[36] Simeon died in 1518. The relations between Vasili and his other brother, Dmitri of Uglich, were likewise strained at times. Vasili reprimanded his brother for his lack of subordination to the grand duke's authority. No open conflict between these two developed, however.[37]

Around 1514 Vasili's brother Iuri (next in seniority to Vasili)

33. *PSRL*, *6*, 255; *13*, 19.
34. *PSRL*, *13*, 21–22; Pskovian Chronicle, p. 98. It is noteworthy that the report on the Orsha battle in the Pskovian Chronicle is in the style of the *Igor Tale*.
35. *Sbornik*, *35*, 629–642.
36. Soloviev, *Istoriia*, *5*, 390.
37. *Ibid.*, 390–391.

conspired with his boyars against Vasili. A retainer of Iuri informed
the grand duke of Iuri's plans. Vasili was about to arrest Iuri when
the latter addressed himself to Iosif Sanin, imploring the aging abbot to intervene in his favor. It should be recalled that in 1513
Prince Fedor of Volok had died, and the Volok apanage was annexed to Moscow. Vasili now went often to Volok to hunt, and in
this way his relations with Iosif were resumed. When Iuri asked
Iosif's help, the latter was ill and not in a position to go to Moscow
personally. He sent, instead, two monks of his monastery to Vasili.
After a stormy talk, Vasili agreed to pardon Iuri. Soon afterward
Iosif died, at the age of 76 (1515).[38]

Not long before his death Iosif wrote a letter to Vasili III in
which he asked the grand duke to keep the Volok Monastery under
his special care and protection. Iosif then asked the friars of the
monastery to select among them a suitable successor to him. They
nominated Daniel, a Riazanian by birth. With Iosif's consent, Metropolitan Varlaam ordained him abbot. Vasili, as he promised Iosif,
favored the Volok Monastery, even hunting in the vicinity of it.
Before long he had established a close friendship with the new
abbot, Daniel. At the same time Vasili's relations with Metropolitan
Varlaam gradually deteriorated. Varlaam's last important act, approved by Vasili, was to invite from Mount Athos a learned Greek
monk to translate into Russian some of the Greek religious manuscript books available in Moscow libraries, and to combat, on dogmatic grounds, the Heresy of the Judaizers (1515). The monk whom
the Muscovites tried to get was old and sickly and did not venture to
travel to Moscow. Instead, the Mount Athos elders sent to Moscow
a young Greek scholar, Michael Triboles, whose monastic name was
Maxim and who became known in Russia as Maxim the Greek. He
arrived in Moscow in 1518.[39] In the following years Vasili grew tired
of Varlaam, partly because of the latter's constant intervention in
favor of persons who had incurred Vasili's disfavor. On December
17, 1521, Varlaam was deposed. Two months after (on February
27, 1522), Vasili appointed Abbot Daniel the new metropolitan.

About this time the principality of Riazan, or rather, the remaining half of it, was annexed to Moscow. The last independent
Riazanian grand duke, Ivan VI, was accused of negotiating with

38. Khrushchov, pp. 249–251; Soloviev, *Istoriia, 5,* 391–392.
39. On Maxim the Greek see Ikonnikov, *Maksim Grek;* Denissoff, *Maxime le Grec et
l'Occident.*

the Khan of the Crimea, Mohammed-Girey, and was arrested by Vasili in 1520. During Mohammed-Girey's raid on Moscow in 1521 Ivan VI succeeded in fleeing to Lithuania, where he received a landed estate. He died in 1534. As had been the case in Novgorod and Pskov, thousands of Riazanians were deported to Muscovy and replaced by Muscovites.[40]

4. THE VICTORY OF THE JOSEPHANS AND THE SECOND MARRIAGE OF VASILI III

With the ordaining of Daniel as Metropolitan of Moscow, Josephism could be expected finally to entrench itself in Muscovy. And, indeed, before long Daniel had eliminated his main opponents. Whenever there was a vacancy in any important position in church administration, Daniel appointed a Josephan. It must be admitted that he knew how to select efficient assistants, and some of his appointments were very good. It was Daniel who ordained Makari Archbishop of Novgorod in 1526. Makari proved one of the enlightened Russian prelates and was to play an important role in the first half of Ivan the Terrible's reign. Daniel supported Vasili's autocracy in many ways and put the authority of the Russian Church firmly behind that of the grand duke. In his turn, Vasili had to renounce any claims on church land.

Church land being barred from confiscation for the pomestie fund, Vasili had no alternative but to turn part of the state (black) land to the pomestiia, although he used every opportunity of expanding the state land fund through annexation, such as of Pskov and Riazan. By 1523 Vasili had succeeded in annexing Severia also. Two Severian princes, descendants of Vasili II's former enemies—Vasili Shemiakin of Novgorod-in-Severia and Vasili of Starodub, grandson of Ivan Mozhaisky—had recognized the authority of Ivan III in 1500 and were left in Severia as apanage princes (see above, p. 94). They hated each other and intrigued one against the other. Vasili of Starodub died around 1518 and his apanage was annexed to Moscow. In 1523 Grand Duke Vasili III ordered Prince Vasili Shemiakin to come to Moscow for explanations, since he was suspected of carrying on secret relations with King Sigismund. Shemiakin was afraid to appear in Moscow, but Metropolitan Daniel

40. Soloviev, *Istoriia*, 5, 386–387.

pledged Shemiakin's safety, giving an oath on the Holy Virgin's icon.[41] Shemiakin was at first well received in Moscow, but soon was arrested and imprisoned. He died in prison six years later, and his apanage was incorporated into Muscovy.[42]

Daniel did not protest against the grand duke's treatment of Shemiakin. Daniel's behavior in this affair irritated many Russians, especially those who followed Nil Maikov's precepts. Grand Duke Vasili, however, was pleased with Daniel's action, or rather lack of action. Before long, Daniel proved useful to Vasili in the latter's family affairs. As has been mentioned (above, p. 135), about this time Vasili became chagrined by the barrenness of his wife Solomonia (née Saburova). Solomonia was a kind and virtuous woman, and Vasili had no complaints against her except that she was sterile. For Vasili this was not merely a family matter but a state problem. In case he died without sons, his brother Iuri would become his successor, and Vasili did not trust Iuri; in fact he despised him.

For state reasons, the major Moscow boyars approved Vasili's decision to divorce Solomonia and marry again. The matter now depended on the metropolitan, without whose decision Vasili could not proceed with the divorce. The divorce, in such a case, was against the precepts of the Gospels and the habits of the Greek Orthodox Church. Daniel at first hesitated to authorize the divorce. Presumably under the influence of Maxim the Greek, he advised Vasili to consult the Eastern patriarchs and the Mount Athos monks. This was done, but no favorable answer was received.[43] Daniel then decided to proceed with the divorce just the same. On November 28, 1525, Solomonia, in spite of her protests, was made a nun under the name of Sophia and sent to the Pokrov Monastery in Suzdal. Soon afterward, Daniel blessed Vasili's second marriage with the young Princess Elena Glinskaia and personally officiated at the wedding on January 21, 1526.

Daniel's role in Vasili's divorce and second marriage aroused the indignation of many of the outstanding Russians, especially the opponents of Vasili III and of Josephism. In a variant of the Pskovian Chronicle Vasili's second marriage is called adultery.[44]

41. Zhmakin, p. 135.
42. Soloviev, *Istoriia, 5,* 387–389.
43. Zhmakin, p. 137.
44. *PSRL, 4,* 295.

Such was also the opinion of Vassian Patrikeev. Maxim the Greek likewise found the divorce and the new marriage uncanonical. Several boyars, including Prince Simeon Fedorovich Kurbsky and Ivan Nikitich Bersen-Beklemishev (long disgraced by the grand duke), sharply criticized both the metropolitan and the grand duke.[45]

Most of those who opposed Vasili's divorce and second marriage were punished in one way or another under various pretexts. Prince Kurbsky was disgraced and died in disfavor in 1527. Bersen-Beklemishev was accused in abusive words against the grand duke, arrested, and tried in February 1525, together with a diak friend of his. Bersen was sentenced to death and the diak to the cutting of his tongue.[46] Bersen was a friend of Maxim the Greek and visited him often. This circumstance was disclosed during Bersen's trial, and Maxim was called for explanation before the meetings of a special conference (sobor) over which the grand duke personally presided and which included not only the bishops and monks but the boyars.

The religious and political views of Maxim the Greek will be dealt with in another volume. Here it would not be amiss to say a few words concerning his position in Russia prior to 1525. When he had been invited to come to Moscow, the immediate task offered to him was to translate commentaries on the Psalms and some other Greek works, as well as to refute the Heresy of the Judaizers. Maxim considered his mission temporary only. The trouble was that when leaving Mount Athos he did not know either Slavic (used by the Russians in their church books), or Russian. He immediately set to learning both languages. As he was a good linguist (knowing Greek and Latin thoroughly), the task was not too hard, but naturally it required time. Two learned Russians, one of them Dmitri Gerasimov, were assigned to work with Maxim. Neither knew Greek; thus Maxim had to translate the original Greek text into Latin, and Gerasimov and his colleague retranslated it into Russian. Later on, Maxim was able to translate directly from Greek to Russian. In both cases, mistakes in translation were unavoidable, and eventually those mistakes served as material for accusations against him by the Josephans.

Maxim was received by Metropolitan Varlaam with great respect.

45. Zhmakin, p. 140.
46. Only part of the *sledstvennoe delo* (official inquiry) concerning Bersen is known. It was published in *AAE, 1,* 141–145. See Zhmakin, pp. 172–173.

Under Varlaam's influence Vasili III was likewise at first favorably disposed toward him; he was regarded as a great reformer, a learned and inspired man who was to advise both the sovereign and the metropolitan how to build up an ideal state and society. Maxim's spiritual and ethical concept of Christianity was congenial to that of the Trans-Volga Hermits (it should not be forgotten that the roots of Nil Maikov's spirituality were also in the wisdom of Mount Athos). The followers of the Trans-Volga Hermits, such as Varlaam and Vassian Patrikeev, could more easily understand and appreciate Maxim than the Josephans. It was but natural, therefore, that Vassian Patrikeev and his friends should establish close relations with Maxim and constantly visit him. In addition to purely religious conversations, some of them, like the disgraced boyar Bersen-Beklemishev, touched on political questions as well. Maxim himself was ready to support wholeheartedly the nonacquirers' opposition to the right of monasteries to own landed estates.

As soon as Varlaam was removed from the Moscow see and Daniel became metropolitan, the nonacquirers lost influence at the grand-ducal court. Daniel at first tolerated Maxim as a learned man but soon changed his attitude, and after Bersen's trial he decided to curb Maxim as well.

At the sobor of 1525 Maxim was accused of wholesale criticism of Russian Church books, of exalting the authority of the Patriarch of Constantinople, and of some dogmatic errors.[47] Accusations on the latter point were the result of misunderstanding based mostly on Maxim's occasional mistakes in Slavic. As regards the authority of the Patriarch of Constantinople, Maxim never concealed his opinion that the Metropolitan of Moscow needed the blessing of the Patriarch. In fact, Maxim considered himself a member of the Greek Church and not subordinated to the authorities of the Russian Church. The trial ended in severe punishment of Maxim, who was imprisoned in the Volok Monastery "for repentance and correction"; he was forbidden to teach anyone, to write anything, or to receive letters.

During his imprisonment Maxim suffered a great deal, both physically and intellectually. Despite the strict regime he found ways to write several epistles in which he defended himself and sharply attacked the deficiences of Russian Church hierarchy. This became known to Daniel, and in 1531 Maxim was subjected to an-

47. Zhmakin, pp. 173–181.

other trial. This time, part of the accusations against him were political. Maxim was accused of pro-Turkish sympathies on the basis of his friendship with a Turkish envoy, the Greek Skinder, who died in Moscow in 1530. At the sobor of 1531 Maxim was found guilty of blasphemy and perversion of the Scripts, and on that ground he was forbidden to partake of the Holy Communion, which was a severe blow to him. He was moved from Volok to the Otroch Monastery in Tver. The Tver bishop was a former monk of the Volok Monastery, and Daniel could be confident that no favors would be shown to Maxim.[48]

After having sealed the fate of Maxim, the sobor of 1531 turned to the alleged crimes of Vassian Patrikeev. Among other things, he was accused by Metropolitan Daniel of following the doctrines of the pre-Christian Greek philosophers, such as Aristotle and Plato. Vassian's sharp polemics against the Josephans on the question of monastery land likewise drew Daniel's wrath. Moreover, Vassian voiced doubts concerning the proposed canonization of Metropolitan Iona and Makari of Kaliazin, both of whom were to be officially canonized in 1547. It seems that in some of his writings Vassian had expressed certain unorthodox views, especially on the divine nature of Christ's body. This enabled Daniel to accuse Vassian of the heresy of Eutychius and Dioscorus—that is, Monophysitism—and of Manichaeism.[49] Vassian was recognized as a heretic by the sobor and sentenced to be imprisoned in the Volok Monastery. There he was thrown into the same prison cell as that formerly occupied by Maxim the Greek, who was now at Tver. Vassian was never allowed to leave the Volok Monastery, and the date of his death there is not known; presumably it was around 1532. The noted opponent of Ivan the Terrible, Prince Andrei Mikhailovich Kurbsky, says that Vassian was "soon starved to death" [50] by the Volok monks, on Vasili III's orders. Kurbsky's explanation of the causes of Vassian's death may be biased, but his dating of the death "soon" after Vassian's imprisonment at Volok seems plausible.

Vasili's second marriage had important results—religious, political, dynastic, and psychological. Religiously and politically, Vasili broke with many people who had been close to him previously. Among these people, as we know, were the spiritual luminary of the

48. *Ibid.*, pp. 185–196.
49. *Ibid.*, pp. 196–232.
50. Kurbsky (Ustrialov's ed.), p. 5.

Orthodox Christianity, Maxim the Greek, and the searcher for religious truth, Vassian Patrikeev. However, the boyar duma as well as the majority of the boyars at large continued to support Vasili and the general policies of Great Russia. There was no change in the position of the boyar council. The new Grand Duchess Elena's uncle—Prince Mikhail Lvovich Glinsky—was soon pardoned by Vasili and came to have great importance in politics. In the duma Glinsky occupied third place, after Prince Belsky and Prince Shuisky.

In 1526 Herberstein accompanied the emperor's envoy to Moscow as a representative of King Ferdinand (brother to the emperor Charles V). The pope also sent his legate. This time Western mediation in the Moscow-Lithuanian conflict proved partly successful, and the truce was renewed for six years, with Smolensk remaining under the authority of Moscow.[51]

As regards the Tatars, the Crimean Horde raided the Moscow border provinces several times but were repulsed each time. They succeeded, however, in doing much harm. Moscow's position in regard to the Khanate of Kazan was greatly strengthened by the building of a new Russian fortress—about halfway between Nizhni-Novgorod and Kazan, on the right bank of the Volga at the mouth of the Sura River, a tributary of the Volga (1522). This fortress, known as Vasil-Sursk (in honor of Vasili),[52] served as a base for further Russian campaigns against Kazan. In 1532 the Kazanians agreed to let Vasili appoint a new khan for them, but they still did not want Shah-Ali. Vasili sent to Kazan Yan-Ali (Enaley), the Tsarevich of Kasimov, Shah-Ali's brother. Moscow's suzerainty over Kazan was thus restored.[53]

Dynastically, Vasili's second marriage solved the problem of succession. On August 25, 1530, Grand Duchess Elena gave birth to her first son, christened Ivan; he was the future Tsar of Russia, Ivan the Terrible. Three years later another son was born to Vasili by Elena: Iuri. The birth of Ivan greatly elated Vasili and brought him a feeling of security in both family and political affairs. He now agreed to the marriage of his youngest brother, Prince Andrei of Staritsa, to Princess Evfrosinia Khovanskaia, who proved to be a very ambitious woman. (The Princes Khovansky were descendants

51. *Sbornik, 35,* 727–731.
52. *PSRL, 13,* 43–44.
53. Veliaminov-Zernov, *1,* 268–271.

of Gedymin). Andrei's and Evfrosinia's wedding was celebrated on February 22, 1533.

For Vasili, the birth of a son was a sign of God's blessing, contradicting the opinion of those who criticized his second marriage, and this made him bolder in his dealings with his opponents. In 1531 he mercilessly crushed both Vassian Patrikeev and Maxim the Greek.

At the time of his second marriage Vasili was forty-seven, and his bride Elena was about half his age. Vasili was apparently greatly enamored of her; under her influence he felt himself younger than he was and wanted to look even younger. Elena had spent her youth in Lithuania and had absorbed many notions and habits of Western civilization and the Western way of life. Vasili, to a certain extent, had now to make concessions to Western habits. He began to shave his beard, which was contrary to the established Muscovite manner.[54] This may seem an insignificant matter to the modern reader, but in view of the extreme conservatism of the Muscovite way of life in the 16th century it had symbolic significance. We should not forget that Peter the Great inaugurated the era of his drastic reforms by personally cutting off the beards of the Russian noblemen in 1698.

Vasili liked to converse with Westerners, such as physicians and engineers. Western ways were closely connected with Western religion. For the Russians of that time—and not only for the Russians, either—religion was the core of culture. Vasili's disappointing experience with Maxim the Greek made him favorably inclined toward Western influence. It was just in Vasili's age that the monolithic grip of the Roman Catholic Church in Europe came to an end, and Protestantism raised its head. The magister of the Teutonic Order became a Lutheran and founded a new lay state, Prussia, in 1525. The new Protestant state was eager to mediate between Moscow and Poland, so that the religious change in Prussia had certain repercussions in the realm of foreign policies.[55] For some time, however, little attention was paid in Russia to Protestantism, and Roman Catholicism remained the symbol of the West there. Throughout Vasili's reign the pope entertained constant hopes that Russia could be converted to the "Roman Faith." [56] In this he was

54. Karamzin, *Istoriia*, 7, 141.
55. See Forstreuter, pp. 101–115.
56. Pierling, *1*, Livre III, chaps. 1–2.

to be disappointed, but undoubtedly Vasili and some of the Russians around him were favorably disposed toward Western learning, as represented by Roman Catholics, even though not ready for conversion to Roman Catholicism.

Vasili's favorite physician was a German from Lübeck, Nicholas Bulev. He was called in Russian sources "Nicholas the German" or "Nicholas the Latin [i.e. Roman Catholic]." Nicholas spent many years in Russia and mastered the Russian language.[57] He was of a lively intellectual disposition and was interested not only in medicine but in astronomy and astrology. As regards religion, he advocated a union between the Eastern and Western churches. He wrote letters to many influential Russians in which he expanded his views, and had many talks with both boyars and prelates. Among his admirers was the boyar Fedor Karpov who learned the Latin language and whom we may call a Russian Westernizer of the 16th century (in terms of 19th-century Russian intellectual history, when the terms "Westernizers" and "Slavophiles" were coined).[58] In short, Nicholas became a popular figure among the Russian intellectual élite of Vasili's time. Nicholas' opinions we know almost exclusively from the polemics against his views by Maxim the Greek as well as by Filofei of Pskov.

On September 21, 1533, Vasili III, together with his consort Elena and their two children, went to the St. Sergius-Trinity Monastery on a pilgrimage. From there Vasili went to Volok for hunting, but soon became ill. His illness started with a boil on his left thigh, which soon grew ominously and caused inflammation. At first Vasili ordered that his illness and blood poisoning be kept secret. He summoned only his physicians and a few boyars to Volok. When Nicholas Bulev arrived, Vasili told him: "Brother Nicholas! You know my great favors to you. Could you not do something, apply some remedy to alleviate my illness?" The physician answered: "Sir, I know your favors to me. If it had been possible, I would gladly injure my own body to help you, but I know no remedy for you except God's help."

Facing the imminence of death, Vasili showed great firmness of spirit. He told those around him: "Brothers! Nicholas was right when he called my illness incurable. Now I have to think how to

57. See Malinin, pp. 256–266.
58. V. F. Rzhiga, "Boiarin-zapadnik XVI veka (F. I. Karpov)," *RANION, 4* (1929), 39–50.

save my soul." Vasili's concerns were to secure the throne for his son Ivan and to be himself ordained monk. He was moved to Moscow, and his wife and children, his two brothers, Metropolitan Daniel, and many boyars gathered in the grand-ducal palace. Daniel and the major boyars were unanimous in recognizing Ivan heir to the throne and in being willing to proclaim him the new grand duke as soon as Vasili would pass away. Vasili's desire to become monk before death was, however, opposed by many. In the confused situation Metropolitan Daniel took the decision upon himself, and the half-conscious Vasili was made monk. He died on December 3, 1533.[59]

Thus a three-year-old boy, Ivan, became the sovereign of all Russia. A regency was established, consisting of Grand Duchess Elena, Metropolitan Daniel, and the major boyars. The success of the regency would depend on the agreement and the cooperation of its members. Such agreement did not last long, and then the troubles started which were to affect painfully not only the boy Ivan but the stability of Great Russia as well.

5. GROWTH OF IMPERIAL IDEOLOGY

The unification of Great Russia and the rise of the authority of the Grand Duke of Moscow under Ivan III and Vasili III resulted, as has been said, in profound changes in the Russian government and administration as well as in the rise of the gentry class that became the cornerstone of the Russian army. The new relations between the grand duke and his subjects, as well as the changed international position of Moscow, could not but be reflected in the growth of new notions on the nature of the power of the grand duke—that is, in a new political ideology. As we know, Ivan III, in the second part of his reign officially established his title in the form of "Sovereign of All Russia." Vasili kept this title. Both of them occasionally used also the title "tsar" (emperor), which was to be formally introduced by Vasili III's son, Ivan the Terrible, in 1547.

Three elements, blending one with another, constituted the contents of the notion of grand-ducal authority. In the first place, we have the traditional idea (now acquiring new meaning) of handing down the grand-ducal power from father to son—that is, the prin-

59. *PSRL*, *6*, 267–276; *13*, 75–77; Soloviev, *Istoriia*, *5*, 395–404.

ciple of *otchina* (heredity). Secondly, Muscovy emancipated herself from the suzerainty of the Mongol khans; the grand duke became thus an independent ruler, a *samoderzhets* (autocrat), in the terms of this period. Here we have the principle of national independence. Thirdly, in 1453 the Byzantine Empire was destroyed by the Ottoman Turks. This brought a far-reaching change in the position of the Great Russian Church as well as in that of the grand duke as an Orthodox Christian ruler. The religious aspects of the power of Moscow's sovereigns were deeply affected by the changes.

While Ivan III had an exalted idea of the dignity of his office, he preferred to proceed cautiously in all his undertakings, as we know. He did not like excessive pomp, or verbose glorification of his power. His main idea, which he expressed in his answer to the German envoy in 1489, was that the "grace of God" was the basic source of the grand-ducal power. "We do not need investiture by anyone else" (see above, p. 13). Ivan never believed that his second wife Sophia gave him any right to the throne of Constantinople; he was interested only in the aggrandizement of the throne of Moscow. He was aware, however, that the disappearance of the Byzantine emperor from the historical stage imposed on him certain responsibilities and obligations, as well as conferred certain rights on him, especially in regard to the administration of the Great Russian Church. From this point of view his role in the installation of Metropolitan Simon, in 1494, is significant (see above, p. 119). It is not accidental that in the late 1490's the Byzantine design of the double eagle became familiar in Moscow as a state emblem. In the last years of Ivan III's reign it was used on grand-ducal seals intermittently with the design of a horseman (with a spear). Under Vasili III the double eagle was represented on one side of the seal, and the horseman on the reverse.[60]

The new notions of the dignity of the sovereign's power were more elaborately expressed in the ceremony of the crowning of Ivan III's grandson Dmitri in 1498 (see above, p. 129). The influence of the Byzantine patterns on this ceremony is obvious. However, the ritual in this case resembled the installation of the Byzantine "caesar"

60. Bazilevich, pp. 87–88. The first representation of the double eagle on a grand-ducal seal known to us dates in 1497. See also *Ocherki*, 2, p, 331. On the archeological background of the emblem of the double eagle see N. P. Kondakov, *Ocherki i zametki po istorii srednevekovogo iskusstva i kultury* (Prague, 1929), pp. 115–119. Cf. A. V. Soloviev, "Les Emblèmes héraldiques de Byzance et les Slaves," *SK, 7* (1935), 119–164.

(*kaisar;* in Slavic, *kesar*), rather than the crowning of the emperor.[61] It should be noted that Dmitri was crowned grand duke, not tsar (emperor), but the term *tsarstvo* (tsardom) was used during the ceremony in the sense of "reign."

In Dmitri's installation the following phases were important: the blessing by the metropolitan; Ivan III's reference to the principles of heredity and seniority; the oration by the metropolitan; the handing of the regalia by the metropolitan to Ivan III and the putting of the regalia on Dmitri by Ivan; an instruction to Dmitri by the metropolitan; and an instruction by Ivan III. This last oration was thus recorded in the chronicle: "Grandson Dmitri! I have favored thee and blessed thee with the grand duchy; do have awe of God, do love truth, mercy, and justice; do care with all thy heart for the whole Orthodox Christianity." [62] Here the love of justice and the care of the Greek Orthodox Church (and people) are pointed out as the basic characteristics of the ideal Russian sovereign. In the beginning of the oration the personal element is emphasized: it was he, Ivan, who "favored" Dmitri with the grand duchy. Apparently Ivan was not able to make a clear distinction between his authority and his person, or rather he believed that the state authority was indissolubly blended with his personality. A great danger could result from this confusion. The difference between the duty of the ruler and the whim of a human being was not established. And indeed, as we know, soon afterward Ivan dismissed Dmitri and "blessed" Vasili with the grand duchy instead. Here obviously lay the weak point of the new authority of the sovereign of all Russia. The danger became only too obvious in the reigns of Ivan's son and grandson.

To confuse the authority of the sovereign and of the man (the bearer of sovereignty) was psychologically easy even for such a great and cautious ruler as Ivan III. In this case, Ivan could also be influenced by the reflections of Byzantine political ideas in Russia. According to Deacon Agapetus of the 6th century, "though an emperor in body is like all the other men, yet in power he is like God." If we suppose that Ivan was influenced by Agapetus, he (or

61. Savva, pp. 118–128. In the Byzantine Empire the term "Caesar" was applied to a secondary rank of office. The Byzantine emperor was known as *Basileus Autokrator*. The Russians used to render *Basileus* as "Tsar" and *Autokrator* as "Samoderzhets," the last term being the literal translation of the word *Autokrator* (Autocrat) into Slavic.

62. *PSRL, 6,* 242.

someone who read it for him) might have found a quotation from Agapetus either in a copy of the Slavic "Bee" (*Pchela*) or in a copy of the Suzdal Chronicle (used there in connection with the death of Prince Andrei Bogoliubsky).[63]

The idea of the divine nature of the sovereign made considerable progress among the Muscovites during the reign of Vasili III. As we know, Herberstein related that the Russians used to say about things uncertain that "God and the Grand Prince know." When the Pskovians were arrested in Novgorod in 1510 by Vasili's order, they were told that they were captured "by God and the Grand Duke."

It was during Vasili's reign that elaborate theories of the high origin of the sovereign's power were developed, mostly by the religious writers. Iosif Sanin, who wrote several epistles to Vasili in connection with the Heresy of the Judaizers, might have called his attention to Agapetus' opinion.[64] No less important were the writings of the former Metropolitan of Kiev, Spiridon, as well as those of Abbot Filofei of Pskov.

Spiridon, a Tverian, was ordained Metropolitan of Russia and sent to Kiev by the Patriarch of Constantinople around 1480. Grand Duke Casimir did not recognize him and had him arrested. Rumors were spread that Spiridon had bribed the Turkish authorities to allow his ordination. Later Spiridon succeeded in escaping to Moscow but was not recognized there either. He was interned in the Ferapon Monastery in the Beloozero region in North Russia. His monastic name was Savva. Spiridon was a learned man and wrote several epistles and religious treatises.[65] Among them was an epistle in which he attempted to place the Russian state in the frame of world history. In this (written in the beginning of Vasili III's reign) he asserted that Rurik, the ancestor of the Russian grand dukes, lived in Prussia and was a descendant of the Roman Emperor Augustus, whose brother Pruss allegedly established himself in the country which after him became known as Prussia. Spiridon also said that the crown (usually called "cap") and other regalia of the Russian

---

63. *PSRL, 1,* Fasc. 2 (2d ed. 1927), col. 370. The quotation there is anonymous but could have been attributed by the readers to St. Paul (a quotation from whom precedes the quotation from Agapetos). On *Pchela* see *Kievan Russia,* pp. 283, 289–290. Cf. Ševčenko, pp. 142–144.

64. *Prosvetitel,* p. 547; Iosif's letters to Vasili III, *AFED,* pp. 513–520; Valdenberg, *Drevnerusskie ucheniia,* pp. 197–220, and "Nastavlenie"; Ševčenko, pp. 156–159.

65. Makari, *9,* 63–68.

grand dukes had been sent to Prince Vladimir Monomakh of Kiev by the Greek Emperor Constantine Monomach.[66] It is probable that Spiridon was acquainted with legends about Rurik that might have originated in Novgorod, as well as with those about the origins of the Russian regalia that probably circulated in Kiev at the time of the Olelkovichi. In any case Spiridon's stories are historical fiction, not pragmatic history. In a sense, however, they made history, since they influenced the development of Muscovite political theories.

Herberstein seems to have been acquainted with the gist of Spiridon's assertions. He said that the cap which belonged to the Russian regalia had been originally worn by Vladimir Monomakh.[67] He also stated that according to the Russians, Rurik and his brothers descended from the Romans.[68] In the 1540's Spiridon's epistle was rewritten and popularized under the name of the "Tale of the Princes of Vladimir." [69] This "Tale" played an important role in the ideology of the Tsardom of Moscow under Ivan the Terrible.

The theory of the Third Rome, as we know (see above, p. 149), was formulated by Abbot Filofei of Eleazar Monastery in Pskov in his letter to Vasili III of 1510. Said Filofei: "Two Romes fell down, the third is standing, and there will be no fourth." [70] Filofei commented that after the fall of the first Rome, the center of true Christianity moved to the second Rome (Constantinople); and after the capture of Constantinople by the Turks, to the Third Rome—Moscow.

In modern times, Filofei's theory has been grossly misunderstood. It has been interpreted in the sense of Moscow's desire to dominate the world—that is, in the sense of Russian imperialism. The theory had no such meaning for Filofei himself. For him, it had an eschatological connotation. As the first two Romes had been destroyed, Moscow remained the only sanctuary of Orthodox Christianity, and the Grand Duke of Moscow was the only remaining Orthodox Christian ruler in the world. Thus new responsibilities and obligations fell on him. He had to guard the last abode of the Orthodox Christian Church and to make Russia a truly Christian power.[71]

---

66. For the text of Spiridon's epistle see Dmitrieva, pp. 159–170.
67. Herberstein–Malein, p. 32.
68. Herberstein–Backus, p. 4.
69. *Skazanie o Kniaziakh Vladimirskikh.* For the text see Dmitrieva, pp. 171–178.
70. Malinin, appendix, p. 55.
71. On the Third Rome see H. Schaeder, *Moskau das Dritte Rom* (Hamburg, 1929); Medlin, *Moscow and East Rome;* O. Ohloblyn, *Moskovska Teoriia III Rimu v XVI–*

It is in this spirit that Vasili III and Metropolitan Varlaam received Maxim the Greek in 1518. But as we know, Maxim believed in the Second Rome, not in Moscow, and was soon repudiated by Vasili. A new experiment of the creation of the Orthodox Christian tsardom was made by Ivan IV, the Terrible, and Metropolitan Makari in the late 1540's and the 1550's. More specifically, Filofei's formula was applied to Ivan IV's coronation.

Be this as it may, ideologically Russia was prepared for tsardom during the reign of Vasili III.

XVII stol. (Munich, 1951); Archimandrite Konstantin [K. Zaitsev], "Chudo Russkoi istorii, I. Vozniknovenie Pravoslavnogo Tsarstva," *Pravoslavnyi Put'* (1951), pp. 108–126; A. V. Soloviev, "Sviataia Rus," *SRAOKS, 1* (1927), 77–113; *idem*, "Helles Russland–Heiliges Russland," *Festschrift für D. Čyževskyj* (Berlin, 1954), pp. 282–289; Oulianoff, "Kompleks Filofeia"; Cherniavsky, "Holy Russia."

Chapter VI

WEST RUSSIA IN THE SIXTEENTH CENTURY

1. Introduction

I

THE MONGOL rule lasted in West Russia for about one century and disintegrated around 1350—that is, one hundred years before it was to come to an end in East Russia. The Mongol domination in West Russia was replaced by that of Poland and the Grand Duchy of Lithuania.

Poland, at first, obtained control over only the westernmost section of the Ukraine by seizing Eastern Galicia in 1349. The balance of Ukraine and the whole of Belorussia recognized the suzerainty of the Grand Duke of Lithuania, who became known as the Grand Duke of Lithuania, Russia and Samogitia [1] (*Veliki Kniaz' Litovsky, Russky i Zhomoitsky*).

While a new political superstructure was thus imposed over West Russia, the Russian people within the framework of the Grand Duchy of Lithuania continued, for some time, to live according to the notions and institutions of the Kievan period. It was only gradually that the new patterns changed the political, religious, social, and economic aspects of life in both Belorussia and the Ukraine.

The interplay of old Russian traditions and new institutions adjusted to the Polish models makes the study of West Russia of the 14th, 15th, and 16th centuries significant for historians and sociologists. The approach of historians to this theme was for many years complicated by the entangled national and religious background in that area of Eastern Europe, which served for centuries as a frontier between the Roman Catholic West and the Greek Orthodox East, and between the Western Slavs and the Eastern Slavs.

1. Samogitia (in Old Russian, *Zhomoit;* in Polish, *Żmudź*) is the name of the north-western part of the Lithuanian area long disputed between the Teutonic Order and Lithuania. It was finally annexed to the Grand Duchy of Lithuania in 1411.

The complexity of the problem, from the historical point of view, is even more accentuated by the fact that this area changed many masters in the course of both the Middle Ages and the modern period, down to our days. In the Kievan period, West Russian lands and principalities were part of the Russian federation centering around Kiev.[2] Then came the Mongols and after them the Lithuanians and the Poles.[3] Ivan III, as we know (see above, p. 86), put forward his claims on the West Russian lands as the legacy of his ancestors, the Kievan Rurikids. By contrast, in the early 17th century, profiting by the "Time of Trouble" in Russia, Poland seemed to have secured the position of undisputed ruler of the whole of West Russia. The Ukrainian Revolution of 1648 greatly undermined the strength of the Polish state and resulted in a union with Moscow of a considerable part of the Ukraine. Through the Polish partitions of 1772–95 the Russian Empire gained all Belorussia and the balance of the Ukraine except for Eastern Galicia, which was annexed by Austria. Following the Russian Revolution of 1917 and the new "Time of Trouble" in Russia, a revived Poland succeeded in seizing back half of Belorussia and the Western Ukraine. After the second World War both Belorussia and the Ukraine were united with Great Russia in the Soviet state. Lithuania, within its ethnic boundaries, likewise became a Soviet republic.

From this brief retrospect of the political destinies of West Russia it is clear that its history is closely interwoven with the development of three states—Russia, Poland, and Lithuania. Within the West Russian area itself two modern East Slavic nations were formed —that of the Belorussians and the Ukrainians.

It is but natural that students of history of all the above nations and states should approach the history of West Russia in the Lithuanian period each from the point of view of his own national historical interest. From the point of view of the Russian historian the main object of study of the Grand Duchy of Lithuania is not so much the history of Lithuania itself as the Russians in the grand duchy, their impact on its policies, and the impact of the Lithuanian administration and Polish institutions on them.

The Russians were legally recognized as one of the two basic nationalities of the grand duchy, the other being, of course, the

2. On the Russian federation of the Kievan period see *Kievan Russia*, pp. 214–240.

3. See *Mongols and Russia*, pp. 233–240, 290–302, 312–332.

Lithuanians. In the Krevo declaration of the Union of the Grand Duchy of Lithuania with Poland, in 1385, King Iagailo (in Polish, Jagiello) declared his intention to "apply" (*applicare*) permanently to the Crown of Poland "his lands of Lithuania and Russia" (*terras suas Litvaniae et Rusiae*).[4]

In the Second Lithuanian Statute of 1566 (Rozdel III, article 9) it is ruled that the grand duke shall never appoint foreigners to the offices of administration but only native Lithuanians and Russians (collectively called *Litva i Rus'*; individually, *Litvin i Rusin*).

Prior to the Union between Poland and Lithuania, the Russian influence in the Grand Duchy of Lithuania was steadily increasing. A number of Lithuanian princes and grandees abandoned paganism and were converted to the Russian Faith (Greek Orthodoxy). Russian methods of administration as well as Russian legal notions were recognized as binding for the entire grand duchy. Russian crafts and agricultural methods continued to follow old traditions. Russian became the language of the grand duke's chancellery, as well as that of many leading Lithuanian princes and nobles, some of whom had Russian wives. It was also the language of administration and courts throughout the grand duchy.

It should be noted that in the 13th and 14th centuries the Lithuanian language was less developed than the Russian in regard to intellectual life, government, administration, and law. It was as late as 1387 that Christianity (in the form of Roman Catholicism) became the state religion of Lithuania. No written literature in Lithuanian existed before that (in fact, not before the 16th century). It was but natural that the Lithuanians had to use the Russian language and script (as they later had to use Latin or Polish).

After the Union of Lithuania with Poland and the conversion of the Lithuanians to Roman Catholicism, a number of Lithuanian nobles and literati began resenting the spread of the Russian language in Lithuania. The Lithuanian author of the 16th century Michalon Litvin (who wrote in Latin) remarked with annoyance that "we [Lithuanians] study the Russian language which contains no urge to valor, since the Russian idiom is foreign to us Lithuanians who are Italians, deriving from Italian blood." Michalon believed that the Lithuanian nation was founded, in the Roman period, by a group of Romans. This legend originated in the 15th century. There are several versions of it. According to one, a few boats

4. *Akta Unji*, p. 2.

manned by Julius Caesar's legionaries were driven by a gale from the North Sea to the southern shores of the Baltic Sea and landed at the mouth of the Nieman River, where they settled and became the forefathers of the Lithuanians. According to another version, the "Roman Prince Polemo," who fled from the wrath of Emperor Nero with his family and retainers, founded the Roman settlement at the mouth of the Nieman.[5]

On the other hand, Maciej Stryjkowski, the Polish writer of the same period as Michalon, advised the Lithuanians not to snub the Russians. He emphasized the fact that the Russians were aboriginal to the land now occupied by the Grand Duchy of Lithuania, and expressed his opinion that the Lithuanians could not even run their courts without the help of the Russians and their language.[6]

Following Lithuania's Union with Poland (1385), Roman Catholicism was proclaimed the state church of Lithuania, and with it came the gradual Polonization of the Lithuanian aristocracy. The Greek Orthodox were at first denied access to the grand-ducal government and administration, and even when the personal rights of the Greek Orthodox princes and boyars were recognized, the tendency to deprive them of their political rights continued in a somewhat modified form. Yet Russian traditions could not easily be eradicated. Although Latin replaced Russian in the relations of the grand duchy with the West, Russian still was used in the state papers and official documents such as ordinances, as well as in the courts.

When the law of the grand duchy was codified, the Lithuanian statutes (the first of them was issued in 1529) were written in Russian. Many of the provisions were based on the traditions of the Russian law of the Kievan period. It is noteworthy that the first Russian printing office was established in Vilna, in 1525—that is, almost three decades before printing started in Moscow.

The negotiations between Lithuania and Moscow were always conducted in Russian. The West Russian language of the 15th and 16th centuries represented a stage in the development of the Belorussian and Ukrainian languages. However, in spite of certain differences, as for example in the vocabulary, between the West Russian and the East Russian (Great Russian), both sides had no difficulty in understanding each other.

5. Lappo, *Zapadnaia Rossiia*, pp. 122, 126.
6. *Ibid.*, p. 122.

II

An important consideration is the numerical strength of the Russian population and its proportion to the total population of the Grand Duchy of Lithuania. Unfortunately, statistical data at our disposal are incomplete. Most of them, belonging to the late 16th and the 17th century, do not give us an adequate picture. But as a basis for tentatively estimating the population of the Russian provinces of the Grand Duchy of Lithuania and Poland in the 14th and the early 15th century we have a list of the Mongol taxation districts of West Russia, the so-called *t'my*. Most of these districts had been originally established in the 13th century, with a few added in the late 14th and early 15th. They do not cover the western part of Belorussia.[7] Another possible angle of approach is by analysis of the numerical strength of the Lithuanian army and an appraisal of its size in proportion to the population of the grand duchy.

In discussing the problem of population, we have to take into consideration the territorial changes of the early 16th century. By the treaty of 1503 the Grand Duchy of Lithuania ceded to Muscovy the Chernigov-Severian area and by that of 1522, Smolensk (see above, pp. 95, 155). In the following estimates the population is considered as of the period after 1522.

Let us now analyze the three bases of calculation indicated above.

(1) Figures of population based on censuses and cadastres of the late 16th century (they refer to Galicia and to the Russian areas incorporated to Poland in 1569 [8]):

Galicia	573,000
Volynia and Podolia	392,000
Kiev and Braslav	545,000
	1,510,000

According to the Ukrainian historian O. Baranovich, the estimate for Volynia and Podolia is too low, since the population of Volynia alone was around 655,000 in 1629.[9]

(2) Figures of population based on the number of the Mongol t'my (200,000 people per one t'ma [10]):

7. See *Mongols and Russia*, pp. 217–218; map, p. 218.
8. Rutkowski, p. 20; Doroshenko, *Narys istorii Ukrainy*, *I*, 139.
9. Doroshenko (n. 8, above).
10. See *Mongols and Russia*, pp. 217–219.

Galicia: 3 t'my	600,000
Volynia and Sokol: 3 t'my	600,000
Podolia: 2 t'my	400,000
Kiev: 1 t'ma	200,000
	1,800,000

As to Belorussia we find in the lists of the t'my one t'ma for Polotsk (and Vitebsk)—of 200,000 people.

(3) Figures which may be computed on the basis of the Lithuanian cavalry army register of 1528.[11] This register includes the Lithuanian and most of the Russian areas of the grand duchy; it does not include Galicia. Kiev and Braslav are not mentioned in the register. The total strength of the mobilized cavalry of the grand duchy amounted to almost 20,000 horsemen. At that time, one horseman was to be mustered from ten "service units" (sluzhby; see below, p. 190). Thus it may be estimated that there existed then about 200,000 sluzhby in the Grand Duchy of Lithuania.

Unfortunately, we do not know how many households the average sluzhba comprised. In fact the sluzhby varied in size in different regions. If we assume that the average figure was three households in a sluzhba and that there were six persons in an average household, then 200,000 sluzhby would mean 600,000 households, indicating a population figure of 3,600,000. To this we have to add the population of the Kiev and Braslav regions (not included in the registry). Thus the figure of the total population of the grand duchy may be tentatively estimated as around 4,000,000.

The breakdown of the figures by provinces and districts shows that the Lithuanian areas of the grand duchy supplied in 1528 about one-half the total number of horsemen. We cannot conclude on this basis, however, that the population of Lithuania proper was equal to that of the Russian provinces of the grand duchy. In the first place, as has been mentioned, the Kiev and Braslav regions did not have to send horsemen to the main Lithuanian army. Presumably the horsemen recruited in these regions were used for the defense of the southern frontier from Tatar attacks. It is possible that only part of the Russian contingents in Volynia were sent to the main army, and most of them were likewise used for the defense of the southern area.

Furthermore, it should be noted that Lithuania and Zhomoit

11. *RIB, 33,* cols. 2–231; Korzon, *1,* 340–341.

usually mustered a higher quota of horsemen than the Russian provinces of the grand duchy. Lithuania had been the cornerstone of the
military organization of the grand duchy in the 14th century, and
continued so in the 15th and the 16th centuries. The grand dukes
considered the Lithuanian contingents the most loyal part of their
army and mobilized them first of all.

When all is said, we may think, then, that the proportion of the
Russian population of the Grand Duchy of Lithuania to the total
population was much higher than can be reckoned on the basis of the
army registry of 1528. Assuming that the total population was
around four million, we may think that the population of the Russian
provinces (not including Galicia, of course, since it was part of
Poland) numbered around three million, and that of Lithuania
proper around one million. This would indicate a ratio of 3 to 1.
In the period between 1450 and 1500 the Russians in the Grand
Duchy of Lithuania must have been considerably more numerous
than this.

III

As regards the political and administrative division of the Russian
area in the Grand Duchy of Lithuania, the old structure of the Russian principalities was gradually shattered by the consequences of
the Mongol invasion and the expansion of Lithuania and Poland in
the late 13th and the 14th centuries. Even though each of the old
Russian lands at first kept its identity, princes belonging to the
House of Rurik gradually lost their sovereign rights and were replaced by the descendants of Gedymin—vassals of the Grand Duke
of Lithuania. The descendants of Rurik—those who did not lose
their rights altogether—remained in some sections of the country as
local dignitaries. It should be noted, however, that many of the new
princes of Lithuanian origin (the Gedyminovichi), accepted the
Russian Faith and Russian culture. Some of them, like the Olelkovichi of Kiev, became prominent champions of the Russian national
movement (see above, p. 46).

By the end of the 15th century the grand duke had succeeded in
eliminating the power of the princes of the large territorial units
(old Russian "lands"), and replacing their reigning princes by
lieutenants appointed by him in concurrence with the *pany rada*
(council of lords) and responsible to him. This was one of the
aspects of gradual transformation of the original loose federation of

"lands," under the suzerainty of the Grand Duke of Lithuania, into an aristocratic monarchy based on the sharp division of society into three sections (*stany*, "orders"), to wit the nobility, the burghers, and the peasants.

The formation of the nobility class with uniform rights and privileges throughout the country, following the Polish pattern, led to the gradual reorganization of local government. Within the class of the nobility there existed a division of interests between the upper aristocratic group and the gentry. The former group consisted of several old princely families as well as nontitled *pany* (lords), some of them of Russian extraction. Members of this group owned large landed estates, filled the most important offices in the government, and constituted the governing council of lords. The members of the gentry (*szlachta*) gradually organized themselves on the provincial level through local assemblies and eventually obtained national representation in the diet.

In the late 14th century and throughout the 15th a number of Russian, or Russianized Lithuanian, princes and noblemen migrated from Lithuania to Moscow and entered the service of the Grand Duke of Moscow (see above, p. 11). Their motives varied. Some resented the curbing of political rights of the Greek Orthodox. Others were dissatisfied with the preponderance of Lithuanian lords over the Russians in the government and administration and the trend toward centralization in the Lithuanian state, to achieve which the grand duke sometimes acted in favor of the lesser gentry in the Russian areas and attempted to contain the authority of the regional princes. Still other West Russian noblemen deserted Lithuania because of family feuds and other personal motives.[12]

2. GOVERNMENT AND ADMINISTRATION

At the time of its formation, in the late 13th and the 14th centuries, the Grand Duchy of Lithuania was a confederation of lands and principalities, Lithuanian and Russian, united by the suzerainty of the grand duke. Each of the lands constituted a sociopolitical unit in itself. In the course of the 15th century the grand dukes attempted to strengthen the authority of the central government over all the territories of the grand duchy.

For a long time, nevertheless, traditions of the old rights of each

12. See Backus, *Motives of West Russian Nobles,* pp. 107–110.

land were hard to eradicate. Each province enjoyed far-reaching autonomy secured by the grand duke's special *privilei* (charter). In the privilei issued to the Vitebsk land in 1561, the grand duke pledged not to compel the inhabitants of this province to move into any other region of the grand duchy (in sharp contrast to the Muscovite policy; see above, pp. 63, 146); not to send the soldiers native to the land to garrison duty in any other land; and not to summon a Viteblianin (inhabitant of the Vitebsk land) to Lithuania for trial. Similar charters were issued to the lands of Polotsk, Smolensk (nine years before its seizure by Muscovy), Kiev, and Volynia.[13] On many occasions the affairs of each of these lands were discussed and conducted by local people—the land-owning nobility and the burghers of the major towns. In Volynia regular provincial assemblies of the gentry functioned on a permanent basis.

The process of strengthening the authority of the central government over the autonomous lands was motivated, as in Muscovy, by both military and financial considerations on the part of the grand duke and the council of lords. In the 14th and early 15th centuries the Grand Duchy of Lithuania was threatened by the Teutonic Order. At the end of the 15th century the Moscow Grand Duke based his claims to West Russian lands on what he regarded as his lawful legacy. Throughout the 15th and 16th centuries the Grand Duchy of Lithuania, as well as Muscovy, was constantly raided by the Tatars, and in the 16th and 17th centuries both West Russia and Poland had to ward off the advance of the Ottoman Turks. Better organization of the economic resources of the country and a more efficient system of administration were needed to meet the ever-increasing difficulties of the Lithuanian state.

One of the first tasks of the grand duke was to put in order those sections of the territory over which he had immediate authority—that is, the *gospodarskie zemli* (crown domains). The bulk of the population of these domains consisted of crown peasants, but part of the crown lands had been turned over to the "crown gentry," those who held sections of crown lands in their capacity of the grand duke's servitors. Their position resembled that of the holders of pomestie in Muscovy, and the very term pomestie was used on many occasions in West Russian documents. Burghers of the smaller towns situated in the area of crown lands likewise were under the direct authority of the grand duke.

13. Liubavsky, *Ocherk*, pp. 86–87.

To make the management of the crown domains more efficient, they were divided into a number of districts, each headed by a grand duke's *namestnik* (lieutenant), known also as *derzhavtsa*. The derzhavtsa was the chief steward and collector of revenue of the crown lands of his district. He was also the military head of the district in charge of mobilization of its people in case of war, and the district judge for the population of the crown lands. The lieutenants were entitled to keep for themselves part of the taxes and court fees they collected, a method of remuneration that corresponded to the kormlenie system in Muscovy.

Outside the bailiwick of the derzhavtsa lay the lands of the nobility—huge domains of the princes and the pany, as well as smaller estates of the gentry. The lords enjoyed the same judicial rights over the population of their estates as the derzhavtsa over that of his district of crown lands. The gentry claimed similar authority over their servitors and the tenant farmers of their lands.

It should be noted that in the second half of the 15th century Polish szlachta had been successful in establishing their right to local self-government, as well as a number of other rights and privileges.[14] The expansion of the gentry rights in Poland could not but accelerate the similar trend in the Grand Duchy of Lithuania. In time of war each lord joined the army with his retainers, and the gentry of each district supplied a separate regiment. For its share in the mobilization of the army the gentry demanded recognition of its political claims, and the grand duke and the council of lords gradually had to yield to these claims. At the same time, however, they tried to establish political and military control of the government over the provinces.

In the middle of the 16th century a balanced system of provincial and district administration was established. The network of districts (*poviety*) constituted the lower stratum of the system. By 1566 the total number of districts was thirty-one. The governor of the district, the starosta, was at the same time the derzhavtsa of the crown domains in the district and the head of the general administration within his district.

For litigation over the gentry land estates a special gentry *sud zemsky* (land court) was established in each poviet. And the gentry of each poviet, when mobilized, constituted a separate military unit

14. Kutrzeba, *1*, 124–127, 168–172; Wojciechowski, pp. 178–183, 252–258.

with its own banner. At the head stood a special officer called a *khorunzhy* of the regiment.[15]

The provinces of the higher layer of provincial administration were called *voevodstva*. Each province included from one to five poviety. At the head of each stood the lieutenant (*namestnik*) or governor general (*voevoda*). Eventually, the latter title was preferred. The voevoda was the derzhavtsa of the central district of the province, the administrative head of the province, the commander-in-chief of all armed forces mobilized within his province in case of war, and the chief justice. His authority extended over the people of the crown lands and the gentry, but not over the lords.

Besides the voevoda, in many a province there was an office of the "commander of the castle" (fortress), called *kashtelian*.

The offices of the voevoda and kashtelian were created in 1413, at first only for Lithuania proper (not including Zhomoit), which was divided on that occasion into two voevodstva, Vilna and Troki. During the principate of Svidrigailo[16] the office of Marshal of Volynia was established. His chief functions were military.[17] In the 16th century Volynia became a regular voevodstvo. In 1471, when Kiev lost the status of principality, the office of the voevoda of Kiev was created. In 1504 the land of Polotsk was made a voevodstvo, and in the 1508 that of Smolensk (seized by the Muscovites in 1514). By 1565, thirteen voevodstva had been established (not counting Smolensk, which at that time belonged to Moscow).

The ethnic composition of three of the voevodstva was predominantly Lithuanian: Vilna (five poviety), Troki (four poviety), and Zhomoit. The latter consisted of only one poviet, and its head was known as starosta not voevoda; his authority, however, was equal to that of the voevody. In all the other voevodstva the Russians constituted the bulk of the population. These provinces were the following:[18]

1. Voevodstvo of Novgorod (Novgorod-Litovsk). This comprised three poviety: Novgorod, Slonim, and Volkovysk.

2. Voevodstvo of Berestie (Brest), consisting of two poviety: Brest and Pinsk.

15. The Slavic word *khorugov* seems to derive from the Mongol term *orunga*, "sign, banner": see Vasmer, *REW, 3,* 206.

16. On Svidrigailo see *Mongols and Russia,* pp. 298–300, 308, 314.

17. Kutrzeba, *2,* 120.

18. Lappo, *Zapadnaia Rossiia,* p. 118.

3. Voevodstvo of Podliashie, three poviety: Belsk, Drogichin, and Melnik.

4. Voevodstvo of Minsk, two poviety: Minsk and Rechitsa.

5. Voevodstvo of Mstislavl, one poviet.

6. Voevodstvo of Polotsk, one poviet.

7. Voevodstvo of Vitebsk, two poviety: Vitebsk and Orsha.

8. Voevodstvo of Kiev, two poviety: Kiev and Mozyr.

9. Voevodstvo of Volynia, three poviety: Lutsk, Vladimir, and Kremenets.

10. Voevodstvo of Braslav, two poviety: Braslav and Vinnitsa.

Two of these provinces, Polotsk and Vitebsk, covered each almost exactly the area of the old Russian principality of the same name. Three of the other voevodstva in the Russian part of the grand duchy (Kiev, Volyn, Minsk) likewise corresponded to the old Russian principalities, in full or in part.

As a result of both the old Russian traditions, still alive in most of the West Russian lands, and the creation of a powerful administrative center in each voevodstvo, provincial government played a much more important role in the Grand Duchy of Lithuania than in Muscovy. On the other hand, the central departments of administration were less developed there than in Moscow.

The main link between the central and the provincial government of the grand duchy was supplied by the aristocracy—the pany. It was they who held the most important offices at both central and provincial levels and who constituted the pany rada (governing council), which not merely advised the grand duke but actually ruled the country.

Juridically, at the top of the Lithuanian-Russian state stood the grand duke. He was traditionally chosen among the descendants of Gedymin, but there was no definite law of succession. After the Union of Lithuania and Poland of 1385 Vitovt, son of Keistut, headed the Lithuanian opposition against his cousin King Iagailo, son of Olgerd, and succeeded in establishing himself as grand duke of Lithuania.[19] Following Vitovt's death (1430), several princes of the House of Gedymin vied for leadership. It was only when Iagailo's youngest son Casimir was proclaimed Grand Duke of Lithuania in 1440 that dynastic peace was restored.[20] In 1447 Casimir was elected King of Poland while remaining Grand Duke of Lithuania. Iagailo's

19. *Mongols and Russia,* p. 240.
20. *Ibid.,* pp. 314–315.

descendants (the Jagellons) thus succeeded in founding a joint Polish-Lithuanian dynasty. The Union between Poland and Lithuania was at first only through the person of the ruler. It was at the Lublin Union of 1569 that the tie between the two states became real (see below, p. 246).

The grand duke was not an autocrat even before the constitutional limitation of his power in favor of the council of lords by the First Lithuanian Statute. It was only in regard to the crown domain that he could act independently, but even in the administration of crown land he actually had to depend on officials who were chosen, by custom, from among the aristocracy. The crown domain was not owned by the grand duke personally, but belonged to his office as sovereign. In addition, the grand dukes and the members of their families owned large landed estates in their own right.

The grand duke also had the authority to collect taxes and fees of various kinds. However, taxes intended for the needs of the army collected from the whole territory of the grand duchy were established by the council of lords and later by the seim. Taxes derived from the exploitation of the crown domains could be imposed by the grand duke himself. Actually, these too were usually approved by individual members of the council of lords, even though not necessarily by the whole council.

The grand duke also possessed certain important royal prerogatives ("regalia") such as for coinage and the selling of salt and alcohol. The prerogative of selling alcoholic beverages was known as "the right of *propinatsia*." The grand duke could and often did transfer his rights of keeping taverns (*korchmy*) to private persons for a suitable fee, or grant it to the persons he wanted to favor. Thus many noblemen were able to acquire the right. In Poland the szlachta received the exclusive right of *propinacja* by virtue of the Statute of Piotrków, 1496.[21]

It may be added that the distilled alcoholic beverage now internationally known under the Russian name of vodka was first mentioned in the documents of the Grand Duchy of Lithuania in the very beginning of the 16th century.[22] It was called *goreloe vino* (distilled wine), hence the Ukrainian word *gorelka* (*horilka*).

The grand duke was assisted by a number of state dignitaries whose offices were established on the Polish model and whose titles

21. Grabieński, p. 94.
22. Dovnar-Zapolsky, p. 426.

were mostly of Polish origin. The Polish offices of this type had been originally connected with the prince's household (court offices, *urzędy dworskie*). In the course of the 13th and 14th centuries they became offices of the royal administration.[23]

Closest to the grand duke among his assistants was the marshal of the land (*marshalok zemsky*). This official was in charge of order and etiquette at the grand duke's court as well as at the meetings of the diet. In case of the grand duke's absence from the meetings of the council of lords, the marshal of the land represented there the person of the sovereign. His deputy was called the marshal of the court. He was at the head of the court servitors (dvoriane). Other court offices were those of the master of the beverages, the carver of the meat, the master of the stables, and so on.

Of greater importance were the chancellor; the treasurer of the land; his deputy, treasurer of the court, who was in charge of the grand duke's treasury; [24] the commander-in-chief; and his deputy, the field commander. In wartime the commander-in-chief had complete control of the army, especially during a distant campaign.[25]

None of these officials had political power; affairs were directed by the council of lords, and the influence some of the highest dignitaries had was based chiefly on their membership in the council. Otherwise they merely executed the council's decision.

The council of lords finally consolidated itself under Casimir and his sons. By that time its membership had expanded so much that the plenary meetings of the council were convoked only when the diet was in session, or on other special occasions.

At the plenary meetings of the council the front-row seats were occupied by the Roman Catholic Bishop of Vilna, the Voevoda of Vilna, the Voevoda and the Kashtelian of Troki, and the Starosta of Zhomoit. In the seats of the second row were the Roman Catholic bishops of Lutsk, Brest, Zhomoit, and Kiev; beside them sat the Voevoda of Kiev, the Starosta of Lutsk, the voevody of Smolensk and Polotsk, the Starosta of Grodno,[26] and the voevody of Novgorod

23. Kutrzeba, *1*, 77 and 154–162; Wojciechowski, pp. 66–69, 241–244, 267–279.

24. The existence of two treasuries reflected the basic division of the revenue of the grand duchy into two categories: the land taxes and the fees collected by the grand duke. In the 15th and 16th centuries both these sources of revenue were used chiefly on state needs. The grand duke's personal income was separated from his income as sovereign. See Dovnar-Zapolsky, pp. 2–6.

25. The commander-in-chief, as well as his deputy, was known as *hetman*. The term "hetman" derives from the German "Hauptmann": see Vasmer, *REW, 1,* 266.

26. The poviet of Grodno belonged to the voevodstvo of Troki.

(Novgorod-Litovsk), Vitebsk, and Podliashie. The highest dignitaries—the marshals and the hetmans—had no specially designated seats, since usually a marshal or a hetman combined his office with that of voevoda or starosta. The lesser court officials had their seats behind the second row.[27]

In the intervals between the plenary sessions of the council, its inner circle, known as the supreme or privy council (*naivysshaia*, or *tainaia*, rada), functioned on a permanent basis. This inner circle consisted of the Roman Catholic Bishop of Vilna (and any other Catholic bishop if he was present at the place of the meeting of the council), all the voevody who were members of the rada, the starosty of Zhomoit and Lutsk, the two marshals, and the secretary of the treasury.

The council of lords, and more specifically its inner circle, was the main driving power of the government. The constitutional authority of the council was formulated in the Charters of 1492 and 1506 and finally guaranteed by the First Lithuanian Statute of 1529. According to this latter, the sovereign (gospodar) pledged to keep intact all of the former laws and to make no new laws without the consent of the council (Rozdel III, article 6).

The lords played a prominent role in the foreign affairs of the Grand Duchy of Lithuania. They represented the duchy in the latter's negotiations with Poland, as well as in those with Muscovy.

In 1492 and 1493, in the preliminary parleys concerning the proposed marriage between Ivan III's daughter Elena and Grand Duke Aleksandr of Lithuania (see above, p. 86), three Lithuanian lords took prominent part, Ian Zaberezinsky, Stanislav Glebovich, and Ian Khrebtovich. Each visited Moscow in turn. Zaberezinsky and Glebovich established friendly relations with the senior Moscow boyar, Prince Ivan Iurievich Patrikeev (who it will be recalled, was a descendant of Gedymin), and some other Muscovite boyars.[28] When Princess Elena arrived in Lithuania and was nearing Vilna, she was greeted by Prince Konstantin Ivanovich Ostrozhsky and princes Ivan and Vasili Glinsky.

In November 1493 a Lithuanian *velikoe posolstvo* (grand embassy) was sent to conclude a peace treaty between Lithuania and Moscow (see above, p. 86). The embassy consisted of three lords: Petr Ianovich (who was Voevoda of Troki and marshal of the land),

27. Liubavsky, *Ocherk*, pp. 184–185.
28. Bazilevich, pp. 306–312, 372.

Stanislav Kezgailo (Starosta of Zhomoit), and Voitekh Ianovich. Simultaneously, the Lithuanian council of lords sent a letter to Prince Patrikeev asking him to sponsor the establishment of friendly relations between the two states. The letter was signed by the Roman Catholic Bishop Ian of Lutsk and Brest, Petr Ianovich (member of the embassy), Prince Aleksandr Iurievich Holshansky (lieutenant of Grodno), and Stanislav Kezgailo (member of the embassy).[29]

Attempts of the Lithuanian council of lords to establish close relation between it and the boyar duma of Moscow were shattered by Prince Patrikeev's disgrace in 1499 (see above, p. 127); but even after that the exchange of envoys between Lithuanian and Moscow often resulted in personal contacts between the nationals of the two countries. Among the Lithuanian envoys who visited Moscow in the first half of the 16th century was a Sapega (in 1508), two Kishkas (1533 and 1549), a Glebovich (in 1537 and again in 1541), a Tyshkevich (1555), and a Volovich (1557). During his sojourn in Moscow in 1555 Iuri Tyshkevich, a Greek Orthodox, visited Metropolitan Makari of Moscow and asked for his blessing.[30]

The council of the lords of the Grand Duchy of Lithuania may be compared to the Polish senate—the upper chamber of the Polish diet (*sejm*). The lower chamber in that diet was the chamber of the deputies from the district gentry—*izba poselska* (chamber of the envoys).

The *sejmiki* (district assemblies) of the Polish szlachta took definite shape in the second half of the 15th century. It is at these assemblies that the gentry elected their deputies to the national diet.[31]

Under Polish influence the gentry of the Grand Duchy of Lithuania likewise began to aspire to both district self-government and national representation. To achieve this the gentry took advantage of political or military circumstances under which the grand duke or the council of lords, or both, were in special need of the active assistance of the gentry. At first, only the representatives of the Lithuanian gentry were called, to help the mobilization of the army for a major war, or to support the interests of the grand duchy in the conflicts and negotiations with Poland. The first national diet (*seim*) [32]

29. *Ibid.*, p. 318.
30. Makari, *9*, 286–287; *PSRL*, *13*, 248–249.
31. See Kutrzeba, *1*, 169–176; Wojciechowski, pp. 252–263.
32. The usual form of the term in West Russian documents is *soim*. I use here the form *seim* since it has entered the modern Russian language and is common in Russian historical literature.

of the grand duchy—in which representatives participated not only from Lithuania proper but from the Russian provinces as well—took place in 1492 after the death of Casimir, for the elections of a new grand duke.[33]

After that, representatives of the gentry participated in the meetings of the diet whenever this was convoked. The voevody were instructed to arrange that two gentry deputies from each poviet be invited to attend the diet. The district electoral diets of the gentry (seimiki) did not function regularly at that time. The gentry deputies were at first not elected but nominated by the provincial or district officials. It was only in the reign of Sigismund II August (1548–72) that the gentry district diets were officially recognized and obtained the right of electing "envoys" to the national diet. This right was granted by the Vilna Charter of 1565 and confirmed by the Second Lithuanian Statute of 1566 (Rozdel III, articles 5 and 6).

What part did the Russians play in the government and administration of the Lithuanian-Russian state? In view of the fact that the majority of the population of the grand duchy was Russian and that the Russian language predominated in both the administration and the courts, it might be expected that Russians would have a major share in the government. Actually, this was not quite the case.

Among the factors that prevented Russian control of the government was the strong position occupied by the Roman Catholic Church. It will be recalled that it was proclaimed the state church of Lithuania in the provisions of the first Union with Poland. Afterward the Lithuanian people were converted to Roman Catholicism. The first Catholic bishopric established in Lithuania was that of Vilna. In 1417 another was created in Zhomoit. Twelve years later two Catholic bishops were instituted in the Ukrainian area—that of Lutsk and of Kiev. One more Catholic bishopric was organized in Brest. As the Ukrainian people at this time belonged to the Greek Orthodox Church, the establishment of Roman Catholic bishoprics in the area could actually serve only small groups of population, chiefly Lithuanians and Poles residing in the Ukraine. However, this action inaugurated an ambitious program of Roman proselytism in the Ukraine.

By the terms of the Charter of 1434 the existence of the Greek Orthodox Church in the grand duchy was recognized, and the Ortho-

33. Kutrzeba, 2, 140.

dox people were promised equality of rights with the Catholics. The promise was repeated by Casimir in 1447. Nevertheless, no Orthodox prelate was ever admitted to the council of lords. On the other hand, as has been mentioned above, all the Catholic bishops were given permanent seats in the council.

As to the lay members of the council, there were both Lithuanians and Russians among them. In the middle of the 16th century the most influential position in state affairs belonged to the Radivils (a Lithuanian clan). However, some of the Russians, like the Princes Ostrozhsky, the Khodkevichs, and the Volovichs were also prominent in the council. The situation in regard to the holders of the offices of central and provincial administration was similar.[34]

In the charter issued at Belsk in 1564 the following Russian (or Russianized) dignitaries were mentioned:[35] Ian Ieronimovich Khodkevich, Starosta of Zhomoit; Prince Konstantin Konstantinovich Ostrozhsky (son of Konstantin Ivanovich), Voevoda of Kiev and marshal of Volynia; Pavel Ivanovich Sapega, Voevoda of Novgorod-Litovsk; Prince Stephan Andreevich Zbarazhsky, Voevoda of Vitebsk; and Ostafi Volovich, marshal of the court and secretary of the treasury. These persons also witnessed the sealing of the charter. Among other Russian witnesses were Grigori Aleksandrovich Khodkevich, Iuri Aleksandrovich Khodkevich, Vasili Tyshkevich, Prince Aleksandr Fedorovich Chartoryisky, and Prince Andrei Ivanovich Vishnevetsky.

Despite the prominent position occupied by some Russian dignitaries, they represented no organized group. There was no "Russian party" in the council of lords. Most of the Russian lords were loyal to the Grand Duchy of Lithuania and satisfied with their own position in the government.

There was, it seems, more national self-consciousness among the Russians in some of the provinces, such as Smolensk, Polotsk, Vitebsk, Kiev, and Volynia. In many cases, however, difference of social and economic interests developed there, as in other parts of

34. For the names of the members of the council of lords, as well as those of the dignitaries in the central and provincial administration, see Liubavsky, *Seim; idem, Oblastnoe delenie;* Leontovich, "Rada"; Lappo, *Velikoe Kniazhestvo Litovskoe, 1;* Hrushevsky, *Istoriia Ukrainy-Rusi, 5.* There are indices of names in all these works except for Leontovich's. There are very useful lists of provincial and district office holders in Backus, *Motives,* pp. 61–78, 153–154.

35. The privilei of Belsk of 1564 is printed above the II Lithuanian Statute, *Vremennik, 23* (1855). For the names quoted above see pp. 6–7 and 10 in that edition.

Lithuania, between the aristocracy and the gentry, which undermined the feeling of ethnic unity. As it became plain at the seim of
Lublin (1569), the dissatisfaction of the Ukrainian gentry with its
position greatly contributed to the transfer of the Ukrainian provinces from Lithuania to Poland at that time.

The nobility of the Russian provinces of the grand duchy constituted but a minority of their population; the majority were
peasants. These latter, however, had no voice in the government. It
was only the nobility who constituted the nation, politically.

3. THE ARMY

There was no standing army in the Grand Duchy of Lithuania.
The armed forces were mobilized whenever an enemy attacked, or
was expected to attack, the confines of the grand duchy, or when an
offensive against an enemy was planned.[36] The First Lithuanian
Statute of 1529, in Rozdel II, ruled that "every landowner is bound
to serve during the war."

Cavalry was the main branch of the army. It was indispensable in
the steppe warfare against the Tatars, as well as in distant campaigns
against the Teutonic Knights, and later against Muscovy. The art of
horsemanship, as well as that of breeding horses, could best flourish
on landed estates, especially the large ones. This was one of the
reasons for the leading role of the aristocracy and the gentry in the
mobilization of Lithuanian armed forces. Besides, each nobleman
was considered a natural military leader of his retainers. The Lithuanian army, therefore, consisted mainly of two categories of horsemen: (1) the lords and their retainers and (2) the district gentry
regiments. It was the lords who mustered the core of the army of the
grand duchy.

On the basis of the army register of 1528 it may be estimated that
the dignitaries mustered about 8,000 horsemen—that is, about two-
fifths of the Lithuanian cavalry army. It would not be amiss to note
here the names of the princes and lords who supplied the largest
contingents, by families. The Kezgailos mobilized 768 horsemen; the
Radivils, 621; the Gashtovts, 426; the Princes Ostrozhsky, 424; the
Ostikovichs, 337; the Glebovichs, 279; the Zaberezinskys, 258;
the Kishkas, 244; the Princes Sanguszko, 170; the Ilyinichs, 160; the
Zenovevichs, 155; the Princes Holshansky, 154; the Sapegas, 153;

36. Liubavsky, *Ocherk*, pp. 207–211; Kutrzeba, *2*, 172–177; Korzon, *1*, 331–343.

Prince Mstislavsky, 152; and so on down the scale.[37] The importance of the share of the lords in the mobilization of the army helps to explain their leading role in the government and administration.

Foot soldiers (*draby*) were rarely used in the regular army except in cases of local or national emergency.

Besides the nobility, the burghers were also expected to muster horsemen for the grand duchy's army (see below, p. 212). Both the noblemen and the burghers who sent their contingents were expected to defray the cost of maintenance throughout the war. When the army invaded a foreign country, it lived off the resources of the land conquered. In the first quarter of the 16th century the customary requirement was to muster one fully equipped horseman per each ten *sluzhby* (service units). In 1529 the ratio was changed to one horseman per each eight service units. The nobleman who controlled only eight sluzhby or less was bound to appear at the mobilization in person. According to the decision of the diet of 1507, a hundred-ruble fine was established for everyone who failed to appear at the mobilization place at the appointed date. Anyone who failed to appear at all or who left the army before the end of the campaign was subject to capital punishment. The diet of 1514 threatened with capital punishment and confiscation of property even those who did not appear in time.

Despite the severity of the laws, the mobilization quota was usually not filled, and if the war lasted long a number of the gentry would go home, arguing that otherwise their estates would be ruined. For this and other reasons the grand dukes tried to strengthen their military forces by hiring professional soldiers, as was done in this period in Poland and Germany. These were known as *zholners*. They were usually recruited in Czechia, Moravia, and Silesia, for a definite term or for the duration of a campaign. Under Sigismund I five thousand were engaged. Part were employed regularly to man the castles erected along the southern border of Ukraine to protect the country against the Tatar raids. These were paid by the quarter of the year. Among the best of the mercenary troops were the companies of Czech soldiers and artillerists who enjoyed high military reputation in both Poland and Lithuania.[38]

The cost of maintaining mercenary troops was high. During cer-

37. *RIB, 33* (1915), 2–231. See also Liubavsky, *Seim*, pp. 355–360; *idem, Ocherk*, p. 135; Hrushevsky (above, n. 34), *5*, 31; Korzon, *1*, 340–341.
38. A. Florovsky, *Chekhi, 2*, 302–322.

tain periods when several thousand officers and soldiers were on the payroll, the yearly expenditure for hired troops amounted from three to six million *groshi* (25,000 to 50,000 rubles). This was a heavy burden on the grand duke, who on many occasions had to mortgage part of the crown estates to meet the expenses. To improve the finances of the grand duchy the diet of 1507 voted a special *sereb-shina* (silver tax) to be paid by all the owners or holders of land estates.

In addition to the mercenary troops, the grand dukes tried to harness to their army machine certain groups of population which were specially fit for military service. In the late 14th century Grand Duke Vitovt settled in the regions of Troki and Novgorod-Litovsk several thousand Tatars, some of whom were prisoners of war and others of whom had gone over to the Lithuanian side because they had participated in the strife between two Tatar khans and their candidate had been defeated.[39]

In the 15th century more Tatars, Nogays, and Chuvashians migrated to Lithuania. All of these eventually became known as Tatars. Their number in the 16th century amounted to four thousand. The Tatars manned the chain of forts west of Vilna and Troki to protect Lithuania from the attacks of the Teutonic Knights. They were granted land estates on condition of military service. Many had servitors and tenant farmers under their control, a quota of whom they had to muster at the time of mobilization. Others, known as Cossacks, could offer only their own persons for military service. The status of the former group was equal to that of the gentry. The regiment formed by them was commanded by an officer of their own who had the title of *khorunzhy*, just like the commanding officer of the district gentry regiments. The Cossacks were organized in companies each headed by an ataman.[40]

---

39. See *Mongols and Russia*, pp. 280–282.

40. For a list of Tatar princes and Cossacks in the Lithuanian army see the army register of 1528, *RIB, 33,* cols. 109–120. See also the registry of the Lithuanian army of 1565, *RIB, 33,* cols. 425–430. On the Tatars in the Lithuanian service see Stökl, pp. 123–135. I am indebted to Mr. S. Szyszman for the following bibliography of the Lithuanian Tatars: S. Kryczyński, *Tatarzy Litewscy* (Warsaw, 1938); M. Tuhan Baranowski, *O muślimach Litewskich* (Warsaw, 1896); A. Mukhlinsky, *Issledovanie o proiskhozh- denii i sostoianii Litovskikh Tatar* (St. Petersburg, 1857); L. Krichinsky [Kryczyński], *Bibliograficheskie materialy o Tatarakh Polski, Litvy, Belorussii i Ukrainy* (St. Petersburg, 1917); D. Aleksandrovich, "Litovskie Tatary," *Izvestiia Obshchestva obsle- dovaniia i izucheniia Azerbaidzhana, 2* (1926), 77–95; Michalon Lituanus, *De moribus Tartarorum, Lituanorum et Moschorum* (Basileae, 1615).

Some of the Tatars settled in cities and occupied themselves with trade in horses and cattle. In the border provinces between Muscovy and Poland on the one hand and the Tatar steppes on the other, Russian Cossacks likewise gradually organized themselves. More about the Cossacks in Lithuania and Poland will be said later (pp. 249–268).

Still another social group, small in size, found its place in the defense system of the Grand Duchy of Lithuania. This was the Karaites (below, pp. 216–219).

4. SOCIAL CLASSES

The role of the nobility—the lords and the gentry—in the formation and activities of the government and administration of the Grand Duchy of Lithuania, as well as in the army, has been delineated in the two preceding sections. The nobility, however, in spite of their political supremacy, were but a fraction of the nation. It is the peasants who constituted the bulk of the people, both in Lithuania proper and in the Russian areas of the grand duchy. The third distinct group was the townspeople. They were neither numerous nor influential politically, but they played a role of considerable importance in the development of commerce, as well as in crafts. Closely connected with the towns were the Jews and the Karaites, who were organized in communities of their own.

It should be noted that outside this system of social classes was a group deprived of personal freedom and personal rights—the slaves. Historically, the slaves in the Grand Duchy of Lithuania, like those in Muscovy, were a leftover of Russia's social structure of the Kievan period.

Apart from the slaves, the evolution of each of the main three social classes—the nobility, the peasants, and the townspeople—presents certain common traits. The general tendency, within each class, was toward uniformity of rights or obligations. In the earlier period, when the unification of the West Russian lands under the suzerainty of the grand duke had been just completed, there was throughout the grand duchy a diversity of rights and variety in the position of the diverse groups of noblemen, peasants, and townspeople, in various parts of the new state. Later the government tried to reduce to a common legal standard, on a Polish model, the rights of different territorial and fragmentary social groups. The nobility itself strove for uniformity of rights and privileges. In that way the nobility became the nation, politically. The only obligation the nobleman recognized was that of military service.

As for the peasants, the new tendency was that of curbing their rights and defining more strictly their obligations. This led finally to restriction of their freedom. The peasants became a downtrodden social class, the main duty of which was to supply to the grand duke or the noblemen either their labor or the proceeds of their labor (in kind or in money), or both. The peasants thus became "men of burden" (*liudi tiaglye*).

The fate of the townspeople in the Grand Duchy of Lithuania was greatly affected by the desire of the Lithuanian government to break the remnants of the old Russian city commune, based as it had been on the veche. The introduction of municipal corporations according to the Magdeburg law considerably changed the life of the towns and the position of the townspeople.

Besides the social classes mentioned above, two more groups should be listed, one old and one newly formed—the clergy and the Cossacks. They will be dealt with below (pp. 249–273).

5. THE ARISTOCRACY

It will be recalled that the aristocracy of the Grand Duchy of Lithuania consisted of families of two categories, the princes and the nontitled lords.[41]

Most of the princes were descendants of either Rurik or Gedymin, but some of them derived from the Lithuanian minor princes who ruled portions of a Lithuanian territory before Gedymin's reign, or under Gedymin as their suzerain. The Princes Glinsky were of Mongol extraction (above, pp. 138–139).

The nontitled lords derived from the Lithuanian or Russian boyars who had been councilors of either Gedymin or the Russian princes of the House of Rurik, such as those of Smolensk, Polotsk, Vitebsk, and Kiev.

The princes possessed inherited suzerainty rights to their domains as well as to the people settled in their lands. The power and

---

41. On the nobility of the Grand Duchy of Lithuania see Kutrzeba, *2*, 45–62; Backus, "Die Rechtsstellung der litauischen Bojaren"; Liubavsky, *Seim*, pp. 311–427; Lappo, *Velikoe Kniazhestvo Litovskoe*, *1*, 254–266; Hrushevsky (above, n. 34), *5*, 27–40; J. Wolff, *Kniaziowie litewsko-ruscy od końca czternastego wieku* (Warsaw, 1895).

prestige of the lords was based on their immense landed estates and wealth. Some of the lords were mightier than princes. The juridical status of the nontitled lords had rested, at first, on old customs and traditions. It took more definite shape, on the Polish model, after the first treaty of Union of Lithuania with Poland in 1385, and the subsequent agreements with Poland as well as the grand duke's *privilei* to Lithuania.

In Poland the "rights of knighthood" (*prawo rycerskie;* in Latin, *jus militare*) comprised the nobleman's immunity from the authority of the king's officers, hereditary ownership of landed estates, and jurisdiction over the population of these estates. Each noble clan received, on the West European model, a coat of arms (*herb*) of its own.[42] The rights of knighthood were soon extended in Poland to the whole gentry (*szlachta*). In Lithuania, at first only the lords received the fullness of these rights (*plenum jus militare*) and full jurisdiction (*judicia maiora*) over the population of their estates.

According to the grand ducal charter of 1387 the Lithuanian boyars were granted the rights and privileges of the Polish szlachta, but the rights of the gentry in Lithuania were not yet defined at that time. By the Charter of Horodlo of 1413 the Lithuanian boyars were entitled to have a coat of arms. Forty-seven Polish noble families "adopted" each a Lithuanian boyar family, extending to it its own (Polish) coat of arms.

The old Russian term "boyar" was replaced by that of *pan*, an old Slavic word for lord. The term "boyar" was still used, but now changed in its connotation, being applied only to certain groups of the lower gentry, except for Smolensk, Polotsk, and Vitebsk, where the term kept its original connotation.

One of the important privileges of the lords was that of providing at the mobilization of the army their own regiments (consisting mostly of their retainers) under their own command and their own banners. In this respect they were known as the "banner lords" (*pany khorugovnye*). Furthermore, the lords were exempted from the jurisdiction of the grand duke's lieutenants and starosty, and subject only to that of the grand duke himself.

As regards the territorial distribution of the main landed estates of the princes and the nontitled lords, a major cluster of princely families was located in Volynia. The enormous estates of nontitled

42. Kutrzeba, *1*, 40–47, 121–127; Wojciechowski, pp. 171–183.

lords were situated chiefly in Lithuania proper and in Podliashie.[43]

Among the princes of Russian extraction settled in Volynia were the Ostrozhskys, the Chartoryiskys, the Vishnevetskys, the Zbarazhskys, and some others. In eastern Belorussia the principality of Mstislavl played a political role of considerable importance because of its location in the border area between Lithuania and Muscovy. The original Princes Mstislavsky ("of Mstislavl") derived from Olgerd. In the late 15th century Prince Mikhail Ivanovich Zaslavsky (Zheslavsky), a descendant of Olgerd's brother Iavnuti, married a Princess Mstislavskaia and assumed the title. In 1526 Prince Mikhail I. (Zaslavsky) Mstislavsky's son, Prince Fedor Mstislavsky, went over to the Muscovite side and was given a prominent position among Moscow boyars. Both these princely families—the Zaslavskys and the Mstislavskys—belonged to the Greek Orthodox Church and were Russianized.

The Russian princes of another border area, the Upper Oka region (the so-called "upper towns," *verkhovskie goroda*), recognized the suzerainty of the Grand Duke of Moscow in the late 15th and early 16th centuries (see above, pp. 86, 95). On the other hand, in the reign of Casimir some of the East Russian princes fled from Muscovy to Lithuania. Of these, the Princes Shemiachich and the Princes Mozhaisky were settled in the Severian land. They were lured to Moscow and their domains confiscated in the reign of Vasili III (p. 157).

Many of the mightiest nontitled lords were Lithuanians. Those of Russian extraction were descendants of old Russian boyars. Thus the Khodkevichs, the Volovichs, and probably the Khrebtovichs (Chreptowicz), derived from the Kievan boyars, and the Sapegas presumably from the Smolensk boyars. According to Liubavsky, the Ilyinichs and the Glebovichs were descendants of the Polotsk boyars, but Hrushevsky doubts it. It is probable that the Kishkas of Podliashie were likewise of Russian ancestry, but there is no definite evidence of it.[44]

Many of the lords were interested not only in the administration and management of their huge landed estates, but in learning and arts as well. They absorbed European culture and were affected by the spirit of the Renaissance and Reformation. They collected books, paintings, and sculpture in their palaces and founded schools and printing presses.

43. Hrushevsky (above, n. 34), *5*, 32–33.
44. *Ibid.*, p. 31.

6. THE GENTRY

As has been said, at the time of the formation of the Grand Duchy of Lithuania there was no unified gentry class in it. In the lands under the suzerainty of the grand duke there were various and different groups of medium size and petty landowners who were ready to give military service whenever necessary and who were either members of local defense organizations or servitors of the grand duke, of princes, or of boyars.

It will be recalled that after the Union of Lithuania with Poland, the rights and privileges of the nobility were defined in terms of the Polish *jus militare,* but this latter was at first applied only to the lords and the upper layer of Lithuanian gentry. It was only gradually that the new rights were extended to the bulk of the gentry in the Russian areas of the grand duchy.

For a long time, local groups of small landowners or landholders lived according to their old customs and were known under traditional group names. Some were called *dvoriane* (court men); others, *slugi* (servitors); still others, *boyare-szlachta* (boyar gentry). A considerable group was known as *zemiane* (land-born people). A number of other terms were also used to designate small local categories of landholders and military servitors.

The two most important groups of all were the zemiane and the boyare-szlachta. The term "zemiane" was widely used in the Kiev land, in Volynia, and in Podliashie, but there were zemiane in other Russian lands of the grand duchy as well. Likewise, the boyare-szlachta are mentioned in Smolensk, Polotsk, Vitebsk, and also in Kiev, but they existed in other regions. The term "boyare-szlachta" (boyar gentry) corresponds to that of *deti boyarskie,* "boyar sons," used in Muscovite Russia (see above, p. 6).

In the First Lithuanian Statute both the zemiane and the boyare-szlachta are mentioned in the sense of members of the szlachta class. (First Statute, Rozdel II, article 10, and Rozdel III, article 11). The term "szlachta" is used in the statute as the generic term for the gentry. Rozdel III of the statute is entitled "On the Liberties of the Szlachta."

From the point of view of state interest, the main function of the gentry was that of military service. On this basis, the gentry of the grand duchy may be classified in two basic categories according to the order in which various groups were mobilized. We may thus discern (1) those who served in the district regiments (*khorugvi*, "banners"), each under the authority of the district commander (*khorunzhi*); and (2) those who served in the "banners" of the lords; in this case the lord was considered the *pan khorugovny* (banner lord).

The bulk of the szlachta served in the district banners, which means that they were under the suzerainty of the grand duke, not of the lords. Some of the members of the szlachta had the right of "eternal" ownership on their ancestral estates. This type of landed estate may be compared to the *votchina* in Eastern Russia. Other noblemen were granted only limited rights on the land—each for his life (*do zhivota*); for "two lives" (*do dvukh zhivotov*)—that is, for the use of the grantee and his son; or for "three lives" (*do trekh zhivotov*)—that is, for the use of the grantee, his son, and his grandson. A grant of this kind was sometimes called pomestie —the same term used in Muscovy (above, p. 116). Its purpose was to enable the noblemen to perform adequately the military service he owed the state. As a matter of fact, even the owner with "eternal" rights on the estate could keep it only if he fulfilled his obligation of military service; if he refused to serve, his land was subject to confiscation. Another limitation of the status of the eternal owner of the estate was that the grand duke could, at his pleasure, release his sovereignty over the estate and its holder to a prince or a nontitled lord. It was only as late as 1529 that the grand duke solemnly promised, for himself and his descendants, never to transfer the gentry estates to the authority of princes or lords.

On the basis of what has been said, it is obvious that the position of the gentry in the Grand Duchy of Lithuania, in regard to its rights on land, was precarious in comparison with that of both the lords and the Polish szlachta.

The situation changed drastically with the adoption of the Second Lithuanian Statute, in 1566, which decreed (Rozdel II, article 2) that henceforth the army should be mobilized only with the approval of the seim, except in the case of sudden enemy attack. Even in such cases no taxes were to be collected before the meeting of the seim. Simultaneously, the grand duke promised that the landed estates of the gentry should not be taken away from their owners or holders (Rozdel III, article 4). As has been mentioned before (p. 187), the Second Statute also gave the szlachta the rights of dis-

trict self-government and of the election of deputies to the seim by
district assemblies (Rozdel III, article 5). The gentry thus received
not only a guarantee of its rights on land but also the control over
the mobilization and financing of the army—that is, the control of
the military service on which the gentry's use of landed estates had
been founded.

Even before 1566 the gentry became a privileged social class, and
its "liberties" were secured by the laws. The nobleman was a free
man, not bound to live in his landed estate if he did not want to;
he could dispose of his land in a particular district and move to
wherever he pleased.[45] He had the right to travel abroad in any
foreign country, except that with which the grand duchy was at war.
He could stay abroad as long as he pleased and "learn the ways of
knighthood" (First Statute, Rozdel III, article 8).

The nobleman was not subject to either capital or corporal punishment, or to imprisonment or confiscation of his property without due trial in the court. For any offense against a nobleman the
guilty party had to pay more than for the offense against a commoner. In court the nobleman was regarded as a more reliable wit-
ness than a commoner, and in many cases his oath was considered
decisive proof.[46]

The Second Lithuanian Statute made the szlachta rights and privileges even more extensive, and the protection of them more effec-
tive.[47] It was decreed, for example, that a commoner who defamed
a nobleman should be punished by the cutting out of his tongue
(Second Statute, Rozdel III, article 18). If a nobleman was killed
by a band of noblemen, only the one who actually committed the
murder was subject to execution, but if a nobleman was killed by
a gang of commoners, all of them were executed (Second Statute,
Rozdel XI, article 12).

While the szlachta rights and privileges were growing, the noblemen attempted to secure the enjoyment of their status as the exclusive top group of the society, on the one hand by undermining the
position of the lords, and on the other hand by establishing a barrier
against the penetration of commoners into the szlachta corporation.
The former objective was reached in 1564–66, the latter in the
1520's.

45. Liubavsky, *Ocherk*, p. 126.
46. *Ibid.*, p. 126; Hrushevsky (above, n. 34), *5*, 54–56.
47. Lappo, *Velikoe Kniazhestvo Litovskoe*, *1*, 515–522; Hrushevsky, *Istoriia*, *5*, 56–
57.

As we know, originally the main state function of the szlachta was military. It was often difficult to draw a definite line between the noble and the non-noble warriors; during a war, all were needed. The defense of the southern frontier against Tatar raids especially called for alert frontiersmen or vigilants, many of whom were local petty landowners or landholders. They were always on the spot and could repel, or try to repel, a Tatar attack before the arrival of regular troops. The same situation existed in East Russia, and was one of the reasons for organization of the Cossack communes and for pressing the Cossacks into service of the government of Poland or Moscow.

The local chieftains of these and similar social groups eventually claimed the same rights that the gentry had had, but the noblemen were reluctant to admit outsiders. The grand duke's government had to comply with the pressure of the nobility and to establish definite rules for preventing the non-nobles from entering the corporation. According to the decision of the council of lords (in 1522) anyone whose right to nobility was challenged had to produce two guarantors, indisputable hereditary noblemen of his clan, who would certify by oath that the claimer had a common ancestor with them.[48] This procedure was sanctioned by the Second Lithuanian Statute (Rozdel III, article 11). The statute added that if the claimer to the nobility could not produce two guarantors from his own clan, he might use instead indisputable noblemen of his neighborhood (even if they were not relatives of his) who would certify his status of nobility.

The army register of 1528 (see above, p. 189), which contained the names of most of the noble families, was important in making uniform the szlachta class in the Grand Duchy of Lithuania. All those families whose names were included were recognized as noble, and their members needed no additional proof of status.

The gentry mansions were spread over the whole territory of the grand duchy. In each region the noblemen's landed estates varied greatly in size. Some of the boyare-szlachta occupied, in respect to the size of their landed estates, an intermediate position between the lords and the lower strata of the gentry. Most of the noblemen of the szlachta class had, however, landholdings of a rather small size. Such was the case especially of the gentry of the southern part of the Kievan land and of Podliashie. Often, a nobleman could muster

48. Liubavsky, *Seim*, p. 440; Hrushevsky (above, n. 34), *5*, 60.

only one horseman for the army at its mobilization, which meant that he controlled only eight or ten service units—that is, from twenty-four to thirty peasant households. There were cases when one horseman was produced by two or three noblemen cooperatively.

7. THE SLAVES

Slavery, which had existed in Russia in the Kievan period, survived in the Grand Duchy of Lithuania as it did in Muscovy. Numerically, slaves constituted a small proportion of population. Economically, they played for a time a role of considerable importance in the large landed estates. Slaves were habitually employed in the master's household as servants. Besides, on the large estates a considerable number of the slaves were used as agricultural laborers, just as in the estates of the Muscovite boyars. The slaves lived either in the buildings of the estate or outside in separate houses alongside peasant homes. The household slave received from his master a monthly allowance of food provisions (*mesiachina*) for his and his family's maintenance. The agricultural slaves, living apart in houses, had small plots of land for petty husbandry, although most of the time they worked in their masters' fields. Their income was also insufficient, and they received the *mesiachina*, though a smaller quota of it than the household slaves.[49] The slaves were known collectively as *cheliad*.[50]

According to the first two Lithuanian statutes, the three main sources of slaves were heredity (birth in the slave family), war captivity, and marriage with a slave, which automatically enslaved the free partner (First Statute, Rozdel XI, article 13; Second Statute, Rozdel XII, article 13). The First Statute also ruled that a criminal extradited for execution to the offended party might redeem his life by offering himself as a slave to the offended. In such a case, his children automatically became slaves (Rozdel XI, article 13).

The slaves, juridically, were not persons but chattels of their masters. The only duty of the master toward his slaves recognized by the law was that of feeding them during a famine. If a lord ousted his slaves from his estate during a famine and they survived by them-

49. On the slaves in the Grand Duchy of Lithuania see Liubavsky, *Ocherk*, pp. 96–97; Hrushevsky (above, n. 34), *5*, 109–115; Kutrzeba, *2*, 73–74.

50. For the origin of this term see *Kievan Russia*, p. 137. Other terms used were *nevolnik* (unfree), *parubok* (boy), and *zhonka* (little woman, from *zhena*, "woman").

selves elsewhere, they would become free (First Statute, Rozdel XI, article 12; Third Statute, Rozdel XII, article 12).

Only Christians were allowed to own Christian slaves; the Jews and the Tatars were expressly forbidden to buy such slaves. However, the First Lithuanian Statute confirmed the privilege of the Tatar gentry to keep those Christian slaves who had been previously granted to them or their forefathers by the grand duke or the latter's ancestors (First Statute, Rozdel XI, article 6). This privilege was annulled by the Second Statute (Rozdel XII, article 5).

It was only the lords who owned large throngs of slaves and were able to assign many of them to agricultural work. The gentry, whose members might own each only a few slaves, used slaves mostly as home servants. For having their land tilled the gentry depended on their tenant farmers—the peasants. Therefore the gentry, as a class, were not so interested economically in preserving the institution of slavery as the lords were.

The lords, in their turn, did not entirely depend on the labor supplied by their slaves. The latter were used on the lord's demesne only, and most of the lord's income derived from payments, in kind or in money, by the tenant farmers he controlled. Here the main problem, from both the lord's and the gentry's point of view, was the effectiveness of this control. The problem was solved in the second half of the 15th and the 16th centuries by attaching a considerable part of the peasants to the soil in order to prevent their moving away from the noblemen's estates at their will. Thus the institution of serfdom was introduced (below, pp. 206–207).

As was the case in Western Europe much earlier, the establishment of serfdom in the Grand Duchy of Lithuania made the institution of slavery less valuable for the landowners in regard to their income from their lands. It should be noted that slavery had disintegrated in Poland much earlier than in Lithuania. In the 14th century most of the former slaves in Poland became peasants, a considerable part of whom were attached to the estates of the gentry in one way or the other.

In the Grand Duchy of Lithuania the process of replacement of slavery by serfdom started in the 15th century and was well along by the middle of the 16th century. This prepared the ground for an attempt to abolish altogether the institution of slavery on the Polish model, or at least to restrict it.

The tight union between Lithuania and Poland that was proclaimed at the Lublin seim of 1569 (below, p. 246) contributed to the policy of limitation of slavery in Lithuania.

The Third Statute (1588) ruled that henceforth the only legal source of slavery was to be war captivity. However, the children of the war prisoners turned to slaves were not considered slaves and were to be settled on land as serfs, like all the former hereditary slaves and their children (Rozdel XII, article 21). The former slaves settled on land and bound to it received the status of *otchichi* —that is, hereditary serfs (below, p. 206).[51] As a result of these legislative measures the number of slaves in the Grand Duchy of Lithuania decreased sharply. Slavery was not, however, completely eradicated. Slaves were occasionally mentioned in the Grand Duchy of Lithuania as late as 1710.[52]

When appraising the legislative attempts to abolish slavery in the Grand Duchy of Lithuania in terms of the growth of personal freedom of the people of the lower classes, we have to take into consideration the simultaneous attachment of a considerable part of the peasants to the landed estates owned by the lords and the szlachta. While trying to raise the status of the slaves, the government of the grand duchy at the same time lowered that of the peasants. The position of these latter will be dealt with in the following section.

8. THE PEASANTS

Just as with the gentry, the formation of the peasant class in the Grand Duchy of Lithuania was a complicated and lengthy process. At its base, historically, lay a variety of different groups of rural population occupied mostly in agriculture, but also in other pursuits, like beekeeping, hunting, and fishing. There was a considerable difference in the land rights of single groups.

In the Kievan period land could be owned by individuals as well as by cooperative commoners. Besides, a man could till a plot of land which juridically belonged not to him but to the prince, the church, or the boyars. The holder of such a plot could use it either by agreement with the owner or on the basis of the agriculturist's customary right to clear, occupy, and till a hitherto wasted and un-

51. Lappo, *Velikoe Kniazhestvo Litovskoe, 1*, 443; Kutrzeba, 2, 74–75.
52. Lappo, *Velikoe Kniazhestvo Litovskoe, 1*, 443.

occupied plot of land. This has become known as the *zaimka* (right of occupancy) or the *trudovoe pravo* (toiler's right).

The generic name for the freemen occupied in agriculture on the land which belonged to them or to a commune in which they were members was *liudi* (men).[53] In Novgorod, a liudin who owned land in his own right was known as *svoezemets* (literally "self-owner of land") (see above, p. 109). A widespread form of land-holding was that of cooperative ownership of an estate by several people, such co-owners being known as *siabry*. They could belong to the same family or clan, but in many cases they were just neighbors.

Beside the liudi and the siabry there was in Russia of the Kievan period a separate group of tillers of land known as the *smerdy*. In the Mongol and early post-Mongol periods the term disappeared in Central Russia but survived in Novgorod and Pskov (see above, p. 40), as well in the Grand Duchy of Lithuania. The smerdy were settled on lands belonging to the state—that is, on the lands of the prince who was the head of the state, or of the city (if it was a city-state, like Novgorod and Pskov).

Alongside those clearly definable groups there was a somewhat fluid class of agriculturists who owned no sufficient acreage for securing their maintenance, or owned no land at all, and because of this had to offer to the landowner their service either as hired laborers or as sharecroppers. In Pskov the latter group was known as *izorniki* (plowers). Men of this class could also settle more or less permanently on the princely or boyar lands in the capacity of tenant farmers.

The terminology of the categories of the agricultural population in the Grand Duchy of Lithuania reflected the original diversity of group names and included a few more variations. In the documents of the Lithuanian period we find the familiar terms of *liudi, siabry,* and *smerdy*. The *liudi* are sometimes qualified as *chernye liudi,* "black men," indicating a lower status. It will be recalled that the term was also used to designate the lower class in Muscovy and Novgorod (above, p. 38). Other terms, not mentioned in the documents of the Kievan period but used in the Grand Duchy of Lithuania, were *muzhiki* (little men), *kmeti,* and *khlopy*. The name *muzhik* denoted a man (*muzh*) of a lower class (the term became familiar in Muscovy after the 16th century). The term *kmet'* was used in most Slavic languages, denoting originally a noble land-

53. *Kievan Russia,* p. 134.

owner or a knight, but later, especially in Poland and Lithuania, a peasant.[54] The term *khlop* is akin to *kholop* which, both in the Kievan period and in Muscovite Russia, denoted a slave. Many other terms were used in the Grand Duchy of Lithuania to designate small groups of the rural population performing specialized duties, such as *bortniki* (beekeepers), *rybolovy* (fishermen), *bobrovniki* (beaver hunters), and so on.

The main trend in the historical evolution of the peasant class was the gradual loss by the peasants of their land rights. All the land which some groups of agriculturists had originally owned as individuals or siabry was eventually appropriated by the grand duke or the noblemen. By the end of the 15th century most of the agriculturists had become tenant farmers either on the crown lands or on the estates of the noblemen.[55]

The peasant had to either work for his master or pay a rent to him (in kind or in money) or both. There were two main taxes the peasants delivered in kind: the *diaklo* and the *mezleva*. The diaklo was paid in grain (rye, wheat, and oats), hay, hemp, flax, and firewood. The mezleva deliveries consisted of heifers, hogs, sheep, chickens, and eggs.

A considerable number of the peasants were liable to corvée on the lord's demesne. These were known as *tiaglye liudi* (men of *tiaglo*, i.e. of burden). At the height of the agricultural season, all the other peasants had to help the tiaglye for a specified number of days to mow the grass, make the hay, mow the corn cereals, and plow the land. Such assistance was called *toloka*. The customary quota for toloka-plowing was six days a year (three days of spring plowing and three days of autumn plowing). For mowing the cereals six more days of work were obligatory (three days for mowing the rye or wheat and three days for mowing the oats or barley). During the hay-making season the helpers had to work through the whole

54. Vasmer, *REW*, *1*, 578. In the *Igor Tale* (*Slovo o Polku Igoreve*) of the late 12th century the term *kmet* denoted a warrior-horseman: see G. Vernadsky, "*The Origins of Russia*," pp. 91, 283.

55. On the peasants in the Grand Duchy of Lithuania see F. I. Leontovich, *Krestiane iugo-zapadnoi Rossii po litovskomu pravu XV i XVI vekov* (Kiev, 1863); idem, "Krestiansky dvor v Litovsko-Russkom gosudarstve," *ZMNP* (1896), *2–4, 7, 10, 12* (1897), *4–5*; I. P. Novitsky, "Ocherk istorii krestianskogo sosloviia iugo-zapadnoi Rossii v XV–XVIII vekakh," *AIZR, 6*, Pt. I (Kiev, 1876); Liubavsky, *Ocherk*, pp. 102–115, 137–143; Dovnar-Zapolsky, *Gosudarstvennoe Khoziaistvo Velikogo Kniazhestva Litovskogo;* Hrushevsky (above, n. 34), *5*, 107–121; Kutrzeba, *2*, 72–85; Grekov, *Krestiane na Rusi*, pp. 250–390.

operation. In addition, all the peasants had to supply labor in an emergency, such as destruction of a mill's dam by flood. The peasants were also required to take part in the battue at the lord's chase, and in handling and dragging the seine to supply the lord with fish.

To secure a more efficient fulfillment of services and payment of taxes required from the peasants, the latter were grouped in teams, each group being considered a service unit (*sluzhba*). In the 15th and the first half of the 16th centuries the size of a sluzhba was not defined in exact terms of either the number of men or of land but varied in different areas and even within the same area. There were sluzhby containing each from two to ten peasant households and from two to ten *voloki* of land.[56] One Lithuanian *voloka* (singular) was equal to about 21 hectares. The average size of a sluzhba may tentatively be estimated as about three peasant households.

The two main categories of peasants were those settled on crown lands and those who were tenant farmers on the noblemen's estates. The peasants of the first category were nominally under the authority of the grand duke but actually under that of the grand duke's local officials, such as the derzhavtsy and their assistants. On the large estates of the lords the latter's bailiffs and stewards managed the peasants. On the smaller estates of the gentry the nobleman often personally supervised the peasants' work.

A barrier was established between the peasants of the crown lands and those of the noblemen's estates by the Grand Duke Casimir's Charter of 1447, which forbade the migration of the peasants from the crown lands to the noblemen's estates and vice versa.[57]

The peasants, irrespective of whose land they were settled on, were divided into two groups: the *pokhozhie* (mobile), who had freedom of movement, and the *nepokhozhie* (immobile), who were attached to the land.

The mobile class was made up of various elements: free men who were in one way or another dispossessed of the land they previously owned or held; landless agricultural laborers; former slaves to whom their owners had granted freedom. Immigrants from East Russia, from Moldavia, or from Poland likewise belonged to this class.

As we know, in the Kievan period all the agriculturists (except the slaves) were free. The process of attaching part of the free peas-

---

56. Dovnar-Zapolsky, pp. 202, 203, 212–216.

57. Vladimirsky-Budanov, *Khristomatiia, 2* (8th ed. Kiev, 1915), 27–28. In this edition the charter is referred erroneously to 1457. See Liubavsky, *Ocherk*, p. 77.

ants to the crown lands or to the estates of the nobility began in Lithuania in the 15th century. The binding of the peasant to the estate was the result, partly at least, of the growth of the privileges of the noblemen, especially of their rights of jurisdiction over the population of their estates.

A peasant who lived on the same plot of land where his father and grandfather had stayed was considered an *otchich*—that is, a hereditary inhabitant of the estate, actually a hereditary serf.

According to the First Lithuanian Statute, a prescriptive term of ten years was established for the claims concerning litigations about land (*davnost' zemskaia*). If a man did not claim ownership of a particular plot of land for ten years, he lost his rights on it (Rozdel I, article 27). This principle was applied to the peasant plots in the crown lands as well as to those in the noblemen's estates. The presumption was that all the land belonged either to the crown or to the noblemen. On this basis, if the peasant could not submit formal proof that the plot of land he tilled had been legally his own and if he notwithstanding stayed on the plot for more than ten years, he was deprived of any rights on the plot. Besides, he was firmly attached to his service unit (sluzhba). The lord would permit him to leave only if he produced a substitute who would agree to perform the amount of work required by his share in the sluzhba.

Such a substitute could be found among the surplus population of the same or another sluzhba—if the families that composed the sluzhba comprised more able-bodied members than were needed— or among the mobile people. An immobile peasant could also exchange his sluzhba with another such peasant who had been attached to a sluzhba in a different place. However, both these sluzhby had to belong to the same master.

The cases of such exchanges were not frequent and occurred mostly among peasants settled on crown lands. As for the peasants on the noblemen's estates, an exchange of two peasants belonging each to a different master could take place only by agreement between the two masters. The initiative in an exchange of such a type likewise was the master's, not the peasant's. The exchange could be done even without any consideration of the wishes of the peasants affected.[58]

When all is said, it is clear that by the middle of the 16th century the majority of the peasants in the Grand Duchy of Lithuania

58. Liubavsky, *Ocherk*, p. 138.

had become either crown serfs or noblemen's serfs. The number of mobile peasants steadily decreased. The Third Lithuanian Statute ruled that if a free peasant had worked on a nobleman's estate for more than ten years, he had no right to leave except by redeeming himself (Rozdel XII, article 13).

The conditions of life of the peasants were different in different areas. As I. P. Novitsky has observed, the burden imposed on the peasants was heavy in the densely populated regions and lighter in those where population was sparse and land plentiful, especially in the "wild prairie" on the left bank of the Dnieper River.[59]

It should be noted that in spite of the loss of their legal rights on the plots of land they tilled, the peasants, while serfs, continued to consider the land their own and for a long time entered among themselves in various transactions about it, such as forming cooperative associations, exchanging plots of land, renting, mortgaging, or selling their lands.

In doing this the peasants acted in the spirit of the old Russian juridical conceptions as well as in the traditions of Russian customary law. From the point of view of the new system of the Grand Duchy of Lithuania such transactions were illegal. The grand duke's officials allowed the pratice, however, provided the transactions affected only the peasants belonging to the crown lands and provided that the efficiency of the service units was not undermined by them. In the grand duke's name, his officials, of course, could always annul any transaction as illegal if it seemed detrimental to the grand duke's interests.

Similar tendencies existed in the attitude toward land of the peasants in the domain of a lord as well as on a gentry estate, but there conditions were much less favorable to the peasants, and the noblemen, especially the petty landowners, could be expected to control the transactions of their peasants more strictly than the grand duke's officials did.

Often the peasants exploited land not each by himself but in groups. Whenever a family grew numerically and became a large group consisting of several generations living in the same homestead of a *zadruga* type,[60] it would form a cooperative association, members of which were known by the traditional name of *siabry*. Such associations could also be formed by neighbors not in blood rela-

59. Novitsky, "Ocherk istorii krestianskogo sosloviia," p. 159.
60. On the zadruga see *Kievan Russia*, pp. 132–133.

tion one with another. In the forest zone, formation of such communes was more often than not dictated by economic necessity. Clearing of woods for making the land fit for plowing was above the strength of an average family and required efforts of a much larger group.

Another way to solve the problem was for an average family to accept into its midst outside laborers not as full members of the enterprise but as having a certain share in the income.

A small cooperative association could be recognized by the grand duke's officials as a separate sluzhba. A large association was counted as two or more sluzhby.

The remnants of the traditional Russian concepts of the rights of the tillers on their lands were tolerated by the authorities until the agrarian reform of the 1550's and the settling of the serfs on the uniform farms shaped on the Polish model (below, pp. 224–226).

9. THE BURGHERS

In Kievan Russia the city was a constituent part of the government of a land. The veche was a branch of the government.[61] In Novgorod and Pskov that branch prevailed over the other two (the prince and the boyars), and the city became a city-state.

In the Mongol period the political importance of the city in East Russia was undermined by the efforts of both the Mongol khans and the Russian princes, and the veche was abolished.[62] Only Novgorod and Pskov were not affected by the change. As we know, however, both those cities were annexed by Moscow in the late 15th and early 16th centuries, respectively.

In West Russia the decay of the cities also started in the Mongol period. A number of them, like Kiev, were destroyed by the Mongols and later looted by the Crimean Tatars. Some of the old Russian cities, like Smolensk, Polotsk, and Vitebsk, escaped the destruction and were able to preserve, for some time, their old constitution. Gradually, however, the veche in those towns lost its original character of a democratic institution. The affairs were discussed by the boyars and the merchants in the name of the whole population.

As we know, the government of the Grand Duchy of Lithuania was based on the rights and privileges of the nobility. The political

61. On the veche see *Kievan Russia,* pp. 185, 186, 198, 199.
62. See *Mongols and Russia,* pp. 345–346.

climate of the grand duchy was not conducive to the preservation of the constitutional rights of the cities. No burgher was admitted to the council of lords, and there were no representatives of the cities in the seim.

Large cities in the Grand Duchy of Lithuania were situated in state territory. Smaller towns belonged either to the crown domain or to the nobles' estates. The city was excluded from any participation in political life, though it maintained its municipal self-government. Gradually, the old Russian institutions were abolished and most of the cities were instead granted municipal government according to the German law.[63]

The population of the cities in Poland and Lithuania was of heterogeneous ethnic origin. In medieval Poland the kings encouraged German colonization in the cities and in the rural areas in order to sponsor the development of commerce, trade, and agriculture. For similar reasons the Russian princes of Galicia and Volynia invited German settlers to their cities in the 13th and early 14th centuries. The grand dukes of Lithuania continued the same policy.

It should be noted that a number of Armenians [64] and Jews had established themselves in Kiev and Lvov in the course of the 11th, 12th, and 13th centuries and even earlier.

Because of the policy of the grand dukes as well as the natural process of migration, many Germans, Armenians, and Jews—merchants and artisans—lived in the 15th and 16th centuries in Russian cities of both Galicia (which at that time belonged to Poland) and the Grand Duchy of Lithuania. However, in most of the old Russian cities the Russians still constituted the majority of the population.

63. On the West Russian towns and burghers see Hrushevsky (above, n. 34), 5, 223–251; Liubavsky, *Ocherk,* pp. 115–117; Kutrzeba, 2, 96–101.

64. The Armenians appeared in the towns of the Kievan region, Galicia, and Volynia in the 11th century. Armenian immigrants continued to move into the Grand Duchy of Lithuania and Poland as late as the 16th century. Most of these Armenians came not directly from Transcaucasia but from the Crimea, where they had stayed for some time and became familiar with the Polovtsian language. Their total number in the Grand Duchy of Lithuania was not large, but they played an important role in commerce by virtue of their business ability and solidarity. They traded mainly in Oriental goods. I am indebted to Mr. S. Szyszman for the following bibliographical references: "Ormijane w Polsce," *Encyklopedyja powszechna, 20* (Warsaw, 1865), 55–60; S. Barącz, *Żywoty sławnych Ormian w Polsce* (Lvov, 1856); T. Kowalski, "Wyrazy kipczackie w języku Ormian polskich," *Myśl Karaimska, 12* (Wilno, 1938), 27–40; B. Baranowski, "Ormianie w służbie dyplomatycznej Rzeczypospolitej," *Myśl Karaimska,* new series, *1* (Wrocław, 1946), 119–132.

The Germans who settled in Poland, in towns or in rural districts, were governed by the German law. Thus the first infiltration of the German law into Poland was connected with German colonization. Later, German municipal law was granted to Polish and Russian cities in Poland because the kings considered it useful for them, mainly for fiscal reasons. There were several variations of the German municipal codes, the most popular in Poland being the Magdeburg law and the Chelmno (Kulm) law. These codes were applied in Poland in somewhat modified form. From Poland the German municipal law penetrated into the Grand Duchy of Lithuania, where it usually was known under the name of the Magdeburg law.[65]

In Lithuania this Magdeburg law was first granted to Vilna (1387). In the course of the 15th century it was extended to Troki, Brest, Lutsk, Kremenets, Vladimir-in-Volynia, Polotsk, Smolensk, Kiev, Minsk, and Novgorod-Litovsk. In the 16th century many other towns received it, Vitebsk being the last Russian city (1593).

In M. Hrushevsky's opinion the Polish government consciously used the Magdeburg law to curb Russian influence in Galicia and prepare the ground for the denationalization of the Russian population.[66] The position of the Russians was much stronger in the Grand Duchy of Lithuania than in Poland, and the Lithuanian government except in a few towns did not succeed in excluding the Russians from the municipal government. However, it attempted, whenever possible, to curb the share of the Russians in the municipalities.

The Magdeburg law was intended for Christian burghers only. The only exception to the rule was made for the Karaites (see below, p. 218). The Jews were excluded from municipal self-government (see below, p. 215).

As for Christians, Roman Catholics were preferred. In Russian cities in Poland the Orthodox were subject to various kinds of discrimination. In Lvov they were entitled to accept the Magdeburg law but were excluded from holding office in the municipal government and were allowed to live only in a special part of the city, called the "Russian Street." [67]

65. On the Magdeburg law in West Russian cities see M. F. Vladimirsky–Budanov, "Nemetskoe pravo v Polshe i Litve," *ZMNP*, *8–12* (1866); F. V. Taranovsky, *Obzor pamiatnikov Magdeburgskoko prava* (Warsaw, 1897); N. P. Vasilenko, "Pravo Magdeburgskoe," *ES*, *48* (1898), 890–896; Hrushevsky (above, n. 34), *5*, 342–355; Liubavsky, *Ocherk*, pp. 148–153; Kutrzeba, *2*, 97–99.

66. Hrushevsky (above, n. 34), *5*, 228.

67. *Ibid.*, pp. 241–242.

When in the early part of the 15th century Grand Duke Vitovt granted the Magdeburg law to a number of towns in the western part of the Russian area of the grand duchy (the Berestie region and Podliashie) he expressly excluded Orthodox Russians from those municipalities.[68]

In most of the other cities of the grand duchy to which the Magdeburg law was granted in the course of the 15th and 16th centuries the Russians were enfranchised, but a rule was established that one-half the members of the city council should be Roman Catholic and one-half Greek Orthodox. Since in many towns the majority of the population consisted of Orthodox Russians, the rule was favorable to the Polish and German minorities.

Under the German law the municipality became a closed corporation. Only those recognized as burghers belonged to it. The West Russian term for burghers was *mieshchane*. The status of burgher was acquired by birth and was hereditary. One could also become a burgher by being accepted into the corporation by the city council or by an artisan guild.

Two main groups may be differentiated among the burghers: the merchants and the artisans. Each of the latter had to belong to one of the guilds called *tsekhi*.[69] Many of the burghers owned land outside the city and supplemented their income by agricultural work.

The city that received the benefits of the Magdeburg law was immune from interference by the grand duke's officials and was placed under its own municipal government. At the head of it originally stood the *voit*,[70] appointed by the grand duke (often chosen by him from among the gentry) as soon as the German law had been granted to a city. The voit could bequeath his office to his heir or sell it to another person. Eventually, many a city bought the office of the voit, after which the voit's rights were transferred to the city council (*rada*).

68. *Ibid.*, p. 229.

69. On *tsekhi* see Vasmer, *REW*, *3*, 291. On the *tsekhi* in West Russian towns see Hrushevsky (above, n. 34), *6*, 109–138.

70. The West Russian term *voit* is usually considered a derivation from the German *Vogt* (the parallel old form is *Voit*). It seems, however, that both the Slavic and the German terms (*voit*) derive from the Greek *boethos* (βοηθός), "assistant, defender" (pronounced *voithos* in medieval and modern Greek). In an old list of Greek words borrowed by the "gallograeci," i.e. Galatians (each word in this list being accompanied by its German and Latin equivalents), we find "βοηθός; voit, vogt; praeses": see W. Lazius, *De aliquot gentium migrationibus* (Basileae, 1572), p. 30. Lazius also published (pp. 748–751) a list of words belonging to a people who came "from Asia and the confines of the Greeks." Most of these words are Slavic. Among them is *foyt*, of which the Greek equivalent is βοηθός (p. 748).

Originally it was the voit who selected the members of the rada (six or twelve, depending on the size of the city) among the candidates whose names were submitted to him by the burghers. The chairman of the rada was called *burmistr*. He served for one year and was selected by the voit and the rada among the *radtsy*. When the rada acquired the voit's rights, the burmistr was elected by the rada. Before long, the elections were replaced by the annual rotation of the members of the rada in the office of burmistr. The rada likewise assumed the task of replacing by cooptation those of its members who either had resigned or had died.[71]

In a number of West Russian cities the rada was in charge only of municipal administration and welfare, not of the judiciary. For the latter, a separate committee was established, known as the *lava* (bench). The *lavniki* (members of the lava) acted as jurors in criminal cases, with the voit, or the burmistr, as the judge. They were appointed by the rada.

The burghers were freed from many duties which they had had to perform alongside the peasants before receiving the Magdeburg law, such as, for example, the *toloka* (on which see above, p. 204). They had to supply their quota of horsemen at the mobilization of the army, however. In the army register of 1528 we find a long list of names of the burghers of Polotsk who had to muster horsemen and a shorter list of the burghers of Vitebsk made for the same purpose.[72] Besides, the burghers had to pay the war tax (*serebshchina*) and supply workers for the building and maintenance of fortresses.

For receiving the benefits of the Magdeburg law the city had to pay into the grand duke's treasury a yearly contribution the amount of which varied from 30 to 100 gold coins.

In its turn, the city had been granted some sources of income of its own. The municipality was allowed to establish in the municipal building (*ratusha*) various stores and shops, for the use of which rent was paid to the city. Moreover, the municipality was entitled to install standard containers for liquid and dry measures as well as a municipal scale. Small fees were collected for the use of all this. More income was derived from the public baths, shops for smelting wax for candles, mills, and wine shops. Selling liquor was the grand duke's prerogative, but he could farm the sale to the city or to individual burghers.

71. Vasilenko, "Pravo Magdeburgskoe," p. 892.
72. *RIB, 33,* cols. 195–198.

As regards outside commerce, the municipality enjoyed the staple right. Outside merchants had to deposit all goods imported by them in the municipal depot. They were allowed only wholesale trading; the burghers alone could conduct retail trade.

Different opinions are voiced in the historical literature concerning the role of the Magdeburg law in the life of West Russian cities. Some scholars, like V. B. Antonovich, considered the introduction of the German municipal law an important attempt to improve the position of the cities and the burghers. Others, like M. F. Vladimirsky-Budanov, emphasized the negative aspects of the influence of the German law.[73]

There is no doubt that under the Magdeburg law the status of the burghers was made more secure and they were freed from many annoying liabilities. Furthermore, some Germans settled in West Russian towns were skillful artisans and, we may think, raised the level of crafts.

On the other hand, the burghers were not sufficiently protected from the competition of the noblemen. The latter had no right of personally participating in trade or in crafts but often did so through their agents. Many artisans worked on the crown lands as well as on the large estates of the nobility, and these were not restricted by guild regulations. Noblemen were granted the privilege of exporting the products of their lands abroad for sale as well as importing goods from abroad for personal use, custom free. The goods so imported were not subject to the municipal staple restrictions.[74]

As has been mentioned, the Jews were excluded from the German law of municipal organization. As a result, they eventually emerged as a separate group in the development of the commerce and crafts in the Grand Duchy of Lithuania and as such proved much more active and successful than the municipal merchants and artisans (see below, p. 215). This could not but undermine the economic activities of the burghers.

While the right of self-government given to the cities looked well on paper, actually the municipal government was controlled by the voit and his cronies and in those cities who bought the voit's office by an oligarchy of a few rich families centering around the rada. The rada members derived much profit from the management of the municipal industrial and commercial establishments. As M. F. Vladimirsky-Budanov observed, the rada subdued the public spirit

73. See Hrushevsky (above, n. 34), 5, 649–650.
74. *Ibid.*, p. 236.

of the burghers and curbed their initiative. It concentrated municipal power and wealth in the hands of its members. Besides, in many towns, the rada proved an instrument of oppression of the Russian nationality and of Orthodox faith.[75]

10. THE JEWS

The Jews constituted an integral part of the population of Poland and Southwest Russia in the early Middle Ages. Their number was small at that time. When the grand dukes of Lithuania acquired Volynia and Kiev, the Jews remained there. In the late 14th century a number settled in Vilna.

In the late 15th and early 16th centuries thousands of Jews migrated to Poland from Germany, Bohemia, and Moravia to escape oppression or persecutions to which they were subjected in their old countries. Some of them moved from Poland to Lithuania, but it was only after the Lublin Union of 1569 that the immigration of the Jews into Lithuania assumed large proportions.[76]

The juridical status of the Jews in Poland was defined by King Casimir the Great's charter of 1367 as well as by subsequent enactments. The Jews were granted extensive personal, religious, and economic rights. Later, on the basis of Casimir the Great's charter, Grand Duke Vitovt granted similar benefits to the Jews of Lithuania.

The benevolent policy of the Lithuanian grand dukes toward the Jews changed abruptly in 1495 when Grand Duke Aleksandr expelled all the Jews from the Grand Duchy of Lithuania, and their property was confiscated. The true motive of this drastic measure is unknown (see above, p. 85). Most of the Jews moved to Poland. Eight years later all were allowed to return, and in 1507 Grand Duke Sigismund I issued a new charter to them, confirming and extending Vitovt's charter. The Jews were entitled to receive back all the houses, stores, gardens, and meadows they had owned before the confiscation. They could claim the debts contracted by their debtors before their exile.

75. Vladimirsky-Budanov, quoted in Vasilenko, "Pravo Magdeburgskoe," p. 892.
76. On the Jews in Poland and Lithuania see Bershadsky, *Litovskie Evrei;* Hrushevsky (above, n. 34), *5,* 254–261; Liubavsky, *Ocherk,* pp. 117–121 ;Kutrzeba, *1,* 152–154, and *2,* 101–105; Wojciechowski, pp. 237–240; *Evreiskaia Entsiklopediia, 10,* cols. 267–271 (Jews in Lithuania), and *12,* cols. 703–733 (Jews in Poland) ; Dubnow, *History of the Jews in Russia and Poland, 1,* 39–102; S. W. Baron, *The Jewish Community* (2 vols. Philadelphia, 1942), *1,* 267–273.

On the basis of the charters granted to them by the grand dukes in various times, the Jews were allowed to conduct all commercial transactions, own stores and pawn shops, and farm liquor sales. They payed the same taxes as the burghers.

The Grand Duke of Lithuania preferred to farm out to the Jews the collection of customs duties and liquor taxes, because they were always efficient and accurate in their payments to the treasury. Besides, the Jews were able to lend large sums of money to the grand duke whenever he was in need of money—and he almost always was. Few Jews at that time had sufficient capital individually, but a group of them would pool their resources. Even many of the poor Jews had small shares in each transaction.

The Jews were organized in self-governing communes centering each around a synagogue or a cemetery. The members of the commune elected the elders who constituted the communal council presided over by the rabbi. This council had the authority of a court for the litigations in which both sides were Jews. The litigations between a Jew and a Christian were subject to the grand duke's officials. The Third Lithuanian Statute ruled that if a Jew were murdered by a Jew, the murderer should be tried by a Jewish court according to Jewish law. If the murderer were a gentile, he should be handed to the grand duke's officials to be executed by them (Rozdel XII, article 7).

When speaking of the position of the Jews in the Grand Duchy of Lithuania, we have to differentiate between the earlier period prior to the influx of masses of Jews from Poland (approximately, prior to the Lublin Union of 1569), and later times. In the earlier period the Jews did not form as yet the exclusive segregated group they later became. In the Russian towns of the Grand Duchy many Jews were familiar with the Russian language and often bore Russian names.[77]

The expulsion of the Jews from the Grand Duchy of Lithuania in 1495, even though the order was revoked in 1503, proved a heavy blow to the Jews, both economically and psychologically. In Poland, where most of the exiled Jews went from Lithuania, they had to rely on the help of their coreligionists—Jews who migrated to Poland from Germany—and were influenced by the latter in many ways. They learned the Yiddish spoken by the Jews from Germany.[78] On

77. Hrushevsky (above, n. 34), 5, 254. It should be noted that part of Hrushevsky's information on the Jews may actually refer to Karaites on whom see below, p. 217.
78. Ibid., p. 255.

the whole the exile of 1495–1503 caused a psychological trauma for the Jews and embittered them against the Lithuanian regime. It showed them the dire necessity of pooling their efforts for survival by any means available. Nevertheless, they resumed their previous occupations and restored their relations with their former neighbors.

It was only after the Lublin Union of 1569 that owing to intensive immigration of thousands of former German Jews from Poland to Lithuania the face of the Jewry in the Grand Duchy of Lithuania changed, and Yiddish became the language of all the Rabbinical Jews in both the Lithuanian and the Russian provinces of the grand duchy.

11. THE KARAITES

Karaism is a denomination of Judaism different in many respects from Rabbinic Judaism. The Karaites do not recognize the validity of the Talmud. In our days the number of Karaites is very small and the denomination is dying out. In the older time, however, Karaism represented a mighty religious current, and the period from the 8th to the 12th centuries was of great spiritual and geographic expansion of Karaism. The doctrine was still very much alive in the 15th and 16th centuries,[79] and more will be said about it in a later volume. What concerns us now is the position of the Karaites in the Grand Duchy of Lithuania.

The Lithuanian branch of the Karaites represents, historically, a fragment of the earlier expansion of Karaite proselytism among the Turkish peoples in Central Asia and South Russia, especially among

---

79. On Karaism and the Karaites see J. Fürst, *Geschichte der Karäerthums von 900 bis 1575* (Leipsig, 1865); A. Harkavy, "Karaimy," *ES*, 27 (1895), 427–431; S. A. Bershadsky, *Dokumenty i regesty k istorii Evreev v Litve* (2 vols., St. Petersburg, 1882); *Sbornik starinnykh gramot i uzakonenii Rossiiskoi Imperii kasatelno prav i sostoiania russko-poddannykh Karaimov* (St. Petersburg, 1890); *Evreiskaia Entsiklopediia, 9,* cols. 268–298; Nemoy, *Karaite Anthology*, pp. xiii–xxiv; Szyszman, "Die Karäer in Ost-Mitteleuropa," pp. 24–54. Mr. Szyszman kindly communicated to me the following additional references on Karaism and the Karaites: I. O. Sinani, *Istoriia vozniknoveniia i razvitiia Karaimizma*, 2 vols. (Simferopol, 1888, and St. Petersburg, 1889); "Karaimy," *Bolshaia Entsiklopediia, 10* (St. Petersburg, 1902), 517; "Karaimy," *BSE, 20,* 110; T. Czacki, *Rozprawa o Karaitach* (Vilna, 1807); T. Kowalski, "Karaimi," *Świat i życie, 4* (Warsaw and Lvov, 1936), cols. 1036–1038; N. L. Cieszyński, "Najmniejsza mniejszość w Polsce," *Roczniki Katolickie* 1930 (Poznań), pp. 323–331; H. Namik, *Türk Dünyasi* (Istanbul, 1932), pp. 179–180; S. Šapšal, "Kırım Karay Türkleri," *Türk yili, 1* (Istanbul, 1928).

the Khazars and later among the Polovtsy.[80] When converted to Karaism, the new faithful accepted Hebrew as their basic religious language, but kept the native Turkic as their spoken tongue. Turkic was used in religious rites as well, in addition to Hebrew. The living language of the Lithuanian Karaites is close to the Polovtsian (Cuman) dialect.[81]

It is usually supposed that the Karaites came to Lithuania from South Russia in the late 14th century—that is, at the same period as the Tatars (see p. 191, above). However, there are indications that some Karaite settlers established themselves in the Russian provinces of the grand duchy much earlier, before the Lithuanian expansion. They must have come from the Crimea and the northern Caucasus.[82]

Since Karaism is a form of Judaism and the religious language of the Karaites is Hebrew, no difference was made between Rabbinic Jews and Karaites in the documents of the Grand Duchy of Lithuania. This makes the study of the Karaites of this period especially difficult, for in many cases it is not clear which our sources mean when they speak of "Jews," and quite a number of scholars have consequently overlooked the Lithuanian Karaites altogether. We find no mention of them in the works on the grand duchy by such outstanding historians as M. K. Liubavsky, M. Hrushevsky, and S. Kutrzeba.

The Lithuanian government, however, had a clear notion of some outstanding traits in the character of the Karaites, namely of their military valor, and knew how to use as soldiers these Turks by blood and speech.

In the late 14th century a number of Karaites were settled in a chain of forts along the northern and northwestern border between Lithuania and the Knights of the Livonian Order to protect the Lithuanian frontier against the Germans.[83] The Karaites were en-

---

80. On Karaism among the Khazars see S. Szyszman, "Le Roi Boulan et le problème de la conversion des Khazars," *Ephemerides Theologicae Lovanienses, 33* (1957), 68–76; *idem*, "Les Khazars: problèmes et controverses," *Revue de l'Histoire des religions, 152* (1957), 174–221.

81. Presumably, the Karaite dialect was also influenced by the Khazar language. On the position of the West Karaite (Troki dialect) in regard to other Turkic languages and dialects see Tadeusz Kowalski, *Karaimische Texte in Dialekt von Troki* (Kraków, 1929), pp. l–lxxi; A. Zajączkowski, *Ze studiów nad zagadnieniem chazarskim* (Kraków, 1947), pp. 61–75; Szyszman, "Karäer," pp. 29–75.

82. Szyszman, "Karäer," pp. 26–35.

83. *Ibid.*, pp. 39–40.

trusted with the defense of the entrance to the bridge connecting the fortress of Troki (situated on an island of a lake) with the main-land,[84] and thus held the key to the fortress.

It is noteworthy that the Karaites, alone of the non-Christians in the grand duchy, received the benefits of the Magdeburg law. They were not merged with the Christian community of Troki, however, but were organized into a separate commune under the same law. The Troki Karaites were entitled to elect the voit, who was confirmed in office by the grand duke and was subordinated to the grand duke. The voit acted as judge in all litigations among the Karaites not only those living in Troki, but also those in other towns in the grand duchy, as well as in Kukizov near Lvov. In litigation between a Karaite and a Christian, the matter was referred to a joint court of the voit and the Voevoda of Troki. The Karaites re-ceived half of the income derived from municipal establishments (such as the municipal scale and the shop for the smelting of wax for candles). Like the Christian burghers in the municipalities under Magdeburg law the Troki Karaites were exempt from a number of taxes and liabilities.[85]

Beside Troki, there were Karaite settlements in Grodno, Lutsk, Smolensk, Starodub, Zhitomir, Kiev, and a number of other towns in the grand duchy.[86] In the 16th and 17th centuries the Karaites proved very useful for the Lithuanian and Polish governments in the wars against the Crimean Tatars and the Ottoman Turks. Heavy casualties in wars must have checked the growth of the Lithuanian Karaites. The Swedish Orientalist Gustaf Peringer, who made a study of the Karaites in 1690, remarked that their number was small because they were accustomed to go to war at a very early age.[87]

In his treatise De duabus Sarmatiis (1517) the Polish writer Maciej of Miechow (Matvei Mekhovsky) says that in Russia (i.e. West Russia) the Jews (he means the Karaites) "are not usurers as the Jews in Christian [i.e. Roman Catholic] lands, but artisans, agriculturists, and wholesale merchants who often farm the custom duties and state taxes." [88] Some Karaites served in the administration

---

84. *Ibid.*, pp. 39–40.

85. *Sbornik starinnykh gramot*, pp. 1–53; Bershadsky, *Dokumenty i regesty, 1*, 28–29; *idem, Litovskie Evrei*, pp. 241–243, 248–250; Szyszman, "Karäer," pp. 37–38.

86. Szyszman, "Karäer," pp. 35–36.

87. Szyszman, "G. Peringers Mission," *ZDMG, 102* (1952), 219–226; *idem*, "Karäer," p. 39.

88. Matthew of Miechow, *De duabus Sarmatiis*, pp. 174 (Latin text) and 96 (Rus-

of the grand duchy. They took an active part in the Oriental trade, and some also had business relations with Warsaw, Danzig (Gdansk), Riga, and Smolensk.[89]

Despite the military service of the Karaites and their general usefulness to the Lithuanian state, the expulsion edict of 1495 was applied to them in the same way as to the Rabbinic Jews. It is usually admitted that most of the Karaites went to the Crimea and returned to Lithuania in 1503. However, in the financial report on the grand duke's castle at Troki for the years 1498–1502 a number of officials, gatekeepers, musketeers, and "cossacks" with typical Karaite names are mentioned. This shows that many Karaites were exempt from the application of the expulsion edict.[90]

---

sian translation). Cf. Szyszman, "Karäer," p. 37. Mekhovsky makes similar statement about the Troki Jews (i.e. Karaites): see pp. 186 (Latin text) and 109 (Russian translation).

89. *RIB, 20,* cols. 909, 1148, 1156, 1181; Szyszman, "Karäer," p. 38.

90. Mr. S. Szyszman called my attention to this document in a letter dated June 12, 1958. In his opinion, the whole question of the expulsion of the Karaites from the Grand Duchy of Lithuania in 1495–1503 should be reconsidered. See also Szyszman, "Karäer," p. 42, n. 61.

CHAPTER VII

DECLINE OF LITHUANIA AND THE RISE
OF THE UKRAINIAN COSSACKS

1. BETWEEN MOSCOW AND POLAND, 1526–66

I

THE ARMISTICE between the Grand Duchy of Lithuania and Moscow, signed in 1526 (see above, p. 162), temporarily eased the tension caused by the war of 1512–22.

In that war the Muscovites suffered a major defeat at Orsha but succeeded in taking Smolensk. According to the provisions of the armistice of 1526, the Muscovites kept Smolensk as well as the Upper Oka towns and Severia, which they had won under Ivan III (see above, p. 95). Following the armistice, Vasili II abrogated the authority of the local princes in Severia and annexed the region (above, pp. 157–158).

The armistice, leaving to Moscow the area she had occupied during the preceding wars, was obviously more favorable to her than to Lithuania. If Lithuania wanted to prevent any further westward advance of the Muscovites, let alone get back the territories she had lost, she had to make a determined effort to strengthen her army and make her administration more efficient.

Besides its military and administrative aspects, the struggle between Lithuania and Moscow in the 16th century should be analyzed from the viewpoint of Russian national problems. It will be recalled that in the middle of the 15th century the consciousness of Russian cultural unity was strong among the Russians in both East and West Russia (see above, pp. 2–3). Politically, the Russian-speaking areas were divided into a number of principalities and city-states. The idea of political unification, in the form of a free federation or in that of a monarchy, was expressed by many Russian literati. Novgorod, as we know, was the main center of the federative idea. In West Russia the plan was apparently favored by some princes and burghers, especially in Kiev.

During the crisis of 1470–71 the hopes of the Novgorod federalists were shattered by the military weight of Moscow and the lack of timely and determinate action on the part of Grand Duke Casimir of Lithuania. Moreover, the latter, after having failed to support Novgorod, crushed the nationalist aspirations of a circle of West Russian princes (above, pp. 75–76). During the war between Lithuania and Moscow in 1500–03 a number of Russian princes along the Lithuanian-Russian border, from Viazma in the north to Chernigov in the south, went over to the Muscovite side.

The whole political picture in the area of the old Russian federation of the Kievan period changed drastically after the fall of Novgorod. Instead of a multitude of Russian states, two major powers now vied for supremacy—the Grand Duchies of Moscow and Lithuania. The latter was handicapped, in its dealing with the Russians, by its Union with Poland and by the influence of the Roman Catholic Church, to which, at that time, the majority of Russians were in opposition and of which they were suspicious. On the other hand, the Russian nobility cherished the rights and privileges it enjoyed in the Grand Duchy of Lithuania and was afraid of the centralized system of government in Moscow. It was the support of the lower classes on which Moscow could chiefly count—in Novgorod and elsewhere.

When in 1508 Prince Mikhail Glinsky revolted against Grand Duke Sigismund I, his original plan was apparently to create a Russian principality within the framework of the Grand Duchy of Lithuania or even to replace the Lithuanian leadership in the rada by the Russian, headed by him. It was only after his plan had miscarried that Glinsky went over to Vasili III's side.

The failure of Glinsky's plan put an end to any consistent Russian attempt to control the government of the Grand Duchy of Lithuania. Afterward the Russians in West Russia had to concentrate their attention on the defense of the Greek Orthodox Church, as well as on education. Politically, both the lords and the gentry in the Grand Duchy, of either Lithuanian or Russian extraction, rallied to the support of their government against the Muscovite danger.

It should be noted, however, that even at the time of the sharp political division of the Russian areas between the grand duchies of Lithuania and Muscovy, many a Russian in both West and East Russia thought in terms of cultural unity between the two parts. In fact, cultural intercourse between the two countries never stopped.

As has been mentioned, the Heresy of the Judaizers was originally sponsored by "Jews" (apparently, Karaites) of West Russia who came to Novgorod under the protection of Prince Mikhail Olelkovich of Kiev in 1470 (above, p. 47). It is from Lithuania that seeds of Protestantism penetrated to Muscovy in the 1540's. Soon afterward, several East Russian religious leaders who had fled from Muscovy helped both the Orthodox and the Protestant movements in West Russia (below, pp. 276–277, 282–283).

In the printing of Russian books in the second half of the 16th century, natives of both West and East Russia took part. Of the two printers who handled the Moscow printing office in 1563–65 one was a native of Moscow and the other of Mstislavl in West Russia. Both of them emigrated to West Russia and continued their work there (below, p. 283).

In the sphere of economics, lively commercial relations were established between East and West Russia. Muscovite merchants regularly visited West Russian towns, such as Smolensk (even prior to its annexation to Moscow), Polotsk, Kiev, and others. Merchants of West Russia, in their turn, traded with Muscovy. As has been mentioned, Karaite merchants established themselves in Smolensk. They continued to stay there after 1514.

In the course of the 15th and 16th centuries many West Russian princes migrated to Moscow and many Muscovite princes and boyars deserted to Lithuania during the "oprichnina" terror regime of Tsar Ivan IV. Psychologically, at the base of these desertions lay the feeling that Lithuania was not a foreign land but part of the Russian milieu.

To return now to the strengthening of the army organization in Lithuania, a number of decrees were enacted by the diet in 1528 and 1529. In the former year the diet ruled that the official at the head of each poviet should appoint two trustworthy noblemen (*zemiane*) to make a census of all the gentry's landed estates, in order to determine the number of men and resources available for the mobilization of the army in case of an emergency. For the crown estates special officials were sent for the same purpose. The lords had to make a census of their respective estates. On the basis of this census, a list of all noblemen was compiled, with the indication of the number of horsemen each nobleman had to muster (see above, p. 189).

At that time it was supposed that one horseman was to be mustered per ten *sluzhby* (service units). In 1529 a new law was passed

by the diet according to which the ratio was changed to one horseman per eight sluzhby. This was enacted, at first, as a temporary
measure for ten years, but the rule was kept in force until 1544 in
spite of the protests of the gentry, who complained that it was too
heavy a burden for them. From the military point of view, the law of
1529 meant a considerable increase in the size of the army. In 1544
the ratio of one horseman per nine sluzhby was introduced. In 1567
it was again changed—one horseman per eleven sluzhby. Also, in
1563 and 1567 the noblemen were required to muster one foot soldier
in addition to each two horsemen.[1]

It should be noted that the Lithuanian government tried to take
care of the financial as well as military problems. Since agriculture
was the mainstay of the grand duchy's national economy, it is understandable that a serious effort should be made to raise the income
from farms. The grand duke led the way by instituting a series of
reforms in the management of the crown estates. The nobility followed suit.

In 1514 and 1529 Grand Duke Sigismund I issued instructions
to the derzhavtsy, ordering them to take a number of measures intended to make the peasants' works in the crown estates more profitable for the grand duke's treasury. Some of the peasants who
formerly had been subject to the corvée now had instead to pay rent
in money for the use of the plots of land they tilled.

In 1548 Grand Duke Sigismund August sent new instructions in
which he ordered the peasants' payments and liabilities to be distributed more equally among the service units. At the same time,
the peasants were forbidden to dispose of their plots by selling or
renting them, as they had been wont to do earlier (above, p. 207).
Thus one of the objectives of the grand duke's instructions was to
crush the passive resistance of the peasants to the legal regime which
deprived them of rights on their lands.

The subsequent agrarian policy of Sigismund August was based
on the principles of German law and German concepts of rational
agricultural economy, long popular in Poland. Besides heeding the
German patterns which penetrated to Lithuania from both Poland
and Prussia, Sigismund August was advised by foreign specialists in
his service, among them Italians who had come to Vilna in the wake
of Queen Bona, Sigismund August's mother. Bona Sforza was the
daughter of a duke of Milan and a Spanish princess. Famous for

1. Kutrzeba, 2, 174.

her beauty and her haughtiness, she was permeated with the spirit of the Renaissance, was fond of the arts and of luxury, and was at the same time a shrewd businesswoman. She introduced new principles of national economy in the huge estates her husband (Sigismund August's father) had bestowed on her at their marriage.[2]

The agrarian reforms Sigismund August undertook reflected the spirit of the age. It was fortunate for him that he succeeded in engaging for service in his Chancellery a number of outstanding specialists in financial administration, among them some Italians previously employed by Queen Bona. It was they who took charge of the reforms.[3]

The German law, as applied to agricultural settlements in Poland, developed chiefly in East Germany in the peculiar conditions of German expansion in the area of the Western Slavs. The communes of the German colonists were exempted from interference by the king's officials as well as from various liabilities with which the native peasants were burdened. New settlements were organized by entrepreneurs with technical knowledge of agriculture who possessed sufficient capital. Such an agent was called a "locator." [4] The locator received a charter from the king on the basis of which he was recognized the hereditary head of the new settlement and was not subordinated to the local lords. In terms of the German law, he would become a judge and overseer of the village, a *Schulze*.

For the agricultural reforms on crown land in the Grand Duchy of Lithuania the most important feature of the German managerial methods was the *folvarok* plan. In modern times (prior to the second World War), the term (*Vorwerk*) was applied in East Germany to a subsidiary establishment on a section of a landed estate. In the late Middle Ages it denoted the chief manor itself. Such farms varied in size from two hundred to over a thousand acres.

The pattern of folvarok became the basis of the agrarian reform instituted by Sigismund August on April 1, 1557. The new land ordinance was called *Ustava na voloki,* "Statute of the voloki." The size of the voloka, a land measure, was standardized and made equal to 33 *morgi* (singular, *morg,* from the German *Morgen*)—that is, about 21 hectares.[5]

2. On Queen Bona see W. Pociecha, "Bona Sforza," *PSB, 2* (1936), 288–294.
3. Dovnar-Zapolsky, pp. 295, 311.
4. See H. Aubin, "The Lands East of Elbe and German Colonization Eastwards," *CEH, 1* (1942), 374–375. On the peasants under German law in Poland see Wojciechowski, pp. 193–203.
5. For the text of the *Ustava na voloki* see *RIB, 30* (1914), cols. 542–585. Cf.

In those parts of the crown estates where the reform was introduced, all tillable land was surveyed and divided into square plots, each being equal to one voloka. The best plots in each group of them were reserved for the local folvarok. Some lots were assigned to the military servitors (each received two voloki), and most to the peasants. A larger peasant household was supposed to receive one voloka. The three-field crop rotation system was to be observed, so that the land in each voloka, or each half voloka in case there were two households on one voloka, was divided into three sections. The peasant's house and barns were to be built in the central field. A small household was entitled to half a voloka.

One of the aims of the reform was to abolish the maze of intermixed peasant strips, so that the land of each household would be all together. This process of consolidation was called *komasacja* in Polish.

The reform, started on crown lands, was later accepted by many noblemen for their estates. Geographically, the main area of the new land settlement comprised Lithuania proper, Zhomoit, Podliashie, Polesie, and Volyn. To a lesser extent it affected the regions along the Dnieper River.

The peasants resettled on the voloki had to pay a tax called *chinsh*. The amount of the chinsh and the accompanying payments in kind varied, depending on the quality of the soil, from 66 to 106 *groshi* per one voloka. The tiaglye peasants—those who were liable to corvée for the folvarok—paid lighter taxes but had to work two days a week and in addition help to mow the meadows and make the hay during the mowing season.

The voloki settlement was a far-reaching agricultural reform; as Mikhail Hrushevsky says, it amounted to a veritable economic revolution.[6] It was based on sound principles from the point of view of agricultural management and technique and raised the grand duke's, as well as the noblemen's, income from the farms.

For the peasants, however, the reform meant the destruction of their traditional ways of husbandry and life and of their basic concepts of rights on land. The new land settlement aimed at the dissolution of all previous forms of peasant cooperative and co-ownership associations. In most cases the peasants had to move from

Hrushevsky, *Istoriia*, 5, 206–209; Dovnar-Zapolsky, pp. 276–311, 322–333; Liubavsky, *Ocherk*, pp. 242–246; Kutrzeba, 2, 85–95. For a recent monograph on the voloki reform see Picheta, *Agrarnaia reforma Sigizmunda-Avgusta*.

6. Hrushevsky, *Istorii Ukrainy-Rusi*, 5, 206.

their old villages to the new voloka lots, which alone meant a complete break with old customs and familiar neighborhood surroundings.

Each peasant was now directly subordinated to the grand duke's or the nobleman's agent, the manager of the folvarok, on crown land known as the voit. He was in a position to impose more liabilities on the peasants in order to squeeze more income from the farm. In the late 16th and early 17th centuries it became usual to require corvée of three days a week from a small peasant household settled on half a voloka. The household on a full voloka had to work four days a week if the peasants supplied their own horses, and five days without horses.[7] Peasant liabilities were lighter in the areas not affected by the reform, especially in the border regions along the Dnieper River south of Kiev and on the fringe of the *Dikoe Pole* (Wild Prairie) east of the Dnieper.[8]

The voloka land reform was conceived as a long-range reform. The initial costs of surveying and resettlement were heavy, and time was required for the adjustment of the peasants to the new conditions. Before long, however, the reform served its purpose financially. By 1566, in the crown domains in the poviets of Vilna and of Troki and in the land of Zhomoit, 57,636 voloki (over 1,000,000 hectares) had been surveyed, and out of this total 42,623 voloka units were already established.[9]

It should be noted that the voloka reform came at the time of important changes in the national economy of the Grand Duchy of Lithuania. Agriculture was oriented toward the ever-growing needs of export to Western markets, which stimulated production. The main items of export to the West from crown land were corn and timber. From Zhomoit these products were carted to Riga and sold to German, Dutch, Danish, and other Western merchants. From the Vilna region and adjacent areas the products of export were transported to Polotsk and other ports on the Western Dvina River and from there shipped down to Riga.[10] As early as 1547 the export of timber became a government monopoly.[11] The voloka land settlement was the cornerstone of the agrarian regime in Lithuania and a considerable part of West Russia for the following three centuries.

7. *Ibid.*, pp. 214–215.
8. *Ibid.*, p. 220.
9. Dovnar-Zapolsky, p. 352.
10. *Ibid.*, pp. 318–320.
11. *Ibid.*, p. 333.

II

Soon after the beginning of the voloka reform a serious international crisis developed that imposed a great strain on the grand duchy's finances and army. The crisis was the result of the clash of interests of Lithuania and Muscovy in the Baltic area.

In the first half of his reign Tsar Ivan IV (1533–84) directed his main efforts against the Tatars. In 1552 Kazan was stormed and the Khanate of Kazan annexed to Muscovy. Two years later the Khanate of Astrakhan was occupied by the Muscovite troops and in 1556 the area of the Khanate incorporated into the Tsardom of Moscow. It might be expected that Moscow's next move would have been against the Khanate of the Crimea.

In May 1555 the Crimean Khan Devlet-Girey sent an envoy to Ivan, expressing his willingness to conclude a treaty of friendship. This proved to be simply a diplomatic maneuver to conceal the khan's preparations for a campaign against Moscow, for by June he was nearing Tula with his army. Although he defeated the Russian vanguard, he hastily turned back to the Crimea as soon as he received news that a strong Russian army had been sent from Moscow to meet him.[12]

The Moscow government decided to counterattack by reconnoitering the approaches to the Crimea via the Dnieper River. In March 1556 the diak Rzhevsky, at the head of a detachment of Putivl Cossacks, reached the Dnieper River below Cherkasy. The Starosta of Kanev and Cherkasy, Prince Dmitri Ivanovich Vishnevetsky, not waiting for the authorization of his sovereign, Grand Duke Sigismund August of Lithuania, decided to cooperate with the Muscovite operations and sent a party of Cherkasy Cossacks to reinforce Rzhevsky's detachment. Rzhevsky descended the Dnieper River down to the Black Sea and raided Ochakov, after which he returned to Putivl. Vishnevetsky's Cossacks returned to Cherkasy.[13]

Encouraged by the raid on Ochakov, Vishnevetsky decided to build up a Cossack stronghold on one of the islands below the Dnieper Cataracts (Zaporozhie). Such a stronghold could serve as an excellent base of operations against the Tatars and the Turks. Vishnevetsky chose for it the Island of Khortitsa, and the Cossack fort was built there in the summer of 1556. This is the first definite

---

12. *PSRL, 13,* 255–258; Soloviev, *Istoriia, 6,* 139.
13. *PSRL, 13,* 271; Golobutsky, p. 74.

information we have about the Zaporozhie *Sech* (in Ukrainian, *Sich*), as the Dnieper Cossacks called their fortress.[14] Vishnevetsky now asked Sigismund August for money and supplies in order to defend Khortitsa against the Tatars, but receiving no help, he abandoned the island and returned to Cherkasy. Soon afterward (September 1557) he went to Moscow and offered his services to the tsar in the latter's struggle with the Tatars. Ivan granted Vishnevetsky the town of Belev on the Upper Oka River for his maintenance. Belev was strategically located as a suitable base for a steppe campaign in the direction of either the Dnieper or the Don area. In January 1558 Vishnevetsky with a detachment of Russian Cossacks and Muscovite musketeers (*streltsy*) was sent to the Perekop Isthmus via the Dnieper River. The expedition was indecisive, and Vishnevetsky went to Khortitsa, where he was joined by reinforcements brought by the diak Rzhevsky. They both made another expedition to Perekop, but their forces proved insufficient to storm it and they returned to the Middle Dnieper area. The tsar ordered Vishnevetsky to come to Moscow, leaving Rzhevsky in the Dnieper region. Apparently, Rzhevsky's camp was on Monastyr Island, above the Cataracts.[15]

It must have become clear to the tsar by this time that any attack on the Crimea via the Dnieper River needed more thorough preparation and a well organized base in the Zaporozhie region. To avoid any misunderstandings with Lithuania he needed an agreement with her before making any new move in the Dnieper area.

In February 1558 Ivan sent to Vilna a "boyar son" (*syn boyarsky*), Roman Olferiev, as his envoy to offer to Sigismund August an alliance against the Crimean Tatars.[16] Olferiev arrived at Vilna in May and was well received there. However, the Lithuanian lords, evidently suspicious of the tsar's connection with Vishnevetsky as well as, on the other hand, of Moscow's interference in Livonian affairs, gave no definite answer. Olferiev was told that the matter of alliance could not be decided now and that the king would send his envoy to the tsar for further talks about it.

The Lithuanians were especially worried about the Livonian situation because they themselves were involved in it. In 1557

14. Golobutsky suggests (p. 77) that by the time Vishnevetsky had built his fort on the Island of Khortitsa, there was already in existence a Cossack *sech* on the Island of Tomakovka, lower down the Dnieper. There is no evidence for his surmise.

15. *PSRL, 13,* 286, 288, 296.

16. *Sbornik, 59,* 538–551.

Sigismund August interfered in a clash between the magister of the Livonian Knights, the aged Wilhelm Fürstenberg, and the archbishop Wilhelm of Riga. The latter's brother, Albrecht, Duke of Prussia, was Poland's vassal. The two brothers were Sigismund August's nephews through their mother, the king's sister. Sigismund led a strong Polish-Lithuanian army into Livonia. Fürstenberg sued for peace and agreed to conclude a military alliance with Poland and Lithuania.[17]

The rapprochement between Livonia and Lithuania must have worried the tsar, since he had had his own plans for Livonia. In 1554 a treaty had been concluded between Ivan IV on the one side and the magister of the Livonian Knights, the Archbishop of Riga, and the Bishop of Dorpat on the other. At that time the magister had pledged not to make an alliance with the King of Poland, and the city of Dorpat had promised to pay a small yearly tribute to Moscow on the basis of an earlier agreement concluded in 1503 (above, p. 95). The alliance between Livonia and Poland signed in 1557 violated this Russian-Livonian agreement of 1554. Moreover, the city of Dorpat had failed to make the stipulated payments to Moscow. Be this as it may, in January 1558 the Muscovite troops invaded Livonia.

Irrespective of the Livonian affairs, Sigismund August was reluctant to conclude an alliance with the tsar against the Tatars because he feared the Ottoman Sultan's interference in favor of the Crimean Khan. Negotiations with the tsar continued, however. In June 1558 Sigismund August sent to Moscow a diplomatic mission consisting of the master of the horse, Ian Volchok, and a secretary of the Chancellery, Lukash Haraburda. No agreement was achieved, and in December of the same year another Lithuanian embassy to the tsar was appointed, which arrived at Moscow on March 3, 1559. One of the Lithuanian envoys was Vasili Tyshkevich, Voevoda of Podliashie; he was accompanied by the marshal of the court, Nikolai Poshushensky, and the secretary, Ian Haiko.

The negotiations proved indecisive, since the Lithuanian envoys insisted on withdrawal of the Muscovite troops from Livonia as the prerequisite of a treaty of alliance between Lithuania and Muscovy, and the tsar refused to comply with the demand.[18] Nevertheless, on April 1, 1559, Ivan, through the mediation of the King of Denmark,

17. Grabieński, p. 113.
18. *Sbornik, 59,* 577–580.

agreed to a six-month truce with Livonia, during which all military operations were to be suspended, each side remaining in the position it held on the day of armistice.

The Magister of the Livonian Knights, Ketler (successor to Fürstenberg, who had resigned in the summer of 1558), decided to use the respite to secure the assistance of Sigismund August against Muscovy. On August 31, accordingly, he concluded an agreement with the king which provided that the latter should recognize Livonia as a protectorate, at the same time recognizing the traditional suzerainty of the German emperor over the Livonian Order.[19]

Following this, Ketler, according to the Russian sources, immediately mobilized his army, preparing himself for continuation of the war against Moscow. In late September or early October 1559 a detachment of Livonian troops invaded part of the territory occupied by the Muscovite troops in the region of Iuriev (Dorpat), without waiting for the expiration of the term of the six-month armistice granted by Ivan in April (the armistice was to expire on November 1).[20] The Muscovites then resumed military operations and raided Livonia several times. Sigismund August did not send any troops to help Ketler but twice dispatched messengers to Moscow urging Ivan to stop war and make peace with Livonia and Lithuania (December 1559 and January 1560).[21]

It so happened that in November 1559 Ivan's consort, Tsaritsa Anastasia, became very ill.[22] Her health was apparently broken and she was not expected to recover. In the event of Anastasia's death, Ivan's second marriage would become feasible, and the idea of using it to further Moscow's diplomatic aims must have occurred to the tsar and his advisers. In fact, the tsar's marriage with one of Sigismund August's sisters, could, as the Moscow leaders might hope, cement a Moscow-Lithuanian alliance and secure Livonia for Moscow.

In the middle of July 1560 a big fire occurred in Moscow. It was with difficulty that the gravely ill Anastasia was moved from Moscow to her village of Kolomenskoe, about ten miles south of the city, where she died on August 7. Anastasia was very popular, and a huge crowd of the Muscovites mourned for her at her funeral in Moscow.

19. Bestuzhev-Riumin, 2, 247; Liubavsky, *Ocherk*, pp. 259–260.
20. *PSRL*, *13*, 320.
21. *PSRL*, *13*, 322–324.
22. *PSRL*, *13*, 321.

It is recorded in the chronicles that Ivan was deeply afflicted by the loss.[23]

Ivan did not let his personal feeling interfere with what he considered his royal duties. The tense international situation required immediate action. By this time the plan of the tsar's diplomatic marriage must have taken definite shape in confidential talks between the tsar and his advisers, and was speedily put in action.

One week after Anastasia's death the first step was taken. On August 14 the boyars and Metropolitan Makari, accompanied by other Russian prelates, called on the tsar and urged him to marry for the second time. The tsar, as probably was expected, answered that he would have to think the matter over. Two days later he called the prelates and boyars to his chambers in the palace and announced his willingness to take a second wife, adding that he intended to choose as fiancée a foreign princess. The metropolitan gave Ivan his blessing, and the tsar declared that he would send envoys for the selection of a suitable bride to three countries: Lithuania, Sweden, and Circassia.[24]

It seems certain that for political reasons the tsar's predilection was for the Lithuanian marriage. Only if this did not materialize was he prepared to accept a Swedish or Circassian bride. From the diplomatic point of view, affiliation with the Swedish royal house could be useful for pressure on Lithuania, and the marital tie with a Circassian princess would encourage the Cirassians' assistance against the Crimean Tatars.

The tsar chose the okolnichi, Fedor Ivanovich Sukin, as his envoy to Lithuania. On August 18 Sukin received proper credentials and instructions. He had to conduct both the official negotiations and the confidential talks concerning the proposed marriage.[25]

Sigismund August had two unmarried sisters, Ann and Catherine. Sukin's first task, according to the tsar's instructions, was to find out discreetly which of the two sisters had the better character and greater beauty. If Ann was over twenty-five, Sukin had to disregard her and demand for the tsar the hand of the younger sister, Catherine. He was also instructed to bring portraits of the sisters to the tsar.

Sukin arrived at Vilna on September 28, where he and his com-

23. *PSRL, 13,* 327–328.
24. *PSRL, 13,* 329.
25. *Sbornik, 71,* 1–10.

panions were warmly received at Sigismund August's court. They presented Ivan's greetings to the king, after which the latter ordered four members of his privy council to enter into negotiations. These members were Valerian, Archbishop of Vilna; Nikolai Ianovich Radivil, nicknamed "The Black" (*Chorny;* in Polish, *Czarny*), Voevoda of Vilna; marshal of the land Ostafi Volovich; and secretary Ian Shimkov. They first discussed with Sukin the matter of Moscow-Lithuanian alliance and, as in previous negotiations, insisted on the withdrawal of Muscovite troops from Livonia.

The matrimonial plan was next given attention. By that time Sukin had collected sufficient confidential information to enable him to select Catherine as Ivan's prospective bride, and he mentioned her name to the members of the privy council. The Lithuanians said at first that it would not be proper for the king to give in marriage the younger sister before the elder, but then agreed to talk about Catherine. They insisted on her remaining Roman Catholic in case of her marriage with Ivan. Besides, they emphasized the necessity of the political alliance before the nuptial.

Sukin asked for an opportunity of personally presenting the tsar's greetings to Catherine. This request was refused, and it was agreed that Sukin and his companions would be given a chance to look at the royal princess from a nearby building at the time she left the cathedral after Sunday mass. On that Sunday, after the mass, the king and his two sisters stood for a while in front of the cathedral. The king chatted with the Voevoda of Vilna. Catherine glanced at the window of the building from which the Muscovite envoys were peeping at her. In his report Sukin remarked: "And we do not know if the *korolevna* (royal princess) was aware of our presence there, or not." [26] She probably was.

Sukin returned to Moscow on November 10, bringing a letter to Ivan from King Sigismund August. The king again mentioned the presence of the Muscovite troops in Livonia as an obstacle to an agreement. On February 6, 1561, the king's envoys Ian Shimkov and Ian Haika came to Moscow to continue negotiations.[27] To parry Moscow's claims on Livonia, the Lithuanian envoys said that the king on his part would be entitled to claim Novgorod, Pskov, Smolensk, and Severia back from Moscow.

In view of these claims and counterclaims no agreement could

26. *Ibid.*, p. 20.
27. *Ibid.*, pp. 23–46.

be reached. The tsar realized the futility of further negotiations with the king and in August 1561 married Princes Maria of Circassia.

In turn, Sigismund August took drastic steps to secure Polish-Lithuanian control of Livonia. In June 1561 his troops entered Livonia.[28] In the fall of the same year the Livonian magister, Ketler; the Archbishop of Riga; and a few other representatives of Livonia came to Vilna and agreed to the incorporation of Livonia into Poland and Lithuania. Lithuania took upon herself the immediate responsibility of defending Livonia (called *Inflanty* in Polish). Kurland became a vassal duchy, with Ketler as the duke, on November 28, 1561.[29]

A full-fledged war between Poland and Lithuania on the one hand and Muscovy, on the other became almost unavoidable. The Lithuanian government began hastily to strengthen the grand duchy's armed forces and finances for the impending crisis. In the course of 1560–61 Sigismund August mortgaged a number of crown estates to princes and lords. The towns were compelled to lend to the grand duke large sums of money by June 29, 1561, the amount of which was determined by the grand duke. In the same year the noblemen were ordered to pay immediately the arrears on the *serebshina* (silver tax) for the years 1559 and 1560. A new collection of serebshina was decreed at the end of 1561 (20 groshi from each voloka). The customs duties were greatly increased.[30] In 1561–62 in its search for new sources of state income the Lithuanian government introduced the salt monopoly. The proceeds from it were to reinforce the existing taxes on salt. Both the population of the crown domain and the szlachta with its dependents had to pay the excise and taxes on salt.[31] The establishment of monopolies and the increase of custom duties resulted in the rapid growth of the state's income. Only partial figures of the state revenue for these years are available, but they are revealing, showing for the decade of 1558–68 an increase of collections from 26 to over 500 per cent.[32]

On the military side, in 1563 a decree was issued according to which the landowners had to muster *draby* (foot soldiers) in addition to horsemen at the rate of one foot soldier per two horsemen.

28. Shmurlo, *2*, Pt. I, 81.
29. Grabieński, pp. 113, 114; Liubavsky, *Ocherk,* pp. 260–261; Kutrzeba, *1*, 201–202.
30. Liubavsky, *Ocherk,* pp. 265–267.
31. Dovnar-Zapolsky, pp. 490–496.
32. *Ibid.,* p. 477.

III

Even with the full exertion of her military and financial resources
the Grand Duchy of Lithuania had little hope to withstand single-
handed the grim trial of a war against Moscow. Therefore, she
strove to receive guaranties of Poland's active support for the loom-
ing conflict.

Although Poland and Lithuania had the same monarch in the person of Sigismund August—king in Poland and grand duke in Lithuania—each state had a separate government and administration,
and the Poles were not bound to support Lithuania in the latter's
wars without a special agreement for each emergency.

Moreover, this weak link of union between the two states was
even more uncertain for the future in view of the fact that Sigismund
August (born in 1520) had no children. In 1543 he married Elizabeth of Austria, but she died suddenly two years later. It was suspected that she was poisoned by her mother-in-law (Sigismund
August's mother), Queen Bona, who was jealous of Elizabeth's influence on the ruler. Soon afterward, in spite of the opposition of
the Polish senate, Sigismund August secretly married a beautiful
Lithuanian widow, Barbara Gashtovt (Gasztold), *née* Radivil
(sister of Nikolai Iurievich Radivil, nicknamed Rudy, "the Rufous";
he was Nikolai Chorny's cousin). Bona hated her second daughter-
in-law no less than the first, quarreled with her son, and went back
to Italy, taking with her all her jewels and money.

In 1550 Sigismund August succeeded in arranging that Barbara
be crowned queen. The coronation, which took place on December
9, was resented by a number of Polish senators. Queen Bona must
likewise have been indignant when she received the news in Italy.
But Barbara was not destined to enjoy her new position for long.
She fell ill before her coronation and died on May 8, 1551. The
courtiers believed that she had had the "French disease" (syphilis).[33]
However, there were rumors that she was poisoned at a banquet by
Bona's agent. Bona herself died in 1557, allegedly poisoned by her
own physician.[34]

In 1553 Sigismund August married for the third time, taking for
his bride Catherine of Austria, his first wife's sister. When he
separated from her, there remained no hope that he would ever have

33. See W. Pociecha, "Barbara Radziwillowna," *PSB, 1* (1935), 294–298.
34. Pociecha, "Bona Sforza," p. 293.

an heir to the throne. Therefore both Polish and Lithuanian statesmen were worried about a possible dissolution of the union between
Poland and Lithuania after his death. In 1562, on the eve of the war
with Moscow, Sigismund was only forty-two, but because of his dis-
solute way of life, his health was seriously undermined.

To secure a continuation of the link between Poland and Lithuania joint action by the diets of the two states was needed. The
necessity of a closer union was fully realized by both the Poles and
the Lithuanians, but their respective approach to the problem was
different. The Polish szlachta insisted on the complete incorporation of the Grand Duchy of Lithuania into Poland. Some of the
Polish senators were in favor of leaving a degree of autonomy to
Lithuania, but they had little chance if any to carry their moderate
views.

In Lithuania the lords wanted to keep the autonomy of the grand
duchy intact and were ready only to pass a new law of succession
to the throne according to which each new sovereign would be elected
jointly by the combined diets of Poland and Lithuania. In addition
they wanted a permanent military alliance with Poland. By contrast
the gentry, especially of some Russian regions of the grand duchy,
were in favor of parliamentary union with Poland. This would give
the szlachta of the grand duchy political preponderance over the
lords.

Thus the discussion of the military aspect of the proposed union
between the two states was complicated by the political rivalry between the aristocracy and the gentry.

In 1562 the szlachta of the Grand Duchy of Lithuania—mobilized
for the war with Moscow and stationed in the camp near Vitebsk—
formed a "confederation" and demanded an immediate convocation
of a joint Polish-Lithuanian diet. The right of forming a confederation of the whole szlachta, or of a group of it, was practiced in
Poland in the late 14th and early 15th centuries to achieve special
political aims. In the 16th century it fell into disuse, since by that
time the szlachta had obtained control of the diet.[35] Now the Lithuanian-Russian szlachta revived the institution.

Its move was seconded by the Polish szlachta, who at the Diet of
Piotrków (1562–63) passed a resolution that a joint Polish-Lith-

---

35. Kutrzeba, *1*, 166–168; Wojciechowski, pp. 264–266. In the 14th and 15th centuries not only the szlachta but also the towns formed confederations on several occasions.

uanian diet be gathered at Warsaw on November 11, 1563, to start negotiations for a full union between Poland and Lithuania. The king complied with the demand and convoked the diet.[36]

By that time the war with Moscow already had begun. Because of this no full representation of the Lithuanian nobility at the diet was possible, and only a delegation of the representatives of the council of lords and of the szlachta envoys could attend the meeting. Since the city of Kraków was entitled to send a delegate to the Polish diet, representatives of the city of Vilna were included in the Lithuanian delegation. Actually, the latter was controlled by the lords, who presented their plan of the union, according to which Lithuania was to keep her autonomy. Nikolai Radivil Chorny was the main spokesman of the Lithuanians at the Warsaw diet.

In contrast, the Polish part of the diet was dominated by the szlachta. The Poles demanded a complete fusion of Lithuania with Poland into one *rzeczpospolita* (commonwealth).

In view of the wide divergence between the Polish and Lithuanian plans of union, the Warsaw Diet of 1563–64 was unable to make any decision.[37]

Meanwhile Lithuania found herself at war. The Lithuanian military leaders had concentrated their main forces in Livonia, expecting that she would become the main theater of war. While part of the Muscovite army was deployed in Livonia, the tsar with his choice troops entered the confines of the Grand Duchy of Lithuania in January 1563 and attacked Polotsk. The city surrendered on February 15. The tsar appointed three lieutenants in Polotsk, whom he instructed to study the old Polotsk customs of justice and administration and to let the Polotsk gentry elect local judges for the area.[38]

On February 20 envoys from the Lithuanian council of lords appeared in Polotsk and were received by the Moscow boyars. Lithuania asked for a truce until August 15, at which time the king was to send an embassy to the tsar to negotiate for peace. The tsar accepted the offer.[39] A few days afterward he went back to Moscow.

In May a Lithuanian envoy came to Moscow for preliminary discussions of an agreement between the two countries,[40] and an envoy

---

36. Liubavsky, *Ocherk*, p. 295; Grabieński, pp. 107, 108, 114. A number of documents of 1563–64 are published in *Akta Unji*, pp. 154–185.

37. Liubavsky, *Ocherk*, pp. 295–298; Grabieński, p. 114.

38. *PSRL*, *13*, 355–364; Karamzin, *Istoriia*, *9*, 41–44; Bestuzhev-Riumin, *2*, 272–273.

39. *Sbornik*, *71*, 121–131.

40. *Ibid.*, pp. 131–151.

of the tsar was received by the king in August. The tsar complained of a Lithuanian raid on Severia.[41] In September a messenger arrived in Moscow to announce that an embassy from the king would arrive in October.[42]

On December 5 the king's embassy, consisting of Iuri Andreevich Khodkevich, Grigori Volovich, and Mikhail Haraburda, reached Moscow. Negotiations continued to January 9, 1564, but proved futile. The tsar now demanded not only Livonia and Polotsk but all his "patrimony"—all the Russian provinces of the Grand Duchy of Lithuania as well as Lvov and Galich. A detailed list of all the Russian cities controlled by Lithuania and Poland was presented to Sigismund August's envoys.[43]

The Lithuanian ambassadors then submitted to the tsar the king's counterdemand of returning to Lithuania her former possessions. The list they presented included Novgorod, Pskov, Chernigov, Smolensk, Polotsk, and a number of other cities.[44]

As a result of these differences the war was resumed, and this time with success on the Lithuanian side. In January 1564 the Lithuanian army headed by Nikolai Radivil Rudy completely defeated the Muscovite troops under the command of Prince Petr Ivanovich Shuisky, who was killed in the melee. The battle took place at Chashniki on the River Ulla, southeast of Polotsk.[45] According to the letter of Cardinal Commendone to Cardinal Borromeo from Warsaw, Shuisky's body was brought to Vilna and buried there with a great solemnity that was resented by the Poles at Sigismund August's court.[46]

Even more ominous for Moscow was Prince Andrei Mikhailovich Kurbsky's desertion to the Polish-Lithuanian forces in Livonia on April 30, 1564. Kurbsky, a descendant of Rurik, was one of Moscow's ablest generals and until 1560 one of the tsar's advisers. Because of the tsar's break with the *izbrannaia rada* (selected council) to which he had belonged, Kurbsky, after about 1562, was afraid of the tsar's disfavor and decided to exercise the Russian boyar's traditional right of freedom to serve any prince he chose. Therefore he went over to Sigismund August.

41. *Ibid.*, pp. 151–163.
42. *Ibid.*, pp. 163–173.
43. *Ibid.*, p. 260.
44. *Ibid.*, p. 267.
45. *PSRL, 13*, 377; Karamzin, *Istoriia, 9*, 29; Bestuzhev-Riumin, *2*, 273.
46. Karamzin, *Primechaniia, 9*, 36 (Note 99).

Kurbsky's desertion increased the tsar's suspicions of the boyars. The tsar now attempted to secure his control over the nation by instituting a special corps of bodyguards known collectively as the *oprichnina*. Its formation was announced by him at Aleksandrovskaia Sloboda on January 5, 1565.

It is noteworthy that the tsar did not want to reveal to the foreign powers the real meaning of the new institution. When a Lithuanian envoy was expected to arrive at Moscow in April 1566, the Moscow officials who had been appointed to meet him received from the tsar the following instruction: "And if he [the envoy] asks you, 'What is the oprichnina?' you must say that there is no such institution. The tsar lives in his palace; those noblemen who serve the sovereign loyally live near him; those who have behaved improperly live farther from the palace . . . Is not the tsar free to build his palace wherever he wishes?" [47]

In spite of the tsar's efforts to conceal the true situation in Muscovy, the Lithuanian lords soon became aware of his conflict with the boyars—for the simple reason that cases of desertion of Moscow servitors started even before Kurbsky's escape to Lithuania. Andrei Klobukov, the tsar's envoy sent to the king in July 1563, was instructed to make in Vilna confidential inquiries about two Princes Cherkassky—Aleksei and Gavriil—who had recently gone over to the king's side.[48] In 1561 Prince Dmitri Vishnevetsky wrote to Sigismund August asking him for permission to return to the grand duchy. Permission was granted and Vishnevetsky returned in the next year.[49] The above-mentioned Andrei Klobukov received precise instructions about what to answer in case the Lithuanians asked him why Vishnevetsky had left the tsar. In case of such a question Klobukov was to say: "Vishnevetsky had come to our sovereign like a dog and fled from him like a dog." [50] He was not, however, asked the question.

The Lithuanian government was not slow in trying to take advantage of the dissension in Muscovy and to attract to Lithuania as many dissatisfied boyars as possible. Thus, in the language of the present time, the Lithuanian lords resorted to methods of creating a fifth column in Muscovy, of supplementing military action with undercover propaganda war.

47. *Sbornik, 71*, 331.
48. *Ibid.*, p. 156.
49. Golobutsky, pp. 82–83.
50. *Sbornik, 71*, 156.

In 1562 the senior Moscow boyar, Prince Ivan Dmitrievich Belsky, received a secret message from Sigismund August urging him to desert the tsar. The correspondence became known to Ivan, and Belsky was arrested, though he was later pardoned after signing a special pledge of loyalty.[51]

Kurbsky likewise had received, before his desertion, secret messages from Sigismund August and Nikolai Radivil Rudy inviting him to come to Lithuania and promising decent maintenance there.[52] The policy of the lords thus proved fruitful and was continued after the Kurbsky case. In 1567 four prominent Moscow boyars—the above-mentioned Prince Belsky, Prince Ivan Fedorovich Mstislavsky, Prince Mikhail Ivanovich Vorotynsky, and Ivan Petrovich Fedorov-Cheliadnin—received secret messages from Sigismund August and Grigori Aleksandrovich Khodkevich inviting them to Lithuania. Each of these boyars immediately referred the matter to the tsar. Ivan ordered them to send back sarcastic and abusive answers, and personally drafted their replies.[53] By doing so he achieved two aims: to insult Sigismund August and Grigori Khodkevich and to discourage further correspondence of the Lithuanian leaders with these boyars.

In attempting to lure the Moscow boyars to Lithuania, the Lithuanian lords were ready to recompense the deserters properly and to treat them with honor. Promises of offices and land grants were made to Prince Belsky in 1562 and again in 1567, as well as to three other boyars at the latter date. It is possible that the honor of the state funeral for Prince P. I. Shuisky at Vilna in 1564 (see above) was part of the same policy. Of course, that honor also might have been an expression of the lords' chivalry and their recognition of the Moscow boyars as fellow aristocrats.

To return to Kurbsky, the latter deserted to Lithuania not alone but at the head of several hundred servitors. He was well received by Sigismund August, to whom he was able to give valuable advise on the conduct of the war against Moscow.[54] Kurbsky expressed a desire to take personal part in the war against Moscow and to muster

---

51. *PSRL, 13*, 339–340; *SGGD, 1*, 477–487 (Nos. 175–177); Soloviev, *Istoriia, 6*, 201; Bestuzhev-Riumin, *2*, 259.

52. Soloviev, *Istoriia, 6*, 203–204.

53. The letters are printed in *Poslaniia Ivana Groznogo*, pp. 241–247.

54. For the following see N. Ustrialov, *Skazaniia Kniazia Kurbskogo* (2d ed.), pp. xviii–xix. See also V. Korsakova, "Kurbsky," *RBS*, Vol. "Knappe–Kiukhelbeker," pp. 589–591.

200 horsemen from among his own followers. For this, Sigismund
August paid him 200,000 groshi. Kurbsky then was appointed one
of the three commanders of the vanguard of the Lithuanian army
in the autumn campaign against Polotsk of 1564. Nikolai Radivil
Rudy was the chief commander of the army.[55]

Polotsk was successfully defended by Kurbsky's former comrade-
in-arms, Prince Petr Mikhailovich Shcheniatev, who was of Lithuanian ancestry. The situation was laden with historical irony: a
Gedyminovich defending Muscovy and a Rurikovich serving Lithuania against Moscow. The Lithuanian army approached Polotsk
on September 16 but was unable to storm it and withdrew on October
4. The Crimean Khan, whom Sigismund August had urged to invade
Muscovy from the south simultaneously with the Lithuanian onslaught in the west, reached Riazan soon after the Lithuanians retreated from Polotsk. The Tatars looted the country around Riazan,
but when the khan received news that Ivan was about to send troops
against him, he retreated in his turn.[56] The combined Lithuanian-
Tatar campaign proved a failure.

During the following winter, Kurbsky was one of the commanders of the Lithuanian division sent, during the Lent of 1565, to
raid the region of Velikie Luki in the former Novgorod territory.
The raid proved futile from the strategic point of view, its only result being the devastation of the region. Many Russian villages and
at least one monastery were looted and burned. In his letter to
Kurbsky from Wolmar, Livonia, written much later (around 1577),
Tsar Ivan accused Kurbsky of burning and defiling many churches
and holy places.[57] In his answer to the tsar, Kurbsky asserted that
during the raid on Velikie Luki he took special care to prevent burning of the monasteries by the soldiers of the Lithuanian army, that
only one church with a monastery was burned by the Moslem
soldiers (Lithuanian Tatars), and that was when he was not present.[58]

Characteristically, neither the tsar nor Kurbsky mentioned the
burning of villages: that was considered normal by all belligerents
at that time. In Kurbsky's case it can only be observed that the
peasants whose villages his soldiers burned had been his compatriots
less than one year ago before the raid.

55. *PSRL, 13,* 390.
56. *PSRL, 13,* 388–389. Cf. Novoselsky, pp. 428–429.
57. Fennell, pp. 192–194.
58. Fennell, p. 208.

King Sigismund August, pleased with Kurbsky's military prowess, rewarded him with the office of Starosta of Krevo in Lithuania and granted him full ownership of landed estates in both Lithuania and Volynia, the latter domain including the rich town of Kovel. Kurbsky, well settled, started a new life in West Russia.

The war came almost to a standstill. Diplomatic negotiations between Moscow and Lithuania continued but brought no peace, since neither side was ready to renounce its claims. In 1566 the tsar convoked in Moscow the *zemsky sobor* (assembly of the land) to decide the dilemma of abandoning Livonia or resuming war. The sobor voted for war.

Simultaneously, the Lithuanian seim gathered at Vilna (1565–66). At that diet the szlachta of the Grand Duchy of Lithuania was granted full recognition of its personal privileges and political rights, and these rights were confirmed by the Second Lithuanian Statute of 1566 (above, p. 198).

At the same time the question of the union of Lithuania with Poland was again discussed. Of the szlachta of the grand duchy's Russian provinces, that of Podliashie and of Volynia were strongly for union. Their argument, which sounds somewhat paradoxical, was that because their respective lands were on the border of Poland, they suffered constantly from encroachment of Polish landowners across the border, from which the government of the grand duchy proved unable to protect them. On that ground they believed that if the union materialized, they would find better justice from the Polish government.

As a result of the deliberations of the seim, Sigismund August agreed to convoke a joint Polish-Lithuanian seim as soon as possible to enact the union with Poland. That fateful diet met at Lublin.

2. THE LUBLIN UNION OF 1569

On December 21, 1568, Sigismund August issued instructions to the Lithuanian representatives concerning the plan of work of the joint Polish-Lithuanian seim. The seim's sessions started in January 1569.[59]

59. On the Lublin Union of 1569 see M. V. Dovnar-Zapolsky, "Polsko-Litovskaia uniia na seimakh do 1569 goda," *DMAO*, 2 (1897); Liubavsky, *Seim*, pp. 815–850; *idem, Ocherk*, pp. 301–303; Lappo, *Velikoe Kniazhestvo Litovskoe*, *1*, 13–85; *idem, Zapadnaia Rossiia*, pp. 134–143; Kutrzeba, *1*, 197–201, *2*, 192–197; Halecki, *Dzieje Unii Jagiellońskiej*, *2*, 248–253. Documents of the Lublin seim are in *Akta Unji*, pp. 189–381, and

At the beginning of the first joint session, the Polish szlachta envoys demanded that all discussions be conducted by the deputies of both sides at the meetings of the seim and that there be no separate conferences of the Lithuanian delegates. The Poles, on the basis of previous seims, were afraid that on such separate conferences the Lithuanian lords would suppress the opposition of their szlachta. The Lithuanians refused to comply with the Polish demand and succeeded in having separate meetings of their own to formulate their plan of the union. As the Polish szlachta envoys had feared, the Lithuanian conferences approved the lords' program. The result was that each of the two sides—the Poles and the Lithuanians—submitted to the joint meetings its own project of the union, and the basic divergency in the respective attitudes of the two sides toward the character of the union led to an impasse.

The Poles insisted on full incorporation of the Grand Duchy of Lithuania into Poland. The very name of Lithuania was to be discarded, and the only title of the monarch would be "King of Poland."

The Lithuanians, instead, offered a close federation of Poland and Lithuania. The common monarch was to be elected at a joint seim taking place on the border between the two states and was to be installed in Kraków as King of Poland and in Vilna as Grand Duke of Lithuania. The joint Polish-Lithuanian seim would meet by turns in Poland and Lithuania on matters of foreign policy, war, and other major affairs bearing on the interests of the two states. Local affairs of each state would be discussed by the Polish seim in Poland and the Lithuanian seim in Lithuania. Lithuania would keep her own laws and judiciary. Only the natives of the grand duchy would be entitled to hold offices in the grand duchy's government and administration. However, Poles would be allowed to buy landed estates in Lithuania, and Lithuanians would be able to do the same in Poland.

The Lithuanian plan caused indignation among the Polish delegates. The Poles argued that Lithuanian had been incorporated into Poland at the time of the first union between the two states in 1385 and that subsequent changes of the status of the union and the concessions to Lithuania did not revoke the basic principle of the union. The Poles' approach to the question was thus legalistic rather

an unofficial diary of the seim in *Dnevnik Liublinskogo Seima,* ed. by Koialovich (St. Petersburg, 1869).

than historical. The Polish delegate Hieronim Ossolinski declared that "the union of the Grand Duchy of Lithuania [with Poland] was defined and confirmed by oath long ago. On that basis the Polish kings ruled Lithuania and granted her various liberties. It only remains to us to make such corrections [in the details of the instrument of the union] as prove necessary and then enforce all the provisions of the union." [60]

The two chief spokesmen of the Lithuanian delegation were the Voevoda of Vilna, Nikolai Radivil Rudy,[61] and the marshal of the land, Ian Ieronimovich Khodkevich. During a conference between the Polish senators and the Lithuanian *pany rada* (*lords in council*), Khodkevich said that "our nations [i.e. Lithuanians and Russians] and we [i.e. the pany-rada] are honest and honorable men and as regards our liberties we are equal to any nation, including you, Messrs. Poles. We would not like to conclude the union before we have established good order in our own commonwealth and have shown you that you are concluding the union with friends equal to you in honor and internal constitution. We have first to settle the matter with our own sovereign [i.e. Sigismund August as Grand Duke of Lithuania]. Only then will we be glad to discuss union with you. The king [i.e. Sigismund August as King of Poland] has nothing to do with the question of union. It is entirely our business, since we are free men and Christians. No one may conduct our affairs except ourselves, as our forefathers did."

Nikolai Radivil, answering Ossolinski, added a historical observation: "Your honor said that the kings of Poland had ruled Lithuania for a long time. I do not think that the requiem has been sung yet for the departed Grand Duke of Lithuania,[62] or that Lithuania received liberties only when the King of Poland began to rule over it." [63]

Khodkevich's and Radivil's defense of Lithuanian autonomy greatly angered the Poles. As the author of the "Diary" of the seim noted, "such conversations brought more mutual irritation than profit."

60. *Dnevnik Liublinskogo Seima*, p. 13. Cf. Lappo, *Velikoe Kniazhestvo Litovskoe*, *1*, 13–14.

61. After the death of Nikolai Radivil Chorny in 1565, Nikolai Radivil Rudy replaced him as the most influential Lithuanian statesman.

62. I.e. the office of the Grand Duke of Lithuania was still in existence.

63. *Dnevnik Liublinskogo Seima*, p. 12; Lappo, *Velikoe Kniazhestvo Litovskoe*, *1*, 18–19.

The position of the Lithuanians was really serious, since, on the one hand, they met with the unwillingness of the majority of the Poles to make any concessions to them and, on the other, the difficult military and diplomatic situation dictated the necessity of an immediate agreement with the Poles. On January 29 Nikolai Radivil said, with bitterness: "When we left for the seim, the enemy [i.e. the Muscovites] was at our backs. We desire that a union with you be cemented with mutual love. We almost came running to conclude it, while our forefathers used to walk slowly on similar occasions." [64]

In February, to end the impasse, the king ordered the Lithuanians to stop their separate conferences and take seats in a common session with the Poles. Instead of complying with the order, the Lithuanian lords decided to boycott further meetings. One by one they started leaving for home. Most of the Lithuanian szlachta delegates followed suit. By March 1 the Poles remained alone at the seim.

It soon appeared that the Lithuanians had miscalculated the situation by underestimating the determined spirit of the Poles and, what was even more fatal to them, overlooking the opposition to them on the part of the Russian (Ukrainian) szlachta of Volynia and Podliashie, which proved ready to separate from the grand duchy.

It is possible that friendly parleys between the Poles and the envoys of the Ukrainian szlachta of those two provinces had been conducted secretly while the seim was still in session.[65] In any case the Poles were well aware of the warm attitude toward union of the deputies of Volynia and Podliashie and decided to take advantage of it.

On March 5 Sigismund August issued an edict of the "return" to Poland of Volynia and Podliashie and the immediate incorporation of these two provinces into Poland.[66] Three days later he ordered the lords and the szlachta envoys of Volynia and Podliashie to arrive at the seim on March 27 to take the oath of allegiance to the Crown of Poland.[67]

The first reaction of the Lithuanians was to oppose the king by force. Orders were sent out by the council of lords to Podliashie and

64. *Dnevnik*, p. 19; Lappo, *1*, 15.
65. Liubavsky, *Ocherk*, p. 304.
66. *Akta Unji*, pp. 193–196.
67. *Ibid.*, pp. 207–209.

Volynia to mobilize for war against Poland.[68] The Poles also prepared to mobilize. Soon, however, the Lithuanians realized that they had no strength to conduct war against Poland, especially since the szlachta of the two provinces of which they had been robbed re-fused to cooperate with them.

The loss of Volynia and Podliashie was a severe blow to Lith-uania, depriving the grand duchy as it did of a considerable part of its military and financial resources. Moreover, many Lithuanian lords owned landed estates in those provinces and occupied adminis-trative offices there. These were immediately required to take oath of allegiance to Poland on the basis of Sigismund August's decree of March 8.

The most spectacular example of the conflict of the spirit of Sigismund's decree with the conscience of the Lithuanian lords was that of Ostafi Volovich, the assistant chancellor of the grand duchy. When the Lithuanians withdrew from the seim in February they left, in Vilna, Volovich and the assistant treasurer of the grand duchy, Nikolai Narushevich, as observers. Volovich owned no patrimonial estates in Podliashie but had been granted three bene-fices there as an award for his previous services to the grand duchy. Immediately after the decree of March 8 the king ordered Volovich to take the oath of allegiance to Poland. Volovich begged the king "to open his other ear" (i.e. as Grand Duke of Lithuania) and to allow him (Volovich) to ask advice of the other Lithuanian lords. For the time being he refused to take the oath and was punished by the confiscation of his Podliashie benefices.[69]

The Lithuanian lords decided to make a last attempt to safe-guard the rights of the grand duchy. On April 5 the Polish senate received a special Lithuanian delegation consisting of Ian Khodke-vich, Ostafi Volovich, and three other lords. They protested against the king's unilateral action of annexing Volynia and Podliashie to Poland and demanded a new election of deputies and a full dis-cussion of the matter by another seim. The Poles reluctantly agreed to new elections in Lithuania on condition that these be held im-mediately and that by May 29 the seim resume its sessions. Mean-while they demanded the "return" to Poland of two more provinces —Kiev and Braslav. On June 6 Sigismund August issued the de-cree of the return of the Kievan land and its incorporation into

68. *Dnevnik*, p. 187; Lappo, *1*, 187.
69. *Ibid.*, pp. 193, 194; Lappo, *1*, 187.

Poland.[70] Concerning Braslav, the king decreed that no new action was necessary, since formerly Braslav had been part of Volynia and its incorporation into Poland was merely a matter of administrative routine. On June 16 the szlachta of the districts of Braslav and Vinnitsa took an oath of allegiance to the Crown of Poland.[71]

By the time the Lithuanian lords and szlachta envoys had returned to the seim, on June 6, the Grand Duchy of Lithuania had been deprived of all its Ukrainian provinces—that is, of about a third of its population. No further resistance to Poland was possible. Pathetically, Khodkevich pleaded before the seim for the return to Lithuania of the illegally separated provinces and insisted on some changes in favor of Lithuania in the Polish draft of the treaty; but the cause of the grand duchy was lost. The despair of the Lithuanian lords was forcefully expressed in Nikolai Radivil's letter to Narushevich, in which the former deplored "the burial and the destruction forever of the previously free and independent state, known as the Grand Duchy of Lithuania." [72]

On July 1, 1569, the Treaty of Union was signed by both the Poles and the Lithuanians. On July 4 Sigismund August confirmed it.[73]

The treaty represented, in its essence, the Polish plan of union. Only in a few details were the desires of the Lithuanians taken into consideration. The basic principles were the following:

1. Poland and Lithuania were to constitute one commonwealth (*res publica*), one state (*unum regnum*), one people (*unus populus*).

2. They would have one sovereign, whose title was to be "King of Poland, Grand Duke of Lithuania."

3. The sovereign was to be elected by the senate and the szlachta of the united nation.

4. The electoral seim would meet in Poland, not in Lithuania.

5. The newly elected king, when accepting the crown, would take the oath of safeguarding the liberties of the two peoples.

6. The king would be crowned in Kraków. He would not be installed as Grand Duke of Lithuania.

7. There would be only one senate and one seim; both would be institutions of the Crown of Poland (*koronnye*, from *korona*, crown).

---

70. *Akta Unji*, pp. 309–319.
71. *Ibid.*, pp. 319–321.
72. Lappo, *1*, 44.
73. *Akta Unji*, pp. 366–379.

8. The foreign policy would be one and the same for the two peoples.

9. Land estates might be acquired by Poles in Lithuania and vice versa.[74]

It was easier to proclaim these principles than to realize them in actual life. Full incorporation of Lithuania into Poland was not achieved, and Lithuania retained her autonomy even after the Lublin Union.

Characteristically enough, there were inconsistencies in this respect in the text of the treaty itself. After proclaiming the fusion of the two peoples, the Poles and the Lithuanians, the treaty continued to mention "two peoples" though united. The title "Grand Duchy of Lithuania" was still used. All the offices of the government and higher administration of the grand duchy were kept intact. The grand duchy still retained its state emblem. Lithuania was allowed to use its own code of laws (statute), even though she was instructed to revise it to coordinate with the Polish legislation.[75]

It is noteworthy also that the status of Livonia was decided by the Lublin seim in the sense that Livonia was incorporated jointly into Poland and Lithuania. This decision likewise presupposed the existence of these two different states even though united.

In the further development of the interrelations of Poland and Lithuania the autonomy of the latter reasserted itself in many respects and on many occasions.[76] The Treaty of Union, as has been said, forbade the continuation of the Lithuanian seim. Actually, this institution was revived as a preliminary conference of the Lithuanian deputies prior to their departure to the sessions of the joint seim in Poland. This conference was called the Chief Seim (*Golovnoi Seim*) of the Grand Duchy. The seim took on the character of a congress of Polish and Lithuanian delegations for settling their differences. On many occasions the Lithuanians presented their "protestations" to the seim. The autonomous status of the Grand Duchy of Lithuania was clearly revealed during interregna when the Lithuanian Chief Seim actually ruled the country.

While, according to the Lublin Union, the Lithuanian Statute of Laws was to be revised to adjust the Lithuanian laws to the Po-

---

74. Shmurlo, 2, Pt. I, 364.
75. Lappo, *Zapadnaia Rossiia*, pp. 141–143; Shmurlo, 2, Pt. I, 364–365.
76. For the following see Lappo, *Zapadnaia Rossiia*, p. 145–151; Shmurlo, 2, Pt. I, 364–365.

lish, the revision was made in Lithuania by Lithuanian-Russian jurists and continued the traditions of the first two statutes. The new Statute—the Third—was approved by King Sigismund III in 1588. Characteristically, the existence of the union was not even mentioned in the Third Statute. Like the first two, the Third Statute was written in Russian (West Russian). The first printed edition of it was published immediately at Vilna.[77]

In his foreword to the first edition of the Third Statute the publisher, Lev Sapega, wrote: "Of all peoples, we should be particularly ashamed not to know our laws since we have them written in our own, not in a foreign, language." [78]

The Russian language remained the official vehicle of the government, administration, and laws of the Grand Duchy of Lithuania for more than a century after the Lublin Union. It was only in 1697 that the Lithuanian government ordered the Russian language replaced by the Polish in the official acts.[79]

Even after its thorough Polonization at the end of the 17th century Lithuania kept her autonomy for almost a century more. It was only by the provisions of the Polish constitution of May 3, 1791, that the remnants of the Lithuanian constitution were abrogated and the incorporation of Lithuania into Poland was finally achieved.[80] This occurred, however, on the eve of the fall of Poland herself. Both nations were reborn after the first World War as two separate states.

Although Lithuania remained autonomous after the Lublin Union, its strength was greatly reduced by the annexation to Poland of all Ukrainian provinces of the grand duchy. The latter retained only the Belorussian lands.

As regards the interrelation of the social groups in Lithuania, the privileged status of the lords was considerably shaken. The szlachta now came to the fore politically, and the council of lords had to accept the new situation.

But curiously, it was the Russians who were dealt the main blow by the Union. Prior to it, only Galicia and part of Podolia were under the direct authority of Poland. Now the whole of West Russia

77. On the Third Lithuanian Statute see Lappo, *Litovskii Statut 1588 goda, 1*, Pts. I–II.

78. Sapega's foreword to his edition of the Third Lithuanian Statute, *Vremennik, 19*, xi. Cf. Lappo, *Zapadnaia Rossiia*, p. 184.

79. Lappo, *Zapadnaia Rossiia*, p. 188.

80. Kutrzeba, *2*, 214–215.

was cut into two parts, one still affiliated with Lithuania and the other dominated by Poland. Belorussia and the Ukraine were politically separated one from the other.

Poland eventually succeeded in Polonizing the bulk of the Ukrainian nobility but failed to assimilate the Ukrainian Cossacks and peasants. Before long, it became obvious that at Lublin, Poland had swallowed more than she could digest.

3. Rise of the Ukrainian Cossacks

Cossackdom as a social phenomenon was a complex product of the frontier life in the intermediate zone between the zone of the forest and the zone of the steppe, between the Slavic states in the North and the Tatar khanates in the South.[81] Cossackdom was a product of the *ukraina* in the original sense of the word, the "borderland." It is from this word that the name Ukraine with its modern ethnic and political connotations derived.

The fringe belt all along the southern border of the Moscow state consisted of a chain of *ukrainy* (plural). One spoke of the Riazan ukraina, the Tula ukraina, the Putivl and the Severian ukrainy (Severia was ethnically a Ukrainian land). Further west the term "ukraina" was applied to the southern border lands of the Grand Duchy of Lithuania, annexed by Poland in 1569. Specifically, the region south of Kiev as well as Podolie were called Ukraina, and this became the nucleus of the Ukraine in a national and political sense.

The frontiersmen were known as Cossacks. The term *Kazak* (also spelled *Kozak*) was used by both the Russians and the Tatars. In Turkic dialects of the 15th and 16th centuries *kazak* meant "free man," "free-lance warrior," "adventurer."

The word derives from the ethnic name *Kas*, an old North Caucasian people now known as Adyge or Circassians. The latter name, in the original form of *Chahar-Kas*, means "four Kas clans." In Russian, since the 15th century, the name has been used in the form of *Cherkasy*.[82] The name appears in the Codex Cumanicus, in the form *cosac* [83] (written around 1294). In the Synaxarion of Sugdaia of the 12th century there is a supplementary entry dated

81. See Vernadsky, *Political and Diplomatic History of Russia*, pp. 137, 159, 160, 165, 166; Stökl, *Die Entstehung des Kosakentums*.

82. G. Vernadsky, "The Riddle of the Gothi-Tetraxitae," *SOF, 11* (1952), 281–283; *Mongols and Russia*, pp. 291–292; *Kievan Russia*, p. 170.

83. On the Codex Cumanicus see D. A. Rasovsky, *SK, 3*, 193–214.

May 17, 1308, concerning a young Christian killed by the sword of the Kazaks.[84] In my opinion, here again the Kasogi (Circassians) are meant.

In the Muscovite documents of the 16th and 17th centuries, both the Circassians and the Ukrainian Cossacks were called Cherkasy, the latter presumably so from the name of the town of Cherkasy on the Dnieper River south of Kiev, which was one of the centers of the Dnieper Cossacks region. The town of Cherkasy must have been originally a Circassian settlement.[85] Consider the similarly formed name of Iasy (in Rumanian, Iaşi), the capital of Moldavia, originally founded by the Alans. In Old Russian *Iasy* meant "Alans." [86]

The Circassian settlement at Cherkasy was probably founded in the 11th century if not earlier. At that time Prince Mstislav of Chernigov and Tmutorokan had a Circassian bodyguard.[87] In the late 13th century new Circassian settlers might have been brought to that region by the Mongol Khan Nogay.[88] It is to the region of Cherkasy that the tsarevich Kasim (later, the first Khan of Kasimov) fled from the wrath of his brother Mahmudek in the fall of 1445, and it is from Cherkasy that he came to the rescue of Grand Duke Vasili II in the fall of 1446.[89]

In the sources of the late 15th century both the Russian and the Tatar Cossacks are mentioned. In many cases the Tatar Cossacks were fighting the Russians or robbing Russian commercial caravans. However, both the Moscow and the Lithuanian governments understood the advantages of using these Tatar Cossacks to strengthen their respective armies. It will be recalled that Tatar auxiliary troops were settled in Lithuania in the late 14th and the 15th centuries, and that one group was known as the "Tatar Cossacks" (above, p. 191). Similarly, the Moscow government used Tatar auxiliaries. The practice gained momentum in the reign of Vasili II and continued afterward (above, pp. 112–113).[90]

84. ξίφη σφαγὴς ὑπὸ καζάκων, see Antonin, "Zametki XII–XIV vekov," *ZOO, 5* (1863), 613; Hrushevsky, *Istoriia Ukrainy-Rusi*, 7, 77; Stökl, pp. 43–44.

85. Allen, *The Ukraine*, p. 69.

86. On the city of Iasy see *Ancient Russia*, pp. 133–134; *Mongols and Russia*, p. 179.

87. *Kievan Russia*, p. 78.

88. G. Pachymeres, *De Michaele et Andronico Paleologis* (2 vols. Bonn, 1835), *1*, 344; N. I. Veselovsky, *Khan iz temnikov Zolotoi Ordy Nogai i ego vremia* (Petrograd, 1922), p. 28; *Mongols and Russia*, pp. 178–179.

89. See *Mongols and Russia*, pp. 320, 324; Stökl, pp. 56–60.

90. See also G. Vernadsky, *Nachertanie Russkoi istorii* (Prague, 1927), pp. 108–111;

Simultaneously with the growth of Tatar Cossacks there developed several groups of Russian Cossacks. The first mention of them in the chronicles is dated in 1444 and refers to the Riazan ukraina.[91]

Besides the Cossack frontiersmen—the "outer Cossacks"—there were also, in both East and West Russia, Cossacks of a different type, whom we may designate "inner Cossacks." Applied to them, the term "kazak" was used not in a military sense but to designate a social category. Thus a kazak (or kozak) was a free man not included in the lists of peasants burdened by taxes and other liabilities to the state. The kazak was not a "man of burden," not a *tiagly*. He could be an agricultural laborer, a teamster, a crewman on a merchant river boat, or a member of a *vataga,* a cooperative company for fishing or hunting.[92] In North Russia as late as the 19th century a year-round handyman or agricultural laborer was known as a kazak.[93]

When the community of outer Cossacks in South Russia and Southern Ukraine started growing, many of the inner Cossacks joined ranks with them. Thus the inner kazaki served as one of the reservoirs which contributed to the growth of the outer Cossacks in the border regions.

In both Muscovy and Poland the rise of the frontier Cossacks was closely connected with the advance of the agricultural Slavic colonization from the forest zone southward into the steppe zone. In spite of the constant danger of Tatar raids, people were attracted to the new area in the South because of its natural wealth—the *chernoziom* (black soil), the abundance of fish and animals, and a climate milder than in the North. Nor were the peasants in the frontier regions overburdened by taxes and liabilities, as they were in the North.

In 1590 a Polish writer described the Ukraine enthusiastically: "the richest part of the Polish state. Its fields are as blissful as the Elysian . . . There are so many cattle, wild animals, and various birds in the Ukraine that one could think her the birthplace of Diana and Ceres. In the Ukrainian apiaries so much honey is produced that one forgets the Sicilian Gela and the Attic Hymettus . . . It is hard to count the Ukrainian lakes teeming with fish. In

idem, Political and Diplomatic History of Russia, p. 137; *Mongols and Russia,* pp. 315–320; Stökl, pp. 64–105.

91. See also *Mongols and Russia,* pp. 280, 288, 289; Stökl, pp. 106–110.

92. Kostomarov, *Bogdan Khmelnitskii, 1,* 6–7.

93. Dal, *Slovar, 2,* 73.

short, the Ukraine is like that land which God promised to the Hebrews, flowing with milk and honey." [94]

The Cossacks, in West Russia as in East Russia, were the pioneers of the Slavic penetration into the area of the steppes. They usually followed the riverways, and their first settlements were on river islands and banks. In the Kievan Ukraine the Dnieper constituted the most convenient channel for them. In Podolia the Southern Bug and the Dniester served the same purpose. The Cossack pioneers at first were engaged mainly in exploitation of animal riches of the steppes—in fishing, hunting, and beekeeping. They formed *vatagi* (cooperative associations), which went down the river usually in April, returning with the catch in October. Each vataga earmarked its own section of river bank, and each group had to be well equipped for its task. The vataga had to prepare boats, fishing seines and nets, cordage, and vessels of various kind for salting and smoking quantities of fish. The salt had to be bought beforehand. In many cases a vataga, before returning home for the winter, would build on the spot where it had worked in the summer a storehouse where part of the equipment was kept in the winter. A few men were left to guard the stores. Such winter quarters (*zimovniki*) eventually became a regular institution.

The equipment of a large vataga required considerable means. Those members of the vataga who had invested money as well as labor in it became the directors of the undertaking, and to them went the largest share of income from the operations. In this way there arose a difference between the "owners" and the laborers; [95] and the cleavage between these two categories in the Cossacks' cooperative associations became one of the predetermining factors of the disparity between the two layers of the Cossack military communes—the officers (*starshina*) and the rank and file.

One of the earliest documents, in which a fishing concern of the Dnieper Cossacks is mentioned, is the Kievan town statute of 1499, which established the amount of customs fees for the fish the Cossacks sold in Kiev. [96]

Fishing was soon supplemented in the advanced steppe settlements by cattle-breeding and then by agriculture. In the coloniza-

94. Doroshenko, *Narys istorii Ukrainy*, *1*, 152.
95. Golobutsky, pp. 56–57.
96. *AZR*, *1*, No. 170; Kostomarov, *Bogdan Khmelnitskii*, *1*, 7; Hrushevsky, *Istoriia Ukrainy-Rusi*, *7*, 81; Stökl, pp. 116–117; Golobutsky, p. 57.

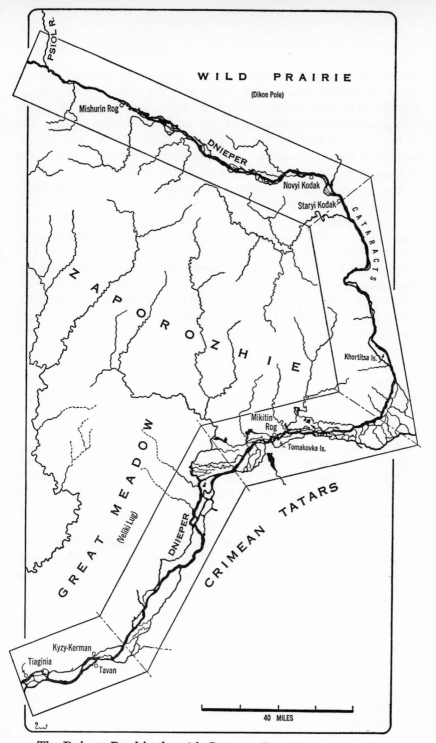

7. The Dnieper Bend in the 16th Century (For insets see Map No. 8)

tion of the southern Ukraine of the 16th century we may discern three component factors: the elemental southward movement of the Cossacks and peasants lured by the fabulous natural wealth of the country; the advance of the nobility's landed estates and of the peasants and tenants working on those estates; and the extension of the state's network of administration taking care of the defense of the southern borders against the Tatars.

The Cossacks formed an important ingredient in all these types of colonization; moreover, by the close of the 16th century they had succeeded in building up a military community of their own more to the south, outside the area of settled agricultural civilization.[97]

Both the lords and the petty gentry acquired landed estates in the region newly opened to agriculture. When necessary, they secured their rights by obtaining a special charter of the grand duke. After the Lublin Union, Polish nobles extended their domains to the Ukraine. But even before 1569 some Polish noblemen, like the Lanckoronskis, who had been connected with the Polish Podolia, took part in the Cossack affairs.

In addition to owning landed estates in the Ukraine, the nobility held offices in the local administration in the capacity of the starosty, or of other officials, and thus were responsible for the defense of the Ukraine from the Tatars. For this task they received no money and few soldiers if any from the grand duke. They had to use the proceeds of the local taxes and fees for building *zamki* (castles) and keeping armed militia. The Cossacks were a suitable type of men for such militia, and for this reason the first moves for using and organizing them as a military force were made by the starosty of the Ukrainian area.

Among the most prominent was Prince Bogdan Fedorovich Glinsky, Starosta of Cherkasy. With a detachment of Cossacks he raided the Turkish fortress of Ochakov in 1493.[98] A later chieftain

97. On the origin of the Ukrainian Cossacks see Kostomarov, *Bogdan Khmelnitskii*, pp. 1–19; Vladimirsky-Budanov, "Naselenie iugo-zapadnoi Rossii ot poloviny XV veka do Liublinskoi Unii"; M. K. Liubavsky, "Nachalnaia istoriia malorusskogo kozachestva," *ZMNP, 300* (1895), 217–244; A. Jablonowski, "Etniczna postać Ukrainy w epoce zjednoczenia jej z Koroną," *KH, 7* (1893), 408–435; Platonov, *Ocherki po istorii Smuty*, pp. 113–120; Hrushevsky, *Istoriia Ukrainy-Rusi*, 66–127; Doroshenko, *Narys istorii Ukrainy, 1,* 144–161; Krupnyckyj, *Geschichte der Ukraine*, pp. 49–64; Allen, *The Ukraine*, pp. 64–72; W. Tomkiewicz, "O składzie społecznym i etnicznym kozaczyny ukrainskiej na przełomie XVI i XVII wieku," *PH, 37* (1948), 249–260; Stökl, *Die Entstehung des Kosakentums;* Golobutsky, pp. 23–63.

98. *Sbornik, 41,* 194–196; Hrushevsky (above, n. 96), 7, 83; Stökl, p. 116.

of frontier Cossacks, Ostafi Dashkevich, was a descendant of Kievan boyars. In 1503 he fled to Moscow to avoid Grand Duke Aleksandr's disfavor and offered his services to Ivan III. In 1508 Ivan's son and successor, Vasili III, sent Dashkevich to Lithuania to assist Prince Mikhail Lvovich Glinsky's rebellion against the Grand Duke of Lithuania (above, p. 139). After Glinsky's failure, Dashkevich went over to the Lithuanian side. In 1514 he was appointed Starosta of Cherkasy, holding the office until his death in 1535. Dashkevich gathered together a detachment of Cossacks, which he used mostly against the Tatars, but occasionally against Muscovy too. In 1515 he joined the Crimean Khan's drive against Moscow, taking upon himself the task of seizing Chernigov and Novgorod-in-Severia. In this, however, he failed.[99] Dashkevich cooperated with the khan against Moscow in 1521 as well (above, p. 153). Among the starosty of Polish Podolia who attempted, in this period, to organize the Cossacks for the defense of the Ukraine were Predslaw Lanckoronski, Starosta of Khmelnik, and Bernat Pretwicz, Starosta of Bar. Both the Lithuanian and the Polish governments, while desiring to use the Cossacks as a frontier military force, were reluctant to grant them an independent organization of their own. Yet without granting such rights to the Cossacks it was difficult to make them a permanent military institution.

The first West Russian grandee who saw in the Cossacks not merely a potential fighting machine in the service of the Lithuanian government but an independent social group was the Starosta of Cherkasy, Prince Dmitri Ivanovich Vishnevetsky. More than that, he tended to identify himself with the Cossacks as their leader. It is hard to say what part his personal ambitions played in his political game, but he apparently had such ambitions.

Be this as it may, Vishnevetsky's attitude toward Cossackdom as an independent force gives us a clue to understanding the pattern of his adventurous and seemingly erratic activities. Vishnevetsky was appointed Starosta of Cherkasy in 1551. Two years later he went to Constantinople and offered his services to the Sultan. The motives of this move can only be guessed at. Hrushevsky thinks that Vishnevetsky attempted to seek the Sultan's protection against the Crimean Tatars.[100] If so, he must have been soon disappointed, since he returned to Cherkasy in 1554. As has been said, Vishnevetsky cooperated with Moscow for five years (1556–61) and then came

99. On Ostafi Dashkevich see W. Pociecha, "Daszkievicz," *PSB, 4* (1938), 444–447.
100. Hrushevsky (above, n. 96), 7, 115–116.

back to Cherkasy again. But not for long: in 1562 he went to Moldavia and intervened in the struggle between two rival candidates for the office of the Moldavian gospodar. A group of Moldavians offered the office to Vishnevetsky himself, but his supporters were soon crushed. Vishnevetsky was taken prisoner and sent to Constantinople, where he was executed in 1563.

From this brief outline of his career it may seem that he was mainly a political adventurer, freely changing his allegiances to various masters. However, a single motive beneath his activities is clearly discernible: to organize the Cossacks for the fight against the Tatars and the Turks (after it had become clear to him that it was not possible to detach the Turks from the Tatars).[101] He cooperated with Moscow as long as he believed that she intended to destroy the Khanate of the Crimea. When he saw that the tsar's attention had shifted from the Crimea to Livonia, he left Moscow and returned to Lithuania. There he found the same situation as in Moscow: the Lithuanian policy was likewise oriented toward Livonia. He then moved to Moldavia, which was under the Sultan's protectorate. By putting a suitable candidate on the gospodar's throne, or obtaining it for himself, Vishnevetsky could hope to detach Moldavia from Turkey.

Vishnevetsky's personality struck the imagination of the Ukrainian people and he became a favorite hero of Cossack epos under the nickname of Baida.[102] Even though his attempt to create a Cossack stronghold in the region of the Dnieper cataracts failed, he created a pattern for the future. We have definite evidence that twenty-five years after Vishnevetsky's venture, the Cossack *sech* (in Ukrainian, *sich*) was firmly established in the region "beyond the Cataracts" (Zaporozhie). From time to time the sech was moved from one Dnieper island to another, but it existed as a permanent institution. The term derives from the identical verb meaning "to hew," "to cut": a place protected by cut trees, a "wooden fortress" as D. I. Doroshenko explains the term.[103]

In 1581 the sech was located in Tomakovka Island, further down

101. Recently M. Golobutsky suggested that Vishnevetsky was a "feudal" lord whose main motive was to suppress the Cossack movement, not to sponsor it (Golobutsky, pp. 71–87). The explanation seems overdrawn and is unacceptable to me.

102. Hrushevsky (above, n. 96), 7, 114–127. Golobutsky denies any connection between the personality of Vishnevetsky and the epic image of Baida (Golobutsky, pp. 84–87).

103. Doroshenko, *Narys istorii Ukrainy, 1,* 155.

the Dnieper than Khortitsa. By 1594 it was moved to Bazavluk Island, a little lower than Tomakovka. It is there that the envoy of Emperor Rudolf II, Erich Lassota, found the Cossacks and negotiated a treaty with them.

According to Lassota, there were 3,000 Cossacks in Zaporozhie and a reserve of several thousand more in the Ukraine. The Zaporozhie authorities reckoned that they had at their disposal 6,000 men ready for a distant campaign. Lassota spent almost one month in the sech (from June 9 to July 2, 1594) and became familiar with the Cossack organization.[104]

On the basis of Lassota's report and other evidence contemporary with it, we may conclude that the sech in this period constituted a military camp and the main center of the independent Cossacks (even though they nominally recognized the sovereignty of the King of Poland). The Zaporozhie community was known as the *kosh*, a term meaning "camp" in Old Russian and apparently deriving from Turkic.[105]

The kosh was divided into several sections each known as *kuren'* (in Ukrainian, *kurin'*). This latter term derives from the Mongol language, in which a *kuriyen* is a camp of tents pitched in a huge circle.[106] The men of each Cossack kuren lived in a barrack of their own. In Lassota's time such a barrack was made of wattles and covered with horsehides, each one housing 150 men. Food consisted of fish and of leavened dough made of millet or wheat flour. While from some of their military raids the Cossacks brought loads of jewels and other booty, they really valued only expensive arms and steeds.

The head of the Cossack army was often referred to as "hetman," the title which the commanders of the Polish and Lithuanian armies bore (above, p. 184). More specifically, the Cossack chieftain was called the kosh ataman (*koshevoi;* in Ukrainian, *koshovy*). The captain of each kuren was known as "kuren ataman." During a campaign the Cossack army was divided into *polki* (regiments), each five hundred strong. At the head of each regiment was the *polkovnik* (colonel). The regiment consisted of five *sotni* (hundreds), each under a *sotnik* (centurion). The sotnia was divided into units of ten *desiatki*. To the higher dignitaries of the Cossack army belonged

104. Lassota, *Tagebuch*, pp. 210–212; Hrushevsky, *Istoriia*, 7, 287–292.
105. Vasmer, *REW*, 1, 650.
106. *Mongols and Russia*, p. 14.

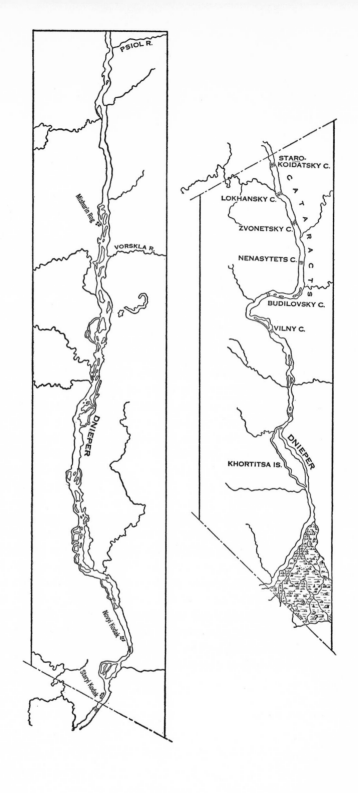

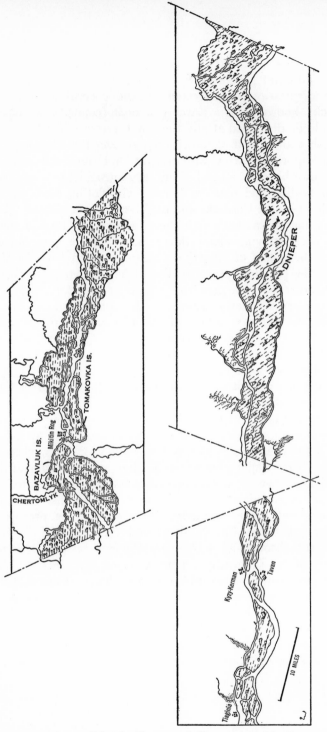

8. The Dnieper: Islands, Forts, and Cataracts, 16th Century

also the *pisar* (secretary), the *obozny* (quartermaster), and the *asauls* (adjutant generals).[107]

The dignitaries were elected by the general assembly of the Cossacks, known as *kolo* (circle) or *rada* (council). All office holders could be dismissed at any time by the rada. During a campaign the kosh ataman had dictatorial power over the whole army.

The Zaporozhie army was even at that time well organized. It had its own banners, a band of military music, its treasury, artillery, a river flotilla, and remount horses. The flotilla consisted of light boats built by the Cossacks and of galleys captured from the Turks. At the time of Lassota's visit the Cossacks had fifty of their light boats, each carrying about thirty men. The remount horses were kept at the Island of Khortitsa. Lassota was told by the Cossacks that in the previous year the Tatars had seized more than 2,000 horses and at that time they had only about 400 left.

In modern scholarly literature the question has been raised whether the military tactics of the Cossacks were influenced by the patterns of Czech companies engaged for military service in Poland and Lithuania on many occasions (above, p. 190).[108] It is possible that some of the Cossacks were acquainted with Czech technique of war, but there is no evidence for any direct Czech influence on Zaporozhie.

Major affairs of the Cossack community, especially treaties with foreign powers, were discussed in a preliminary way by the council of the dignitaries, known as *starshina* (seniors). Thus, when Lassota brought to the Zaporozhie Cossacks the emperor's offer of alliance, they divided themselves into two *kola,* that of the starshina and that of the *chern* (menials). There was at first much discord among the two kola, but finally the advice of the starshina prevailed. The dichotomy between the starshina and the rank-and-file Cossacks was to run through all subsequent Cossack history. Nevertheless, we can call the Zaporozhie regime a democracy, since the starshina had as yet no firm constitutional or hereditary rights. The right of holding an office belonged to every member of the Cossack fraternity.

The sech Cossacks called themselves the "Free Zaporozhie Army" or the "Fellowship of Knights." The sech was a military fraternity; no woman was allowed to appear there. Married Cossacks had to leave their wives home when coming to the sech. Access to the

107. Vasmer, "esaul," *REW, 1,* 405.
108. A. Florovsky, *Chekhi, 2,* 323–331.

fraternity was free, and anyone could join. The only obligations were loyalty to the fraternity and observance of its rules. From the incomplete statistical data we have it may be supposed that in the late 16th century around 80 per cent of the Zaporozhie Cossacks were West Russians (Ukrainians and Belorussians); the balance consisted of Muscovites, Poles, Moldavians, and Circassians. In addition, Tatars, Serbians, and Germans joined the Cossacks occasionally, but they probably constituted only an insignificant minority in the Zaporozhie community.[109]

The Zaporozhie Cossacks were a small group in comparison to the unorganized Cossackdom of the Ukraine, not to mention the Ukrainian peasants, among whom sympathy toward the Cossacks was steadily growing. We have to take into consideration, however, that the figure of the Zaporozhie Cossacks as given in Lassota's report (6,000) is not a permanent fixed quota. During a major military undertaking the ranks of the Cossacks were rapidly swollen by the influx of outsiders, Cossacks and peasants. Then, too, we should not forget that the contingent of the Zaporozhie commune was fluid. Cossack casualties in the struggle with the Tatars and the Turks were heavy. Besides, many of the married Cossacks returned to their homes after spending a year or two in the sech, being rapidly replaced by newcomers. Thus, if we take a period of ten years, the total number of men who participated in the commune at one time or another within such a period was considerably more than 6,000.

The formation of the sech as an independent center of Cossackdom could not but worry the Polish government. In the first place, the Zaporozhie Cossacks undertook frequent raids on the Crimean Tatars and the Turkish garrisons on Black Sea coastal forts like Ochakov and Akkerman. Beginning with Dmitri Vishnevetsky's leadership, the Cossacks intervened in Moldavian affairs and so came into conflict with Turkey. This endangered the peace between Poland and Turkey, which Poland at that time was eager to keep. The Sultan considered the Cossacks Polish subjects and threatened Poland with war.

The Polish government, which assumed control over the Ukraine after the Lublin Union, attempted to curb the Cossacks by making of them a regular frontier militia loyal to the king and commanded

109. Hrushevsky (above, n. 96), 7, 155–157; Doroshenko, *Narys istorii Ukrainy, 1,* 158.

by officers appointed by the king. The first attempt of this kind was made in 1572, in the last year of the reign of Sigismund August. The Polish hetman, Jerzy Jazlowiecki was entrusted with the task. He established a small detachment of Cossacks (300 men) and appointed a Polish nobleman to command them. The Cossacks were promised a salary.[110] The detachment, it seems, existed for only three years and then was disbanded, presumably because of lack of funds to pay the salary.

In 1578 King Stefan Batory organized a Cossack *polk* (regiment) of 500 men under the command of the Starosta of Cherkasy, Prince Mikhail Vishnevetsky (a relative of Prince Dmitri Vishnevetsky).[111] This proved a modest beginning of the institution of the "registered" Cossacks in the service of Poland.

During Batory's war with Moscow (1579–81) Mikhail Vishnevetsky and other Ukrainian grandees undertook several raids on Severia. Both registered and other Cossacks served under Vishnevetsky. Other noblemen recruited bands of Cossacks under their own authority. These groups of Cossacks were each commanded by its own *vatazhok* (petty ataman). Part of these Cossacks were horsemen, but the majority were foot soldiers; [112] their number probably was about two thousand. They thoroughly looted the region around Starodub and other parts of Severia. Batory urged the Zaporozhie Cossacks to join his main army, which was engaged in besieging Pskov, but they refused to cooperate. It should also be recorded that around 500 Don Cossacks were at that time in Pskov helping the Pskovian and Muscovite troops to defend the city. Their ataman was a Dnieper Cossack from Cherkasy whose name is given in Polish sources as Misko.[113]

After the end of the war, the supernumerary Cossacks who attacked Severia under the command of M. Vishnevetsky were disbanded. Many of them were now in search of other adventures. Meanwhile the Zaporozhie Cossacks, who did not participate in Batory's war against Russia, had their own plans for fighting the Tatars and Turks. It so happened that just at that juncture they received encouragement from the West. Both the pope and the emperor looked for allies against the Turks. News of the Cossack ex-

110. Hrushevsky, 7, 142–143; Doroshenko, 1, 157.
111. Hrushevsky, 7, 154–155; Doroshenko, 1, 158.
112. Hrushevsky, 7, 163.
113. Golobutsky, p. 94.

ploits reached the West from Poland through the Roman Catholic clergy and in many other ways. In 1584 a Cossack chieftain escaped from the Turkish captivity and fled to Italy. There the Italian Gamberini interviewed him and wrote down his information on the Cossacks. He noted that the Cossacks were good soldiers, both as cavalry and as infantry, and that they were able to muster 15,000 men for war in an emergency.[114]

Not all the Cossacks' attention was directed toward the Turkish war, however. Conscious of their new strength, the Cossacks also proved ready to occupy themselves with domestic affairs. While recognizing the King of Poland (at least theoretically) as their suzerain, they were eager to shatter the grip of the king's local officials and of the nobility on the population of the Ukraine. The Ukrainian peasants were eager to support the Cossacks against the landlords. Besides, looting of the nobles' estates could bring the Cossacks easy booty and plenty of it. The booty of the Cossacks who participated in the raids on Severia made them all eager for more.

Be this as it may, the Cossacks now turned their attention to civil war. In 1591 a Cossack uprising took place in the Kievan area, led by Krishtof Kosinsky, presumably a petty nobleman from Podliashie. It is known that in 1586 Kosinsky was in Zaporozhie.[115] In the winter of 1592–93 the Cossacks penetrated into Volynia. In January 1593 they were defeated near Zhitomir by the mobilized nobility of Volynia, at the head of which stood the aging Prince Konstantin Konstantinovich Ostrozhsky. The Cossacks are said to have lost two thousand men and twenty-six cannon.

Kosinsky surrendered and was pardoned by Ostrozhsky. The Cossacks promised to return to Zaporozhie and to stay there quietly. They went, but immediately began preparations for another uprising against Poland, apparently asking Moscow for assistance. The Starosta of Cherkasy, Prince Aleksandr Vishnevetsky, reported to the Polish government that Kosinsky and the whole Zaporozhie army had petitioned Tsar Fedor to accept the Cossacks under his protection. This was refused, but, according to A. Vishnevetsky some money and provisions were sent from Moscow to Zaporozhie. In the summer of 1593 two thousand Zaporozhie Cossacks, headed by Kosinsky, went up the Dnieper River in boats and besieged Cherkasy. Vishnevetsky's report to the chancellor, Jan Zamoyski,

114. Hrushevsky, 7, 293; Doroshenko, 1, 159–160.
115. LSZ, No. 18 (p. 34); Golobutsky, p. 100.

says he made a successful sortie and defeated the Cossacks. Kosinsky was killed in the battle. According to other sources, Kosinsky and a group of Cossacks were invited by Vishnevetsky to Cherkasy for negotiations, and Kosinsky was slain by Vishnevetsky's retainers.[116] His Cossacks returned to Zaporozhie.

At that juncture the diplomacy of the West attempted to channel the Cossack energy against the Turks. In 1592, on the initiative of Pope Clement VIII and Emperor Rudolf, plans for a coalition of Christian states against Turkey were revived. Both the Catholic Bishop of Kiev, Josef Verescinski, and Prince Ianush Ostrozhsky (Konstantin Konstantinovich's eldest son) sympathized with these plans. In 1593 the pope sent to the Cossacks the Croatian priest Aleksandr Komulović with 12,000 ducats as an advance payment for their equipment for the Turkish war. Komulović went to Podolia, where he met two Cossack chieftains, to whom, as it seems, he handed the money. The name of one of these Cossacks was Severin Nalivaiko.[117]

It will be recalled that in the next year the emperor's envoy, Lassota, reached the sech and negotiated a treaty of alliance with the Cossacks. When Lassota first mentioned the emperor's offer, the rank and file Cossacks immediately agreed to enter the service of *Ego Tsesarskoe Velichestve* ("His Majesty the Caesar," literally "His Caesarial Majesty"). It should be noted that both the Southern and Western Slavs called the Austrian emperor Caesar (*Tsesar*). In this form the Western imperial title was also used in Muscovite diplomatic language. (The Byzantine emperor was called Tsar.) [118]

The council of the Cossack seniors refused, however, to agree to the emperor's proposal without first determining the exact conditions of the agreement. They emphasized the difficulties of the campaign against the Turks and the need for a substantial subsidy for buying cannon, horses, and other equipment. Lassota handed the Cossacks the emperor's presents: two imperial banners, trumpets, and 8,000 ducats cash, but they were dissatisfied and demanded more money. Lassota, in the emperor's name, promised them a

116. *LSZ*, No. 17 (p. 27); Hrushevsky, *Istoriia*, 7, 191; Golobutsky, pp. 105–106.
117. Hrushevsky, 7, 198–199; Doroshenko, 1, 190. On Komulović see Pierling, 2, 329–360; Halecki, "Possevino's Last Statement," pp. 296–297.
118. The Tatar khans of Kazan, Astrakhan, and the Crimea were likewise recognized as tsars. The modern Russian form of the imperial title, "Imperator," was first used in Russia by Pseudo-Dmitri I in 1605–06, was introduced again by Peter the Great in 1721, and was used by him and his successors to 1917.

further subsidy. The Cossacks decided to send their own envoys to the emperor to make a definite agreement about the amount of subsidy and to receive at least an advance payment. Consequently, two envoys were sent to the emperor in Lassota's train when he left for home.

Meanwhile Severin Nalivaiko succeeded in building up a strong group of Cossacks in Podolia, presumably with the help of money he received from Komulović. Nalivaiko was a Volynian burgher (according to some sources, a petty nobleman). His elder brother, Damian Nalivaiko, was a priest of the church at Prince Konstantin Ostrozhsky's estate. Severin himself had served for some time in Prince Ostrozhsky's retinue and in that capacity had participated in the battle against Kosinsky in January 1593. In view of Prince Ianush Ostrozhsky's sympathy to the anti-Turkish league we may think that Nalivaiko was instructed by Ostrozhsky to get in touch with Komulović and to recruit Cossacks for an expedition against the Turks.

In 1594 Nalivaiko established connection with the hetman of the Zaporozhie Cossacks, Grigori Loboda. Loboda was a Ukrainian landowner of the northern section of the Kievan land, known as the Kievan *Polesie* (Forest Region). His wife belonged to the Ukrainian gentry. Before going to the sech, Loboda for some time had commanded a reserve detachment of the registered Cossacks. The Zaporozhie Cossacks were bound to fight the Turks by virtue of their treaty with the emperor. Loboda and Nalivaiko decided to combine their detachments for a campaign against the Turkish-dominated Moldavia. The total of their forces was 12,000. The two Cossack groups, while closely cooperating, retained their own identities.[119]

In the fall of 1594 the Cossacks invaded Moldavia, defeated the troops of the Moldavian gospodar Aron, seized the city of Iasy, and devastated the whole country. Under the pressure of the Cossacks, Aron renounced Turkish suzerainty and took the oath of allegiance to Emperor Rudolf. As allies of Aron the Cossacks then made a raid on the Turkish fortresses Tiaginia, Belgorod (Akkerman), and Kilia. They did not succeed in seizing the fortresses but thoroughly looted the country around. Following that, they retired to the Braslav region in Podolia.

119. On the Cossack rebellion of 1594–96, see Hrushevsky, 7, 200–239; Doroshenko, 1, 191–194; Golobutsky, pp. 127–146.

The Poles were not inclined to cede to the emperor the protectorate over Moldavia. Consequently, Hetman Jan Zamoyski led Polish troops into Moldavia, ousted Aron, and installed as a new gospodar the Moldavian boyar Ieremia Mogila (in Rumanian, Movila; in Ukrainian, Mohyla) as a vassal of the King of Poland. Being a shrewd politician, Mogila concluded an agreement with Turkey and recognized the sultan's protectorate over Moldavia as well.

To return to Loboda and Nalivaiko, Zamoyski ordered them not to invade Moldavia any more and to retire to Zaporozhie; instead, they began a civil war, establishing quarters in Braslav province and requiring contributions from estates of nearby nobles. When met with a refusal, they took by force what they needed. The city of Braslav recognized the authority of the Cossacks. The king finally had to send against them a Polish army under the command of Hetman Stanislaw Żołkiewski, one of the ablest Polish generals of the period. It was only in the autumn of 1595 that Żołkiewski reached Braslav. The city surrendered, and the Cossack forces separated. Nalivaiko raided several towns in Belorussia, including Mogilev, and Loboda moved to the Kievan Polesie, with which he was well familiar. Before long, Nalivaiko returned to Volynia. In the spring of 1596 both of them were pressed by Żołkiewski's army and had to retreat hastily to the Dnieper area and call reserve troops from Zaporozhie. Several Cossack detachments attempted to make a stand against the Poles at Belaia Tserkov, but soon news came that new troops from Poland and Lithuania were on their way to reinforce Żołkiewski's army. The position of the Cossacks seemed hopeless, and some of their leaders, including Loboda, must have understood it. In March 1596 Żołkiewski sent a messenger to Loboda urging him to desist from the rebellion. It is not known whether Loboda sent back any answer.[120]

The Cossacks crossed the Dnieper River eastward, followed by many peasants, fleeing east with their families. Discord started among the Cossacks depressed by their failure. At the tumultuous rada at Pereiaslav, Nalivaiko was ousted from power and Loboda was proclaimed the sole commander of the Cossack troops. On May 16, 1596, Żołkiewski's army surrounded the Cossack camp at the Solonitsa River not far from the town of Lubny. There was in the camp only about 3,000 Cossacks fit for battle. Gathered there were many wounded and sick Cossacks and peasants, some of them

120. *LSZ*, No. 45 (p. 69); Golobutsky, p. 137.

women and children. The Cossacks had only 20 cannon left by that time, and new dissension had started among their leaders. Loboda, who was suspected of secret negotiations with Żołkiewski, was killed by the partisans of Nalivaiko, and Colonel Krempsky was elected the new hetman.

Żołkiewski had plenty of artillery and battered the Cossack camp. For two weeks the Cossacks repulsed the Poles, but finally a group of them decided to surrender. According to the conditions of surrender, the Cossacks had to yield to the Poles Nalivaiko and other ringleaders, as well as their banners and weapons. Krempsky refused to accept these conditions and succeeded in escaping to Zaporozhie with 1,500 horsemen. The remaining Cossacks and their families were promised pardon, but the Polish soldiers, angered by the stubborn resistance, butchered most of the disarmed crowd. The ringleaders were brought to Lvov and executed there—except for Nalivaiko, who was taken to Warsaw, tortured in prison, and then publicly beheaded.

The Poles tried to clinch their victory by extraordinary enactments intended for the complete suppression of the Cossack danger. In the spring of 1597 the seim proclaimed the Cossacks *perduelles et hostes patriae* (public enemies and foes of the fatherland). The Polish hetman was instructed to destroy them once and for all, and to confiscate their property. The program was unrealistic and could not be carried out; four years later the seim had to abrogate the proscription.

As a matter of fact, it was not easy to penetrate to Zaporozhie to destroy the sech, the strength of which was not in its wooden walls but in its people's support. If destroyed, it would be revived within a short time, since there were always enough men for whom it was a necessity. In a sense the sech was imperishable. Behind the small group of militant Zaporozhie Knights stood the rapidly growing population of the southern Ukraine. Not only the peasants but the petty gentry and many of the burghers sympathized with the Cossacks. In fact, all who were tired of the burdens imposed by the government and nobility began to look to the Cossacks as potential defenders of the rights of the common man.

The only way for the Poles to undermine the strength of the Cossacks was to improve the conditions of life which vexed the Ukrainian peasants and had made them sympathetic to the Cossack movement. But that the Poles were not able to do, since their rule over the

Ukraine was based on the privileges of the szlachta and subjugation of the peasants.

Behind this social conflict loomed the religious and national problem. A considerable part of the Ukrainian szlachta was gradually attracted to the Polish ways of life and to Roman Catholicism. On the other hand, most of the petty gentry and the burghers as well as all the peasants kept their Orthodox faith. It seemed to many a Pole that the surest way to assimilate psychologically the West Russian peasants into the Polish regime would be to undermine the traditional religious independence of their church and to subordinate that church to the authority of the pope.

CHAPTER VIII

THE CHURCH UNION OF BREST

1. INTRODUCTION

THE UNION of the Roman Catholic and the Greek Orthodox churches, as an ideal, seems natural and lofty to any believer in the unity of the Universal Christian Church. In its actual application to the Eastern Europe of the 16th century the ideal was distorted by political passions and took the form of the subordination of a part of the Slavonic Church to Rome.

From the Roman Catholic point of view the union which had been announced at the Council of Florence of 1439 [1] was still valid, in spite of the unwillingness of the Russian population of Poland and Lithuania to accept it. Its reintroduction at the close of the 16th century was the result of an interplay of various factors—spiritual, social, political, and economic.

In order to understand better the historical background of the Union of Brest of 1596 we must briefly examine at least some of the aspects of the complex situation, such as the position of the West Russian Orthodox Church in Lithuania and Poland; the inner contradictions in that church; the upsurge of the Protestant movement in Poland and Lithuania; and the Catholic Counter Reformation.

2. PLIGHT OF THE ORTHODOX CHURCH
IN WEST RUSSIA

After the separation of the West Russian Church from the East Russian (above, p. 33), the former remained a diocese of the Patriarchate of Constantinople. Following the destruction of the Byzantine Empire by the Ottoman Turks the Patriarch of Constantinople found himself in a difficult and humiliating position. It was not easy for him to guide and protect the West Russian Orthodox

1. See *Mongols and Russia*, pp. 306–309.

Church even if he had tried hard to do so. As a matter of fact, the patriarchs did not even try to do this until the late 16th century. Yet the Orthodox Church in Poland and Lithuania needed such protection, since it existed within the framework of two states in which the Roman Catholic Church occupied a predominant and privileged position. The situation became, if anything, less favorable to the Russian population when, after the Lublin Union, Ukrainian provinces of the Grand Duchy of Lithuania were transferred to the Crown of Poland.

The King of Poland was in position to intervene in the life of the West Russian Church in many ways. In the first place he could, and in many cases did, nominate and appoint the Orthodox metropolitans of West Russia. It should be noted that in regard to the Roman Catholic Church in Poland, the appointment of a new bishop was usually a result of an understanding of the king with the pope. In 1589 the pope officially recognized the right of the king to nominate bishops.[2] In the case of the Orthodox Church in Poland and Lithuania the king's hands were practically free, since the Patriarch of Constantinople had no way to prevent the king's appointment of the metropolitan.

The king had vast powers in church administration through his right of patronage. That right existed in the practices of the Roman Catholic states in Europe, including Poland.[3] In the case of the Orthodox Church of West Russia, the anomaly of the situation was that the right of patronage belonged to a sovereign of a different religious denomination. This could and did lead to a variety of incongruities and abuses.

The king's right of patronage included his care not only of the parish churches and monasteries but of bishops' sees as well. Originally, a West Russian Orthodox bishop was elected by the council of prelates and laymen. Gradually this practice was discontinued, and the king began to dispose of the sees at his will. Some of the bishoprics were richly endowed and had good incomes. The grant of a see was in such cases as good a reward to a nobleman as the grant of a lay *derzhava* (beneficium). The king used such grants to reward those he owed a favor to, not considering the candidate's spiritual integrity as a potential church leader. The king's appointees

---

2. Kutrzeba, *1*, 128, 131.
3. N. Suvorov, *Uchebnik tserkovnogo prava* (4th ed. Moscow, 1912), pp. 395–396; J. B. Sagmüller, "Patron and Patronage," *The Catholic Encyclopaedia, 11* (1911), 560–561.

were usually noblemen, who more often than not had been laymen before the appointment. Such a layman was hurriedly made monk and then ordained bishop. In some cases the appointee had no desire to take monastic vows and would remain a layman and rule the see, as its administrator, for several years before agreeing to be ordained. Most of these noblemen, even after becoming church prelates, remained laymen in spirit and continued to lead the boisterous life of the szlachta. Like the lay dignitaries, they kept in their castles a large retinue of servitors, armed guards, and even cannon.

The patronage over parish churches and monasteries was exercised not only by the king but by noblemen and towns. Originally, the right of patronage over a church or monastery belonged to the lord, or to a town, who built the church (or monastery). To secure the functioning of it, the founder usually endowed it with landed estates. On his part, he reserved for himself the right of selecting the priest (or abbot). Private founders of the Orthodox monasteries and churches were, as a rule, Orthodox themselves. The kings founded a number of Orthodox monasteries in Galicia in order to sponsor colonization of thinly populated areas.[4] However, the landed estate with which the monastery or church was endowed was subject to the general laws of the country. The estate, including the religious establishment on it, could be mortgaged, sold, or exchanged for another one, and the new holder of such an estate acquired with the land the right of patronage over the church. In such a way a non-Orthodox individual could become the patron of an Orthodox monastery or church.[5]

The Russian term for the patron of a religious establishment is *ktitor* (founder).[6] A good and conscientious *ktitor*, if belonging to the same religious denomination as the church people, could be very useful to the church or monastery under his patronage. A non-Orthodox *ktitor*, or an Orthodox who did not have a sense of responsibility, could be very harmful.

It was through the disposal by the king of the Orthodox sees that the greatest harm to Orthodoxy in West Russia was done. Consider, for example, the case of the Bishop of Kholm, Feodosi Lozovsky, a nobleman by birth. He coveted the lucrative see of Vladimir-in-Volynia while the incumbent was still living. The king had beforehand appointed as that holder's successor the nobleman Iona

4. Hrushevsky, *Istoriia Ukrainy-Rusi, 5,* 262.
5. Shmurlo, *2,* Pt. I, 383.
6. Vasmer, *REW, 1,* 676.

Krasensky and had issued the proper patent to him. However, after the incumbent's death in 1563, the king changed his mind and appointed Bishop Feodosi to the Vladimir see (presumably, for a consideration). Iona Krasensky was not willing to let the Vladimir see slip from his hands. Taking the king's previous patent with him, he rushed to Vladimir and established himself there in the bishop's castle. Then, leaving his son Vasili as a guardian of his interests, he went to the king to seek justice. Meanwhile Bishop Feodosi set forth for Vladimir with an army of around 2,500 soldiers with nine cannon. Vasili Krasensky fled from the bishop's castle and surrendered to Feodosi. The king thereupon ordered Feodosi to appear before him for trial of the case, but Feodosi disregarded the order and remained Bishop of Vladimir until his death in 1589.[7]

Iona Krasensky, having to satisfy himself with the bishopric of Lutsk, which he had been granted in 1567, imposed heavy taxes on the parish priests under his authority, and if a priest refused to pay ordered his church sealed. Iona's son Vasili and the latter's two sons also appropriated everything they wanted from the estates belonging to the see, taking bells, icons, and books from the churches. In addition to the see of Lutsk, King Sigismund August had granted Iona the abbacy of the Monastery of Zhidichin, and Iona disposed of the treasury and the estates of the monastery as if they were his own, eventually reducing the monastery to poverty. In 1580 King Stefan Batory ordered Prince Konstantin Ostrozhsky, Voevoda of Kiev and marshal of Volynia, to take the monastery from Iona and hand the abbacy to Bishop Feofan of Meglin. Iona refused to obey Ostrozhsky, who seized the monastery by force and installed Feofan there. The king then appointed the Starosta of Lutsk, Prince Aleksandr Pronsky, guardian of the monastery. In 1583 Iona re-established his control. Pronsky's first attempt to oust Iona failed. The next year Pronsky led a detachment of 300 soldiers, equipped with cannon, against Iona and seized the monastery once more. Feofan returned to Zhidichin, but not for long, since in 1585 the Bishop of Lvov, Gedeon Balaban, sent his brother to the monastery at the head of a company of soldiers; they ousted Feofan and announced that the monastery was under Gedeon's authority. Feofan complained to the king but the latter finally granted the abbacy to Gedeon.[8]

7. *AIZR, 1*, Pt. I, Nos. 4 and 5, and pp. xvi, xxi; Makari, *9*, 337–339; Shmurlo, *2*, Pt. I, 384–385.

8. *AIZR, 1*, Pt. I, Nos. 25–29, 31–34, 40–42, 46, 50, 53; Makari, *9*, 445–448, 451, 452; Shmurlo, *2*, Pt. I, 385.

The king's appointments of the highest dignitaries of the West Russian Orthodox Church—the metropolitans—proved hardly more beneficial. Among the five metropolitans in the period between 1534 and 1589 one owed his see to the intervention of Queen Bona in his favor; another was almost illiterate; still another was a bigamist. On many occasions the metropolitans quarreled with the bishops, and both sides, complaining to the king, gave him ample pretext to intervene in church affairs. Of all the metropolitans of this period only one was a good administrator and provided adequately for the material needs of the church. None was able to give spiritual leadership to the faithful.[9]

We should not, however, consider the decay of the West Russian Orthodox hierarchy as proof of the moribundity of the body of the West Russian Church. There were conscientious Christians and honest men among the parish priests and the monks as well as among the laymen. Membership was constantly growing numerically, and the percentage of parishes to the number of believers, especially in the rural districts, was probably higher in West Russia than in East Russia in this period. Mikhail Hrushevsky compiled a long list of monasteries founded in Galicia, Volynia, and the Kiev region in the 15th and 16th centuries.[10] The number of parish churches in the 1560's, computed on the basis of taxation lists, was in Galicia, 1,270 in rural districts serving 2,491 villages and 190 in 125 towns.[11] The data for Volynia and the Kiev region are incomplete.

Because of the delinquency of the West Russian hierarchy, the laymen had to sponsor the cause of Orthodoxy in West Russia in regard to both protection of church institutions and the spread of education. Prominent among the laymen were several Orthodox lords, like the Princes Ostrozhsky and the Khodkevichs, and the associations of burghers known as *bratstva*.

3. PROTESTANT INTERLUDE

It is probable that the efforts of the Roman Catholics to subordinate the West Russian Church to the pope would have led to the imposition of the church Union much earlier than it actually occurred, had it not happened that in the middle of the 16th century

9. Shmurlo, 2, Pt. I, 386–387.
10. Hrushevsky (above, n. 4), 5, 261–268.
11. *Ibid.*, p. 271.

the grip of the Catholic Church over Poland and Lithuania was temporarily loosened by the rapid spread of Protestantism.

Even before the Reformation introduced by Luther in Germany, the pre-Reformation Protestant currents reached Poland and Lithuania from Bohemia through the Hussite and post-Hussite movements, and especially through the evangelical community known as the Czech Brethren (in English, usually, the Bohemian Brethren) founded by Peter Chelčický in 1467. Their influence was not great at first, but had assumed more importance by 1560.[12]

The ideas of the German Reformation penetrated into Poland and Lithuania pretty soon after the beginning of the movement in Germany. Many of the Polish and Lithuanian notables used to send their sons to German schools and universities for education, and some of them eagerly absorbed the new ideas. An important political fact that helped the spread of Protestantism in Poland and Lithuania was the secularization of the Teutonic Order in Prussia (1525) and then of its branch in Livonia. When the former great magister Albrecht repudiated the pope and became a lay duke of Prussia, he also became the Polish king's vassal. After 1550 Calvinism was fashionable among the Lithuanian lords, and Arianism (Anti-Trinitarianism, Unitarianism) found many adherents.[13]

Among the Lithuanian and Russian lords who took active part in the Calvinist movement was the powerful statesman Nikolai Radivil Chorny, who had renounced Catholicism and accepted Calvinism in 1553. His conversion, followed by that of many others, made Calvinism an influential factor in the council of lords. In 1558 the Russian lord Ostafi Volovich (Orthodox) sent a confidential message to the Moscow state diak, Ivan Mikhailovich Viskovaty, in which he reported that "Lutheranism" (as all Protestant denominations were called in Moscow) had firmly entrenched itself in Sigismund August's government. From Volovich's message it is

12. On the Czech Brethren see A. Florovsky, *Chekhi*, *1*, 370–376 and 382–392. See also P. Brock, *The Political and Social Doctrines of the Unity of Czech Brethren* (The Hague, 1957).

13. On the Reformation in Poland and Lithuania in the 16th century see N. N. Liubovich, *Istoriia reformatsii v Polshe: Kalvinisty i Antitrinitarii* (Warsaw, 1883); S. Kot, ed., *Reformacja w Polsce* (a quarterly published in Kraków), *1* (1922–); idem, "L'Influence de Michel Servet sur le mouvement Antitrinitarien en Pologne et en Transylvanie," in B. Becker, ed., *Autour de Michel Servet et de Sebastien Castillion* (Haarlem, 1953), pp. 72–115; Brückner, *2*, 120–121; Makari, *9*, 311–328; Lappo, *Velikoe Kniazhestvo Litovskoe, 1*, 232–235; Shmurlo, *2*, Pt. *I*, 387–389; E. Kupsch, "Der Polnische Unitarismus," *JGOE, 5* (1957), 401–440.

plain that while personally he abhorred Lutheranism, he was cautious not to oppose it publicly. Volovich asked Viskovaty to explain the situation to Tsar Ivan and to assure the latter that he was not a Lutheran.[14] However, around 1574 Volovich helped collect money to buy a house in Vilna that was to be converted into a Calvinist chapel.[15] If this does not prove in itself that he formally joined the Calvinist Church, at least it shows that he was at that time rather favorably disposed toward Calvinism. When Prince Kurbsky received news of Volovich's new attitude, he wrote him a letter (in 1574 or 1575) urging him to keep the faith of his ancestors.[16]

In 1564 Nikolai Radivil Rudy (originally a Roman Catholic) was converted to Calvinism. About the same time Ian Ieronimovich Khodkevich repudiated Orthodoxy and likewise accepted Calvinism. Of the princes of Russian extraction, Prince Simeon Pronsky (a descendant of the Riazan branch of the Rurikids) was converted to Calvinism in 1564 and changed his first name to Frederick.

The chief promoter of the *Socinian* (Antitrinitarian) movement in Lithuania was Ian Kishka. In the late years of his life Nikolai Radivil Chorny turned to Socinianism from Calvinism.

Under the patronage of the lords, the Protestants of the Grand Duchy of Lithuania were able to establish many churches and prayer houses, found schools, and publish books. It is noteworthy that the first book printed in the Lithuanian language was the translation of Luther's Catechism (published in Königsberg, Prussia, in 1547). Chorny sponsored a Russian translation of the Calvinist manual by Simeon Budny that was published in 1562 in Nesvizh under the title *Catechism for the Plain Russian Folk* (*Katekhizis dlia prostykh liudei iazyka Russkogo*). Radivil also gave funds to publish the Polish translation of the Bible prepared by the Socinians (Brest, 1563). Nine years later Simeon Budny's Polish translation of the Bible came out in Nesvizh.[17] The protestants opened several high and primary schools, for example in Novgorod-Litovsk, Nesvizh, Kovna, and Vitebsk. Among the Socinian institutions of learning, a high school was established by the brothers Goisky in Goshchi, Volynia. It is in this school that later (in 1602–03) the Pretender Dmitri studied Latin.

14. *Sbornik, 59,* 550–551.
15. Lappo, *Velikoe Kniazhestvo Litovskoe, 1,* 233–234.
16. Ustrialov, *Skazaniia Kniazia Kurbskogo,* pp. 287–288.
17. On Simeon Budny see S. Kot, "Budny Szymon," *PSB, 3* (1937), 96–99. In the later years of his life Budny became an anti-Trinitarian.

In 1500 there were 700 Roman Catholic parishes in the Grand Duchy of Lithuania. In 1566, according to the Jesuit Cichowius, only one-thousandth of the former parishioners remained in the fold of the Catholic Church. (This was probably a rhetorical exaggeration.) In the whole of Zhomoit there remained, in 1566, only six Catholic priests.[18] When there was wholesale conversion of Roman Catholic parishes to Protestantism, the Protestants usually turned Catholic churches into their own prayer houses, throwing away the statues of the saints and sometimes, in their zeal, destroying the church buildings.

Protestantism spread among the Orthodox as well as among the Roman Catholics. It was said that 650 Orthodox churches were adapted to the needs of the Protestants, or destroyed, in the province of Novgorod-Litovsk alone.[19]

In that province, of 600 Orthodox szlachta families only sixteen remained faithful to Orthodoxy.[20] Prince Andrei Kurbsky wrote to Konstantin Ostrozhsky that "almost the entire Volynia was infected with the cancer [of Protestantism]." [21]

Geographically, the area of the spread of Protestantism in the Grand Duchy of Lithuania included Lithuania proper as well as Zhomoit; the province of Novgorod-Litovsk; Volynia; and the towns of Brest, Zaslavl (in Minsk province), Polotsk, and Vitebsk.

It so happened that Arian ideas found support not only from the Western preachers or their pupils but likewise from a few religious radicals who had emigrated to Lithuania from East Russia. In 1555 a Russian monk—Feodosi Kosoy ("the Squint")—who deviated from Orthodoxy fled from Moscow after his ideas had been found heretical by the church council of the preceding year. Coming to Lithuania with several associates, he first appeared in Vitebsk and then moved to Polotsk, in both of which towns he organized Protestant communities. Afterward, with a companion, Ignati, he proceeded farther west to Novgorod-Litovsk province, leaving another of his associates, Foma, as minister of the Protestant community in Polotsk. Feodosi himself wanted to meet the leaders of the Socinian movement in Lithuania.

As we know, the Muscovites took Polotsk in 1563, following

---

18. Makari, *9*, 321–322.
19. *Ibid.*, p. 323.
20. Skarga, *Synod Brzeski* (see n. 56, below); Makari, *9*, 322.
21. Ustrialov, *Skazaniia Kniazia Kurbskogo,* p. 285.

which the Russian Protestant community there was dissolved. In his comments on Slavic religious history compiled in 1650, Andreas Węgierski relates that Tsar Ivan ordered the minister Foma to be executed, and that Foma was drowned in the river accordingly.[22] It is supposed that in his account of the Protestant movement in Lithuania in the 16th century Węgierski used as his source oral traditions of the Polish Protestants, and possibly some written records. However, his story contains several chronological and other errors, and we cannot be sure that the execution of Foma actually took place. If Foma had been killed by the tsar's order, the official Russian chronicle would have registered the event, but Foma's execution is not mentioned there.[23]

Feodosi and Ignati settled in Volynia and continued their religious activities there, apparently with much success. The Novgorodian monk Zinovi Otensky (i.e. of the Otnia Hermitage), in his polemical treatise against Protestantism, called Feodosi a predecessor of Antichrist. Zinovi wrote that "the Devil corrupted the East through Mohammed, the West through Martin the German [Luther], and Lithuania through the Squint [Feodosi]." [24]

There are no statistical data concerning the number of West Russians converted to various Protestant demoninations. It is obvious that the highest percentage of conversions occurred among the nobility, and the younger generation of the Khodkevichs, the Volovichs, the Sapegas, the Princes Vishnevetsky, and many other prominent clans renounced Orthodoxy. In the cities, as in Vitebsk and Polotsk, Protestants constituted, it seems, a minority of the population.

The attitude of the peasants we can only guess. In provinces like Novgorod-Litovsk—where, according to Skarga, hundreds of Orthodox churches ceased to function—the peasants must have been deprived of the care of the Orthodox priests. Whether they resented it we do not know. As to Volynia, when Kurbsky said that it became Protestant, he probably meant the nobility only. Judging from later events—the opposition of the peasants to the Union of Brest for example—we may think that the peasants were less disposed than the nobility to change their religious affiliation.

---

22. Adrian Regenvolscius (Andreas Węgierski), *Systema historico-chronologicum ecclesiarum Slavonicarum* (Trajecti ad Rhenum, 1652), p. 263, Russian translation in *Chteniia, 8* (1847), 3; Vilinsky, p. 101.

23. For the report of the seizure of Polotsk see *PSRL, 13*, 353–359.

24. Zinovi, *Istiny pokazanie* (Kazan, 1863), pp. 48–49.

There is, likewise, no evidence that the Orthodox parish priests were deeply affected by Protestantism. The majority of them, in any case, remained Orthodox.

The success of Protestantism in Poland, Lithuania, and West Russia may partly be ascribed to the high intellectual level and personal integrity of their leaders, both foreign and native. It should be noted that Faustus Socinus himself came to Poland in 1579 and settled near Kraków. The chief weakness of the Protestant movement was the lack of unity among its followers. Each of the main currents—Lutheranism, Calvinism, and Anti-Trinitarianism—broke into a number of smaller groups, or sects. In 1592 there were 72 different Protestant groups in Vilna alone.

4. THE CATHOLIC COUNTER REFORMATION

At first neither the Roman Catholics nor the Orthodox in the Grand Duchy of Lithuania proved capable of withstanding the Protestant proselytism on a high enough intellectual level.

The Roman church, worried by the spread of Protestantism, insisted on repressive measures against it. In 1557 King Sigismund August issued an edict forbidding conversion of Catholic churches into Protestant prayer houses. Seven years later the king promulgated two more decrees. The first banned from the country all foreigners preaching against Roman Catholicism; the second urged Poles to maintain the Catholic faith. All such measures proved futile. Personally, Sigismund August did not care for religious matters and was not inclined to enforce his decrees against the dissidents. Besides, the two Radivils—Chorny and Rudy—had great influence with him, and Radivil Rudy's sister Barbara was, as we know, Sigismund August's second wife.

Obviously, Roman Catholicism in Poland could be saved not by oppression of the dissidents, in any case not by such measures alone, but by vigorous spiritual effort and intelligent leadership. Such leadership was provided by the Jesuits. They first appeared in Poland in 1564 and in Lithuania in 1569. Their emphasis was on education. Within twenty years they had created a number of excellent schools and colleges, to which even non-Catholics were eager to send their children. The first Jesuit college in Lithuania was founded in Vilna in 1570; eight years later it was expanded into a university (called "academy"). The Catholic Counter Reformation thus began in Poland and Lithuania.[25]

A prominent role in the Catholic movement of the period was played by the talented Polish writer and orator Peter Skarga, who became a Jesuit in Rome in 1569 and four years later returned to Poland. Besides founding schools, the Jesuits organized Catholic societies and brotherhoods, staged public religious ceremonies which attracted thousands of participants and spectators, and led open religious discussions arguing against both Orthodoxy and Protestantism. As a result of their skillful proselytism, the nobility, especially the younger generation, began turning away from Protestantism and Orthodoxy and toward the Catholic fold. In 1574 Skarga succeeded in converting Radivil Chorny's eldest son Nikolai Krishtof (then 25) to Catholicism. Chorny's next son, Iuri (then 18) soon followed the eldest brother's example. Next year the pope appointed Iuri coadjutor of the Bishop of Vilna; and in 1579, Bishop of Vilna. In 1581 Bishop Iuri organized in Vilna an *auto-da-fé,* publicly burning anti-Catholic books, many of which had been published by his late father. As regards the prominent Orthodox families, both Prince Konstantin Ostrozhsky's eldest son Ianush and Prince Andrei Kurbsky's only son Dmitri were likewise converted to Catholicism.

Sigismund August died in 1572. After an interregnum of four years, the Hungarian nobleman voevoda of Transylvania Stefan Batory (the Hungarian spelling is "Báthory") was elected king on condition he marry Sigismund August's sister Anna, which he did. Batory, an able military leader and forceful ruler, gave full support to the Counter Reformation. In 1576 Poland and Lithuania became the site of a full-fledged Jesuit "province." When Batory took Polotsk in 1579, he immediately founded there a Jesuit college, granting to the Jesuits all but one of the Orthodox churches and all the Orthodox monasteries in Polotsk, with the landed estates that had belonged to them. The Warsaw seim of 1585 confirmed the king's action.[26]

In their anti-Orthodox propaganda the Jesuits paid considerable

25. On this Counter Reformation see N. N. Liubovich, *Nachalo katolicheskoi reaktsii i upadok reformatsii v Polshe* (Warsaw, 1890); Makari, *9,* 350–373; Shmurlo, *2,* Pt. I, 389–393; Brückner, *2,* 155–163.

26. Makari, *9,* 404–405.

attention to the promotion of the idea of church union. In 1577, in the Catholic printing office founded in Vilna by Nikolai Krishtof Radivil, Peter Skarga's book *On the Unity of God's Church (O jednosci Kosciola Bożego)* was published in Polish. During the same year the Jesuit Antonio Possevino founded a Russian seminary in Rome to educate young Russians in the Catholic spirit.[27] In 1583 a Russian translation of a Catholic Christian manual by Peter Canisius was published in Rome, and a Catholic Catechism was published in Vilna in 1585, likewise in Russian translation.[28]

In October 1582 Pope Gregory XIII introduced the new (so-called Gregorian) calendar. It was done without a preliminary agreement with the Eastern Church, and the Orthodox in West Russia refused to accept it. This seemingly minor technical matter caused confusion and irritation in West Russian Church affairs; in the opinion of Oskar Halecki, "it probably was a tactical mistake to insist upon the immediate acceptance of a change which affected the daily life of the conservative Orthodox people." [29]

The Jesuits working in Moldavia convinced the Holy See that it was advisable not to make the acceptance of the Gregorian calendar a condition of the Union with Rome. However, Possevino, who in the period between 1581 and 1587 was Rome's chief agent in Russian affairs, worked hard for the adoption of the new calendar and deeply resented the West Russian opposition against it.[30] It should be borne in mind that Possevino's main goal was the conversion of Muscovy to Catholicism, and he regarded the conversion of West Russia as a preliminary move in that direction.

After Batory's death in 1586 there was a new interregnum in Poland. In the lively electoral campaign to choose the new king three potential candidates were put forward: Sigismund of Sweden, Maximilian of Austria, and Tsar Fedor (son of Tsar Ivan) of Moscow.[31] The latter had many supporters among the szlachta. By that time Possevino had lost any hope of converting to Catholicism either West Russia or Muscovy, and in his letter to Stanislav Gomolinski of May 5, 1587,[32] he warned against the danger to Po-

---

27. *Ibid.*, p. 421; Shmurlo, 2, Pt. I, 391.
28. Karataev, No. 95 (pp. 204–206) and No. 98 (p. 210).
29. Halecki, "Possevino's Last Statement," p. 285.
30. *Ibid.*, pp. 284.
31. K. Lepszy, *Walka stronnictw w pierwszych latach panowania Zygmunta III* (Kraków, 1929); Halecki, "Possevino's Last Statement," p. 289.
32. Published in Halecki, "Possevino's Last Statement," pp. 298–302.

land of electing a non-Catholic king and specifically opposed electing the tsar. The supporters of Sigismund of Sweden prevailed, and
the latter was elected king of Poland as Sigismund III. He was the
son of King Johannes III of Sweden and the Polish princess Catherine, whom Tsar Ivan IV had unsuccessfully wooed in 1560. Sigismund III reigned in Poland from 1587 to 1632, and proved an even
more stanch supporter of the Jesuits than Batory had been.

5. THE ORTHODOX REVIVAL IN WEST RUSSIA

Caught between Protestantism and Catholicism, Orthodoxy in
West Russia had to struggle for its survival. As has been said, the
Orthodox hierarchy was not able to offer any guidance to the faithful. Among the parish priests, only a few had sufficient learning
and capabilities to be concerned about raising the intellectual level
of the congregations. As for the West Russian monks, those of the
Derman Monastery in Volynia occupied themselves with translation (from the Greek and Latin) of religious literature, but they
lacked money and initiative.

In these circumstances it was the Orthodox laymen who had to
take upon themselves the burden of the task of defending their faith
and promoting education and learning. In this movement both
Orthodox lords and townspeople participated. A number of Orthodox
brotherhoods were founded in the cities for the purpose of the support of the church.[33] It should be noted that, as in the case of the
development of Protestantism in West Russia, émigrés from East
Russia played a considerable role in the movement.

Prominent among the West Russian Orthdox lords active in promoting Orthodox learning and literary activities were Prince Konstantin Konstantinovich Ostrozhsky and Grigori Aleksandrovich
Khodkevich. Of the Orthodox burghers, Kuzma and Lukash
Mamonich of Vilna are best known. Konstantin Ostrozhsky founded
a school of higher learning in Ostrog, where both Church Slavic
and Greek were taught, and two printing presses, one in Ostrog
and one at the Derman Monastery. It was at the Ostrog press that
the first complete Bible was published in Slavic in 1581. Grigori

33. On the educational activities of the Orthodox lords and town brotherhoods
see Makari, 9, 409–419, 446–477; K. V. Kharlampovich, *Zapadnorusskie pravoslavnye
shkoly XVI i nachala XVII veka* (Kazan, 1898); Hrushevsky, *Istoriia, 6,* 479–498, 516–
520; Shmurlo, *2,* Pt. I, 394–397; G. Florovsky, *Puti Russkogo bogosloviia,* pp. 34–35.

Khodkevich likewise sponsored the publication of several religious books in Zabludovo. Other Orthodox religious books were published in Vilna at the Mamonich brothers' printing office. The Mamonichs were printers for the Lithuanian government, and it was their office that published the Third Lithuanian Statute of 1588.[34]

Turning now to the activities of the city *bratstva* (brotherhoods), small associations of this kind had existed in Russian towns, both in East and in West Russia, since the Middle Ages. In connection with the religious crisis in West Russia, brotherhoods of a new type were now organized, with religious education as their main purpose.[35] The first such brotherhood was created in Lvov in 1586. Two years afterward a similar association was organized in Vilna. These two were the leading organizations of their kind. Later, brotherhoods of the same type were opened in Kiev, Lutsk, Minsk, Vitebsk, Polotsk, and other West Russian towns. The Orthodox brotherhoods founded schools, printing presses, and hospitals; published religious books; and supported Orthodoxy in many ways. In most of the schools Latin and Polish were taught in addition to the Church Slavonic.

Of the émigrés from East Russia, the stanchest supporter of Orthodoxy in West Russia was Prince Andrei Mikhailovich Kurbsky, who established close relations with Prince Ostrozhsky and the brothers Mamonich, and encouraged Orthodox people to stand firm against both Protestantism and Catholicism. He undertook to enrich collections of the Orthodox libraries with new translations of basic works of church fathers. Although in the days of his youth he had known Maxim the Greek and admired him, he had at that time known neither Greek nor Latin. He studied the latter language after coming to West Russia and mastered it sufficiently to undertake the translation into Russian from Latin of works by John Damascene, John Chrysostom, and other Byzantine religious authorities. Kurbsky convinced his nephew Prince Mikhail Obolensky, to enroll as a student in Kraków University and after that to complete his education in Italy. Obolensky helped his uncle with some of the translations. Kurbsky died in 1583.[36]

34. On the Mamonich Brothers' printing office see Lappo, *Litovskii Statut 1588 goda, 1,* Pt. II, 257–309.

35. On the West Russian town brotherhoods see Makari, *9,* 412–419; A. Papkov, *Bratstva* (Moscow, 1900); Hrushevsky (above, n. 4), *6,* 500–538; Vlasovsky, pp. 211–222.

36. For Kurbsky's works see "Sochineniia Kniazia Kurbskogo," *RIB, 31.* On Kurb-

A remarkable spiritual leader from East Russia was the monk Artemi.[37] Artemi (born after 1500) was a Pskovian and in his youth was connected with the Pskov-Pechersky Monastery. Like Kurbsky, he was an admirer of Maxim the Greek. He belonged to the mystic branch of Orthodoxy and followed the traditions of Nil Sorsky. The Moscow Church Council of 1554–55, which condemned Feodosi Kosoy (who actually had broken with Orthodoxy), also accused Artemi of heresy; and Artemi, like Feodosi, fled to Lithuania. In West Russia, Artemi's Orthodoxy was not put in question, and he took active part in the Orthodox movement, conversing with various people and writing many epistles. Like Nil Sorsky, he valued prayer and meditation more than the ritual of the church, but dogmatically he was Orthodox and could accept neither Lutheranism nor Calvinism, writing several epistles against Protestantism. He died shortly before 1575. Kurbsky had a high opinion of him, and a prominent West Russian Orthodox writer of the 17th century, Zakhari Kopystensky, in his book *Palinodia* (written around 1622) said that "Artemi had turned many people in Lithuania away from the Arian and Lutheran heresies, and it was through him that God did not let the Russian people in Lithuania accept the heresy." [38]

We should also not forget the Muscovite Ivan Fedorov, who managed the printing office in Moscow from 1563 to 1565 and then, at the time of the oprichnina, fled to Lithuania and worked as a printer of Russian books there—first in Zabludovo under the patronage of Grigori A. Khodkevich, then in Lvov, and finally in Ostrog under the protection of Prince Konstantin Ostrozhsky.[39] Although Ivan Fedorov was not a religious writer, he contributed greatly to the Orthodox literary movement by his printing activity. While working in the Moscow printing office, he was assisted by a West Russian, Petr Mstislavets (i.e. of Mstislavl). Petr fled from Moscow with Ivan, and they continued working together in West Russia.

---

sky's literary activities in Lithuania see I. Iasinsky, "Sochineniia Kurbskogo kak istorichesky istochnik," *KiUnIzv* (1888), Nos. 10–11; Makari, *9*, 422–423; A. S. Arkhangelsky, Supplement, pp. 3–166; V. Korsakova, "Kurbsky," *RBS*, Vol. "Knappe-Kiukhelbeker" (1903), 594–595; G. Florovsky, *Puti Russkogo bogosloviia*, pp. 32–33. Before coming to Lithuania, Kurbsky wrote a biography of Maxim the Greek: see E. Denissoff, "Une Biographie de Maxime le Grec par Kourbski," *OCP, 20* (1954), 44–84.

37. Artemi's epistles are published in *RIB, 4*, cols. 1201–1448. See also Vilinsky, *Poslaniia startsa Artemiia*. On Artemi see G. Florovsky, *Puti*, pp. 31–32.

38. *RIB, 4*, 913.

39. On Ivan Fedorov see *Pervopechatnik Ivan Fedorov* (Moscow, 1935); R. Jakobson, *Ivan Fedorov's Primer* (Cambridge, Harvard University Press, 1955).

6. Seeds of Conflict between Bishops
and Laymen

Although at the height of the Protestant movement in Lithuania the Orthodox paid as much attention to the polemics against the Protestants as they did to those against the Roman Catholics, the attitude of the Orthodox to Protestantism changed considerably when the Catholic Counter Reformation started in Poland and Lithuania and both the Orthodox and the Protestants had to defend themselves against the attacks of the Jesuits. It was the Protestants who bore the brunt of the parliamentary fight to confirm the right of existence of the non-Catholic churches at the Warsaw seim of 1573. A special confederation of the szlachta was formed, in which the Catholics also participated, and a religious truce was proclaimed.[40]

It was obvious to both the Protestants and the Orthodox that more Catholic pressure on both dissident denominations lay ahead, and it was but natural that some attempts should be made to coordinate the activities of both these denominations to withstand Jesuit ascendancy. Among the Orthodox who advised cooperation with the Protestants was Prince Konstantin Ostrozhsky himself. He invited several Protestant writers to his court at Ostrog and commissioned one of them, the Arian Motovila, to write in Russian a refutation of the Jesuit Peter Skarga's treatises. Ostrozhsky also asked another Protestant to translate into Polish Kurbsky's Russian translation of John Chrysostom's discourse on faith, hope, and love. When Kurbsky learned of this cooperation with the Protestants, he severely criticized Ostrozhsky's action. Other friends of Ostrozhsky likewise were disturbed by his friendly relations with the Protestants. Ostrozhsky answered that he considered it useful to have the Protestants' assistance against the Jesuits.

Although dogmatically the Orthodox remained true to their traditional faith, there were certain peculiarities in the Orthodox movement in West Russia of this period that irritated the hierarchy of the West Russian Church because, from its point of view, they smacked of Protestantism. While not being able to supply spiritual leadership to the faithful, many an Orthodox hierarch objected to the ever-growing active interference of the laymen in church affairs.

40. Grabieński, pp. 118–119.

They especially objected to the activities of the brotherhoods.

Besides the questions of principle, unavoidable personal conflicts between the hierarchs and members of the brotherhoods aggravated relations between the two sides. The West Russian Orthodox hierarchs found themselves in a difficult situation between the increasing pressure on them from above, which emanated from the Catholic government, and the increasing hostility toward them from below of the Orthodox laymen. This psychologically prepared the ground for the inclination of some of the hierarchs toward acceptance of the Union with Rome.

At that juncture the Patriarch of Constantinople found it necessary to inspect personally the West Russian Church (which, it will be recalled, was a diocese of the Patriarchate of Constantinople) and correct the most obvious defects in its organization.

In 1588 Patriarch Jeremiah II decided to visit both West Russia and Moscow. The Church of Moscow, as we know, became autocephalous in 1448 and was no longer canonically subordinated to the Patriarch of Constantinople. However, the Patriarch of Constantinople, as well as the three other Eastern patriarchs, were esteemed in Moscow as the highest prelates of the Orthodox Church. Jeremiah's motives in his decision to visit Moscow were manifold. Among other things, he expected to receive in Moscow large donations from the tsar and the Russian Church for the needs of the Constantinople see, which was in pitiful condition at this time.[41]

Jeremiah reached the Polish frontier in May 1588. He was received in Poland with due esteem to his office. On advice of the chancellor, Jan Zamoyski, King Sigismund III issued a charter to Jeremiah authorizing him to travel in Poland and Lithuania. (It should be noted that Zamoyski, like many Poles at that time, objected to the Jesuits, whose activities he considered harmful to Catholicism as well as to Poland.) On June 3 Patriarch Jeremiah arrived at Vilna, where he was solemnly met by the Orthodox flock there. Jeremiah blessed the recently formed Orthodox brotherhood in Vilna and then proceeded to Smolensk, going from there to Moscow.[42]

Jeremiah returned to Lithuania in July 1589. By that time many priests and all the West Russian prelates, headed by the metropol-

41. Makari, 9, 14; Shpakov, *Uchrezhdenie patriarshestva v Rossii*, pp. 277–278, Supplement, pp. 113–116.
42. *HRM*, Supplement, No. 60; *AZR, 4*, No. 5; Makari, 9, 458–460.

itan Onisifor, had gathered in Vilna. The patriarch conferred with the clergy about the disorders in the West Russian Church. When he received many complaints that some clergymen were guilty of bigamy, he issued an order that all guilty be unfrocked. On this ground he deposed Metropolitan Onisifor himself (July 21, 1589).

Six days later King Sigismund appointed Mikhail Ragoza, a monk of noble origin, the new metropolitan. The patriarch ordained him, even though he had doubts about his fitness for the office.[43] From Vilna, Jeremiah went to Brest, where he appointed Bishop Kirill Terletsky of Lutsk his exarch in West Russia.[44] By this action the patriarch apparently showed he wanted to keep track of Metropolitan Mikhail. The latter, understandably, resented Jeremiah's move. On his return voyage home the patriarch stopped in Tarnopol, where the metropolitan and five bishops came to see him off and receive his blessing. In Tarnopol the patriarch confirmed the privileges of the Lvov brotherhood and ruled that it be exempted from the authority of the Lvov bishop, Gedeon Balaban, and have the authority of appointing and dismissing priests in the Church of Dormition in Lvov, over which the brotherhood had the right of patronage (November 13, 1589).[45] Because the relations between Bishop Gedeon and the Lvov brotherhood had been strained even before the patriarch's charter, the bishop was greatly offended by the patriarch's ruling.

7. THE WEST RUSSIAN BISHOPS TURN TO ROME

The measures taken by Patriarch Jeremiah in his effort to reorganize the administration of the West Russian Church proved ineffective. The patriarch's support of the brotherhoods was especially resented by the bishops.

In 1591 four West Russian bishops, including the patriarch's exarch, Kirill Terletsky, and the Bishop of Lvov, Gedeon Balaban, sent a confidential letter to King Sigismund III informing him that they were ready to accept union with Rome on condition that the Slavonic ritual of the West Russian Church be not changed.[46] Thus the patriarch's trust of Kirill proved misplaced, for Kirill preferred

---

43. *AZR, 4*, No. 20; Makari, *9*, 460–461, 482–485.
44. *AIZR, 1*, Pt. I, No. 60, 250; *AZR, 4*, No. 20; Makari, *9*, 488–490.
45. Makari, *9*, 493–495.
46. For the story of the preparation of the Church Union of Brest see Makari, *9*, 478–652; Hrushevsky (above, n. 4), *5*, 508–605; *6*, 445–467, 539–544; Shmurlo, *2*, Pt. I, 397–402; K. Chodynicki, pp. 194–346; G. Florovsky, *Puti*, pp. 30–46; G. Hofmann, "Die Wiedervereinigung der Ruthenen mit Rom," *OC, 12* (1924–25), 125–172;

to make up with both Metropolitan Mikhail and Bishop Gedeon and to seek protection from the pope. The Catholics now began, systematically, to prepare the ground for organizing the supporters of the idea of union among Orthodox leaders before announcing the union publicly. In 1593 the king appointed one of the Russian lords, the Kashtelian of Brest, Adam Potei (in Polish, Pociej), Bishop of Vladimir-in-Volynia. He became a monk and received a new personal name, Ipati.[47]

Potei was born in 1541 in an Orthodox family and received good education in a Calvinist school and then in Kraków University. In his youth he had been converted to Calvinism but in 1574 returned to Orthodoxy. By 1590, however, he had become disappointed in the disorderly state of West Russian Orthodox Church administration and inclined toward the union with Rome. As soon as he was ordained bishop, he began to propagandize the idea of union. In education and personality Potei was far above the other West Russian hierarchs and became the main leader of the Uniate movement. He was probably the only West Russian hierarch of the period who joined the movement because he believed in its religious value and not merely because of personal considerations.

Prince Konstantin Ostrozhsky, who had known Potei long before the latter's appointment as bishop, proved ready to discuss the problem of union with him. On June 21, 1593, Ostrozhsky wrote to Potei a long letter in which he expounded his attitude toward the church union.[48] In this letter Ostrozhsky expressed his willingness to accept the union in principle, but declared that union with Rome should be concluded not by the West Russian diocese alone, but only by the whole Greek Orthodox Church, to achieve which result it was necessary that the union be approved by the Eastern patriarchs, the Muscovites, and the Moldavians.[48a]

A. M. Ammann, pp. 169–184; Halecki, "Possevino's Last Statement." Halecki has announced in his study that he is preparing a book on the origins and background of the Union of Brest. [O. Halecki, *From Florence to Brest, 1439–1596* (Rome, 1958; New York, Fordham University Press, 1959). This work appeared too late for me to use it for this volume.]

47. On Potei see Makari, *9*, 534–536; Shmurlo, *2*, Pt. I, 398–399; Hrushevsky, *Istoriia Ukrainskoi literatury*, *5*, 380–402.

48. *AZR*, *4*, No. 45; Makari, *9*, 537–539.

48a. The problem of the union of Christian churches has come to the fore in our own time, assuming international significance. On January 25, 1959, Pope John XXIII announced that he would call an ecumenical council aimed at seeking unity "between the Roman Catholic Church and other Christian communities throughout the world . . . The new Pope is understood to be convinced that the time has come for a move for reunion, above all between Rome and the Eastern Christians" (*New York Times,*

Ostrozhsky's point of view was unacceptable to Potei and other West Russian bishops who had already advised King Sigismund III that they favored the union. They now decided to act without delay. In May 1594 Kirill Terletsky announced that the king was sending him and Ipati Potei to Rome. In December of the same year Potei and Kirill composed and signed a declaration by West Russian bishops of their adherence to the union. They succeeded, after much delay, in obtaining the signatures of Metropolitan Mikhail and the bishops of Polotsk, Pinsk, and Kholm.[49] In January 1595 Bishop Gedeon of Lvov convoked an assembly of the clergy of his eparchy, which decided to accept union. On June 1 Metropolitan Mikhail, Bishop Ipati Potei, and the Bishop of Lutsk signed the draft of the "Articles of the Union," which they sent to the king and to the pope.[50]

In the "Article" the signers insisted on the autonomous status of the West Russian Church under the pope's supremacy, and on the integrity of the traditional Slavonic ritual. They insisted that the church estates should be safeguarded and the Uniate metropolitan and bishops should be given seats in the senate.

As soon as Prince Ostrozhsky received news of the Uniate bishops' action, he issued, on June 24, a declaration addressed to all the Orthodox people of Poland and Lithuania, protesting against this kind of church union and urging the Orthodox to stand firm against it.[51]

Ostrozhsky's declaration produced a deep impression on the Orthodox laymen and on most of the clergymen. On July 1 Bishop Gedeon of Lvov announced that he had never agreed to the union formally and that Bishop Kirill had twice misused (in 1591 and 1594) the blanks with his signatures that he had given Kirill for

January 26, 1959). In April, 1959, the Patriarch of Constantinople, Athenagoras I, made the following statement: "No synod can be called ecumenical unless it is truly such, that is, pan-Christian. If the Orthodox Church is invited, it will be represented only if the entire Christian world is invited to send representatives" (*New York Times,* April 23, 1959). It may be seen that Patriarch Athenagoras' attitude toward the union of churches in 1959 is similar to that of Prince Konstantin Ostrozhsky in 1595, but is of larger scope, since the Patriarch makes the participation "of the entire Christian world" (that is, including the Protestants) a prerequisite for the discussion of the Union.

49. *AZR, 4,* No. 53; Makari, *9,* 551–552.

50. For the Polish text and the Latin translation of the "Articles" see Hofmann, "Die Wiedervereinigung," pp. 142–158; Latin translation previously published in Theiner, *Vetera Monumenta, 3,* No. 185, 234–235. For the accompanying letter of the metropolitan and the two bishops to the pope, see *AZR, 4,* No. 68; cf. Makari, *9,* 571–579.

51. *AZR, 4,* No. 71; Makari, *9,* 584–586.

another purpose, a proposed petition to the king to stop the abuses of the Catholics against the Orthodox. Gedeon registered an official statement on this matter in the files of the City of Lvov.[52] It is hard to say whether this statement is correct, since there is enough evidence to show that he had been inclined to the union in 1591–94. Whatever the previous situation, Gedeon now decidedly broke with the Uniate movement.

On July 13 the Orthodox burghers of Vilna protested against union. The head teacher of the Vilno brotherhood's school, Stefan Zizani, wrote a pamphlet in Russian against union under the title *A Booklet against the Roman Church*. Metropolitan Mikhail, now a Uniate, excommunicated Zizani. The latter declared that since Mikhail had left the Orthodox Church, he no longer had authority over the Orthodox. Zizani was arrested and imprisoned but succeeded in fleeing from the prison.[53]

Disregarding the opposition of the Orthodox, King Sigismund now announced the union of the West Russian Church with Rome (September 24, 1595). On December 23 Pope Clement VIII received bishops Kirill Terletsky and Ipati Potei in audience and blessed them. The "Articles of the Union" submitted to the pope were revised in order to bring the West Russian Uniate Church into greater conformity with the Roman Catholic Church.[54]

In May or June 1596 the king issued an edict in which he authorized Metropolitan Mikhail to convoke in Brest a council of the West Russian Church for the purpose of completing the union. The king expressed his belief that the Orthodox would wholeheartedly accept the union. In August the metropolitan announced to the West Russian clergy and laymen that the church council would convene in Brest on October 8.[55]

8. The Council of Brest and the
Proclamation of Union

Both the Uniates and the Orthodox gathered in Brest October 5, 1596.[56]

52. *AIZR, 1,* Pt. I, No. 109; Makari, *9,* 586–588.

53. Makari, *10,* 705; Shmurlo, *2,* Pt. I, 401.

54. For Ipati's and Kirill's letter to Bishop Gedeon of Lvov, see *AIZR, 1,* Pt. I, No. 416, 482–485; Theiner, *Vetera Monumenta, 3,* No. 185, 240–260; Makari, *9,* 620–628.

55. *AIZR, 1,* Pt. I, No. 120; *AZR, 4,* Nos. 97 and 100; Makari, *9,* 643–644.

56. On the Church Council of Brest see Makari, *9,* 652–674; Soloviev, *Istoriia, 10,* 55–59; Hrushevsky (above, n. 4), *5,* 605–613; Doroshenko, *Narys istorii Ukrainy, 1,*

The Uniates were headed by Metropolitan Mikhail Ragoza, assisted by five bishops—Ipati Potei of Vladimir-in-Volynia, Kirill Terletsky of Lutsk, German of Polotsk, Iona Gogol of Pinsk, and Dionisi Zbiruisky of Kholm. On their side were at least three archimandrites and several other clergymen. The pope appointed seven representatives to the council: Jan Dymitr Solikowski, the Catholic Archbishop of Lvov; the Catholic bishops of Lutsk and Kholm; and four Jesuits, including Peter Skarga. The king sent to the council, as his envoys, three Catholic lords: Nikolai Krishtof Radivil, Lev Sapega, and Dymitr Chalecki.[57] They were accompanied by numerous noblemen and attendants.

The Orthodox delegation was headed by the exarch of the Patriarch of Constantinople, Nicephorus, and that of the Patriarch of Alexandria, Cyril Lukaris. They were accompanied by two abbots from Mount Athos. Only two West Russian bishops were on the Orthodox side: Gedeon Balaban of Lvov and Mikhail Kopystinsky of Peremyshl. Nine West Russian archimandrites, two abbots, and no less than 100 priests supported them.

The Orthodox laymen were led by Prince Konstantin Ostrozhsky. With him was his son Aleksandr (Voevoda of Volynia) and several lords, mostly Volynian dignitaries. In addition there were many delegates representing the laymen of the provinces and districts of Vilna, Kiev, Galicia, Volynia, Braslav, Peremyshl, and Pinsk; the delegates of the cities—Vilno, Lvov, Pinsk, Belsk, Brest, Kamenets-in-Podolia, Kiev, Vladimir-in-Volynia, Minsk, Slutsk, and some other towns; and finally, representatives of the Orthodox brotherhoods of Vilna and Lvov. Several Protestants, apparently Brest burghers, at-

---

182–183; Ammann, p. 181; Vlasovsky, *1*, 248–275. Works written on the Council of Brest by contemporaries include the following. *A. Roman Catholic viewpoint:* Piotr Skarga, *Synod Brzeski i iego obrona* (Kraków, 1597); Russian translation, *Opisanie i oborona Sobora Beresteiskogo* (Vilna, 1597), on which see Karataev, *1*, No. 133, 260–261. Both the Polish and the Russian texts are reprinted in *RIB, 19*, cols. 183–328. *B. Greek Orthodox viewpoint: Ekthesis* (outline of the proceedings of the Council) (Kraków, 1597), published anonymously in Polish (it is supposed that a Russian translation was printed simultaneously, but no copy of it has been found as yet); Polish text reprinted in *RIB, 19*, cols. 329–376; Khristofor Philalet (pseudonym), *Apokrisis ili Apologiia* (1598 or 1599); printed probably in Ostrog, see Karataev, No. 136, pp. 263–265). Polish translation appeared in 1600. Both the Russian and the Polish texts are reprinted in *RIB, 19*, cols. 477–982. It was supposed that either Khristofor Bronsky or Martin Bronevsky was the author of *Apokrisis*, but there is no direct evidence to prove either surmise. (Additional reference: Halecki, *From Florence to Brest*, pp. 287–419.)

57. On D. Chalecki see O. Halecki, "Chalecki Dymitr," *PSB, 3* (1937), 247–249.

tended the Orthodox meetings, although they did not vote. As a matter of precaution, Prince Ostrozhsky and other Orthodox lords came each with a throng of armed attendants, Cossacks, and Tatars, even bringing some artillery.

On the eve of the opening of the council the exarchs of the Eastern patriarchs and Prince Ostrozhsky sent their greetings to Metropolitan Mikhail Ragoza and asked a joint meeting with him to settle the agenda. The metropolitan gave no definite answer, but on October 6 called all the Uniate delegates to the Brest Cathedral for the mass, registering this act with the public notary of Brest as the official opening of the Congress.

Not only were the Orthodox not invited to the cathedral, but by the order of Bishop Ipati Potei all Russian churches in Brest were locked for the duration of the council. The Orthodox gathered in a private home, that of Lord Raisky, where there was a large hall that served as a Protestant prayer chapel. There the Orthodox spent the day in suspense, waiting for an answer from Metropolitan Mikhail. As none came, the Orthodox decided to organize their own council, dividing themselves into two *kola,* that of the clergy and that of the laymen.

Thus instead of one church council two were formed in Brest—the Uniate and the Orthodox—each meeting separately. On October 8, the Orthodox council declared that the question of the union with Rome could not be decided by the West Russian Church alone, but only by an agreement of the Eastern patriarchs and of all Orthodox churches. At that juncture Peter Skarga brought to the Orthodox the demand of the king's representatives in the Uniate council to send deputies to hear the king's orders. Skarga demanded and received a private interview with Prince Konstantin Ostrozhsky. While the latter was not convinced by Skarga's arguments, the Orthodox council agreed to send its delegation to the king's representatives. Prince Ostrozhsky was a member of this delegation. The king's envoys tried to convince them to accept the union, but they only agreed to refer the matter to the Orthodox council. The latter, in its message to the king's envoys, reiterated its basic principle, insisting that the question of the union could be decided only by the whole Orthodox Church.

On October 9 the Uniate council solemnly proclaimed the Union of the West Russian Church with Rome and excommunicated Bishop Gedeon Balaban and all the Orthodox monks and priests who refused to accept it. On the same day, at the meeting of the Orthodox council, the patriarch's exarch, Nicephorus, proclaimed the Uniate metropolitan and bishops divested of their offices and of their right to conduct church services. The Orthodox council then announced its refusal to accept the union.

Both councils petitioned the king, each asking him to approve its decisions. The king's position had been, taken long ago, of course: he confirmed the rights and privileges of the Uniate Church as the only legal church of the Russian population of Poland and Lithuania.

The Uniates accused Nicephorus of being a Turkish spy. He was tried but acquitted by the court. Nevertheless, by the king's order he was arrested and imprisoned in Marienburg Castle, where it was reported he soon died of hunger.

As the only legally approved West Russian Church, the Uniate Church now claimed for itself all church buildings and landed estates of the Orthodox Church. The Uniates succeeded in acquiring many Orthodox monasteries. The Uniate drive was intensified in 1599 when the first Uniate metropolitan, Mikhail Ragoza, died and was replaced by Ipati Potei. The Orthodox were somewhat protected only in those towns and districts that were under the authority of Prince Konstantin Ostrozhsky and other—now not numerous—Orthodox lords. In 1599 the Orthodox concluded an agreement with the Protestants for the joint defense of the rights of the religious dissidents.[58]

After the declaration of the Union of Brest many of the West Russian noblemen either joined the Uniate Church or were converted to Roman Catholicism outright. However, among the townspeople and especially among the peasants a stubborn opposition to the union continued for a long time.

Throughout the 17th century most of the Ukrainian peasants had kept their traditional faith, and the pressure of the Uniates on the Orthodox was greatly resented by the latter. Thus the organization of the Uniate Church did not result in the acceptance by the Ukrainian peasants of the Polish regime. The introduction of the union actually divided the West Russian Church into two parts: the Uniate Church and the Orthodox Church. The union brought confusion and nurtured irritation. It added a religious motive to the social opposition of the peasants and the Cossacks. Before long, the latter came to the fore as champions of Orthodoxy.

58. Hrushevsky (above, n. 4), 6, 568–569.

NOTE ON THE SPELLING OF
RUSSIAN NAMES

THE TRANSLITERATION of Russian names in this book follows the
system of transliteration of the Yale University Library, with the
following exceptions:

In Russian family names ending in *-skii* the spelling *-sky* is
preferred.

In both the masculine personal names ending in *-ii* and the feminine names ending in *-iia* simplified transliterations *-i* and *-ia* are
used. Thus Makari, *not* Makarii; Maria, *not* Mariia.

Personal names of Russians are used in their Russian forms. Thus
Ivan, *not* John; Feodosia, *not* Theodosia. However, in a few cases
when Russian names are similar to the corresponding English names,
the English form has been kept. Thus Daniel, *not* Daniil; Sophia,
not Sofia.

NOTE ON RUSSIAN PATRONYMICS
AND FAMILY NAMES

Family names in modern sense were rarely used in Russia in the
15th and the 16th century. When used, they derived mostly from the
personal name (or nickname) of one's father or grandfather. A man
of the boyar class was identified by his patronymic rather than by
his family name.

See, for example, in Genealogical Table IV, below. An ancestor of
the Romanovs was called Fedor Andreevich (i.e. son of Andrei). He
was nicknamed Koshka (meaning "cat"). His son Ivan was known
as Ivan Fedorovich Koshkin. The family name (if we can call it
that) Koshkin was used for two or three generations only and then
was replaced by Koshkin-Zakharin (Ivan F. Koshkin's son was
called Zakhari). The family name subsequently changed to Zakharin, then to Iuriev-Zakharin, and finally to Romanov.

The princely family names derived usually from the name of the
apanage town of the progenitor of the particular branch of the family

in question. Thus, in Genealogical Table V, the family name of the princes Shuisky derived from the name Shuia, the apanage town of the progenitor of the family. Some branches of princely families were identified by the nickname of the progenitor of that branch. Thus, in Table V, Prince Ivan Vasilievich Shuisky was called Skopa ("Osprey"). His descendants became known as the Princes Skopin-Shuisky.

For family names of women (of both titled and nontitled families) the Russian feminine gender form is retained in this book. Thus: Prince Riapolovsky, but Princess Riapolovskaia; Isaak Boretsky, but Marfa Boretskaia; Iuri Saburov, but Solomonia Saburova.

Patronymics of women likewise are given in their feminine forms. See Genealogical Table IV: Anastasia Romanovna Zakharina, sister of Nikita Romanovich Zakharin.

GENEALOGICAL TABLES

THE PURPOSE of the following tables is not to give the full genealogy of each Russian princely and boyar family but to help the reader to identify the family background of some of the leading rulers and statesmen mentioned in this volume.

I. IVAN III'S ANCESTRY

Rurik of Jutland

Igor = Olga of Pskov (*presumably a Norse princess*)

Sviatoslav = Malusha (*Olga's stewardess; presumably a Slav*)

Vladimir the Saint = Rogned of Polotsk (*Norse princess*)

Iaroslav the Wise = Ingigerd of Sweden

Vsevolod I = Byzantine princess of the House of Monomach (*name unknown*)

Vladimir Monomach = 2d (*or 3d*) wife (*name unknown*)

Iuri I = Polovtsian princess (*name unknown*)

Vsevolod the Big Nest = Maria (*Ossetian princess*)

Iaroslav I of Suzdal and Vladimir = Feodosia of Riazan

Aleksandr Nevsky = Aleksandra of Polotsk

Daniel of Moscow = (*origin and name of his wife unknown; presumably a Russian*) (*progenitor of the Danilovichi*)

Ivan I = Elena (*origin unknown; presumably a Russian*)

Ivan II = Feodosia of Briansk

Dmitri Donskoy = Evdokia of Suzdal

Vasili I = Sophia of Lithuania (*daughter of Vitovt*)

Vasili II = Maria of Borovsk

Ivan III = 1st wife, Maria of Tver
= 2d wife, Sophia Paleologus

II. IVAN III'S DESCENDANTS

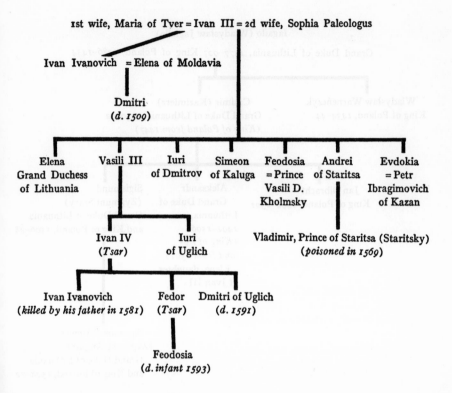

1st wife, Maria of Tver = Ivan III = 2d wife, Sophia Paleologus

Ivan Ivanovich = Elena of Moldavia

Dmitri
(*d. 1509*)

Elena
Grand Duchess
of Lithuania

Vasili III

Iuri
of Dmitrov

Simeon
of Kaluga

Feodosia
= Prince
Vasili D.
Kholmsky

Andrei
of Staritsa

Evdokia
= Petr
Ibragimovich
of Kazan

Ivan IV
(*Tsar*)

Iuri
of Uglich

Vladimir, Prince of Staritsa (Staritsky)
(*poisoned in 1569*)

Ivan Ivanovich
(*killed by his father in 1581*)

Fedor
(*Tsar*)

Dmitri of Uglich
(*d. 1591*)

Feodosia
(*d. infant 1593*)

III. THE JAGELLONS

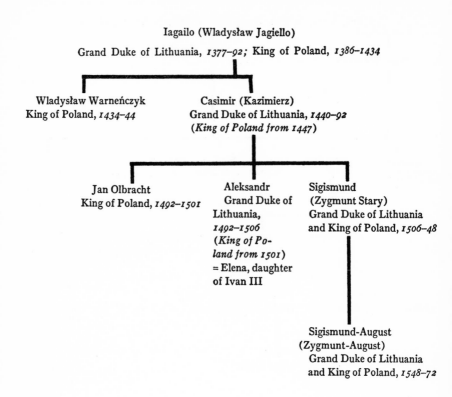

Iagailo (Wladysław Jagiello)

Grand Duke of Lithuania, *1377–92;* King of Poland, *1386–1434*

Wladysław Warneńczyk
King of Poland, *1434–44*

Casimir (Kazimierz)
Grand Duke of Lithuania, *1440–92*
(*King of Poland from 1447*)

Jan Olbracht
King of Poland, *1492–1501*

Aleksandr
Grand Duke of
Lithuania,
1492–1506
(*King of Po-
land from 1501*)
= Elena, daughter
of Ivan III

Sigismund
(Zygmunt Stary)
Grand Duke of Lithuania
and King of Poland, *1506–48*

Sigismund-August
(Zygmunt-August)
Grand Duke of Lithuania
and King of Poland, *1548–72*

IV. THE ANCESTRY OF THE ROMANOVS

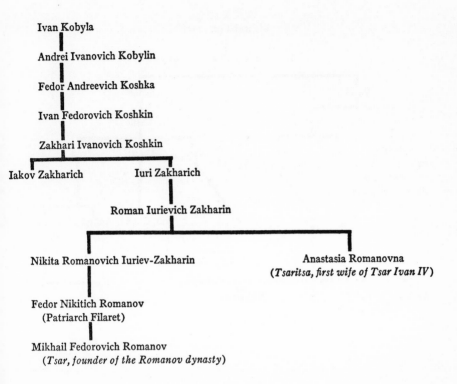

Ivan Kobyla

Andrei Ivanovich Kobylin

Fedor Andreevich Koshka

Ivan Fedorovich Koshkin

Zakhari Ivanovich Koshkin

Iakov Zakharich   Iuri Zakharich

Roman Iurievich Zakharin

Nikita Romanovich Iuriev-Zakharin   Anastasia Romanovna
                                                 (*Tsaritsa, first wife of Tsar Ivan IV*)

Fedor Nikitich Romanov
  (Patriarch Filaret)

Mikhail Fedorovich Romanov
  (*Tsar, founder of the Romanov dynasty*)

V. THE PRINCES SHUISKY

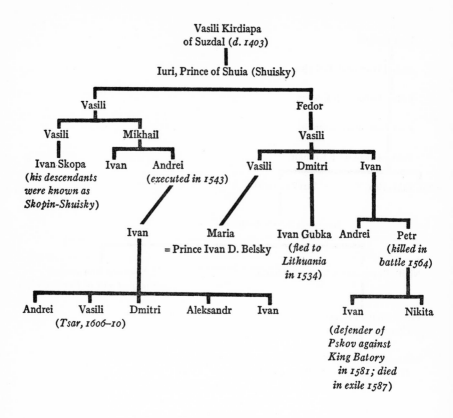

VI. THE PRINCES GLINSKY

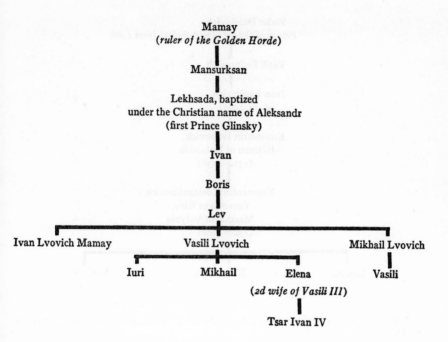

Mamay
(*ruler of the Golden Horde*)

Mansurksan

Lekhsada, baptized
under the Christian name of Aleksandr
(*first Prince Glinsky*)

Ivan

Boris

Lev

Ivan Lvovich Mamay   Vasili Lvovich   Mikhail Lvovich

Iuri   Mikhail   Elena   Vasili
(*2d wife of Vasili III*)

Tsar Ivan IV

VII. THE PRINCES OSTROZHSKY *

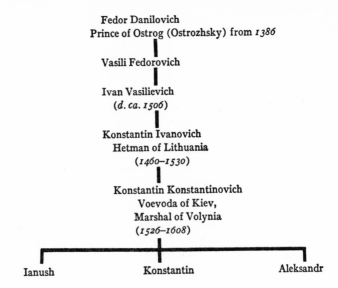

Fedor Danilovich
Prince of Ostrog (Ostrozhsky) from *1386*

Vasili Fedorovich

Ivan Vasilievich
(*d. ca. 1506*)

Konstantin Ivanovich
Hetman of Lithuania
(*1460–1530*)

Konstantin Konstantinovich
Voevoda of Kiev,
Marshal of Volynia
(*1526–1608*)

Ianush   Konstantin   Aleksandr

* The princes Ostrozhsky belonged to the House of Rurik, presumably to the branch of Turov.

VIII. THE PRINCES VISHNEVETSKY *

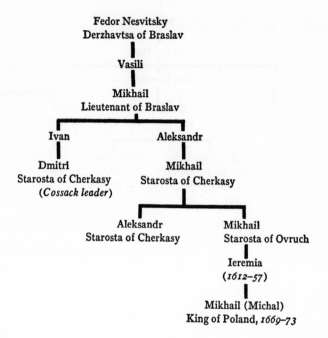

Fedor Nesvitsky
Derzhavtsa of Braslav

Vasili

Mikhail
Lieutenant of Braslav

Ivan

Aleksandr

Dmitrí
Starosta of Cherkasy
(*Cossack leader*)

Mikhail
Starosta of Cherkasy

Aleksandr
Starosta of Cherkasy

Mikhail
Starosta of Ovruch

Ieremia
(*1612–57*)

Mikhail (Michal)
King of Poland, *1669–73*

---

* Presumably descendants of Koribut, son of Olgerd. See *Mongols and Russia*, p. 434, Table X.

IX. THE RADIVILS *

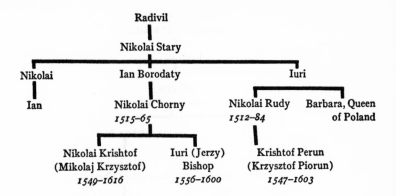

* The Polish spelling of the name is Radziwiłł.

X. THE KHODKEVICHS

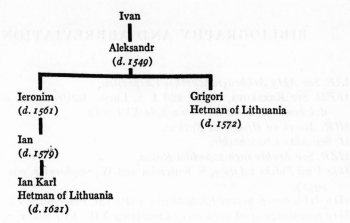

Ivan

Aleksandr
(*d. 1549*)

Ieronim
(*d. 1561*)

Grigori
Hetman of Lithuania
(*d. 1572*)

Ian
(*d. 1579*)

Ian Karl
Hetman of Lithuania
(*d. 1621*)

BIBLIOGRAPHY AND ABBREVIATIONS

AAE. See *Akty Arkheograficheskoi Ekspeditsii.*
AFED. See Kazakova, N. A., and I. S. Lurie, *Antifeodalnye ereticheskie dvizheniia na Rusi XIV—nachala XVI veka.*
AHR. American Historical Review.
AI. See *Akty istoricheskie.*
AIZR. See *Arkhiv iugo-zapadnoi Rossii.*
Akta Unji Polski z Litwą, S. Kutrzeba and W. Semkowicz, eds. (Kraków, 1932).
Akty Arkheograficheskoi Ekspeditsii (AAE) (St. Petersburg, 1836). 3 vols.
Akty feodalnogo zemlevladeniia i khoziastva XIV–XVI vekov, S. V. Bakhrusin and L. V. Cherepnin, eds., *1* (Moscow, 1951).
Akty istoricheskie (St. Petersburg, 1841–42). 5 vols.
Akty otnosiashchiesia k istorii iuzhnoi i zapadnoi Rossii (St. Petersburg, 1863–92). 15 vols.
Akty sotsialno-ekonomicheskoi istorii severo-vostochnoi Rusi kontsa XIV—nachala XVI v., B. D. Grekov and L. V. Cherepnin, eds., *1–2* (Moscow, 1952–58).
Akty zapadnoi Rossii (AZR) (St. Petersburg, 1846–53). 5 vols.
Alef, G., "The Political Significance of the Inscriptions on Muscovite Coinage in the Reign of Vasili II," *Speculum, 34* (1959), 1–19.
Allen, W. E. D., *The Ukraine: A History* (Cambridge, Cambridge University Press, 1940).
American Historical Review (AHR).
American Slavic and East European Review (ASEER).
Ammann, A. M., *Storia della chiesa Russa* (Torino, 1948). German ed., *Ostslavische Kirchengeschichte* (Vienna, 1950).
Ancient Russia. See Vernadsky, G., *Ancient Russia.*
Andreyev, N., "Kurbsky's Letters to Vasyan Muromtsev," *SEER, 33* (1955), 414–436.
———— "The Pskov-Pechery Monastery in the 16th Century," *SEER, 32* (1954), 318–343.
Annuaire. Annuaire de l'Institut de Philologie et d'Histoire Orientales et Slaves.
Archiwum. See *Archiwum Towarzystwa* . . .
Archiwum Jana Zamojskiego, 1–4 (Warsaw and Kraków, 1904–48).
Archiwum Towarzystwa Naukowego we Lwowie (Archiwum).

Arkhangelsky, A. S., *Ocherki iz istorii zapadno-russkoi literatury XVI–XVII vekov* (Moscow, 1888).
Arkhiv iugo-zapadnoi Rossii (Kiev, 1859–1911). 24 vols.
ASEER. American Slavic and East European Review.
Aubin, H., "The Lands East of Elbe and German Colonization Eastwards," *CEH, 1* (1942), 361–397.
AZR. See *Akty zapadnoi Rossii.*
Backus, O. P., *Motives of West Russian Nobles in Deserting Lithuania for Moscow, 1377–1514* (Lawrence, University of Kansas Press, 1957).
———— "Die Rechtsstellung der litauischen Bojaren 1387–1506," *JGOE, 6* (1958), 1–32.
Barbaro. See *Travels to Tana and Persia.*
Baron, S. W., *The Jewish Community* (Philadelphia, The Jewish Publication Society of America, 1942). 3 vols.
Baumgarten, N. de, "Généalogies des branches régnantes des Rurikides du XIII-me et XVI-me siècle," *OC, 94* (1934).
Bazilevich, K. V., *Vneshniaia politika Russkogo tsentralizovannogo gosudarstva. Vtoraia polovina XV veka* (Moscow, 1952).
Becker, B., ed., *Autour de Michel Servet et de Sebastien Castellion* (Haarlem, 1953).
Belokurov, S., *Snosheniia Rossii s Kavkazom* (Moscow, 1889).
Bershadsky, S. A., *Dokumenty i regesty k istorii Evreev v Litve* (St. Petersburg, 1883).
———— *Litovskie Evrei* (St. Petersburg, 1898).
Bestuzhev-Riumin, K. N., *Russkaia istoriia, 2,* Pt. I (St. Petersburg, 1885).
Bielski, Marcin, *Kronika Polska* (Kraków, 1597).
Black, C., ed., *Rewriting Russian History: Soviet Interpretations of Russia's Past* (New York, F. A. Praeger, 1956).
Brock, P., *The Political and Social Doctrines of the Unity of Czech Brethren* (The Hague, Mouton & Co., 1957).
Brockhaus-Efron, *Entsiklopedicheskii Slovar' (ES).* References are to the half-volume edition.
Brückner, A., *Dzieje Kultury Polskiej* (Kraków, 1930–31). 3 vols.
BSE. Bolshaia Sovetskaia entsiklopediia (2d ed.).
Budovnits, I., *Russkaia publitsistika XVI veka* (Moscow, 1947).
Cambridge Economic History (CEH).
Cambridge History of Poland, 1 (Cambridge, Cambridge University Press, 1950).
CEH. Cambridge Economic History.
Cherepnin, L. V., *Russkaia paleografiia* (Moscow, 1956).
———— *Russkie feodalnye arkhivy XIV–XV vekov, 1–2* (Moscow, 1948–51).
Cherniavsky, M., "Holy Russia," *AHR, 63* (1958), 617–637.

Chodynicki, K., *Kościoł prawosławny a Rzeczpospolita Polska, 1370–1632* (Warsaw, 1934).

Chteniia. See Moscow, Universitet . . . *Chteniia.*

Chubaty, N., "Derzhavno-pravne stanovischche Ukrainskykh zemel Litovskoi derzhavy," *ZNTS* (1926), 134–135, 144–145.

Comitato Internazionale di Scienze Storiche, X Congresso Internazionale di Scienze Storiche, Roma, 1955, *Relazione, 1–7* (Florence, 1955).

Contarini. See *Travels to Tana and Persia.*

Dal, V., *Tolkovyi slovar' zhivogo Velikorusskogo iazyka* (St. Petersburg, 1881; new impression, Moscow, 1954). 4 vols.

DDG. See *Dukhovnye i dogovornye gramoty velikikh i udelnykh kniazei XIV–XVI vekov.*

Denissoff, E., "Une Biographie de Maxime le Grec par Kourbski," *OCP, 20* (1954), 44–84.

—— *Maxime le Grec et l'Occident* (Louvain, 1942).

Dewey, H. W., "The 1497 Sudebnik," *ASEER, 15* (1956), 325–338.

—— "The White Lake Charter: a Medieval Russian Administrative Statute," *Speculum, 32* (1957), 74–83.

Diakonov, M. A., *Ocherki obshchestvennogo i gosudarstvennogo stroia drevnei Rusi* (4th ed. St. Petersburg, 1912).

—— *Vlast' Moskovskikh Gosudarei* (St. Petersburg, 1889).

Dlugosz, J., *Opera omnia*, ed. A. Przezdiecki (Kraków, 1873–78). 15 vols.

DMAO. Drevnosti Moskovskogo Arkheologicheskogo Obshchestva. Trudy Slavianskoi Kommissii.

Dmitrieva, R. P., *Skazanie o kniaziakh Vladimirskikh* (Moscow and Leningrad, 1955).

Dnevnik Liublinskogo Seima 1569 goda, M. I. Koialovich, ed. (St. Petersburg, 1869).

Dolgorukov, Prince P. D., *Rossiiskaia rodoslovnaia kniga* (St. Petersburg, 1854–55). 4 vols.

Doroshenko, D., *Narys istorii Ukrainy* (Warsaw, 1932–33). 2 vols.

—— *A Survey of Ukrainian Historiography;* Supplement, O. Ohloblyn, "Ukrainian Historiography 1917–1956" (New York, 1957).

Dovnar-Zapolsky, M. V., *Gosudarstvennoe khoziaistvo Velikogo Kniazhestva Litovskogo pri Iagellonakh* (Kiev, 1901).

—— "Polsko-Litovskaia uniia na seimakh do 1569 goda," *DMAO, 2* (1897).

Drevnosti Moskovskogo Arkheologicheskogo Obshchestva. Trudy Slavianskoi Kommissii (DMAO).

Dubnow, S. M., *History of the Jews in Russia and Poland* (Philadelphia, The Jewish Publication Society, 1916–20). 3 vols.

Dukhovnye i dogovornye gramoty velikikh i udelnykh kniazei XIV–XVI vekov (DDG), S. V. Bakhrushin and L. V. Cherepnin, eds. (Moscow and Leningrad, 1950).

EI. Encyclopedia of Islam.

Ekzempliarsky, A. V., "Glinskii, kniaz' M. L.," *ES, 16* (1893), 866–867.

――*Velikie i udelnye kniazia Severnoi Rusi v tatarskii period* (St. Petersburg, 1889–91). 2 vols.

Eliashevich, V. B. [B. Eliachévitch], *Istoriia prava pozemelnoi sobstvennosti v Rossii, 1–2* (Paris, 1948–51).

Encyclopedia of Islam (EI).

Entsiklopedicheskii Slovar' (ES). See Brockhaus-Efron.

ES. See Brockhaus-Efron.

Evreiskaia Entsiklopediia, A. Harkavy and L. Katsenelson, eds. (St. Petersburg, 1906–13). 15 vols.

[Fedorov, I.] *Pervopechatnik Ivan Fedorov* (Moscow, 1935).

Fedotov, G. P., *Sviatye drevnei Rusi* (Paris, YMCA Press, 1931).

Fennell, J. L. I., ed., *The Correspondence between Prince A. M. Kurbsky and Tsar Ivan IV of Russia, 1564–1579* (Cambridge, Cambridge University Press, 1955).

Finkel, L., *Bibliografia historii Polskiej* (new impression, Warsaw, 1956). 3 vols.

First Novgorodian Chronicle *(Novgorodskaia Pervaia Letopis'),* A. N. Nasonov, ed. (Moscow and Leningrad, 1950).

Florinsky, M. T., *Russia: A History and an Interpretation, 1* (New York, Macmillan, 1955).

Florovsky, A. V., *Chekhi i Vostochnye Slaviane* (Prague, 1936–47). 2 vols.

Florovsky, G., *Puti Russkogo bogosloviia* (Paris, 1937).

Forsten, G. V., *Borba iz-za gospodstva na Baltiiskom more v XV–XVI stoletiakh* (St. Petersburg, 1884).

Forstreuter, K., *Preussen und Russland* (Berlin and Frankfurt, 1955).

Fourth Novgorodian Chronicle *(Novgorodskaia Chetvertaia Letopis'),* PSRL, 4 (2d ed. Petrograd, 1925).

Fürst, J., *Geschichte des Karäerthums von 900 bis 1575* (Leipzig, 1865).

GNP. Gramoty Velikogo Novgoroda i Pskova.

Golobutsky, V. A., *Zaporozhskoe Kazachestvo* (Kiev, 1957).

Golubinsky, E. E., *Istoriia Russkoi Tserkvi* (Moscow, 1901–17). 2 vols., each in 2 parts.

Grabar, I., *Istoriia russkogo iskusstva.* 6 vols., not completed (Moscow, n.d. [1909–12]; 2d ed. *1–3,* Moscow, 1953–55).

Grabieński, W., *Istoriia Polskogo Naroda,* Russian translation, N. Iastrebov, ed. (St. Petersburg, 1910).

Gramoty Velikogo Novgoroda i Pskova (GNP), S. N. Valk, ed. (Moscow and Leningrad, 1949).

Grekov, B. D., *Krestiane na Rusi do XVII veka* (Moscow and Leningrad, 1946).

Grekov, B. D., and A. I. Iakubovsky, *Zolotaia Orda i ee padenie* (Moscow and Leningrad, 1950).

Gudzii, N. K., *Istoriia drevnei russkoi literatury* (2d ed. Moscow, 1941).
Halecki, O., *Dzieje unii Jagellońskiej* (Kraków, 1919–20). 2 vols.
—— *From Florence to Brest, 1439–1596* (Rome, 1958; New York, Fordham University Press, 1959).
—— "Possevino's Last Statement on Polish-Russian Relations," *OCP* (1953), pp. 261–302.
Hamilton, G. H., *The Art and Architecture of Russia* (Baltimore, Penguin Books, 1954).
Harkavy, A., "Karaimy," *ES, 27* (1895), 427–431.
Harvard Slavic Studies (HSS).
Herberstein–Backus. Herberstein, S. von, *Commentaries on Muscovite Affairs*, O. P. Backus III, ed. and trans. (Lawrence, University of Kansas, 1956).
Herberstein–Malein. Herberstein, S. von, *Zapiski o moskovitskikh delakh*, A. I. Malein, ed. and trans. [into Russian] (St. Petersburg, 1908).
Historica Russiae monumenta (HRM), A. I. Turgenev, ed. (St. Petersburg, 1841–42; Supplement, 1848). 2 vols.
Hofmann, G., "Die Wiedervereinigung der Ruthenen mit Rom," *OC, 12* (1924–25), 169–184.
HRM. See *Historica Russiae monumenta.*
Hrushevsky (Grushevsky), M., *Istoriia Ukrainskoi literatury* (Kiev, 1923–27). 5 vols.
—— *Istoriia Ukrainy-Rusi* (Kiev and Lvov, 1898–1937). 10 vols.
HSS. Harvard Slavic Studies.
IA. Istoricheskii Arkhiv.
Iasinsky, I., "Sochineniia Kniazia Kurbskogo kak istoricheskii istochnik," *KiUnIzv* (1888), Nos. 10–11.
Igor Tale (Slovo o Polku Igoreve). H. Grégoire, R. Jakobson, M. Szeftel, J. A. Joffe, "La Geste du Prince Igor," *Annuaire, 8* (1948).
Ikonnikov, V. S., *Maksim Grek* (Kiev, 1866).
—— *Opyt issledovaniia o kulturnom znachenii Vizantii v Russkoi istorii* (Kiev, 1869).
—— *Opyt Russkoi istoriografii* (Kiev, 1891–98). 2 vols., each in 2 parts.
Ioasafovskaia letopis' (Moscow, 1957).
Iosif (Sanin), *Prosvetitel ili oblichenie eresi zhidovstvuiushchikh* (3d ed. Kazan, 1896).
Istochnikovedenie istorii SSSR, 1, M. N. Tikhomirov, ed. (Moscow, 1940).
Istoricheskie Zapiski (IZ).
Istoricheskii Arkhiv (IA).
IZ. Istoricheskie Zapiski.
Jablonowski, A., "Etniczna postać Ukrainy w epoce zjednoczenia jej z Koroną," *KH* (1893), 408–435.
Jablonowski, H., *Westrussland zwischen Wilna und Moskau* (Leiden, 1955).
Jahrbücher für Geschichte Osteuropas (JGOE).

Jakobson, R., *Ivan Fedorov's Primer* (Cambridge, Harvard University Press, 1955).

JGOE. Jahrbücher für Geschichte Osteuropas.

Jireček, H., *Svod Zakonův Slovanských* (Prague, 1880).

Kalugin, F., *Zinovi, inok Otensky* (St. Petersburg, 1894).

Karamzin, N. M., *Istoriia Gosudarstva Rossiiskogo* (6th ed. St. Petersburg, A. Smirdin, 1851–53). 12 vols.

—— *Primechaniia k istorii Gosudarstva Rossiiskogo* (Notes to *Istoriia Gosudarstva Rossiiskogo*) (6th ed. St. Petersburg, A. Smirdin, 1852–53). 12 vols.

Karataev, I., *Opisanie slaviano-russkikh knig, 1* (St. Petersburg, 1878).

Kazakova, N. A., and I. S. Lurie, *Antifeodalnye ereticheskie dvizheniia na Rusi XIV–nachala XVI veka (AFED)* (Moscow and Leningrad, 1955).

Kazanskaia istoriia, V. P. Adrianova-Peretts and G. N. Moiseeva, eds. (Moscow and Leningrad, 1954).

KH. Kwartalnik Historyczny.

Kharlampovich, K. V., *Zapadnorusskie pravoslavnye shkoly XVI i nachala XVII veka* (Kazan, 1898).

Khrushchov, I., *Issledovanie o sochineniiakh Iosifa Sanina* (St. Petersburg, 1868).

Kievan Russia. See Vernadsky, G., *Kievan Russia.*

Kievskaia Starina (KiSt).

KiSt. Kievskaia Starina.

KiUnIzv. Kiev, Universitet, *Izvestiia.*

Kliuchevsky, V. O., *Boiarskaia Duma Drevnei Rusi* (4th ed. Moscow, 1910).

—— *Drevnerusskie zhitiia kak istoricheskii istochnik* (Moscow, 1871).

—— *Kurs Russkoi istorii* (American Council of Learned Societies Reprints, Russian Series, No. 14). Reproduction of the 1937 Moscow edition. 5 vols.

Kondakov, N. P., *Ikonografiia Gospoda Boga i Spasa nashego Iisusa Khrista, 1* (St. Petersburg, 1905).

—— *Ocherki i zametki po istorii srednevekovogo iskusstva i kultury* (Prague, 1929).

—— *The Russian Icon,* E. H. Minns, ed. (Oxford, Clarendon Press, 1927).

Konstantin, Archimandrite [K. I. Zaitsev], "Chudo Russkoi istorii, I. Vozniknovenie Pravoslavnogo tsarstva," *Pravoslavnyi Put'* (1951), pp. 108–126.

Kopanev, A. I., A. G. Mankov, N. E. Nosov, *Ocherki istorii S.S.S.R. Konets XV–nachalo XVII vv.* (Leningrad, 1957).

Korsakova, V., "Kurbskii," *RBS,* Vol. "Knappe–Kiukhelbeker," pp. 589–591.

Korzon, T., *Dzieje wojen i wojskowosci w Polsce, 1* (Kraków, 1923).

Kostomarov, N. I., *Bogdan Khmelnitskii* (4th ed. St. Petersburg, 1884). 3 vols.

────── *Severnorusskie narodopravstva* (St. Petersburg, 1863). 2 vols.

Kot, S., "Budny Szymon," *PSB, 3* (1937), 96–99.

────── "L'Influence de Michel Servet sur le mouvement antitrinitarien en Pologne et en Transylvanie," in Becker, B, ed. (q.v. above).

────── ed., *Reformacja w Polsce* (a quarterly published in Kraków), *1* (1922–).

Kovalevsky, P., *Manuel d'Histoire Russe* (Paris, 1947).

────── "Messianisme et millénarisme Russes," *Archives de Sociologie des Religions, 5* (1958), 47–70.

Kowalski, T., *Karaimische Texte im Dialekt von Troki* (Kraków, 1929).

Kromer, M., *De Origine et rebus gestis Polonorum libri XXX* (Basileae, 1568).

Krupnyckyj, B., *Geschichte der Ukraine* (2d ed. Leipzig, 1943).

Krymsky, A. E., *Istoriia Turechchiny* (Kiev, 1924).

Kupsch, E., "Der Polnische Unitarismus," *JGOE, 5* (1957), 401–440.

Kurat, A. N., *Topkapı Sarayi Muzesi Arşivindeki Altın Ordu, Kırım ve Türkistan Hanlarına ait Yarlık ve Bitikler* (Istanbul, 1940).

Kurbsky, Prince A. M., "Sochineniia," G. Z. Kuntsevich, ed., *RIB, 31* (1914).

Kutrzeba, S., *Historja ustroju Polski* (2d ed. 2 vols. *1*, Kraków, 1931; *2*, Lvov, 1914).

Kwartalnik Historyczny (*KH*).

Lappo, I. I., *Litovskii Statut 1588 goda, 1* (Pts. I–II), Issledovanie; *2*, Text (Kaunas, 1934–37).

────── *Velikoe Kniazhestvo Litovskoe za vremiia ot zakliucheniia Lublinskoi Unii do smerti Stefana Batoriia, 1–2* (St. Petersburg, 1901).

────── *Zapadnaia Rossiia i ee soedinenie s Polsheiu* (Prague, 1924).

Lassota von Steblau, E., *Tagebuch* (Halle, 1866).

Lazius, W., *De aliquot gentium migrationibus* (Basileae, 1572).

Leontovich, F. I., *Krestiane iugo-zapadnoi Rossii po Litovskomu pravu XV i XVI vekov* (Kiev, 1863).

────── "Krestianskii dvor v Litovsko-Russkom gosudarstve," *ZMNP, 2–4, 7, 10, 12* (1896), *4–5* (1897).

────── "Rada velikikh kniazei Litovskikh," *ZMNP, 9–10* (1907).

Lepszy, K., *Wałka stronnictw w pierwszych latach panowania Zygmunta III* (Kraków, 1929).

Lewicki, K., "Książe Konstanty Ostrogski a unja Brzeska 1596 r.," *Archiwum*, Ser. 2, Vol. *11*, Fascicle 1 (Lvov, 1933).

Liashchenko, P. I., *Istoriia narodnogo khoziaistva SSSR, 1* (Moscow, 1947).

Likhachev, D. S., *Russkie letopisi* (Moscow and Leningrad, 1947).

Likhachev, N. P., *Razriadnye diaki XVI veka* (St. Petersburg, 1888).

Listy Stanisława Żołkiewskiego, 1584–1620 (*LSZ*) (Kraków, 1868).
"Litovskaia Metrika," *RIB, 20* (1903), *27* (1910), *30* (1914), *33* (1915).
"Litovskii Statut." First (1529): H. Jireček, *Svod Zakonův Slovanských* and *Vremennik, 21*. Second (1566): in *Vremennik, 19*. Third (1588): in *Vremennik, 18*. For the recent edition of the Third Statute see Lappo, *Litovskii Statut 1588 goda, 2*.
Liubavsky, M. K., *Litovsko-Russkii Seim* (Moscow, 1901).
——— "Nachalnaia istoriia kozachestva," *ZMNP, 300* (1895), 217–244.
——— *Oblastnoe delenie i mestnoe upravlenie Litovsko-Russkogo gosudarstva* (Moscow, 1892).
——— *Obrazovanie osnovnoi gosudarstvennoi territorii Velikorusskoi narodnosti* (Leningrad, 1929).
——— *Ocherk istorii Litovsko-Russkogo gosudarstva* (2d ed. Moscow, 1915).
Liubovich, N. N., *Istoriia reformatsii v Polshe: Kalvinisty i Antitrinitarii* (Warsaw, 1883).
——— *Nachalo katolicheskoi reaktsii i upadok reformatsii v Polshe* (Warsaw, 1890).
Lobanov-Rostovsky, Prince A. B., *Russkaia rodoslovnaia kniga* (2d ed. St. Petersburg, 1895). 2 vols.
Long, John, *Modern Russia: An Introduction* (London, Gerald Duckworth and Co., 1957).
LSZ. Listy Stanisława Żołkiewskiego.
Lurie, I. S., "Iz istorii politicheskoi borby pri Ivane III," Leningrad University, Section of Historical Sciences, *Uchenye Zapiski, 10* (1940), 90–91.
Makari (Bulgakov), Metropolitan, *Istoriia Russkoi tserkvi* (St. Petersburg, 1877–91). 12 vols.
Maksimovich, E. F., "Pervosovetnik Dumy Boyarskoi," *ZRIOP, 2* (1930), 141–162.
Malinin, V., *Starets Eleazarova Monastyria Filofei i ego poslaniia* (Moscow, 1901).
Materialy po istorii SSSR, 2, A. A. Novoselsky, L. V. Cherepnin, L. N. Pushkarev, eds. (Moscow, 1955).
Matthew of Miechow (Miechowita, Mekhovsky), *Traktat o dvukh Sarmatiiakh* (*De duabus Sarmatiis*), S. A. Anninsky, ed. and trans. into Russian (Moscow and Leningrad, 1936).
Medlin, W. K., *Moscow and East Rome* (Neuchâtel, Switzerland, 1952).
Mekhovsky. See Matthew of Miechow.
MGH. Monumenta Germaniae Historica.
MHH. Monumenta Hungariae Historica.
Michalon Lituanus, *De Moribus Tartarorum, Lituanorum et Moschorum* (Basileae, 1615).

Miechowita. *See* Matthew of Miechow.

Miliukov, P., *Ocherki po istorii Russkoi kultury, 2–3* (Paris, 1930–31).

Mongols and Russia. See Vernadsky, G., *The Mongols and Russia.*

Monumenta Germaniae Historica (MGH).

Monumenta Hungariae Historica (MHH).

Moscow, Universitet, Obshchestvo Istorii i Drevnostei, *Chteniia.*

Nemoy, L., *Karaite Anthology* (New Haven, Yale University Press, 1952).

Nikitin, Afanasi, *Khozhenie za tri moria Afanasiia Nikitina 1466–1472 gg.,* B. D. Grekov and V. P. Adrianova-Peretts, eds. (Moscow and Leningrad, 1948).

Nikitsky, A., *Istoriia ekonomicheskogo byta Velikogo Novgoroda* (Moscow, 1893).

—— *Ocherk vnutrennei istorii Pskova* (St. Petersburg, 1873).

—— *Ocherk vnutrennei istorii tserkvi v Velikom Novgorode* (St. Petersburg, 1879).

Nikon Chronicle (*Nikonovskaia letopis*), *PSRL, 9–13* (1862–1906).

Nosov, N. E., *Ocherki po istorii mestnogo upravleniia Russkogo gosudarstva pervoi poloviny XVI veka* (Moscow and Leningrad, 1957).

Novgorodian Chronicles. See First Novgorodian Chronicle; Third Novgorodian Chronicle; Fourth Novgorodian Chronicle.

Novitsky, I. P., "Ocherk istorii krestianskogo sosloviia iugo-zapadnoi Rossii," *AIZR, 6,* Pt. I (Kiev, 1876), 1–161.

Novoselsky, A. A., *Bor'ba Moskovskogo gosudarstva s Tatarami v pervoi polovine XVII veka* (Moscow, 1948).

OC. Orientalia Christiana.

Ocherki 2, Ocherki 3. Ocherki istorii SSSR. Period feodalizma: [2] *XIV–XV vv.;* [3] *Konets XV–nachalo XVII v.* (Moscow, 1953–55).

OCP. Orientalia Christiana Periodica.

Ohloblyn, O., *Moskovska teoriia III Rymu v XVI–XVII stol.* (Munich, 1951).

Okinshevich, L., *The Law of the Grand Duchy of Lithuania: Background and Bibliography* (New York, Research Program on the U.S.S.R., 1953).

Orientalia Christiana (OC).

Orientalia Christiana Periodica (OCP).

OSP. Oxford Slavonic Papers.

Oulianoff [Ulianov], N. I., "Kompleks Filofeia," *Novyi Zhurnal, 45* (1956), 249–273.

Oxford Slavonic Papers (OSP).

Pachymeres, G., *De Michaele et Andronico Paleologis* (Bonn, 1835). 2 vols.

Pamiatniki diplomaticheskikh snoshenii (PDS), 1 (St. Petersburg, 1851).

Pamiatniki Russkogo prava (PRP), 1–4, S. V. Iushkov, L. V. Cherepnin, A. A. Zimin, eds. (Moscow, 1952–56).

Pamiatniki starinnoi Russkoi literatury (*Pamiatniki SRL*), published by Count G. Kushelev-Bezborodko. Vols. *1, 2, 4,* N. Kostomarov, ed.; Vol. *3,* A. N. Pypin, ed. (St. Petersburg, 1860–62).

Papkov, A., *Bratstva* (Moscow, 1900).

Pavlov, A. S., *Istoricheskii ocherk sekuliarizatsii tserkovnych zemel v Rossii* (Odessa, 1871).

Pavlov-Silvansky, N. P., *Feodalizm v udelnoi Rusi* (St. Petersburg, 1910).

PDS. See *Pamiatniki diplomaticheskikh snoshenii.*

Peresvetov, I., *Sochineniia I. Peresvetova,* D. S. Likhachev and A. A. Zimin, eds. (Moscow and Leningrad, 1956).

Petukhov, E. V., *Russkaia literatura, drevnii period* (Iuriev, 1912).

PH. Przegląd Historyczny.

Picheta, V. I., *Agrarnaia reforma Sigizmunda-Avgusta v Litovsko-Russkom gosudarstve* (Moscow, 1958).

Pierling, P., *La Russie et le Saint-Siège, 1–2* (Paris, 1896).

Pis'ma. Pis'ma Russkikh gosudarei (Moscow, 1848).

Platonov, S. F., *Lektsii po Russkoi istorii* (6th ed. St. Petersburg, 1909).

——— *Ocherki po istorii Smuty* (St. Petersburg, 1899).

Pociecha, W., "Barbara Radziwiłłowa," *PSB, 1* (1935), 294–298.

——— "Bona Sforza," *PSB, 2* (1936), 288–294.

——— "Daszkievich," *PSB, 4* (1938), 444–447.

Polčin, S., "La Mission religieuse du Père A. Possevin, S.J., en Moscovie (1581–1582)," *OC, 150* (1957).

Polnoe sobranie Russkikh letopisei (*PSRL*).

Polski Słownik Biograficzny (*PSB*), *1–4* (not completed) (Kraków, 1935–38).

Porfiridov, N. G., *Drevnii Novgorod* (Moscow and Leningrad, 1947).

Poslaniia Ivana Groznogo. Text prepared by D. S. Likhachev and I. S. Lurie and edited by V. P. Adrianova-Peretts (Moscow and Leningrad, 1951).

Potemkin, V. P., ed., *Istoriia diplomatii, 1* (Moscow, 1941).

Povest' o prikhozhenii Stefana Batoriia na grad Pskov, V. I. Malyshev, ed. (Moscow and Leningrad, 1952).

Presniakov, A. E., *Lektsii po Russkoi istorii, 2,* fasc. 1 (Moscow, 1939).

——— *Obrazovanie Velikorusskogo gosudarstva* (Petrograd, 1918).

Prosvetitel. See Iosif (Sanin), *Prosvetitel ili oblichenie eresi zhidovstvuiushchikh.*

PRP. See *Pamiatniki Russkogo prava.*

Przegląd Historyczny (*PH*).

PSB. See *Polski Słownik Biograficzny.*

Pskovian Chronicle (*Pskovskie letopisi*), *1,* A. Nasonov, ed. (Moscow and Leningrad, 1941). See also *PSRL, 4.*

Pushkarev, S. G., *Obzor Russkoi istorii* (New York, Chekhov Publishing House, 1953).

—— "Tselovalniki v sude i upravlenii Moskovskoi Rusi," *ZRNIB*, *9* (1953), 17–53.
—— "Vnitřní zřizení a vnější postavení Pskovského státu," *SVPS, 25* (1925).
RANION. Rossiiskaia assotsiatsia nauchnykh institutov obshchestvennykh nauk. Institut istorii.
Rasovsky, D. A., "K voprosu o proiskhozhdenii Codex Cumanicus," *SK, 3* (1929), 193–214.
RBS. See *Russkii biograficheskii slovar'*.
Regenvolscius, A. (Andreas Węgierski), *Systema historico-chronologicum ecclesiarum Slavonicarum* (Trajecti ad Rhenum, 1652). Excerpt in Russian translation, *Chteniia, 8* (1847), 3.
Relazioni. Comitato Internazionale di Scienze Storiche, *Relazioni.*
Revue historique de droit Français et étranger (RHDFE).
REW. See Vasmer, M., *Russisches etymologisches Wörterbuch.*
RHDFE. Revue historique de droit Français et étranger.
Rhode, G., *Die Ostgrenze Polands* (Cologne and Gratz, 1955).
Riasanovsky, V. A., *Obzor Russkoi kultury, 1–2* (New York, 1947–48). Vol. *2* in 2 parts.
RIB. See *Russkaia istoricheskaia biblioteka.*
Rodoslovnaia Kniga ("Barkhatnaia Kniga") (Moscow, 1787). 2 vols.
"Rodoslovnaia Kniga," *Vremennik, 10* (1851), 1–286.
Rossiiskaia Assotsiatsia Nauchnykh Institutov Obshchestvennykh Nauk (RANION).
Russkaia istoricheskaia biblioteka (RIB) (St. Peterburg, 1872–1927). 39 vols.
Russkii biograficheskii slovar' (RBS) (St. Petersburg, 1896–1918). 25 vols., not completed.
Rutkowski, Jan, *Histoire économique de la Pologne avant les partages* (Paris, 1927).
Rzhiga, V. F., "Boiarin-Zapadnik XVI veka (F. I. Karpov)," *RANION, 4* (1929), 39–50.
Sadikov, P. A., *Ocherki po istorii Oprichniny* (Moscow and Leningrad, 1950).
Sagmüller, J. B., "Patron and Patronage," *The Catholic Encyclopedia, 11* (1911), 560–561.
Sarkisyanz, E., *Russland und der Messianismus des Orients* (Tübingen, 1955).
Savva, V., *Moskovskie tsari i Vizantiiskie vasilevsy* (Kharkov, 1901).
Sbornik. Sbornik Imperatorskogo Russkogo Istoricheskogo Obshchestva.
Sbornik Russkogo Arkheologicheskogo Obshchestva v Korolevstve S. Kh. S. (SRAOKS).
Sbornik starinnykh gramot i uzakonenii Rossiiskoi Imperii kasatelno prav i sostoianiia russko-poddannykh Karaimov (St. Petersburg, 1890).

Sborník věd právních a státnich (SVPS).

Schaeder, H., *Moskau das Dritte Rom* (Hamburg, 1929).

SEER. The Slavonic and East European Review (London).

Seminarium Kondakovianum (SK) (Prague).

Sergeevich, V. I., *Drevnosti Russkogo prava* (St. Petersburg, 1908–11). 3 vols.

Ševčenko, I., "A Neglected Byzantine Source of Muscovite Political Ideology," *HSS, 2* (1954), 141–179.

——— "Intellectual Repercussions of the Council of Florence," *Church History, 24*, No. 4 (1955). Reprint.

SGGD. See *Sobranie gosudarstvennykh gramot i dogovorov.*

Shakhmatov, M. V., "Gosudarstvenno-natsionalnye idei chinovnykh knig venchaniia na tsarstvo Moskovskikh Gosudarei," *ZRNIB, 1* (1930), 245–278.

——— "Ispolnitelnaia vlast' v Moskovskoi Rusi," *ZNIOP, 1*, No. 5 (1935).

——— "Politická ideologie Josefa Volokolamského," reprint from *SVPS* (Prague, 1928).

Shmurlo, E., *Kurs Russkoi istorii, 2*, Pts. I–II (Prague, 1933–34).

Shpakov, A. I., *Uchrezhdenie patriarshestva v Rossii, 1* (Odessa, 1912). Supplement: *Prilozheniia* (Odessa, 1912).

SK. See *Seminarium Kondakovianum.*

Skarga, P., *Synod Brzeski* (Kraków, 1597).

Slavonic and East European Review (SEER) (London).

Smirnov, I. I., *Ocherki politicheskoi istorii Russkogo gosudarstva 30— 50–kh godov XVI veka* (Moscow, 1958).

Smirnov, N. A., *Rossiia i Turtsia v XVI–XVII vekakh, 1* (Moscow, 1946).

Smirnov, V. D., *Krymskoe khanstvo pod verkhovenstvom Ottomanskoi Porty* (St. Petersburg, 1887).

Smolitsch, Igor, *Das Russische Mönchtum* (Würzburg, 1953).

Sobranie gosudarstvennykh gramot i dogovorov (SGGD) (St. Petersburg, 1813–94). 5 vols.

SOF. See *Südost-Forschungen.*

Soloviev, A., "Les Emblèmes héraldiques de Byzance et les Slaves," *SK, 7* (1935), 119–164.

——— "Helles Russland—Heiliges Russland," *Festschrift für D. Čyzhevski* (Berlin, 1954), pp. 282–289.

——— "Sviataia Rus'," *SRAOKS, 1* (1927), 77–113.

Soloviev, S. M., *Istoriia Rossii s drevneishikh vremen* (1st ed. Moscow, 1851–79). 29 vols.

——— *Ob otnosheniiakh Novgoroda k velikim kniaziam* (Moscow, 1845).

Spassky, I. G., *Russkaia monetnaia sistema* (Moscow, 1957).

Speransky, M. N., *Istoriia drevnei Russkoi literatury, 2* (Moscow, 1921).

SRAOKS. Sbornik Russkogo Arkheologicheskogo Obshchestva v Korolevstve S. Kh. S.

Stökl, G., *Die Entstehung des Kosakentums* (Munich, 1953).

—— "Russische Geschichte von der Entstehung des Kiever Reiches bis zum Ende der Wirren," 3, *JGOE, 6* (1958), 468–488.

—— "Russland von der Mongolenzeit bis zu Peter dem Grossen," *Historia Mundi, 7* (1958), 392–438.

Struve, P., "Nabliudeniia i issledovaniia iz oblasti khoziaistvennoi zhizni i prava drevnei Rusi," reprint from *Sbornik Russkogo Instituta v Prage, 1* (Prague, 1929).

—— *Sotsialnaia i ekonomicheskaia istoriia Rossii* (Paris, 1952).

Stryjkowski, M., *Kronika Polska, Litewska, Żmodzka i wszystkiej Rusi* (Warsaw, 1846). 2 vols.

Sudebniki. Sudebniki XV–XVI vekov, B. D. Grekov, ed. (Moscow and Leningrad, 1952).

Südost-Forschungen (SOF) (Munich).

Suvorov, N., *Uchebnik tserkovnogo prava* (4th ed. Moscow, 1912).

SVPS. Sborník věd právnich a státnich.

Szeftel, M., "Le Justicier (Sudebnik) du Grand Duc Ivan III," *RHDFE* (1956), pp. 531–568.

—— "The Sudebnik of 1497: Paleographical Analysis, Composition and Sources," *For Roman Jakobson* (The Hague, 1956), pp. 547–552.

Szyszman, S., "G. Peringer's Mission," *ZDMG, 102* (1952), 219–226.

—— "Die Karäer in Ost-Mitteleuropa," *ZOF, 6* (1957), 24–54.

—— "Les Khazars: problèmes et controverses," *Revue de l'histoire des religions, 152* (1957), 174–221.

—— "Le Roi Boulan et le problème de la conversion des Khazars," *Ephemerides Theologicae Lovanienses, 33* (1957), 68–76.

Taranovsky, F. V., *Obzor pamiatnikov Magdeburgskogo prava* (Warsaw, 1897).

Tavricheskoe Obshchestvo Istorii, Arkheologii i Etnografii (Simferopol), *Izvestiia (TOIAE).*

Theiner, A., *Vetera Monumenta Poloniae et Lithuaniae, 3* (Rome, 1863).

Third Novgorodian Chronicle, *PSRL, 3,* 205–279.

Tipografskaia Letopis (The Synodal Printing Office Chronicle), *PSRL, 24* (1921).

TODRL. See *Trudy Otdela Drevnerusskoi Literatury.*

TOIAE. See Tavricheskoe . . . , *Izvestiia.*

Tomkievicz, W., "O składzie społecznym i etničnym kozaczyny Ukraińskiej na przełomie XVI i XVII vieku," *PH, 37* (1948), 249–260.

Travels to Tana and Persia by Josafa Barbaro and Ambrogio Contarini (London, Hakluyt Society, 1873).

Trudy Otdela Drevnerusskoi Literatury (TODRL) (Akademiia Nauk, Institut Russkoi literatury).

Tupikov, N. M., "Slovar' drevne-russkikh lichnykh sobstvennykh imen," *ZORSA, 6* (1909), 58–913.

Übersberger, H., *Österreich und Russland seit dem Ende des 15. Jahrhunderts, 1* (Vienna, 1906).

Ustiug Chronicle (*Ustiuzhskii letopisnyi svod*), K. N. Serbina, ed. (Moscow and Leningrad, 1950).

Ustrialov, N., ed., *Skazaniia kniazia Kurbskogo* (2d ed. St. Petersburg, 1842).

Vakar, N. P., *Belorussia* (Cambridge, Harvard University Press, 1956).

—— *A Bibliographical Guide to Belorussia* (Cambridge, Harvard University Press, 1956).

Valdenberg, V., *Drevnerusskie ucheniia o predelakh tsarskoi vlasti* (Petrograd, 1916).

—— "Nastavlenie pisatelia VI v. Agapita v russkoi pismennosti," *Vizantiiskii Vremennik, 24* (1926), 27–34.

Vasilenko, N. P., "Litovsko-russkoe gosudarstvo," *ES, 34* (1896), 818–827.

—— "Pravo Magdeburgskoe," *ES, 48* (1898), 890–896.

Vasmer, M., *Russisches etymologisches Wörterbuch* (Heidelberg, 1950–58). 3 vols.

Veliaminov-Zernov, V. V., *Issledovanie o Kasimovskikh tsariakh i tsarevichakh* (St. Petersburg, 1863–87). 4 vols.

Vernadsky, G., *Ancient Russia* (New Haven, Yale University Press, 1943).

—— "Feudalism in Russia," *Speculum, 14* (1939), 300–323.

—— "The Heresy of the Judaizers and the Policies of Ivan III of Moscow," *Speculum, 8* (1933), 436–454.

—— *Kievan Russia* (New Haven, Yale University Press, 1948).

—— *Medieval Russian Laws* (New York, Columbia University Press, 1947).

—— *The Mongols and Russia* (New Haven, Yale University Press, 1953).

—— *Nachertanie Russkoi istorii* (Prague, 1927).

—— *The Origins of Russia* (Oxford, Clarendon Press, 1959).

—— *Political and Diplomatic History of Russia* (Boston, Little, Brown, 1936).

—— "The Riddle of the Gothi-Tetraxitae," *SOF, 11* (1952), 281–283.

—— "Serfdom in Russia," *Relazioni, 3* (1955), 247–272.

Veselovsky, N. I., *Khan iz temnikov Zolotoi Ordy Nogay i ego vremia* (Petrograd, 1922).

Veselovsky, S. B., *Feodalnoe zemlevladenie v severovostochnoi Rusi* (Moscow and Leningrad, 1947).

—— "Vladimir Gusev, sostavitel sudebnika 1497 goda," *Istoricheskie Zapiski, 5* (1939), 31–47.

Vilinsky, S. G., *Poslaniia startsa Artemiia XVI veka* (Odessa, 1906).

Vladimirsky-Budanov, M. F., *Khristomatiia po istorii russkogo prava* (St. Petersburg and Kiev). 3 vols. Vol. *1*, 6th ed. (1908); Vol. *2*, 5th ed. (1915); Vol. *3*, 4th ed. (1908).

────── "Naselenie iugo-zapadnoi Rossii ot poloviny XV veka do Liublinskoi Unii," *AIZR, 7,* Pt. II (Kiev, 1891).

────── "Nemetskoe pravo v Polshe i Litve," *ZMNP, 8–12* (1866).

────── *Obzor istorii Russkogo prava* (7th ed. St. Petersburg and Kiev, 1915).

Vlasovsky, I., *Narys istorii Ukrainskoi pravoslavnoi tserkvy, 1* (New York, 1955).

Voskresensk Chronicle (*Voskresenskaia letopsis*), *PSRL, 7–8* (1856–59).

Voyce, A., *Russian Architecture* (New York, Philosophical Library, 1948).

Vremennik. Vremennik Obshchestva Istorii i Drevnostei.

West Russian Chronicles (*Zapadno-russkie letopisi*), *PSRL, 17* (1907).

Wojciechowski, Z., *L'Etat Polonais au Moyen Age* (Paris, 1949).

Wolff, J., *Kniaziowie Litewsko-Ruscy od konca czternastego wieku* (Warsaw, 1895).

Zajączkowski, A., *Ze studiów nad zagadnieniem Chazarskim* (Kraków, 1947).

Zapiski Nauchno-Issledovatelskogo Ob'edineniia (ZNIOP) (Prague).

Zapiski Naukovogo Tovarystva imeni Shevchenka (ZNTS).

Zapiski Odesskogo Obshchestva Istorii i Drevnostei (ZOO).

Zapiski Otdeleniia Russkoi i Slavianskoi Arkheologii Russkogo Arkheologicheskogo Obschestva (ZORSA).

Zapiski Russkogo Istoricheskogo Obshchestva v Prage (ZRIOP).

Zapiski Russkogo Nauchnogo Instituta v Belgrade (ZRNIB).

ZDMG. Zeitschrift der Deutschen Morgenlandischen Gesellschaft.

Zeitschrift der Deutschen Morgenlandischen Gesellschaft (ZDMG).

Zeitschrift für Ostforschung (ZOF).

Zherela do istorii Ukrainy-Rusi (Lvov, Archeographic Commission of the Shevchenko Scientific Society, 1895–1919). 16 vols.

Zhmakin, V., *Mitropolit Daniil i ego sochineniia* (Moscow, 1881).

Zhurnal Ministerstva Narodnogo Prosveshcheniia (ZMNP).

Zimin, A. A., *I. S. Peresvetov i ego sovremenniki* (Moscow, 1958).

Zinovi of Otnia (Otensky), monk, *Istiny pokazanie* (Kazan, 1863).

ZMNP. Zhurnal Ministerstva Narodnogo Prosveshcheniia.

ZNIOP. Zaposki Naucho-Issledovatelskogo Ob'edineniia (Prague).

ZNTS. Zapiski Naukovogo Tovarystva imeni Shevchenka.

ZOF. Zeitschrift für Ostforschung.

Żołkiewski, S. See *Listy Stanisława Żołkiewskiego.*

Zolotaia Orda. See Grekov, B. D., and A. I. Iakubovsky, *Zolotaia Orda i ee padenie.*

ZOO Zapiski Odesskogo Obshchestva Istorii i Drevnostei.

*ZORSA. Zapiski Otdeleniia Russkoi i Slavianskoi Arkheologii Russkogo
   Arkheologicheskogo Obshchestva.*

Zotov, R. V., *O Chernigovskikh kniaziakh po Liubetskomu Sinodiku* (St.
   Petersburg, 1892).

ZRIOP. Zapiski Russkogo Istoricheskogo Obshchestva v Prage.

ZRNIB. Zapiski Russkogo Nauchnogo Instituta v Belgrade.

Zurov, L., *Otchina* (Riga, 1929).

INDEX OF AUTHORS CITED

GLOSSARIAL INDEX

The second of two consecutive forms separated by a comma is plural. Parentheses denote variant or alternative spellings.

altyn, coin, equal to 6 *dengas*, 76, 77

asaul (esaul, iasaul), adjutant (in Cossack armies), 260. From the Turkic

ataman, leader of a Cossack company; among the Don Cossacks the commander of the army, 113

baisa, badge of authority (in Mongol administration), 73, 76

barmy, part of the regalia of the Moscow tsars; a collar of broad form made of black silk overlaid with gold and jewels (Herberstein's description), 125

basma, stamp, impression, 72–74

bereg, river bank, specifically the bank of the Oka River used by the Russians as a fortified line against the inroads of the Tatars, 154

besy, evil spirits, 9

bobrovnik, bobrovniki, beaver hunter, 204

bortnik, bortniki, beekeeper, 204

boyarin, boyare, boyar (noble). See General Index

boyare szlachta, gentry (West Russia), 196

boyarskie zemli, boyar land (on which the owner had full rights), 108–109

bratstvo, bratstva, brotherhood, 273, 282

burmistr, mayor (West Russia), 212. From German *Bürgermeister*

byliny, epic tales, 9

Chahar-Kas, four *Kas* clans (Circassians), 249

cheliad', household slaves (collectively), 200

Cherkas, Cherkasy, Circassian; Cossack, 249. Modern Russian *Cherkesy*, Circassians

chern', menials, 260. See also *chernye liudi*

chernoziom, black soil, 3, 251

cherny bor, a tax (presumably collected in silver), 44

chernye liudi, black people (lower classes), 38, 203

chernye zemli, black land (state land in Muscovy), 108

chestno i grozno, in esteem and respect (the Novgorodians pledged so to keep the power of the Moscow grand dukes), 43

chinsh, tax on land (West Russia), 225. Polish *czynsz*. From German *Zins*, from Latin *census*

cosac, Cossack, 249

dar, gift, 35

davnost', prescriptive term for claims, 206; *davnost' zemskaia*, claims about land, 206

denga, dengi, silver coin (half a kopek), 10, 76, 77. In Modern Russian *dengi* means "money"

derzhavtsa, derzhavtsy, lessee; holder of a benefice; a prefect (West Russia), 180. From Polish *dzierżawca*

desiatina, desiatiny, land measure (about 2.7 acres), 115, 116

desiatok, desiatki, unit of ten (military or administrative), 257

deti boyarskie, boyar sons (gentry), 6, 196. See also sing. form *syn*

diak, diaki, state secretary, 4, 58, 104

diaklo, a tax in kind on peasants (West Russia), 204

dikoe pole, wild prairie (South Russian and Ukrainian), 226

do dvukh zhivotov, grant of land for two "lives," 197

do trekh zhivotov, grant of land for three "lives," 197

do zhivota, grant of land for one "life," 197

dobrye liudi, good men (i.e. reliable men), 104

starshina, officers of the Zaporozhie Cossack army (collectively), 252, 260

stepennyi posadnik, senior mayor (Novgorod), 38 n.

stiag, banner, standard. See *vladychnyi stiag*

strelets, streltsy, shooter (musketeer), 228

sud, court, justice; *sud zemski,* land court, provincial court (West Russia), 180

sudebnik, law manual, code of laws, 103

svoezemets, svoezemtsy, owner of land in his own right, 109, 203

syn boyarsky, boyar son, 228. See also plural form *deti boyarskie*

szlachta (*shliakhta*), nobility (West Russia), 6, 51, 178, 180. *Szlachta* (Polish) from German *geschlecht*

tainaia rada, privy council, 185. See also *naivysshaia rada*

tamga, customs duties, 10, 143

tapkana, a kind of carriage, 88

tiaglo, burden (total of peasants' taxes and liabilities), 204; *tiaglye liudi,* men of burden, i.e. men subject to *tiaglo,* 204, 251

t'ma, t'my, military and taxation district (in Mongol administration), 175

toloka, assistance (given by peasants or neighbors) in agricultural work, 204, 212

trudovoe pravo, toiler's right, 7, 203

tsarevichi, tsar's sons, 112

tsarstvo, tsardom, 167

tsekh, tsekhi, artisan guild (West Russia), 211. From Polish *cech.* Old German *Zech*

Tsesar, Caesar (title of the Austrian Emperor in Old Russian and Ukrainian), 264

tysiatsky, tysiatskie, chiliarch (commander of the unit of *tysiacha,* thousand), 30, 42

uboitsa, assassin; armed insurgent, 106 n. See also *gosudarskii uboitsa*

ukraina, ukrainy, borderland, 154, 249

ukrainnik, ukrainniki, inhabitant of a borderland; frontiersman, 154

ulitsa, ulitsy, street; street commune (in Novgorod), 37

urzędy dworskie, court offices (Polish), 184

Ustava na voloki, land ordinance of *1557*

(Lithuania), 224 (*Ustava,* statute, in West Russian)

ustavnaia gramota, statutory charter, 103 (*ustav,* statute, in Russian)

vataga, vatagi, cooperative association (for fishing, hunting, or other purposes), 252

vatazhok, chief of the *vataga,* petty ataman, 262

veche, city assembly, 5. See also General Index

vechnye gramoty, charters enacted by the *veche* (Novgorod), 35

veliki kniaz', grand duke (literally, grand prince); *Veliki Kniaz' Litovsky i Russky,* Grand Duke of Lithuania and Russia, 86; . . . *i Zhomoitsky,* 171

velikoe posolstvo, grand embassy, 185

verkhovskie goroda, upper towns (specifically towns in the Upper Oka River basin), 195

vladychnyi stiag, bishop's banner, specifically the banner of, and the military unit mustered under this banner by, the Archbishop of Novgorod, 42. *Vladyka,* bishop

voevoda, voevody, commander of an army (or an army division); governor of a province, 50, 112, 181

voevodstvo, voevodstva, office of the governor, province, 181

voit, mayor (West Russia), 211 and n. Cf. German *Vogt*

voloka, voloki, measure of land in West Russia, consisting of 33 *morgi* (about 21 hectares,) 205

volost, volosti, possession; rural district, 6, 35, 40, 115

volostel, volosteli, official in charge of a rural district (under the *kormlenie* system), 4, 102

votchina, votchiny, patrimonial estate, 108, 197. See also *otchina*

vsia voi svoia, "all his warriors," 50

vykhod, tribute (paid to the Tatars), 77

yarlyk, charter, patent (Tatar term), 16, 110

zadruga, "greater family" commune, 207

zaimka, right of occupancy, 203

Zavolzhskie Startsy, "Trans-Volga Hermits," a group of Russian monks supporting the mystical trend in Orthodox spirituality (15th and 16th centuries) 71, 119

zemianin, zemiane, native of the land; landowner (gentry), 196. From *zemlia,* land. In medieval Latin *terrigena,* meaning (in classical Latin) "earth-born"

zemsky sobor, assembly of the land (in Muscovy), 51, 241

zhena, woman, wife, 200 n.

zhityi liudi, well-off men, middle-class burghers (in Novgorod), 38, 39, 55, 115

zhivot, life (in Modern Russian, belly). See *do zhivota*

zholner (Polish, *żołnierz*), professional soldier (West Russia), 190. From German *Söldner*

zhonka (diminutive of *zhena*), a female slave (West Russia), 200 n.

zimovnik, zimovniki, winter quarters of a *vataga* or of a Cossack company, 252

GENERAL INDEX